C000064394

# HISTORY OF

# A DISGRACEFUL SURRENDER [2021]

## by

## INAM R SEHRI

REAL FACTS ABOUT A
HUMILIATING DEFEAT

Sourced From

AMERICA'S *'OFFICIAL'* DOCUMENTS

AND

THE WESTERN MEDIA

Grosvenor House
Publishing Limited

All rights reserved
Copyright © Inam R Sehri, 2022

(However, scholars & students are permitted
to use material of this book by quoting the exact reference)

The right of Inam R Sehri to be identified as the author of this
work has been asserted in accordance with Section 78
of the Copyright, Designs and Patents Act 1988

The book cover picture is copyright to Klenger

This book is published by
Grosvenor House Publishing Ltd
Link House
140 The Broadway, Tolworth, Surrey, KT6 7HT.
www.grosvenorhousepublishing.co.uk

This book is sold subject to the conditions that it shall not, by way of
trade or otherwise, be lent, resold, hired out or otherwise circulated
without the author's or publisher's prior consent in any form of binding or
cover other than that in which it is published and
without a similar condition including this condition being imposed
on the subsequent purchaser.

A CIP record for this book
is available from the British Library

ISBN 978-1-80381-004-1

# Other Books from

# INAM   R   SEHRI

## *KHUDKUSHI*
(on Suicide) [in Urdu] (1983)
{Details of historical perspective of 'Suicide' in various societies; & investigation techniques differentiating in Murder & Suicides}

## *WARDI KAY ANDAR AADMI*
(Man in uniform) [in Urdu] (1984)
{Collection of short stories keeping a sensitive policeman in focus}

## *AURAT JARAIM KI DALDAL MEIN*
(on Female Criminality) [in Urdu] (1985)
{Describing various theories and cultural taboos concerning Female Criminal Behaviour}

## *POLICE AWAM RABTAY*
(on Police Public relationship) [in Urdu] (1986)
{Essays describing importance of mutual relationships}

## *DEHSHAT GARDI*
(on Terrorism) [in Urdu] (1987)
{Various theories and essays differentiating between Freedom Fighting & Terrorism in Middle Eastern perspective}

## *QATL*
(on Murder) [in Urdu] (1988)
{The first book written for Police students & Lawyers to explain techniques of investigation of (difficult) Murder cases}

## *SERVICE POLICING IN PAKISTAN*
[in English] (1990)
{A dissertation type book on which basis the PM Benazir Bhutto, in 1990, had okayed the Commissionerate System of Policing in Pakistan. Taking Karachi as the pilot project, later, it was levied for all major cities and still going on as such}

## *SHADI*

(on Marriages) [in Urdu] (1998)

{A detailed exposition of Marriage explained in various religions, cultures, countries and special groups; much applauded & commented upon on PTV in 1998-99}

All the above URDU books were published by
Pakistan's one of the top publishers

## *SANG E MEEL PUBLICATIONS,*
## *25 - The Lower Mall LAHORE, Pakistan*

And are normally available with them in latest re-prints.

**Judges & Generals in Pakistan VOL-I**
[in English] (2012)

**Judges & Generals in Pakistan VOL-II**
[in English] (2012)

**Judges & Generals in Pakistan VOL-III**
[in English] (2013)

**Judges & Generals in Pakistan VOL-IV**
[in English] (2013)

**The Living History of Pakistan Vol-I**
[in English] (2015)

**The Living History of Pakistan Vol-II**
[in English] (2016)

**The Living History of Pakistan Vol-III**
[in English] (2017)

**The Living History of Pakistan Vol-IV**
[in English] (2017)

**The Living History of Pakistan Vol-V**
[in English] (2017)

**The Living History of Pakistan Vol-VI**
[in English] (2018)

**The Living History of Pakistan Vol-VII**
[in English] (2018)

{The **FOUR** volumes of *'Judges & Generals in Pakistan'* are not the stories or facts about only the honourable judges or respectable military Generals of Pakistan but also an authentic record of contemporary history.

*Living History of Pakistan* Vol-1 *to* 7 are the continuation of the same series with only a change in name of the same product. It is just for the change of taste otherwise the SCENARIOS and the PAGE NUMBERS are in the same continuity. All the above books deal with Pakistan's chequered history of massive financial & intellectual corruption, abortive rule by two political parties in succession with higher judiciary's gimmicks during 1971 onwards; Constitutional Amendments which made political parties as family businesses & apex court's nexus making the politicians more corrupt.}

The above mentioned 4+7 volumes in English are published by

*Grosvenor House Publishing Ltd*
*LINK HOUSE, 140 THE BROADWAY,*
*TOLWORTH*
*SURREY UK    KT6 7HT*

*It's me; my Friends!*

## Inam R Sehri

- Born in Lyallpur (Pakistan) in April 1948

- First Degree from Government College Lyallpur (1969)

- Studied at Government College Lahore & got first Master's Degree from Punjab University Lahore (1971);

- Attachment with AJK Education Service (1973-1976)

- Central Superior Services (CSS) Exam passed (batch 1975)

- Civil Service Academy Lahore (joined 1976)

- National Police Academy Islamabad (joined 1977)

- LLB from BUZ University Multan (1981)

- Master's Degree from Exeter University of UK (1990)

- Regular Police Service: District Admin, Police College, National Police Academy, the Intelligence Bureau (IB), Federal Investigation Agency (FIA) [1977-1998] then migrated to the UK permanently.

A part-script copied from the earlier volumes:

Just spent a normal routine life; with hundreds of mentionable memoirs allegedly of bravery & glamour as every uniformed officer keeps, some times to smile at and next moment to repent upon but taking it just normal except one or two spills.

During my tenure at IB HQ Islamabad I got chance to peep into the elite civil and military leadership of Pakistan then existing in governmental dossiers and database.

During my stay at FIA I was assigned to conduct special enquiries & investigations into some acutely sensitive matters like Motorway Scandal, sudden expansion and build-up of Sharif family's industrial empire, Sharif's accounts in foreign countries; Alleged Financial

Corruptions in Pakistan's Embassies in Far-Eastern Countries; Shahnawaz Bhutto's murder in Cannes (France); Land Scandals of CDA's Estate Directorate; Ittefaq Foundry's 'custom duty on scrap' scam, Hudaibya Engineering & Hudaibya Paper Mills enquiries, Bhindara's Murree Brewery and tens more cases like that.

> [*Through these words I want to keep it on record that during the course of the above mentioned, (and also which cannot be mentioned due to space limits) investigations or enquiries, the then Prime Minister Benazir Bhutto, or [late] Gen Naseerullah Babar the then Federal Interior Minister, or G Asghar Malik the then DG FIA, had never ever issued direct instructions or implicit directions or wished me to distort facts or to go malafide for orchestrating a political edge or other intangible gains.*
>
> *Hats off to all of them!*]

I should feel proud that veracity and truthfulness of none of my enquiry or investigation could be challenged or proved false in NAB or Special Courts; yes, most of them were used to avail political compromises by Gen Musharraf's government.

That's enough, my dear countrymen.

# Contents

**Scenario 241**

# THE 12ᵀᴴ SUBMISSION

In the end, we all have witnessed the state of affairs in Afghanistan during the America's two decades occupation against the will and resolve of the general populace especially the rural tribal masses. After wasteful investment of countless billions of dollars of the American tax payers in the name of nation building measures on Afghan soils – what results – horrific embarrassment, humiliation, disgrace, mortification and dishonour coupled with defeat & degradation from the super-power ranking. See the opening paragraphs of an article in London's **THE ECONOMIST** of 22ⁿᵈ August 2021:

> "......*AMERICA announced that it would not save its client state (Afghanistan)...... As the enemy [Afghan Taliban] seized province after province, government soldiers [Afghan Army] shed their uniforms and ran. On paper the army had hundreds of thousands of well-equipped fighters. In reality its few loyal commanders had to buy ammunition from crooked supply officers [?] and pay in cash for artillery support; regular troops were often commanded by politicians' incompetent relatives. Soldiers went unpaid as officials pilfered military budgets. The [Afghan] state was a* **Potemkin village** *constructed to please its American sponsors. When they left - it fell.*
>
> *So it went in South Vietnam in 1975, and again last week in Afghanistan. The similarities between the two collapses are striking. They go beyond intelligence failures, mendacious speeches and abandoned allies.* **Ultimately, both states fell because they had been hollowed out by corruption,** *an ancient disease of governance..... (Think also of Iraq, Kosovo, Bosnia and Haiti)."*

In the eyes of many media gurus and think-tanks, the Americans were not sincere in helping out the underprivileged people or the deprived communities – in 2001 they had chosen Afghanistan as another business venue, the Tribal Warfield – thus invested their time and money in it as new war-project and simply suffered with multiple losses. Why to worry now; every thing is fare in love [*in the given scenario – US business*] and war.

**Pakistan's Inter-Services Intelligence [ISI]** played its role to save its own country first – a natural demand of nationalism. Some historians held that the real US-Taliban war started in 2001 BUT then restarted in 2009 after Obama's take-over. The US kept its carrot and stick approach for Pakistan amidst the swelling of 60,000 US troops in Afghanistan, with another 30,000 in-line to be sent later, coupled with greater *'all sorts of assistance'* for India – thus distances increased. Pakistan had been helping the US since 2001, more precisely since 1979, though had continuously been fooled in one way or the other in connivance with its own rogue leadership in army and politics.

*The world media is crying that in fact Pakistan's ISI won the war –* not the Taliban alone. Let the myth prevail because the ISI has been doing its home-work dedicatedly since the US allocated the task to the Pak-Army in 1980s. During America's so-called **WAR ON TERROR** which country offered the human, financial, trade and social sacrifices more than Pakistan – **NO ONE**; not even the US and NATO countries collectively.

**On 18<sup>th</sup> November 2018;** in an interview with Fox News, President Trump accused Islamabad of receiving billions in US aid. The contents of the telecast and his statement were: '*.....Pakistan doesn't do a damn thing for the US'*. President trump also said that:

> "*.....he [Osama Bin Laden] was living in Pakistan right next to the military academy; everybody in Pakistan knew he was there [but the CIA came to know it in 2011 – astonishing]. We're supporting Pakistan, we're giving them $1.3 billion a year, which we don't give them anymore, and by the way, I ended it because **they don't do anything for us, they don't do a damn thing for us.**"*

Just next day, a tweet from Pakistan's PM Imran Khan appeared on media pages which had shaken the whole world; see the details:

- *"No Pakistani was involved in 9/11 but Pakistan decided to participate in US War on Terror.*

- *Pakistan suffered 75,000 casualties in this war & over $123 billion lost in economy. 'US aid' was a miniscule $20 bn – and that too (against our bills) for Military Operations done by Pak-Army.*

- *Pakistan's tribal areas along the border with Afghanistan were devastated and millions of people had been uprooted from their homes.*

- *Pakistan continued to provide free lines of ground and air communications [GLOCs / ALOCs]; which other ally provided such facilities to the US?*

- *Why, despite 140,000 NATO troops plus 250,000 Afghan troops & reportedly $1 trillion spent on war in Afghanistan, the Taliban today are stronger than before; instead of making Pakistan a scapegoat for their [the US & NATO] failures, the US should do a **serious assessment of factors involved**."*

.....AND in this book the same factors have been highlighted.

See an article titled **'Does the great retreat from Afghanistan mark the end of the American era?'** appeared in a US magazine *New Yorker* penned down by Robin Wright after the American quit from the region:

> *"The United States of America is reeling from both the loss of war and loss of face. It's not just an epic defeat for the US. The fall of Kabul may serve as a bookend for the era of US global power.*
>
> *For the United States, the costs do not end with its withdrawal from either Afghanistan or Iraq. It could cost another two trillion dollars just to pay for the healthcare and disability of veterans from those wars. And those costs may not peak until 2048. America's longest war will be a lot longer than anyone anticipated two decades ago."*

In fact, the cost of the humiliating defeat in the two-decades-long 'war on terror' launched by president George Bush was more steep than Bush and his successors could have imagined. Pakistan was in delicately promising position after the relatively peaceful transition of power in Kabul.

In the next pages, I've identified the other dynamic causes and grounds of the US failure in Afghanistan – ISI's patriotic character may be found unsuitable for some Western political philosophers or rulers – BUT it cannot be blamed as the whole responsible factor for loosing 20 years long war by the successive American rulers, war-strategists and policy makers.

In the pages ahead, I've based my conclusions on the analytical notes and articles from the Western press & media, mostly the American policy documents and reports which are available to any research student of war histories – nothing unusual; each script is mentioned with proper references.

**Inam R Sehri**
Manchester UK
12th February 2022

# SUMMARY OF THE DEFEAT PROCESS

President Biden's decision of early QUIT was not unanticipated, even if the timing and extent of the drawdown were not settled until the last minute. The US was initially motivated after the 9/11 attacks to defeat al-Qaeda, then got based in Afghanistan but lost its whole honour, prestige and history after two decades. Referring to **Dhruva Jaishankar**'s analysis in *Hindustan Times* dated 13<sup>th</sup> July 2021:

> *"......intervention resulted in over 2,400 US military deaths [one can add 13 American soldiers killed in two suicide attacks on Kabul Airport on 27<sup>th</sup> August 2021], some 20,000 US troops injured, and over $776 billion spent between 2001 and 2019 according to the Pentagon......... the Taliban have returned [again] ........"*

The US misadventure in Afghanistan did not necessarily have to end this way. Let us look into the past: The initial US troop commitment after 2001 was small but soon after increased enormously. In 2003, a sizeable army from here was moved to Iraq leaving only 8,000 troops on the Afghan grounds. After 2006, Washington's relations with allies and the Afghan government grew strained on the issues related with *'Taliban resurgence'*.

The 2011-13 periods marked another phase of transition. After OBL's killing, President Obama announced the beginning of troops' withdrawal, intra-Afghan negotiations restarted but suddenly the former Afghan President and peace negotiator Burhanuddin Rabbani was assassinated. Pakistan boycotted the **Second Bonn Conference** due to its own reasons or preferences. By 2013, the US and NATO handed over primary security responsibilities to the Afghan National Security Forces [ANSF], and the US military limited itself to special operations, missions and training.

President Trump initially announced [in 2017] a redoubling of efforts amidst increasing suicide bombings in Kabul and the growing profile of the Islamic State [IS]; but subsequently he reversed the course, indicating his preference for a US withdrawal before the 2020 elections. In February 2020, the US signed the famous **Doha Accord** with the Taliban telling the whole world about total withdrawal from Afghan soils. Moreover, hasty transfers of resources to NATO and the ANSF proved fatal for the core US policies of finding strong footing in Asia.

Another crucial factor remained the **under-estimated hidden power of Pakistan, its ISI,** which had record of the most successful activities and achievements in Afghanistan during initial five years of the War on Terror – of course in association with the CIA but at the cost of it's own high human losses in Pakistan. The US could have acknowledged the Pak-Army & the ISI seriously [and NOT hypocritically or dishonestly]; particularly thinking about troubled US relations with Iran and Russia then.

Pakistan deserved truthful recognition due to realities on ground that all military and food logistics were coming into Afghanistan through them. On the contrary, knowingly that Pakistan is also a nuclear power, the US preferred far-off placed **India as its *'Strategic Partner'*** developing a false belief that the Pak-Army and the ISI could be cajoled or coerced into cooperation by filling coffins of its corrupt ruling political elite.

In 2017-18, in an arena of high relations between President Trump and Imran Khan, the writing on the wall was noticeable for India. Then Trump's reversal had confirmed that a complete US withdrawal was only a matter of time. After the US, India was amongst the largest investors in Afghanistan but its widespread consular contingents and the RAW couldn't go deep into the ground realities. Indian security presence on Afghan soils was politically undesirable for Afghan masses. Especially when India's geographical access to Afghanistan was limited; they could go there only via air, Iran, or some Central Asian corridors.

For 20 years, India posed itself as major trade partner of Afghan governments at Kabul. The Taliban's sudden takeover this time resulted in an abrupt meltdown of India-Afghanistan trade; the Taliban preferred to shut the trade routes immediately while ending bilateral trade worth $1.5 billion. During these years, India had emerged as an important destination for Afghan exports such as dry fruits. Likewise, India's exports to Afghanistan, totalling almost $1 billion, included tea, cement, sugar, and pharmaceuticals – but all vanished within days because of the sudden fall of Kabul. *'As a solution [and revenge] India opted to agitate the international law to hold the Taliban accountable for the illegal shutting down of the trade routes. Let us wait for the outcome'*; **Prabhash Ranjan**'s essay on media pages *dated 3rd September 2021* is referred.

The world order phenomenon is changing rapidly. America's old world order has moved back into crawling phase. Russia is re-appearing on the globe as a loud voice for the under-developed while **China** has emerged as a **New Super Power** and as if the America is winding up its chaotic fronts to retain its survival – starting from Afghanistan.

# Scenario 221

## <u>DON'T BLAME PAKISTAN-I</u>

As Washington ponders how the US lost its
**longest war in Afghanistan.**
....worth considering that it was the America's own choice
to jump into the Afghan sand-grave.

- **The world media's FALSE cry:** Pakistan, nominally a US partner
  in the war, had also been the Afghan Taliban's main patron.

Now find the answer below –
see the *Washington Post* of 27<sup>th</sup> September 2021 with a big caption:

**PM Imran Khan: Don't blame Pakistan
for the outcome of the war in Afghanistan**

It's PM Khan's **reality-opinion** over the gloomy ending of America's
longest war in Afghanistan. The PM said that:

- '....I was surprised to see that no mention was made of Pakistan's
  sacrifices as a US ally in the war on terror for more than two decades.
  Instead, we were blamed for America's loss.'

- Let me put it plainly. Since 2001, I have repeatedly warned that the
  Afghan war was un-winnable. Given their history, Afghans would
  never accept a protracted foreign military presence, and no outsider,
  including Pakistan, could change this reality.

- Unfortunately, successive Pakistani governments after 9/11 sought
  to please the United States instead of pointing out the error of a
  military-dominated approach.

- Desperate for global relevance and domestic legitimacy, Pakistan's
  Gen Musharraf agreed to every American demand for military
  support after 9/11. This cost Pakistan, and the United States,
  dearly.

- The United States asked Pakistan for help to train certain Afghani groups, jointly by the CIA and our intelligence agency, the ISI, to defeat the Soviets in Afghanistan in the 1980s.

- Back then, these Afghans were hailed as freedom fighters performing a sacred duty. President Ronald Reagan even entertained the *mujahedeen* at the White House.

- Once the Soviets were defeated, the United States abandoned Afghanistan and sanctioned my country, leaving behind over 4 million [*on documents; illegal entrants may be double*] Afghan refugees in Pakistan and a bloody civil war in Afghanistan. From this security vacuum emerged the Taliban, many born and educated in Afghan refugee camps in Pakistan.

- Fast forward to 9/11, when the United States needed us again — but this time against the very actors we had jointly supported to fight foreign occupation against the Soviets. Gen Musharraf offered Washington logistics and air bases, allowed a CIA footprint in Pakistan and even turned a blind eye to American drones bombing Pakistanis on our soil.

- For the first time ever, our army swept into the semi-autonomous tribal areas on the Pak-Afghan border, which had earlier been used as the staging ground for the anti-Soviet *jihad*. The fiercely independent *Pashtun* tribes in these areas had deep ethnic ties with the Taliban and other Islamist militants.

- For the Afghan people, **the United States was a 'foreign occupier' of Afghanistan just like the Soviets, deserving of the same treatment.**

- As Pakistan was now America's collaborator, we too were deemed guilty and attacked. This was made much worse by over 450 US drone strikes on our territory, making us the only country in history to be so bombed by an ally.

- These strikes caused immense civilian casualties, riling up anti-American [and anti-Pakistan army] sentiment further.

- The die was cast. **Between 2006 and 2015, nearly 50 militant groups declared *jihad* on the Pakistani state, conducting over 16,000 terrorist attacks on us. We suffered more than 80,000 casualties and lost over $150 billion in economy.**

- The conflict also drove 3.5 million of our citizens from their homes.

- **The militants** escaping from Pakistani counter-terrorism efforts entered Afghanistan and were **then supported and financed by Indian and Afghan intelligence agencies, launching even more attacks against Pakistan.**

- Pakistan had to fight for its survival.

- A former CIA station chief in Kabul wrote in 2009, Pakistan was **"beginning to crack under the relentless pressure directly exerted by the US."**

- Yet the United States continued to ask us to **DO MORE – DO MORE** for the war in Afghanistan.

- In 2008, I met the then Senators Joe Biden, John F Kerry and Harry M Reid [among others] to explain this dangerous dynamics.

- President Asif Zardari, undoubtedly the most corrupt man to have led my country, told the Americans to continue targeting Pakistanis in the name of **'collateral damage'** – for no reason.

- Nawaz Sharif, our next prime minister, was no different.

- While Pakistan had mostly defeated the terrorist onslaught by 2016, the Afghan situation continued to deteriorate.

- Why the difference? Pakistan had a disciplined army and top intelligence agency, both of which enjoyed popular support of the general populace of Pakistan [– *in fact the whole world*].

- In Afghanistan, the lack of legitimacy for an outsider's protracted war was compounded by a corrupt and inept Afghan govt, seen as a puppet regime without credibility, especially by rural Afghans.

- **Tragically, instead of facing this reality, the Afghan and Western governments created a convenient scapegoat by blaming Pakistan, wrongly accusing us of providing safe havens to the Taliban.**

- If it had been so, would the United States not have used some of the 450-plus drone strikes to target these supposed sanctuaries?

- Still, to satisfy Kabul, Pakistan offered a joint border visibility mechanism, suggested biometric border controls, advocated fencing the border [which we have now largely done on our own] and other measures.

- Each idea was rejected. Instead, the Afghan government intensified the 'blame Pakistan' narrative, aided by Indian-run fake news networks operating hundreds of propaganda outlets in multiple countries.

- A more realistic approach would have been to negotiate with the Taliban much earlier, avoiding the embarrassment of the collapse of the Afghan army and the Ashraf Ghani government.

- Surely Pakistan is not to blame for the fact that 300,000-plus well-trained and well-equipped Afghan security forces saw no reason to fight the lightly armed Taliban – numbering c 60,000+ only.

- The underlying problem was an Afghan government structure lacking legitimacy in the eyes of an average Afghan.

- We must look to the future to prevent another violent conflict in Afghanistan **rather than perpetuating the blame game of the past.**

- Had we done this right, we could achieve what the Doha peace process aimed at all along, where Afghans could finally dream of peace after four decades of conflict.

- **Abandoning Afghanistan** — has been tried before. As in the 1990s, it will inevitably lead to a meltdown, Chaos, mass migration and a revived threat of international terror.

NOW BEHOLD: Much before the Taliban's re-capture of Kabul in August 2021 -

On 8th June 2021; *SHASHI THAROOR,* AN INDIAN MP AND THEIR CELEBRITY STATE MINISTER, wrote for the media that:

> *"With the Taliban more powerful than ever and poised to reclaim power in Afghanistan, the only external victor will be Pakistan's Inter-Services Intelligence agency [ISI]."*

India knew the facts since long. BUT it's astonishing that the mighty CIA of America had not advised Obama in 2009 to refrain choosing India as their strategic partner while letting down Pakistan.

Once the head of Pakistan's powerful ISI agency, late **Lt Gen Hameed Gul,** was found boasting that:

> *"....when Afghanistan's history would be written, **it would record that the ISI, with the help of America, defeated the Soviet Union.** And next, very shrewdly, historians would also state that the **ISI, with the help of America, defeated America."***

Gen Hameed Gul's boast was not the shallow words; he was right to argue that it was the ISI's policies - arms supplied and financed by the US – against the Soviets in Afghanistan that forced the Kremlin to withdraw at last un-ceremonially. During the same days, America came on the back of *mujahedeen* of 1980s out of which the Taliban appeared as a separate faction being PURE *PASHTUNS* but much later; ultimately took over Afghanistan and ruled for 1996-2001.

President Biden announced that US forces would withdraw completely from Afghanistan by 11<sup>th</sup> September [2021], the 20th anniversary of 9/11 attacks – but Taliban's speedy victories in other parts of Afghanistan forced the US to retreat and vacate their lands nearly a month earlier.

Indian Minister *Shashi Tharoor* had rightly commented; [again] much earlier on 8<sup>th</sup> June 2021, that:

> *"Whatever, face-saving successor arrangements the US may put in place to mask its capitulation, **its withdrawal from Afghanistan,** with none of its long-term objectives achieved, **is a defeat."***

[.....but INDIA had not believed in his own Minister's words.]

## PAKISTAN's ON-GROUND PRIORITIES:

The ISI had long been obsessed with the idea that friendly government in Afghanistan would give Pakistan the *'strategic depth'* needed to challenge its main adversary, India. A Taliban regime [*or even a Taliban-dominated coalition government*] in Kabul could be the best guarantee of that. But the ISI Generals were wise enough to tone down their celebrations on various counts.

Mainly that, as the ISI knows, the problem with taking sides and sponsoring militant groups may go un-controllable; they don't always remain under one's charge – think the *'Pakistani Taliban';* while the Afghan Taliban needed Pakistani refuge, the Pakistani Taliban started attacking their own erstwhile godfathers on the wake of insufficient steps taken by Pakistan governments to make the country a True Islamic State.

President Trump reviewed its plans to manage the war in Afghanistan; Washington was on track to modestly increase the number of military personnel deployed to Afghanistan as a stop-gap measure indicating that the US presence in the country was unlikely to end soon. Secretary of Defense Jim Mattis was named for delegated decision making on the Afghan war and chalk out a suitable strategy.

Referring to an article of *Kassel and Philip Reiner* at **foreignaffairs.com** dated 14<u>th</u> July 2017; this strategy was based on:

> *".....it is clear that the Taliban [group] is better equipped, funded and more operationally efficient today than ever before and that senior Pakistani military leaders are well versed in how to support such groups covertly. Evidence of the ISI's direct support for the militants is thin, but ...it is through the ISI that these groups, which have targeted American, Afghan, and coalition forces, survive and operate."*

The intelligentsia could read in between the lines that the US had no direct evidence of Pakistan's negative involvement in the Taliban's uprising but propaganda was being fed to media by the US and India's agencies. The US had never asked India to help them in Afghanistan with identifying and locating the Taliban's hide-outs or planning strategies. It was an 'out of bound' area for the successive US military commanders posted there because the India was shielding their lions' shares of corrupt $88bn spending in the name of *'Training Afghan Security forces in India'* – that trained force could not stop, even for an hour against the Taliban's taking-over the whole of Afghanistan including Kabul.

President Obama administration became increasingly critical of Pakistan over his entire tenure in office; however, Trump's strategy didn't fully buy Obama's arguments and policies. The Trump administration's approach remained mostly unclear – till it announced for DOHA NEGOTIATIONS in ending 2018. But it was clear that any approach would be a mistake to manage the war in Afghanistan without addressing the role and concerns of Pakistan was bound to fail – and it happened so at last. Some observers, such as the former US National Security Advisor Stephen

Hadley and the political scientist Moeed Yusuf, had argued that the US must address Pakistan's insecurities with respect to India to gain its cooperation in Afghanistan – however, President Trump didn't bother to heed.

President Trump was also advised by some so-called media gurus who were quite ignorant of the Afghan-Pak history that:

> *"....combination of carrots and sticks has been considered but never pursued by previous administrations. It would help eliminate the militants' safe haven and preserve bilateral ties by addressing Pakistan's fear of India."*

But the subsequent developments and ultimately the America's humiliating exit from Afghanistan proved that those Indian sponsored media people were living in fool's paradise.

However, the mainstream Pakistanis mostly thought positively; the other way around. Let the Taliban settle down; peace would be restored, and the Pakistani Taliban would stop targeting Pakistani army installations and convoys, and would assure the ISI to lead a peaceful life. It was a 50/50 possibility – Pakistani Taliban's viewpoint was straight that if Afghanistan could be run as an Islamic emirate, then why can't they do the same in Pakistan? Let us wait for the time to decide. May be true, the Pakistani Taliban – without a state sponsor of their own – has less chance of success than their Afghan counterparts but, of course, could still do considerable damage.

Just a day after the Taliban took Kabul on 15<sup>th</sup> August 2021, their flag was flying high above the RED MOSQUE in Pakistan's capital; conveying an open message to the people that the US-Afghan War was won by the Pakistani Taliban [TTP] as well. It was also a gesture intended to tease the Pakistan's ISI and the defeated Americans both. But who were the real victors in that Afghan war which aimlessly lasted for long 'Twenty Years', remained a question to answer by any.

Pakistan was supposedly America's partner in the war against Al Qaeda and the Taliban. The US contended that the Pak-Army had got billions of dollars in US-aid over the two decades; whereas Pakistan argued that the US still owed their bills for the military operations which were accomplished either jointly or solely with US-planned strategic roles. Also that instead of paying off Pakistan's due bills, the US had chosen India for those strategic operations knowingly that India was NOT able to deliver any performance being at a far off place. However, many alleged that:

> '.....*the American Generals adopted this policy to make the US money disappeared into unaccounted sinkholes; both parties enjoyed the booty smilingly.*'

See **Jamie Dettmer**'s essay at *voanews.com* dated 25<sup>th</sup> August 2021:

> *"President Obama revealed publicly after he left office that he ruled out involving or informing Pakistan of the raid on bin Laden's hideout because it was an open secret that certain elements inside Pakistan's military, and especially its intelligence services, maintained ties with the jihadists, sometimes using them as strategic assets **against India** and regionally.*
>
> *In 2018, the Trump administration stopped military aid to Islamabad, accusing Pakistan of failing to take action against the Taliban. Pakistan denied harbouring terrorists (– AND Taliban were not terrorists)."*

That was the level of trust between two 'war-allies', then how a partnership could survive. Trust is a two way game. Pakistan was not so foolish state not to understand such below the belt hits.

It was a story of divided interests; the US blamed that the Afghan Taliban were fighting on Pakistan's intelligence service [ISI]'s planning and control whereas the ISI contended that Pakistan's military aided the US forces as per their plans whatsoever.

In media gurus' opinion, even most Americans didn't know about the secret **'Afghan-War Papers'** released after investigations & interviews by an American watchdog from 2014-19, the SIGAR, while documents were first released in Dec 2019. In an overall assessment the US military lost war due to lethargic, incompetent, sluggish and inept Afghan Army on which the US spent $88 billion for getting it trained.

Secondly the defeat came speedily than expected because the US and Indian intelligence agencies deployed in Afghanistan proved them totally useless. *Gen Stanley A. McChrystal*, the then commander of all American troops in Afghanistan, told in an interview that:

> *".... But the facts were that the fledgling Afghan military performed poorly in the field and [thus] the American 'clear, hold, build' counter-insurgency strategy had little hope of succeeding."*

The tension between rosy public statements and the reality on the ground had been one of the enduring elements of that war. *Jeffrey Eggers*, a former Navy SEAL and later an Adviser to Gen McChrystal, told the SIGAR investigators that:

> *"One of McChrystal's hardest lessons was his government-in-a-box program which typified the American wartime machinery, and he thought you could simply wave a magic wand and POOF!"*

*Barnett Rubin*, a senior Adviser during 2009 to 2013, described the American strategy in much starker terms; saying in 2017:

> *"....But we were doing counter-insurgency as colonial power. Afghans [army commanders] knew this influx of funds wouldn't last, and they wanted to make the best of the windfall without endangering themselves. It was a fantasy that we could do that."*

*'Pakistan's ISI'* may not be the correct reason for American failure in Afghanistan. One would have to dig out the real causes; see the following paragraphs in this context.


## US *vs* TALIBAN IN RURAL AFGHANISTAN:

In 'the Washington Post' dated 5th October 2021, see an article penned down by *Sudarsan Raghavan* titled as *'Everyone here hated the Americans': Rural Afghans live with the Taliban and a painful US legacy'*, in which he openly admitted after visiting the Afghan villages named *Sinzai* and *Samarda* in *Wardak* province, 25 miles southwest of the Afghan capital – that the general populace were happy with the Taliban.

In *Wardak* province, the US military, the CIA and the ruthless Afghan militias, armed and Indian trained, fought against the Taliban for years, but trapped in the crossfire were villagers and farmers. Many became casualties of US counter-terrorism operations, drone strikes and gun battles.

What was the state of affairs in rural Afghanistan; how the Taliban won hearts in the respective areas of rural Afghanistan — why the white flags fluttered in the apple orchards of this calm settlement in between ringed mountains – it's a point to ponder.

The columnist *Raghavan* wrote that the Afghanis had marked the precise spots where US air-strikes in 2019 killed 12 villagers and their families.

In the village centre still the destroyed shell of a big building stands that once housed shops; down the road was a mangled, rusted car – AND there were white flags, too. Such reminders of legacy the US left in many rural areas across Afghanistan would remain there; *Raghavan* noted his opinion:

> *"The US military murdered civilians and committed atrocities. In Kabul and other Afghan cities, the US will be remembered for enabling two decades of progress in women's rights, an independent media and other freedoms. But in the nation's hinterlands, the main battlegrounds of America's longest war, <u>most Afghans view the US primarily through the prism of conflict, brutality and death</u>."*

*Sinzai* and the surrounding *Nerkh* District offered a glimpse of life in a post-American rural Afghanistan, home to nearly three-quarters of the population, where peace emerged in 2021; after 20 years of war. The visit offered clues to how the Taliban would govern the country and it helped explain how the militants were able to seize power across the rural areas so swiftly.

The towns and villages were abetted by the harsh tactics of US forces and their Afghan allies and by the corruption and ineffectiveness of the US-backed Afghan government. No justice or compensation from the US military or the government for the killed civilians - thus the killings of their relatives and the lack of accountability drove many villagers to support the Taliban – and it seemed plausible.

Rural Afghan society is largely conservative, and residents mostly agreed with the Taliban's harsh interpretation of Islam. They never got to see the face of American aid because hardly a dollar out of the billions was spent in *Sinzai*, less than two hours' drive from Kabul. Reconstruction efforts outside the capital were thwarted by insecurity, corruption and inefficiency - the homes in *Sinzai* and nearby villages still don't have power or running water.

The Americans left nothing for the villagers of Afghanistan – but only the empty bases. With the departure of US forces and the fall of President Ghani's government, there was calm unlike the villagers had experienced in two decades. **With the conflict ended and the Taliban in control, the violence disappeared; and brutal killings of the people totally stopped.** The village imam, said in front of a mosque peppered with bullet holes. *"You can move freely now anywhere. Death has disappeared."*

WP's *Lorenzo Tugnoli* reported another factual position:

> *"The family of Sher Mohammed was inside their home in the village of Sarmarda in April 2019 when Afghan forces raided the compound. When his son, Mohammed said, refused to come out an air-strike was called on the house. His son, his son's wife, their three children and two other relatives were killed at the spot."*

However, the security relief got tempered by new miseries. The Taliban takeover triggered freezing in funds in Afghanistan's Central Bank and elsewhere abroad. Humanitarian aids finished; international charities got pulled out of the district, and the economy seen in free fall. One villager sadly explained that:

> *"There are no air-strikes, no night raids, no bombings - but the problem now is there is no work and no money. People here are facing hunger."*

This villager named Haideri's shop and 16 other people businesses were air-bombed years before and the people of Wardak were stuffed with resentment. Occasion was that nationwide protests had erupted in 2009 after US soldiers allegedly burned Qur'an, Islam's holiest book, during a raid in Wardak. Thereafter an Army Special Forces teams raided at different times and killed at least 18 Afghan civilians during 2012-13, prompting President Hamid Karzai to order the said team out of Wardak and the Pentagon to launch an investigation – but with no results.

## MORE AMERICAN ATROCITIES:

See a high profile research paper, written by John H Akins and published in 2019 by an accredited American University:

> *"ABSTRACT: Nearly two decades after the declaration of the War on Terror, global terrorist attacks have increased. Beginning in 2005, the levels of domestic terrorism have drastically increased while international terrorism has not. This is a result of U.S. counter-terrorism policy shifting towards 'dis-aggregation' in which the US government would focus on breaking up the global al Qaeda network into disconnected groups....*
>
> *Domestic terrorism within partner states rose as a result of revenge attacks from the targeted communities and groups in the periphery in*

*response to the offensive military actions of the state, especially when they resulted in civilian casualties......*

*This led partner states to sink deeper into a terrorism trap. This study uses quantitative analysis of a global dataset and case studies of Pakistan, Yemen, Mali, and Egypt to demonstrate and test the terrorism trap theory."*

Referred to **the Terrorism Trap:** *the Hidden Impact of America's* **WOT** by *John H Akins* University of Tennessee, Knoxville USA published in <u>August 2019</u>.

On **5<sup>th</sup> August 2011**, Taliban fighters shot down a Chinook military helicopter in the *Tangi* Valley, killing 31 US military personnel, seven Afghan National Forces members and an Afghan interpreter. By 2015, US forces had quit that province. The Taliban, since then, controlled much of the *Nerkh* district. The government was entrenched in the district's centre and the villagers were caught in between. **'Whenever we left our homes we told our families - goodbye, we didn't know whether we would return home alive'.**

One villager confided:

[*Even mundane tasks become matters of life or death here. If Haideri shaved, for example, would the Taliban consider him loyal to the foreigners and the government? If he grew out his beard, would the government or the US forces consider him a Taliban?*]

Whenever the Americans conducted raids or any operations against the Taliban in that geographic area, they indiscriminately fired at anyone. That's why they all supported the Taliban. The Americans were killing the people while the Taliban protected them.

In Kabul, Afghans were waiting to see how the Taliban would govern; but in Wardak province the residents already knew it; by strict *Sharia* law — which the villagers embrace. *'It is acceptable here as it is divine and according to our Afghan values,'* said Omar, the imam.

*Sudarsan Raghavan* - referred earlier, narrated facts in his article which are not known to many Westerns. He wrote [shortened to save space]:

*"The Taliban has a 3-level court system and a police force, typically fighters not in uniforms. Thieves who are first-time offenders are given*

*public whippings – not by amputating a hand. The Taliban regime taxes the villagers, usually 10% of their farm production or store revenue.*

*The Taliban are relatively lenient by its hard-line standards to avoid alienating villagers. Villagers may listen to music or watch movies inside their homes or on smart-phones.*

*The militants have not enforced a requirement that men grow long beards. The Taliban's morality police patrol the village, but they preach about their dictates rather than use force, residents said."*

The Taliban victory was an achievement for the rural masses. One villager, Shafiqullah Zakir of Sinzai said:

*".....he was so enraged by the night raids and air-strikes that he joined the insurgency to wage jihad against the Americans. People who haven't seen each other in two decades are now travelling to far-flung areas to see relatives."*

But he [Zakir] acknowledged the challenges faced by the Taliban – foremost stands **'poverty'**, deeply rooted here since long. *'A few Western aid agencies that provided food, health care and other necessities have left; medicines are scarce.'*

Some people were hardly getting food for their families; many had to boil potatoes and eating for days to survive. That made villagers more resentful of the urban elites in Kabul; watching millions of dollars flow to shady contractors and corrupt politicians in the capital. They knew that those who left Kabul, they did not leave Afghanistan due to hunger - they collected a lot of wealth – so that's why no one liked the Americans here.

America's legacy kept on haunting one Shukrullah Khail whose younger brother, Nasratullah, was victim of the US unit. The Special Forces unit raided their home and grabbed him on a cold night and took him to the US base. *Two days later, they found Nasratullah's body near a bridge, badly tortured.* Months later, the remains of 10 missing Afghan villagers were uncovered in graves near the base. Two years later, a criminal investigation was opened but the Pentagon never responded to his emails. *'There was no justice done. What can we do now when they have all gone?'*

Coming back to **Jane Perlez's** assessment in **NEW YORK TIMES** dated 26th August 2021:

*"During the whole Afghan war the Americans had no choice, preferring to fight a chaotic war in Afghanistan **to frighten the nuclear-armed Pakistan** - EVEN though, Pakistan's ports and airfields provided the main entry points and supply lines for American military equipment needed in Afghanistan; AND the official bills of Pak-Army were only partially paid.*

*Though Pakistan was supposed to be an American ally, it mostly worked toward its own interests, as nations should do. Those interests did not include a large American military presence on its border. It was basically autonomous Afghanistan's, with a democratic government, responsibility and prerogative to act for its interests.*

*Truly, Pakistan's one goal in Afghanistan was to keep an eye over activities sponsored by its enemy, India – as the later always used separatist groups like the Balochistan Liberation Army [BLA], operating from havens in Afghanistan, to stir dissent in Pakistan."*

The Pakistani army believed that the US encouraged India to support the American-backed Afghan governments after 2001, and a fact too, which inter-alia fuelled the Pak-Army's suspicion. The Pakistanis had also felt bitter when President Obama visited India in 2015 but conspicuously boycotted Pakistan. Then Pakistan preferred to go a mile forward.

*[During a visit to Washington in spring 2021 (the Taliban took over much after), Moeed Yusuf, the national security adviser to Pakistan's PM Imran Khan, stressed the need to eliminate the Indian presence in Afghanistan,]*

While Indian diplomats were among the first foreigners to evacuate from Kabul, their departure was played correctly in the Pakistani media as a singular victory.

**Douglas London,** a former CIA counter-terrorism Chief for South and Southwest Asia, however, felt bad about the reality factor that the Tliban had taken over the government in Kabul. He said:

*"All the time Gen Bajwa [Pak-Army Chief] was pressed by the US to give up Khalil Haqqani and two other Haqqani leaders, and all the time, Bajwa would say, 'Tell us where they are.' My favourite quote was when Gen Bajwa said: You just have to come to my office and we will go in a helicopter and pick them up.*

*The Afghan Taliban would not be where they are without the assistance of the Pakistanis."*

It remained a fact that Washington's relationship with Pakistan cooled as per Obama's 'other' priorities but touched its heights after Navy SEALS killed Osama bin Laden [OBL] in May 2011 in Pakistan. Top American officials stopped visiting Pakistan and its bill-payments stopped. In the mean time, Pakistan stopped American war supplies from transiting Pakistan, increasing the cost of the war for America. However, it proved to be a temporary measure; in countries where rogue and corrupt leaderships like Zardaris sit in Presidency – every facility comes on sale.

# Scenario 222

## THE BLAME GAME-II

### WEST's NEW SCAPEGOAT FOR DEFEAT:

Referring to *Irfan Raja*'s article in **Daily Sabah** dated <u>27<sup>th</sup> October 2021</u>:

> *"Pakistan is Western media's new scapegoat in Afghanistan. Ever since the fall of Kabul, many US officials are campaigning to threaten Pakistan with sanctions and accusing it of contributing to the defeat in Afghanistan. Americans believe that because of Pakistan's role and support, the Taliban retook Kabul."*

Raja mentions that correspondingly, 22 influential US senators passed a **bill** in the House, *'giving a hefty bipartisan endorsement to open an independent investigation of US failure in Afghanistan.'*

Additionally, a Canadian politician and former diplomat, **Chris Alexander,** started a Twitter campaign to put sanctions on Pakistan for its role in Afghanistan. One simple question here:

- Between 2006 and 2015, nearly 50 militant groups declared war on Pakistan, conducting over 16,000 terrorist attacks on its territories. It suffered more than 80,000 casualties and lost over $150 billion in the economy.

- The conflict also drove 3.5 million of Pakistani citizens from their homes.

### WHAT SACRIFICE WAS OFFERED FOR AFGHANISTAN BY CANADA?

BUT....what sacrifices the Canada offered during 20-years being a NATO ally.

It was shameless move by Mr Alexander who didn't know even an iota about the contemporary history and wars.

*Daniel Markey* in his write-up in the **Foreign Affairs** [discussed in next paragraphs] raised two important questions as to:

- 'How could the US failed so completely to engineer a change in Pakistan's behaviour in Afghanistan?

- Why couldn't Washington convince or coerce Pakistan to join its side?'

In the next paragraphs, the writer *(Daniel Markey)* himself replied these two questions with justification [shortened for space constraints]:

This situation recalls the US defeat in **Vietnam,** after which **Cambodia** was blamed for the setback. Despite repairable losses in Afghanistan, evidently, the US had not learned any lessons from the costly and deadly war in Vietnam and Iraq. In the same vein, the Western media was not ready to admit that its irresponsible role in propagating a designed propaganda campaign of **Weapons of Mass Destruction [WMD]** had destroyed an entire Iraqi nation along with the so called prestige of a super power.

Following the fall of Kabul, most sections of Western media played the same old game of finding a neighbour and blaming it for the US 'MISSION FAILURE' in Afghanistan. 20 years is such a long time to build a nation and, even if it was not a US mission, **the US has no excuse for its failure – being a superpower.** Once again, history repeated itself for America: but its whole machinery remained busy in searching for a new scapegoat to cover their follies in Afghan-War.

For a long time now, the US and Pakistan maintained a *fragile relationship* – exhaustive reasons are placed in coming chapters. In a **Harvard Business Review** article, *Nir Eyal* poses a question, *'Why you need an imaginary scapegoat'* that is built upon an internet theme of *DJ Khaled,* a man who warns his social media followers about a group of villains. After learning this, the Western media opted to fit Eyal's analysis of the *'imaginary scapegoat'* in Afghan-War situation. Several American officials, strategists and media commentators were bent upon to demonize Pakistan's role in the US's WAR ON TERROR [WOT] – the reply lies in the beginning above.

The Western media raised this hue and cry against Pakistan and its ISI because of their opposing thoughts about ISLAM. They played it more on the instance of Indian media lobby knowing well that Pakistan and India are die-heart rivals in all spheres of international forums. India had very nefarious and wicked plans in association with Afghan President Ghani – they wanted an access to hot waters of Arabian Sea through breaking Balochistan [Pakistan's biggest 4th province]. Now their plans: India's $3 bn investment on infrastructure and American's $87bn investment on training of Afghan Security Forces have gone into vain plus both countries lost their prestige.

## AMERICA FAILED TO WIN ISI; WHY?

There cannot be two opinions that the US completely failed in Afghanistan and wasted its two decades time, finances and honour as well. But the intelligentsia also held the opinion that the US Pentagon and CIA miserably crashed and collapsed in terms of Washington's approach to Pakistan, its army and the ISI.

Why some Pakistani groups cheered the Taliban's return to power in Kabul. How the US failed so completely to engineer a change in Pakistan's behaviour about Afghanistan? Why couldn't Washington convince or coerce Pakistan to join its side – simply because since a decade the US continuously humiliated Pakistan by keeping India dearer and making two puppet Afghan regimes subservient to Indian domain. **It was, of course, a battle of survival for the fittest.**

US-Pakistani dialogues after President Biden's speech announcing their quit and on the allied issues showed clear signs of friction: Pakistani officials earned great public praise for their assistance in evacuating third-country officials from Kabul, while US diplomats remained less optimistic about Taliban reprisals; they remained concerned about threats of resurgent al Qaeda and Islamic State [ISIS] affiliates in Afghanistan.

Cool minded think tanks in Washington appreciated just how little leverage the US often held with Pakistan, particularly when it tried to push an overlong list of priorities and made demands that scampered counter to Islamabad's interests. If the relationship had to gain vital American national interests, as it did after the 9/11 attacks, the US policymakers could level credible threats to ensure Pakistan's compliance with their agenda, too.

Alternately, the US should have lowered its ambitions with Pakistan to transactional cooperation on issues where the two sides could see eye to eye. This could include some counter-terror operations in Afghanistan, as well as regional diplomacy and crisis management.

Let us return to the recent history of Afghanistan for a while. In the chaotic aftermath that followed the Soviet withdrawal from Afghanistan in early 1989, Islamabad had no plans to expand its influence westward but the US dragged it in the battlefield – perhaps to negate Iran. Then some Pakistani security officials started supporting the Taliban out of ideological sympathy.

Pakistan withdrew its official support to the Taliban only after 9/11 event and it became sanctuary for fleeing Taliban leaders because they were mostly *Pashtuns* and their step families were [still they are] residing in tribal belt areas [FATA] all along Pak-Afghan border where Islamabad had no writ then. Within months, the whole country was depleted with bombing and terror activities – loosing about 50,000 civilians and 5000 army troops within a span of first 5-6 years of war.

Pakistan became a safe haven for the Taliban because the two countries have about 2500+ miles shared border, mountainous and barren highlands with tribal way of living. Additionally, the dummy political order that the US created in Afghanistan offered fertile ground for insurgency, as the government in Kabul was endemic with corruption and made enemies of many of its own citizens.

New **Afghan forces, especially trained in India,** wasted all American funds – could not stay for even a day to defend Kabul in August 2021. Washington totally failed in tackling the Taliban especially in its last years of stay – and thus preferred to negotiate an earlier withdrawal.

The American policy makers knew that the US rarely placed Afghanistan at the top of its list of priorities; 1$^{st}$ position always given to India – just to make it stand against China. Pakistan always kept at number 3 which was the hatred level for the West. This priority order clearly explains why Pakistani leaders repeatedly doubted Washington's seriousness of purpose in Afghanistan. These doubts were only compounded after 2003, when the US focused greater attention on Iraq.

- *Another reality that every American administration since 2001 preferred to work with Pakistan's military directly after buying the ruling [mostly corrupt] elite – politician and bureaucracy both – then why complaints.*

The US collaborated closely with the Pak-army and its ISI to capture or kill al Qaeda operatives – but simultaneously patronising Indian RAW to launch its offensives in Balochistan, Kashmir and Tribal regions. Washington rarely found exploitable fractures within the Pak-army and even feared that sowing such divisions would risk collapsing the most effective institution of a nuclear state. No matter the implications for Afghanistan, that was never considered a plausible risk.

Referring to an essay titled *'Why Washington Failed to Win Over Islamabad...'* by <u>Daniel Markey</u> appeared on all media pages on 9th **September 2021** *[words & phrases re-arranged]*:

> "........*an important contingent within the Pak-army straightaway opposed any cooperation with the US and rather attacked Pakistanis who collaborated with Washington, including fellow officers in the army and the intelligence services. In December 2003, Gen Musharraf escaped two assassination attempts traced to military officers within the organization; and several other plots were also reportedly foiled.*
>
> *Over the next few years, that opposition to the US materialised into a domestic insurgency under the banner of the Pakistani Taliban [TTP]. The group initially enjoyed sympathy from many quarters in Pakistani society, including serving and retired military officers; the violence had spiked against the Pakistani state itself to an unprecedented level."*

It remained a fact that even those Pakistanis who were working with the US in previous times were not convinced that Washington's lead could be fruitful for Afghanistan's future; truth being that US officials never demonstrated much sympathy for Pakistan's concerns. They were never serious about Islamabad's anxiety *vs* Kabul-based puppet governments. Both Kabul and the US were often seen siding with India - rather routinely preferred strategic partnerships with the later.

Immediately after the famous 9/11 episode, **Pakistan was** *'threatened to be taken into the stone-age'* – US Secretary Powel's phone call is still remembered by the whole Pakistani nation. Then the US many times tried to impose coercive measures to win Pakistani support—frequently adopting carrot and stick policies but such efforts never provided any soothing effect for any party.

Later, Washington often talked about the sale of F-16 fighter jets but got the issue melted in extensive congressional debates which ultimately lost its utility – thus the US suffered in the long run. *'Reimbursements for Pakistan's military operations'* amounting to millions of dollars were unnecessarily delayed; or tied with strings - leaving Islamabad internally bleeding.

Once an opportunity came immediately before President Obama's 2009-10 rush into Afghanistan; the US could have forced Islamabad into serious negotiations. Washington instead chose to delay negotiations in the hope that its military advances would deliver a sweeping victory over the Taliban. That was a crucial moment to take Pakistan into confidence before actual despatch of forces – but the US lost it due to its fake and false ego.

On 2nd May 2011, the US SEALs killed OBL in a raid near Abbot Abad; the whole Pakistani nation knew that the said act was accomplished with President Zardari-CIA-Gen Shuja [the then ISI Chief] nexus whereas the rest of the Pak-army was betrayed in humiliating mode. However, rather than following up with new threats of what would come up in return, the US officials preferred to play a blame-game more vigorously.

The US officials kicked the Pakistani military when it was already down. Contrarily they hoped to maintain good relations with Pakistan by continuing the US military access through its roads and airspace into Afghanistan; they also believed that Pakistan's situation could get worse. In fact the worst days were ahead for the US due to its short sightedness coupled with their failed diplomacy and proud intelligence both.

The Biden administration and its associates had known about the black and hollow media propaganda of their companions – Kabul and India; openly felt that none of Afghanistan's other neighbours could hold as much influence as Pakistan. Within years, the conclusion appeared that Islamabad went more attached to China and seen less inclined to trust Washington's commitments. Washington learnt very soon that a strategic partnership with Islamabad became out of reach at least for the time being.

Very few people knew that the US forces had already developed working relationship with the Taliban to counter ISIS in recent years. In the given scenario, the US had already started efforts to calibrate its relationship with Pakistan; but it's a future story.

## ISI HOSTED 7 INTELLIGENCE CHIEFS:

On 11th September 2021; Pakistan's Inter-Services Intelligence [ISI] DG Gen Faiz Hameed welcomed participation of the heads of intelligence of China, Russia, Iran, Kazakhstan, Tajikistan, Turkmenistan and Uzbekistan to discuss the Afghan situation in detail and planned unified strategy to cooperate with the Taliban government in Afghanistan.

Notably, the foreign ministers of all the countries mentioned above had met earlier the same week for the same purpose. The high-level meeting was convened days after Gen Faiz Hameed's return from Afghan capital Kabul, which he visited on the invitation of the Taliban. The seven chiefs discussed the immediate future of Pakistan and Afghanistan's security, economic and trade ties with the Taliban leadership.

Russia and other central Asian countries had been monitoring the rapid developments in Afghanistan since the Taliban began its offensive against the US-backed Afghan government, which culminated in President Ghani's collapse amid the pullout of American troops and the Taliban seizing power.

Few days before, the Taliban announced its new interim government, headed by Mohammad Hasan Akhund, with Abdul Ghani Baradar as his deputy. The Taliban invited only six countries to the inaugural ceremony of the new government -- Russia, China, Turkey, Iran, Pakistan and Qatar – just to put another slap on the western and American faces. However, the inauguration event was cancelled after the Taliban was pressurised by allies not to conduct that ceremony in the back-drop of the anniversary of 9/11 terror attacks in the US.

As the five participants exchanged views on the security situation in Afghanistan, it may be recalled that about a week back, the ISI chief had visited Afghanistan and especially met *Hizb-e-Islami* head Gulbaddin Hekmatyar. On a similar note, foreign ministers of countries neighbouring Afghanistan held a virtual conference on 8th September 2021, to discuss the latest developments in the war-torn country.

## PM PAKISTAN's 'ABSOLUTELY NOT':

On 14th September 2021; in a public hearing in Congress since collapse of the US in Afghanistan, the US Secretary of State Blinken said to the Foreign Affairs Committee that US IS ANGRY ON PAKISTAN, adding:

> *"Pakistan has a multiplicity of interests some that are in conflict with ours. It is one that is involved hedging its bets constantly about the future of Afghanistan; it's one that's involved harbouring members of the Taliban; it is one that's also involved in different points cooperation with us on counter-terrorism."*

Blinken categorically told the lawmakers that Washington would re-examine its relationship with Pakistan. The US would re-evaluate the role that Pakistan played over the last 20 years but also the role we would want to see it play in future. Blinken also called on Pakistan to deny legitimacy to the Taliban unless they meet global demands. He said that *'Pakistan needs to line up with a broad majority of the international community in working toward those ends and in upholding those expectations'*.

However, during the hearing, the furious lawmakers **accused the White House** of presiding over a historic disaster. Mr Blinken stayed cool as he faced the toughest grilling of his career at the first congressional hearing on President Joe Biden's end to the 20-year war, which brought a swift victory by the Taliban. However, Blinken continued to speak that:

> *"Former president Donald Trump had set the withdrawal from Afghanistan. We inherited a deadline; we did not inherit a plan.*
>
> *After Trump's February 2020 deal with the Taliban and drawdown of US troops, the movement was in the strongest military position it had been since 9/11.*
>
> *Biden administration was intensely focused on the safety of Americans. Even the most pessimistic assessments did not predict that Afghan forces in Kabul would collapse."*

The United States and its allies ultimately evacuated 123,000 people out of Afghanistan, one of the largest airlifts in history.

America's anger on Pakistan was exactly not on the terms Mr Blinken narrated; most analysts and media gurus had complete knowledge of the background reason. The real reason was Pakistani PM Imran Khan's media interview in which the US was bluntly refused any access to any facility on Pakistani soils in connection with the Afghan-war. PM Khan's famous dialogue **ABSOLUTELY NOT** became talking point for the whole world then.

**On 19th June 2021;** Pakistan's PM Imran Khan conveyed a big NO to the United States on its request of military bases for future operations in Afghanistan. The statement from the premier came during an interview with Jonathan Swan of **HBO Axios,** which was then aired two days later, on 21st June 2021 instant.

PM Imran reiterated Pakistan's stance on the use of military bases and categorically stated that Islamabad would not allow it.

PM Khan was asked by the American journalist for his comments on giving access to the Central Intelligence Agency [CIA] to Pakistan military bases as was permitted during Gen Musharraf's tenure. The proposal was floated to land the CIA in Pakistan to conduct cross border counter-terrorism missions against Al Qaeda, ISIS and the Taliban. **ABSOLUTELY NOT,** PM Imran Khan had spontaneously responded and added:

> *"There's no way we're going to allow any bases or any sort of action from Pakistani territory into Afghanistan – [asserting once more] Absolutely not."*

Axios on HBO is a documentary-news program that combines the reporting of Axios journalists with the expertise of HBO filmmakers to explore the collision of tech, media, business, and politics. The US was in talks with Pakistan and other regional countries for cooperation in future operations in the war-torn country, Afghanistan, to keep a check on its militancy. Pakistan had also officially conveyed to Washington that it was NOT possible.

Pakistan's ISI DG Lt Gen Faiz Hameed was in Kabul during the first week of September 2021 and as having meetings with the Taliban leadership as well as other Afghan leaders including Gulbadin Hekmatyar. There was no government in Afghanistan then; in such a situation, Pakistan's political high-ups could not visit Kabul because there was no counterpart. Pakistan showed a good gesture by sending its ISI Chief in person there to show the solidarity with the Afghan people.

As Pakistan and Afghanistan shared deep strategic, economic, political and social relations, Islamabad could not abandon ordinary Afghans and close its eyes to the likely impacts to be caused to the country in case of instability in Kabul. Negating the impression that the country was following an Afghan policy different from the rest of the world, Fawad Chaudhry, **a Federal Minister of Pakistan,** said the only difference was that Pakistan had been calling for a political solution to the Afghan crisis for years, while the US and other world powers realised the importance of the option only recently – after getting defeated after 20 year's war.

Forming a government in Kabul was the right of the Afghan people only and Pakistan supported the idea of an inclusive government there. He said Islamabad could only play a role in the stability of the war-torn country and that the new government there would be recognised in consultation with regional countries and world powers. Indian taxpayers and Lok Sabha should question Modi government's Afghan strategy in which it had wasted billions of dollars in Afghanistan while this amount could have been used for the welfare of the marginalised people in India.

Question arises that why the Indian government and media were presenting Afghanistan as the biggest issue though *the two countries shared not a single inch of border*. India could not be given any role in Afghanistan, for it had always used Afghan soil for sponsoring terrorist activities against Pakistan.

## EUROPE's BEST PAL IN 2021 CRISIS:

While the whole Europe including the UK was desperate to repatriate its citizens from Taliban's new regime in Afghanistan – they wanted to avoid another refugee crisis - Europe turned to Islamabad for help which was honoured by the PM Imran Khan's government.

Referring to SAIM SAEED's essay in *POLITICO.EU* of 3<u>rd</u> September 2021:

> *"Meet Europe's unexpected new best friend.*
>
> *As the Continent scrambles to evacuate its citizens from Afghanistan and prevent a potential wave of refugees on its borders, Europe is reaching out to Pakistan — long seen as a recluse state — (now) for help with both.*
>
> *In only one week, the foreign ministers of Germany, the Netherlands and the UK visited Islamabad. They asked Pakistan for its assistance in the humanitarian crisis next door, and showered praise on the country for its help evacuating thousands of diplomatic staff and Afghan workers from Kabul."*

Germany's Ambassador to Pakistan Bernhard Schlagheck said it would not have been possible to fly out German and Dutch staff without Islamabad's assistance, while Pakistan also received friendly calls from the EU Council's President Charles Michel, EU foreign policy chief Josep Borrell, the Austrians, and the Slovenes.

> This newfound affection for Pakistan is a significant shift in the diplomatic tides from this spring when the EU had eyes only for Pakistan's arch-enemy India. In April 2021, the <u>EU committed to an Indo-Pacific strategy</u> that meant to see increased **European cooperation with India** against Pakistan's ally, China. In May 2021, **Brussels**

**also launched free-trade talks with New Delhi.** However, Pakistan gracefully avoided bargaining with any EU member for its hardships and sufferings in the field of economics, trade incentives, diplomatic support for the disputed region of Kashmir or travelling concessions for UK or the EU countries.

Pakistan looked to invest only in cordial relationships with Europe, which was caught flat-footed by the US's heuristic decision to withdraw; they were all trying to secure their own interests in the region without the American help and so-called 'US's flimsy directions'. Before the Afghan crisis, Pakistan was not at all popular in Brussels though it had been supporting the NATO.

The EU mostly posed as a major trading partner of Pakistan but in fact had placed the later much low in the EU's priority list – especially in comparison with India. With the Taliban's take over in mid-August [2021], the whole scenario changed suddenly. Islamabad played its role in helping European and foreign officials leave Kabul, including **294 Dutch** citizens, **201 Belgians, 216 Italians, and 273 Danes.** In addition, Pakistan also helped evacuate more than **4,000 Afghan nationals** who worked with the US and allied forces in Kabul.

> [.....*interestingly, on 17th August 2021, the UK government had announced plans to welcome an additional 5,000 Afghans fleeing the Taliban in a new resettlement programme prioritising the women. It had already got plans to relocate 5,000 people as part of an* **Afghan Relocation Programme** *designed to help present and past employees of the UK government. Home Secretary Priti Patel wrote in* **Daily Telegraph** *that day:*
>
> *"I want to ensure that as a nation we do everything possible to provide support to the most vulnerable fleeing Afghanistan so they can start a new life in safety in the UK.*
>
> *The UK is also doing all it can to encourage other countries to help. Not only do we want to lead by example, we cannot do this alone."*]

But how fast the developed nations eat their own words, no one can guess. Just two weeks later, the four Foreign Ministers of EU and UK were there in Islamabad to shift their burden and follies on poor Pakistan's shoulders.

Pakistan did its moral duty bravely; PM Mr Khan's prime thinking brought fruit. He immediately launched talks with Taliban leadership the day they captured Kabul Palace. Pakistan's that 'welcome gesture' allowed it to continue flights and keep its embassy open, even as most countries were scrambling to leave the country. See the Dutch Foreign Minister **Sigrid Kaag**'s address at a press conference in Islamabad on the very next day:

> *"We have tremendous admiration and respect for Pakistan and we would like to reiterate our gratitude."*

UK's Foreign Secretary Dominic Raab told the media that: *"Pakistan is a vital partner for the UK."*

Hosting refugees has been a toxic issue in Europe, and the Continent was to avoid the animosity it experienced over the last influx of 2015-16. Austria loudly announced not to take in any Afghan refugee after the Taliban took over, and **French President Macron said:**

> *"Europe must anticipate and protect ourselves against major irregular migratory flows that would endanger those who use them and feed trafficking of all kinds."*

That's where they sought Pakistan's help – which has been loosing its own economy since 1980s when millions of Afghan refugees were there on its soils – and not a single person went back. In good days, the EU prefers India to trade along with pointing towards Pakistan's depressed economic state, its repressive blasphemy laws and the lack of protection for minorities. Then the stances changed suddenly in August 2021 when the **Dutch Foreign Minister Kaag** said in Islamabad:

> *"We're mindful and grateful for the longstanding hosting role Pakistan has played for the refugees over the years. We will explore ways in which we can assist Pakistan in its role as a hosting nation to refugees and wanting to invest and make use of the improving climate to attract business and invest in Pakistan itself."*

BUT the Pakistanis were mindful even in that changed arena – knowing that all countries would forget Pakistan when the dust would settle down. UK continued to keep Pakistan in RED list in the name of coronavirus sanctions; no EU country promised to remove Pakistan from the **"grey list"** of the Financial Action Task Force [**FATF**]; no EU country called Pakistan to join their trade scheme called the **GSP+**; no EU country allowed Pakistan's national carrier, **the PIA,** to fly up to their airports – but this time there was no President Musharraf or Zardari in place; nothing was on sale now.

## GOVERNING PAKISTAN IS NOT JOKE:

On 26th October 2021; One Usama Siddique interestingly wrote on media pages that: *'Governing Pakistan isn't a joke'* and he was more than 100% true. Usama continued saying that the External Forces tried and failed in destabilising Pakistan with numerous attempts; that spanned over years. However, at the internal front, the country was badly beaten by:

- Target Killings
- Suicide Attacks & Terrorism
- Corruption & Economic Stranglehold
- TTP & BLA through Indian secret funding
- Indian infiltrations through Afghanistan

In this Asian region, the US & EU were encountered with 3 major problems since decades

- CPEC [BRI]
- Pakistan's Nuclear Capability
- Pakistan's mostly dishonest & 'ON SALE' rulers

The West was able to strike a blow to CPEC in the past two corrupt ruling regimes but not through 2018-22, while there's a ruler in place in Pakistan; loyal to the safety and integrity of Pakistan at least.

> *PM IK and the Army Chief Bajwa sent a crystal clear message to the West that Pakistan was no more available for hire to fight wars at the behest of others. No more slaughtering of Pakistanis in the killing fields of unjust clashes.*

The Western bugle of war against CPEC and BRI was up; look at the statement made by the US Deputy Secretary of State **Wendy Sherman** while visiting India during 5-7th October 2021:

> *'.....we don't see building broad-based relationship with Pakistan.'*

It was a wake-up call for the whole Pakistani leadership. Pakistan had clearly conveyed a message that it would not restrict CPEC, rout to

Central Asia would go ahead - no border closures. However, the opposition in Pakistan was bent upon to play usual notorious gimmicks.

Pak-Army, the powerhouse in Pakistan, also understood that PM IK was mentally and psychologically tough – a rare breed in the third world. President Biden played mind games with IK; he tried to outsmart and humiliate IK because he, being a Vice President with Obama, knew the Pakistani leaders Sharif brothers, AAZ and IK personally.

On 19th November 2018; newly elected Pakistani PM Imran Khan, in response to disparaging and critical comments made by President Trump, had courage to tweet:

> *"No Pakistani was involved in 9/11 but Pak decided to participate in US War on Terror. Pakistan suffered 75,000+ casualties in this war & over $123 bn were lost to economy…Our tribal areas were devastated & millions of people uprooted from their homes. The war drastically impacted lives of ordinary Pakistanis."*

Quoting the above phrase, one **American researcher John Akins** wrote in his thesis submitted to *University of Tennessee*, Knoxville USA in <u>August 2019</u> that:

> *"Like so many partner states drafted into America's fight against al Qaeda, the previous two decades have left an indelible impact on Pakistan's domestic political landscape, particularly given the key strategic role Pakistan played in US counter-terrorism efforts.*
>
> *…..this chapter shows how the use of the military in Pakistan's north-western border region, given the prevailing conditions of this periphery, led to a violent backlash in the form of domestic terrorism. As terrorist violence intensified, U.S. officials continued to press Pakistan to '<u>DO MORE</u>,' with the resulting 169 military operations by the Pakistani army making worse the local conditions that contributed to the dramatic rise in domestic terrorism, trapping the country in a deadly cycle of violence."*
>
> [*The Terrorism Trap: the Hidden Impact of America's WOT* by *John H Akins* is referred]

## ISLAMIC STATE - Khorasan [IS-K]

As the *Islamic State-Khorasan* [IS-K] started ramping up attacks in Afghanistan; Pakistan used its network of informal channels to feed intelligence and technical support to the Taliban rulers to combat the threat.

Pakistan has been passing the Taliban raw information as well as helping it monitor phone and Internet communication to identify IS-K members and their operational hubs but the communication between the two sides remained confined to informal discussions, rather than an established intelligence-sharing partnership. However, this uphill task could only be undertaken by brave countries like Pakistan not like the US or India.

It remained unclear how much intelligence countries like the US would be able to share. Without an embassy or military presence in Afghanistan, US intelligence gathering capabilities stand crippled, and the Taliban had previously denounced the US for flying drones over Afghan territory. Referring to *S George*'s essay in '**The Washington Post**' dated 23rd October 2021:

> "*Despite those regional concerns, the Biden admin is struggling to create stronger military and intelligence partnerships with Afghanistan's close neighbours. **Pakistan and Tajikistan have so far refused to host US bases; dis-allowing the US to maintain 'over-the-horizon' pressure on terrorist threats in Afghanistan*".*

**Lisa Curtis,** a former adviser to the White House NSC and now director at the Centre for New American Security said:

> "*There are shrinking options regarding countries on which the US could rely for staging counter-terrorism operations. Currently, the bulk of the US military assets available for a possible strike in Afghanistan remain in Qatar, some 1,200 miles away, making their use expensive and risky.*"

The head of the US Central Command **Gen Kenneth McKenzie** told the lawmakers a month earlier that:

> "*It's yet to be seen if the Taliban could stop the IS-K or al-Qaeda from using Afghan territory to launch international terrorist attacks. We could get to that point, but I do not yet have that level of confidence.*"

Afghanistan's close neighbours were equally concerned about the rise of the IS-K in Afghanistan, despite a reluctance to work with the US because of numerous conflicts. At a meeting held in Moscow during the 3ʳᵈ week of October 2021, Soviet Foreign Minister *Sergei Lavrov* said that:

> *"Russia's Central Asian friends have assured him that they do not want US military units stationed in their countries. While the US military had established temporary bases in Uzbekistan and Kyrgyzstan after 9/11 of 2001's attacks, those agreements have long since been vacated.*
>
> *The situation right now is very different than it was when that post-9/11 cooperation took place."*

For Central Asia, it could have been a very costly thing to agree to have something like that on their territories. The possibility of militant spill-over was seen in Iran, which shares a 570-mile border with Afghanistan, and China, which always feared increased IS recruitment of Uyghurs, a Muslim minority in western China under relentless pressures from Beijing including 're-education camps' that have since been denounced by the West.

Russian President Vladimir Putin also charged that there was a clear 'concentration of extremist and terrorist groups' near Afghanistan's northern borders, focusing on inciting ethnic and religious conflicts and hatred.

The IS-K had, till then, far fewer fighters in Afghanistan than the Taliban — roughly 2,000 according to the latest UN estimate, compared to Taliban ranks estimated at more than 60,000 — but many feared it could grow if the Taliban fractured or if disaffected Taliban members sought a return to the battlefield to join other groups.

After the fall of Kabul, the IS-K launched a campaign of direct assaults on Taliban security forces as well as escalating violence against Afghanistan's Shiite minority, which it regards as their orthodox rivals.

> {*In a month-long spree beginning in mid-September 2021, the Islamic State carried out 47 attacks, ranging from assassinations and assaults on military checkpoints to suicide bombings at Shiite mosques that killed dozens. All but seven of the attacks targeted Taliban fighters.*}

Referring to an article of **Henry Kissinger** on *why America failed in Afghanistan;* published in **The Economist** dated 25<u>th</u> <u>August 2021</u>; the former American statesman said:

> *"It was not possible to turn the country into a modern democracy, but creative diplomacy and force might have overcome terrorism.*
>
> *THE TALIBAN takeover of Afghanistan caused an immediate concern on the rescue of tens of thousands of Americans, allies and Afghans stranded all over the country - their salvage needed our urgent priority.*
>
> *The fundamental question remained that how America planned to withdraw **without much warning or consultation with allies** or the people most directly involved in 20 years of sacrifice. And why the basic challenge in Afghanistan has been conceived and presented to the public as a choice between full control of Afghanistan or complete withdrawal."*

The US had risked the lives of its military, staked its prestige and involved other countries, without any home work on strategic and political objectives. Strategic - to make clear the circumstances for which the US opted to fight; political - to define the governing framework to sustain the outcome of the war. *The US lost primarily because of its inability to define achievable goals* and to link them in sustainable foot-steps by the future American regimes.

Henry Kissinger rightly pointed out that in this US-Afghan war, the US military objectives were too absolute and unattainable while the political ones too theoretical and vague. The failure to link them to each other involved America in conflicts and domestic controversies. The US entered Afghanistan amid wide public support in response to the al-Qaeda's attack on America. The initial military campaign prevailed with great effectiveness but *then tensions developed with Pakistan amidst carrot & stick policies which didn't work this time unfortunately;* Henry Kissinger had floated a very bold statement.

However, soon the US lost its strategic focus. The White House got convinced that ultimately the re-emergence of terrorist bases could only be prevented by transforming Afghanistan into a modern state with democratic institutions and government. But there was no timetable for such major reforms because Afghanistan has never been a modern state. There was no sense of common obligation and concept of central authority. The whole Afghan soil has been in tribal pigeon holes indeed since centuries. It was precisely Afghanistan's inaccessibility and absence of central authority that made it an attractive base for terrorist groups.

Afghan entity could have been analysed in the light of its past and historical notes; the people live in ethnic groups and tribal clans, in basically a feudal structure where the decisive power brokers are the organisers of clan defence forces. Typically in latent conflict with each other, these warlords unite in broad coalitions primarily when some outside force—such as the British army that invaded in 1839 and the Soviet armed forces that occupied Afghanistan in 1979—sought to impose centralised governments. Both retreats, British and Soviets, sufficiently prove that the Afghan people are only willing to fight for themselves.

The fact remained that the Taliban could be contained but not eliminated during this longest war. And the introduction of unfamiliar western-like government weakened the US political commitment and enhanced already widespread corruption to unparalleled heights.

Moreover, the counter-insurgency side of the American debate was defined as progress, the political one treated as disaster. The two Administrative and military groups tended to paralyse each other during successive policy discussions in White House and else where. An example was decision in 2009 to declare a surge of troops in Afghanistan with a simultaneous announcement that they would begin to withdraw in 18 months. Here, the counter-insurgency was reduced to the containment, rather than the destruction of the Taliban.

In fact political goals were not co-ordinated with counter-insurgency efforts. India, China, Russia and Pakistan often had divergent interests then; so the US needed a creative diplomacy to have distilled common measures for overcoming terrorism in Afghanistan. But this alternative was never explored. Having campaigned against the war, Presidents Trump and Joe Biden undertook peace negotiations with the Taliban and committed for withdrawal plans for which the US had induced allies to help.

America couldn't escape being a key component of international order because of its capacities; sudden withdrawal tarnished its honour and images both. The US could have recognised that no dramatic strategic move was available in the immediate future to offset this self-inflicted setback; thus its rashness brought disappointment among allies, encouraged adversaries, and caused confusion among the media from all around the world.

### 20 years long chapter was closed

### IN FACT,
### AFGHAN PEOPLE SUFFERED WAR FOR NEARLY 4 DECADES

### BUT
### HOW IT STARTED
### HOW FINISHED –
### SEE DETAILS IN NEXT PAGES

# Scenario 223

## AFGHANISTAN – AS COUNTRY:

Afghanistan is approximately 653,000 sq km, out of which arable land is only a little less than 12%, amounting to 78,360 sq km. One sq km has 247 acres. In America one acre feeds about 1-2 people. In Afghanistan, if one acre fed 10-15 people, then less than 2 million people get food out of a population of about 38 million. The other 36 million have to be fed from Pakistan, because it is the cheapest source of surplus wheat. Pakistan's 882,000 sq km has more than 40% arable land and it normally produces surplus wheat and rice.

Afghanistan needs Pakistan for its access to the sea, food security and building up a modern defence capability. If Afghanis keep practicing pure Afghan nationalism, and Pakistan continues to keep practicing Uncle Tom's backward ideologies from the bygone days of European enlightenment, both will remain adversaries. Pakistan will remain poor and Afghanistan will starve to death. Better for Afghanistan to partner up with Pakistan's various sectors, except politics; if not, Pakistan would let its neighbour down for its own security.

An important factor to be remembered by ruling Afghan Taliban, that the Muslim women have been leading the armies of men in Islamic history. Islam produced female scholars before any other civilization could do so – so education should be opened up equally for all. Better to follow enlightened Islamic injunctions and protect your women. Disallow man-hating feminist ideologies to protect the family unit; community's wellbeing depends on the wellbeing of mothers, sisters, daughters and wives and on various roles performed by them.

Afghan government should reject all pressure from abroad on this account but it can gradually re-engineer its society in which women will be modest but fully participating in Islamic empire at local as well as national levels.

## THE EARLY HISTORY:

Most Americans don't know that the phenomenon of tense US-Afghan relations has its deep roots. In American libraries still one can find a press-photo of **16th December 1955**, originated by the AP, in which Sardar M Daoud Khan, the then prime minister of Afghanistan, is seen with Soviet Minister of Defence Marshal Nikolai Bulganin in Kabul in a state celebration. In fact, these Soviet ties brought a slow escalation of conflict with the US in the Cold War.

During Daoud Khan's rule, Afghanistan increasingly saw in Pakistan both a competitor and a threat. Indeed, Daoud's quest for arms from Russia was in large part motivated by Afghanistan's own cold war with Pakistan. However, it was Daoud's support for a *'Pashtun Nationalist Movement'* in Pakistan that left the greatest lasting repercussions. Though issue of the *Pashtunistan* has roots in 1893 when Sir Henry M Durand, foreign secretary of India, demarcated what became known as the **Durand line,** setting the boundary between British India and Afghanistan; thus dividing the *Pashtun* tribes into two countries BUT Daoud Shah flared up the problem more intensively.

In 1955, Pakistan re-ordered its administrative structure to merge all provinces in West Pakistan making it a single unit. Daoud Khan interpreted the move as an attempt to marginalize the Pashtuns of the North West Frontier Province [NWFP] now the Khyber PK.

**In March 1955,** Afghan mobs attacked Pakistan's embassy in Kabul, and ransacked the Pakistani consulates in Jalalabad and Kandahar. In return, Pakistani mobs retaliated by sacking the Afghan consulate in Peshawar. Afghanistan mobilized its reserves for war but Kabul and Islamabad agreed to approach an arbitration commission - the process provided time for tempers to cool.

Twice, in 1960 and in 1961, Daoud Khan sent Afghan troops into Pakistan's NWFP; in September 1961, Kabul and Islamabad disengaged diplomatic relations and Pakistan sealed its border with Afghanistan. Pakistan, meanwhile, got disturbed with a Moscow-New Delhi-Kabul alliance. For the next two years, Afghanistan and Pakistan traded venomous and hurtful radio and press propaganda as Afghan insurgents fought Pakistani units inside Pak-territory.

On 9th **March 1963,** Daoud Khan stepped down. Two months later, with the mediation of the Shah of Iran, Pakistan and Afghanistan re-established their diplomatic relations – but remained confined to lip-services only.

In those days, Afghanistan was going through a series of modernizing projects; attempting to really build into a modern nation-state under two consecutive leaderships: King Zahir Shah, and followed by his cousin President Daoud Khan - amidst the rogue curse of the Cold War.

Both the Soviet Union and the United States were involved in Afghanistan through infrastructure building. The Soviet Union built the much needed *Salang* Tunnel, which connected northern Afghanistan to Kabul. The US got involved in the *Helmand* Valley project - an irrigation and agricultural project about building dams in southern Afghanistan. Both super powers were funnelling significant amounts of money from the '50s till much late.

In brief, during that Cold War era, both the US and the Soviet Union sought to gain footholds in Afghanistan; first through infrastructure investments and then military intervention. One power had to escape from that soil in February 1989 leaving the country with inheritance of a civil war — a backdrop to the rise of Taliban.

While the US took a back seat in Afghanistan during much of the '90s, it invaded it after the 9/11 event in 2001 and assumed a two-decade project to end on 31st August 2021 with humiliations and losses of all sorts. Then a wide spread notion appeared on world media horizon – who were the Taliban and how the group managed the only super power's defeat.

For the answer, one can follow the new conceptions developed in most American minds soon after 9/11 attacks. A testimony titled as **"WHO IS RESPONSIBLE FOR THE TALIBAN"** by Michael Rubin appeared at *Washingtoninstitute.org* website on **1st March 2002**, just about 5 months after America's attack on Afghanistan. The essay starts with:

> *"As the United States prepared for war against Afghanistan, some academics or journalists argued that Osama bin Ladin's al-Qa'ida group and Afghanistan's Taliban government were really creations of American policy run amok. A pervasive myth exists that the United States was complicit for allegedly training Osama bin Ladin and the Taliban.*
>
> *For example;*
> ***Jeffrey Sommers***, *a professor in Georgia, has repeatedly claimed that the Taliban had turned on 'their previous benefactor.'*

*David Gibbs, a political science professor at the University of Arizona, made similar claims.*

*Robert Fisk, widely-read Middle East correspondent for <u>The Independent</u>, wrote of 'CIA camps in which the Americans once trained bin Ladin's fellow guerrillas.'*

*Mort Rosenblum, <u>Associated Press</u> writer, declared that 'Osama bin Ladin was the type of Soviet-hating freedom fighter that US officials applauded when the world looked a little different'."*

The same type of opinions again started appearing in media pages, might be sponsored by the US government, after a decade to win the public opinion: see **TO WIN IN AFGHANISTAN-DESTROY PAKISTAN's ISI** written in <u>American Intelligence Journal</u> - Vol. 30, No. 2 (2012), pp. 120-124 (5 pages) by <u>Howard Kleinberg</u> - Published By: **National Military Intelligence Foundation**: Ref: https://www.jstor. org/stable/26202023

In above write up, it was argued that neither Osama Bin Ladin [OBL] nor Taliban spiritual leader Mullah Omar were direct products of the CIA.

Linguistic and Tribal divisions have been the peculiar characteristics of Afghan whirlpool. The Pashtuns are divided among the Durrani, Ghilzai, Waziri, Khattak, Afridi, Mohmand, Yusufzai, Shinwari, and numerous smaller tribes. Further, each tribe is divided into subtribes. For instance, the Durrani are divided into seven sub-groups: the Popalzai, Barakzai, Alizai, Nurzai, Ishakzai, Achakzai, and Alikozai. These, in turn, are further divided into numerous clans. Zahir Shah, ruler of Afghanistan between 1933 and 1973, belonged to the Muhammadzai clan of the Barakzai subtribe of the Durrani tribe. Such clan, sub-tribal, and tribal divisions mostly contribute towards intense rivalries.

Religious diversity further complicated internal Afghan politics and relations with neighbours. Once home to thriving Hindu, Sikh, and Jewish communities till the mid-twentieth century, Afghanistan today is overwhelmingly Muslim. The vast majority – 84% are Sunni Muslims; amongst the rest the Hazaras are Shi'a Muslims, and so have sixty million Shi'ites in Iran. In the north-eastern Badakhshan region, there are many *Isma'ili Shi'a*. Further; the *Pashtun* Muslims of Kandahar traditionally look toward their compatriots in Pakistan while people in northern Herat keep links with Iran.

The contemporary political history of Afghanistan starts with a bloodless coup of 1973 when government of King Zahir Shah was toppled by his cousin Daoud Khan. Daoud Khan had served as prime minister of Afghanistan since 1953 and promoted economic modernization, liberation of women, and *Pashtun* nationalism – the last phenomenon was though developed amidst Pak-Afghan armed clashes as mentioned in above paragraphs.

Till early 1970s, the US was quite hesitant to support any type of military project on Afghan soils. However, Daoud Khan started inclining more towards the Soviet Union. He could not stick to his own famous phrase:

> *"I feel happiest when I light my American cigarette with Soviet matches".*

Pakistan continuously felt threatened for two decades while facing with its own restive Pashto-speaking population. Pakistan viewed *Daoud's Pashtunistan* rhetoric - and his simultaneous support for *Baluchi* separatists - as well as his generally pro-India foreign policy, as a serious threat to country's security.

In mid-1970s Pakistani PM Zulfiqar Ali Bhutto [ZAB] responded Afghanistan by supporting an Islamist movement there – in fact that strategy later developed into Taliban myth. PM Bhutto started encouraging Afghan Islamic leaders; it was from this Islamist movement that Pakistan's Inter-Services Intelligence [ISI] introduced the US to important *Mujahedeen* leaders as Burhanuddin Rabbani, Ahmad Masud, and Gulbuddin Hikmatyar.

Under Daoud's rule, Afghanistan became increasingly polarized. Just as Pakistan backed the Islamist opposition, the Soviet Union threw its encouragement behind the People's Democratic Party of Afghanistan [PDPA] but soon withdrawn its support without showing any anger.

## DECADE OF *MUJAHEDEEN* VS RUSSIAN ARMY:

On 27th April 1978; there was another bloody coup in Afghanistan; Daoud Khan was formally overthrown and a communist government was established in Kabul; two days later, a Revolutionary Council declared Afghanistan to be a *Democratic Republic*. The US started funding some resistance groups but without any unified policy.

In the US government, the then Security Adviser Zbigniew Brzezinski and his group-mates were seen more interested in getting involved. They thought if the US got involved, the Soviet Union would come open – so the cold-war era should be ended. In 1979, they started funnelling cash & arsenal to Pakistan's intelligence services; especially the ISI, that US policy eventually induced formal Soviet invasion on Afghanistan through its northern borders; the US got more involved, too.

**US involvement** with Islamic groups remained uneven. Brzezinski used to say proudly: *'We created the Mujahedeen.'*

In reality, the *Mujahedeen* were already there in various pockets but the US exploited them strategically; used them to their advantage. Money was passed on through Pakistan's ISI - mostly going into the hands of the group-leaders of the *Mujahedeen*. Ordinary people didn't receive training from the CIA or Pakistan's ISI; they had guns in their houses; picking up their guns and fighting - nothing beyond. But these were the reactionary elements that the US got allied with.

[AMERICA's 1st MISTAKE ON AFGHAN SOILS: The critics held that the US made some horrific blunders, too. It pressurised Egypt to release a group of Islamists that they had arrested including one *Ayman al-Zawahiri,* who happened to be the second-in-command of al-Qaeda then. The US inadvertently imported him — or it might be intentional to bolster the *Mujahedeen* by calling in foreign fighters. They were accompanied by Arabs, later called *Arab Mujahedeen;* in fact they were the people from **Egypt's Muslim Brotherhood,** from Yemen and Saudi Arabia - who later became fighter members of al-Qaeda.

Additionally, the US, either inadvertently or intentionally, ended up funding for groups of foreign fighters who were allied with organized factions of the *Mujahedeen*. It was a sudden decision. For more than a decade the funding was being done via Pakistan's ISI and sometimes through direct cash payments; once the process stopped, Afghanistan fell into civil wars. The unintended consequence of such meddling brought chaos – thus another class of fighters emerged, of course, with American training manuals, funds and guns.]

In 1978, Daoud Khan was killed in a coup by Afghan's Communist Party, his former partner in government then known as the **People's Democratic Party of Afghanistan [PDPA].** The PDPA pushed for a socialist transformation by abolishing arranged marriages, promoting mass literacy, and reforming land ownership. This undermined the traditional tribal order and provoked opposition from Afghani Islamic leaders across rural areas, but it was particularly the PDPA's crackdown that contributed to open rebellion.

On **11th September 1979;** while the PDPA was besieged by internal leadership differences it went totally destabilized by an internal coup in which Hafizullah Amin ousted Nur Muhammad Taraki, the then ruler.

**In December 1979;** the Soviet Union, sensing PDPA's weakness, got involved militarily in Afghanistan's internal affairs, to depose Amin and install another PDPA faction. In fact the Soviets had welcomed the new regime of Democracy-lovers in Afghanistan with a massive influx of aid. However, the old rivalries between Hafizullah Amin's faction [*Khalqis*], who dominated the new government and its rival group [*Parchamis*], crippled the regime. Rule through brutal force and terror was rejected; so Russia sought to salvage its influence there through altered leadership, but Hafizullah Amin straightaway refused to relinquish power.

America immediately planned to get engaged in Afghanistan because he had lost Iran as its most trusted ally in the region due to Khomeini's successful Islamic Revolution of 1978-79. In December 1979, Premier Brezhnev sent the Soviet Red Army to Kabul; punished Hafizullah Amin by storming his palace and then executed him – installed Soviet client regime and controlled the city. Like in American stay during 2001-21, the Soviets were never fully able to gain control over the countryside; pockets of resistance continued to remain and exist with full hidden force.

When the Red Army contingents flew on Aeroflot planes into Kabul, and as Soviet tanks rolled across the Friendship Bridge [in Uzbekistan now], the Afghan *mujahedeen* were already there. Many of them had been and were in Pakistani exile since their failed uprising four years before. The US decided at once to arm the Afghan *mujahedeen* and they launched resistance afresh which quickly gained momentum. In 1980, President Carter sent only $30 million to help that resistance movement but President Reagan enhanced the amounts steadily reaching $250 million in 1985 while Saudi Arabia had contributed an equal amount. Contrarily, Moscow invested about $5 billion per year in Afghanistan.

Entry of the Soviet Union into Afghan political arena had also prompted [besides the US] its other Cold War rivals like Pakistan, Saudi Arabia and China, to support rebels fighting against the Soviet-backed PDPA factions in Afghanistan.

In comparison to the secular and socialist government backed by Soviets, which controlled the cities well, religiously motivated *mujahedeen* held influence in much of the countryside. Beside *Rabbani* and *Hekmatyar*, other *mujahedeen* commanders including *Jalaluddin Haqqani* also jumped in.

Historians noted that PDPA was a progressive regime in Afghanistan; a government that expanded women's rights, it extended literacy; it brought agricultural reforms in the economy and adequate health care. But, like in other communist states, no one was allowed to speak against the government; such critics were arrested, thrown in jail or declared *'disappeared'*.

*Mujahedeen* was in fact a Resistance Movement; it was not a single group – but actually four different groups who were roughly aligned for resisting ruling PDPA's harsh government. Amongst them was a more organized **'the Islamist Faction'**, led by *Gulbuddin Hekmatyar*. Even before the Soviet invasion, he carried out a series of horrific acid attacks against un-covered women.

Another adequately organized group was allied with the moderate **Ahmad Shah Masoud**; not involved in acid attacks; not regressive – only wanted egalitarian Islamic Republic. One group was of **Maoists and leftists** who were angry with ruling PDPA government simply because they weren't being heard. Then the fourth group comprised of **just ordinary people** — that they just *'pick up arms and fight'*. They didn't have an ideology; no particular vision of the government or its functions. They were slower but when the Soviets invaded, this group of ordinary people grew up dramatically and became leading fighters.

Referring to Milton Bearden [the **CIA station chief in Pakistan** during 1986-89]'s thesis **"Afghanistan - Graveyard of Empires,"** published in *'Foreign Affairs'* of <u>December 2001</u>:

> *"By 1985, the occupying 40$^{th}$ Soviet army had swollen to almost 120,000 troops and with some other elements crossing into the Afghan theatre on a temporary duty basis.*
>
> *Initially, the CIA refused to provide American arms to the resistance, seeking to maintain plausible deniability. The State Department had also opposed providing American-made weapons for fear of antagonizing the Soviet Union."*

The American CIA, a cold-war rival of the Soviets, worked closely with Pakistan's Inter-Services Intelligence [ISI] to funnel foreign support for the *mujahedeen*. The war also attracted Arab volunteers [later called Afghan Arabs] headed by Osama bin Laden [OBL] and his reactionary companions.

The US provided Stingers to the *mujahedeen* through Pakistan till 1983 at least. Covertly; millions of dollars were spent to purchase Chinese, Warsaw Pact, and Israeli weaponry for *mujahedeen*. In March 1985, President Reagan formally decided to switch their strategy from 'mere harassment of Soviet forces' to driving the Red Army completely out of the country – also opted [in September 1986] to provide the *mujahedeen* with the Stinger anti-aircraft missile - thereby breaking the embargo on *'Made in America arms'*. Under the guidance and supervision of the CIA, Pakistan's ISI distributed those weapons to the Afghan warriors through Karachi, Quetta and *Ojhari Camp in Rawalpindi*.

[*Washington had considered India a lost entity then and Pakistan's role was hailed at all levels. However, the differences plagued in mujahedeen did not surface until after the withdrawal of the Soviet army from Afghanistan; the country had become a bleeding wound for the Soviet Union. Each year, the Red Army suffered thousands of casualties; plentiful Soviets died of disease and drug addiction and huge economic drain out compelled Russian troops to wind up & go back in 1988; Soviet Premier Gorbachev had to announce it.*]

It was alleged by the US, throughout the 1980s & 90s that the ISI used its position to promote its own national interests; the ISI refused to recognize any Afghan resistance group that was not religiously based. The ISI only dealt with seven groups which were more concerned and adequately charged to fight in the field bravely. Indeed, the ISI tended to favour *Gulbuddin Hekmatyar,* perhaps the most militant Islamist of the *mujahedeen* commanders and having history of fighting fearlessly.

Ahmed Masoud, the most effective *Mujahid* commander, later developed his own group named **THE NORTHERN ALLIANCE**, being a Tajik received only eight Stingers from the ISI during the war; *Pamela Constable*'s essay 'Pakistani Agency Seeks to Allay US on Terrorism' in **The Washington Post** dated **15th February 2000** is referred.

The war between the rural based Afghan tribal clergy and cities controlled PDPA government backed by the Soviet Army continued for a full decade but the Soviets on Afghan soils remained throughout in turmoil; they were unable to get complete writ over the whole country. Under the new leadership of Mikhail Gorbachev, the Soviet Union [USSR] attempted to consolidate the PDPA's hold over power in the country but could not succeed due to varying strategies.

The Russians immediately started planning to move out of Afghanistan in an honourable way. The main strategy revolved around measures to save face while withdrawing troops. During this period, the military and intelligence organizations of the USSR worked with the Afghan government of Mohammad Najibullah to improve relations between the government in Kabul and the leaders of rebel tribal factions.

**On 14 April 1988;** Geneva Accords in this respect were signed by the USSR, the US, Pakistan and Afghanistan which provided a framework for the departure of Soviet forces, and established a multilateral understanding between the signatories regarding the future of international involvement in Afghanistan.

> [**Geneva Accords** *consisted of several instruments; a bilateral agreement between Pakistan and [the Republic of] Afghanistan on the principles of mutual relations, particularly based on non-interference and non-intervention; a declaration on international guarantees signed by the Soviet Union and the US; a bilateral agreement between Pakistan and Afghanistan on the voluntary return of Afghan refugees; and an agreement on the inter-relationships for the settlement of Afghanistan, signed by Pakistan and Afghanistan and witnessed by the Soviet Union and the US.*]

The agreements also contained provisions for the timetable of the withdrawal of Soviet troops from Afghanistan; to start on 15ᵗʰ May 1988 and to end by 15ᵗʰ February 1989, thus putting an end to a nine-year-long Soviet occupation and Soviet–Afghan War.

The Afghan resistance groups - *Mujahedeen*, were neither party to the negotiations nor to the Geneva accords and so refused to accept the terms of the agreement. As a result, the civil war continued even after the completion of the Soviet withdrawal. The Soviet-backed regime of Najibullah [confined to Kabul city mainly] failed to win popular support, rural territory, or international recognition but was able to remain in power until 1992, when it collapsed and was overrun by the *Mujahedeen*.

The Russians finally worked out their exit; a complete withdrawal of Soviet forces from Afghan soils was there before the given date - **15ᵗʰ February 1989.**

## HOME WARS - *MUJAHEDEEN* DIVIDED:

*Mujahedeen,* the coalition of groups with different aims & goals - they only aligned when the Soviets were there. Once the Soviets left in February 1989, the four groups turned towards their individual agendas to lead Afghan Civil Wars of the 1990s in all corners of their country, Afghanistan.

After May 1989, though the PDPA regime under Najibullah held on **until 1992** – but the history was to see collapse of the Soviet Union in its own and was torn into new independent countries – after which Afghan regime could not get aid of any kind from Russia; the defection of Uzbek Gen Abdul Rashid Dostum played its role to approach Kabul. With the political stage cleared of Afghan socialists, the remaining Islamic warlords started competing for power.

It remains a fact that the Afghans fought their own war and outsiders of any band of colour or race were kept on the sidelines. Then the Osama bin Ladin [OBL]'s role was confined to build and guard roads, dig ditches, and prepare fixed positions only. The battles were fought by the real Afghans while the Afghan Arabs were generally viewed as nuisances by *mujahedeen* commanders.

Most of the Afghan Arabs were from the *'Muslim Brotherhood'* of Egypt and the Saudia-based Islamic Coordination Council [ICC]. In Pakistan, Arab volunteers staffed numerous Saudi Red Crescent offices near the Afghan borders. The Arab volunteers were also allied with the *Ittihad-e-Islami*, led by Al-Rasul Sayyaf, a Pashtun scholar and long lived in Saudi Arabia. It was estimated that during 1982-92, some 35,000 members of *Ittehad-e-Islami* served in Afghanistan as volunteers.

*After Russia's withdrawal, the US had only planned to support the mujahedeen for one year* but Saudi and Kuwaiti donors provided $400 million to them as emergency aid. While the US budgeted $250 million for the collective *mujahedeen* in 1991, the following year President Bush allocated no money for them.

Like the sudden exit of the US from Afghanistan in August 2021, the Americans had walked away from Afghanistan within two years after the Russians' quit in 1988. A journalist named Ed Girardet then noted with anger then: *"The United States really blew it. They dropped Afghanistan like a hot potato."* Indeed, that was the time when the Pakistan's ISI filled the vacuum firstly created by the Russia and then by Washington.

**On 2nd August 1990;** Iraqi troops invaded Kuwait. Washington's attention and resources both shifted to that nearby battle ground. Islamist commanders like *Hikmatyar,* who were already upset with the US, broke with their Saudi and Kuwait patrons and found new patrons in Iran, Libya, and Iraq. The tables got turned around.

The CIA supported Arab volunteers who had come to Afghanistan to wage *jihad* against the Soviets, eventually used those American arms in terrorist activities around. Pakistan provided strong support to the Taliban to achieve their early victories in 1994; p 352 of Amin Saikal's book *Modern Afghanistan: A History of Struggle and Survival (2006 1st ed.)* is referred. Other suggested readings are here:

- Ahmed Rashid's essay in the *daily Telegraph* London dated 11th September 2001-

- "Pakistan's support of the Taliban" in *Human Rights Watch [2000]* &

- An article titled "The elite force who are ready to die" in *the guardian* of 26th October 2001.

# Scenario 224

## US-AFGHAN HISTORY AFTER 9/11

Let us travel to the earlier decades for a while – see an article titled as *Soviet Union invades Afghanistan* available at **History.com; published** on <u>24<sup>th</sup> November 2009</u>:

> [*On 24<sup>th</sup> December 1979; the Soviet Union invades Afghanistan, under the pretext of upholding the Soviet-Afghan Friendship Treaty of 1978.*
>
> *As midnight approached, the Soviets organized a massive military airlift into Kabul, involving an estimated 280 transport aircraft and three divisions of almost 8,500 men each. Within a few days, the Soviets had secured Kabul, deploying a special assault unit against **Tajberg Palace**. Elements of the Afghan army loyal to Hafizullah Amin put up a fierce, but brief resistance.*
>
> *On 27<sup>th</sup> December 1979; Babrak Karmal, exiled leader of the Parcham faction of the Marxist People's Democratic Party of Afghanistan (PDPA), was installed as Afghanistan's new head of government, and Soviet ground forces entered Afghanistan from the north.*
>
> *The Soviets, however, were met with fierce resistance when they ventured out of their strongholds into the countryside. Resistance fighters, called mujahedeen, saw the Christian or atheist Soviets controlling Afghanistan as a defilement of Islam as well as of their traditional culture.*
>
> *The mujahedeen employed guerrilla tactics against the Soviets. They would attack or raid quickly, then disappear into the mountains, causing great destruction without pitched battles. The fighters used whatever weapons they could grab from the Soviets or were what were given by the US.*
>
> *The tide of the war turned with the 1986-87 inductions of US shoulder-launched anti-aircraft missiles. **The Stingers** allowed the mujahedeen to shoot down Soviet planes and helicopters on a regular basis. With*

*this weapon, the mujahedeen were able to limit Soviet air capabilities.*

*New Soviet leader Mikhail Gorbachev decided it was time to get out. Demoralized and with no victory in sight, Soviet forces started withdrawing in 1988. The last Soviet soldier crossed back across the border on <u>15 February 1989</u>.*

*It was the first Soviet military expedition beyond the Eastern bloc since World War II and marked the end of a period of improving relations (known as détente) in the Cold War. Subsequently, the SALT II arms treaty was shelved and the US began to re-arm.*

***15,000 Soviet soldiers were killed** [in this expedition].*

*The long-term impact of the invasion and subsequent war was profound. First, the Soviets never recovered from the public relations, [diplomacy] and financial losses, which significantly contributed to the **fall of the Soviet empire in 1991.***

*Secondly, the war created a breeding ground for terrorism and the rise of Osama bin Laden [and AL-QAEDA]. During 1980s the US passed on millions of dollars and ammunition through Pakistan to Afghanistan's mujahedeen as part of that anti-communist effort.]*

On 15th February 1989; as said in above paragraphs, the Soviets pulled their last troops out of Afghanistan – however, the US continued to patronise the Islamist *mujahedeen.*

## US SCHOLARS CONDEMNED 9/11 WAR:

In 2003, there was a documentary on Western media titled *'TRUTH AND LIES in THE WAR ON TERROR'* which had shaken the whole world. It was compiled and directed by one John Pilger, an award-winning journalist who had investigated the discrepancies between American and British claims for those atrocities they played in Afghanistan in the name of 'war on terror'. He collected the relevant facts on the ground as then available in Afghanistan and Washington.

Within two years of the *topi-drama* of 9/11 in 2001, the US had its military bases in 'liberated Afghanistan'. Amongst other warlords there was one woman named **Condoleezza Rice** in Washington - *in many ways worse than the Taliban.* In Washington, there were leading Administration officials like Douglas Feith, the Under Secretary of Defence for Policy;

and John Bolton, the Under Secretary of State for Arms Control and International Security and the other architects of the New American Century, who were dismissed as 'the crazies' by the first Bush Administration in the early 90s when they first floated their plans for world domination by the Americans and its close allies.

Now recall the words of a son of the same soil - *Henry Kissinger*:

> *"What we in America call terrorists are really groups of people that reject the (new) international system [aka the New World Order]".*

Most Americans don't take 9/11 at its face value; they believe that George Bush brought down the towers and killed hundreds of the Americans and used it to start his war to begin the Democrats climb towards world conquest. There could have been a rebellion on the spot but the US citizens were too late to understand the inside political intrigues. See one American's [**Jeffrey Norris**] feelings available on the world media pages of 5ᵗʰ August 2016:

> *"I was born in 1960. I never thought there would be a day when 'American' was a dirty word. It's here! Washington D.C. is a cesspool of scum - lies, greed and a quest for some imaginary power. I'm sure Prescott Bush is in the bowels of hell waiting on his son and grandson too."*

And also; most Americans were infuriated that Obama campaigned on *Guantanamo,* and didn't do bend about it; most felt ashamed to be the Americans – they were being kept in dark.

See an editorial note of the *New York Times* dated 12ᵗʰ September 2001 – the next day of agonizingly and painfully known 9/11 episode – carrying the notion:

> *'......the events of the previous day are identified as one of those moments in which history splits, and we define the world as "before" and "after"; also termed as 'The War against America'.*

The said event single-handedly changed the course of international history – a sudden conflict - the so-called *'Global War on Terror'* – it was said. Then there were 100s of opinions, articles, books and media events followed by up-rise of torturing dens of *Guantánamo, Baghram* and *Abu Ghraib* etc. Then the world saw mass slaughtering in Afghanistan & Pakistan, Iraq and Syria – just like an endless horror movie on a universal screen – America's image was distorted more in fact.

A little later, historians had to extend their list of *'sickening images and narratives'* to the *'horrors'* associated with the rise of the Islamic State of Iraq and Syria [ISIS] and the cycle of violence and counter-violence that was set in motion by the military interventions in Afghanistan and Iraq. The ensuing humanity crisis continuously expanded its geographical reach, leading to further destruction and deaths across the Middle East and South Asia as well as to continuing terrorist incidents in the West. In the process, the 'War on Terror' gradually superseded the memory of 9/11 as an isolated event, and this was especially taken as true if we abandon George Bush and Obama's misleading narratives for a while.

In the wake of 9/11 War on Terror, **Dr Paul Craig Roberts** [an Assistant Secretary of the US Treasury for Economic Policy and Associate Editor of The Wall Street Journal & a well known columnist for Business Week] had once written in his essay **'Taliban the Wrong Target'** published on 13th November 2001 that:

> *'The war on terrorism has lost its focus. It has become a military campaign against the Taliban.* **The Taliban are not terrorists.** *Defeating them will have very little effect on terrorism.*
>
> **The Taliban are a group of Afghans focused on their own country, NOT on the West. We are [otherwise] Israel's ally and are perceived as the power behind a corrupt Saudi royal family.**
>
> *If the U.S. becomes bogged down in an Afghan civil war between the Taliban and the Northern Alliance, we will achieve our own demoralization and embolden terrorists unimpaired by our efforts.'*

Dr Paul had further elaborated that by using the authority of Islam to create a national unity in place of tribal consciousness, the Taliban were engaged in what the Council of Foreign Relations, the State Department, and the World Bank called "nation building." **The Taliban did not participate in the attacks on the World Trade Centre and the Pentagon. The anthrax letters were postmarked in the US not in Afghanistan."**

For more details see
**JUDGES & GENERALS IN PAKISTAN VOL-III**
by *Inam R Sehri* [2013]; Scenario 58; pps 755-772,
*GHP Surry* [UK]

The re-alignment of geopolitical power relations after the two rogue interventions; the formation of new terrorist networks [like ISIS] and regional alliances [Iraq / Syria]; the growing number of terrorist incidents in the West; the changing discourses on security and technologies of warfare; the leveraging of fundamental constitutional principles; and the ethical anxieties surrounding the lack of accountability for the violence carried out in the name of countering terrorism – became the leading areas of study for future generations of the West. The Western new generations gathered evidences to identify the disgruntled faces of Bush, Tony Blair and Obama as the biggest enemies of humanity and human values.

For the future, the political students of the Western hemisphere would study the levels of their leaders' intellectual corruption, i.e. from 'Ground Zero novels' to 'post-9/11 literature'; they would reach a unanimous conclusion that how empty minded their earlier leaders were – and then there would be nothing left behind except curses and irritations.

History is so cruel, we all know; for many it would be a historical rupture - more narrowly be characterised as Ground Zero Fiction.

## BACKGROUND OF AMERICAN DREAM:

However, the story of two decades' defeat and humiliation starts from the **11th September 2001** [9/11] attacks on Twin Towers in New York. The United States of America [US], supported by its close allies mainly the United Kingdom [UK], invaded Afghanistan on 7th October 2001.

Following the 9/11 attacks, allegedly orchestrated by al-Qaeda, the US under the Bush administration issued an ultimatum to Afghanistan to hand over Osama bin Laden [OBL] with his top companions and shut down all al-Qaeda training camps within the country.

In an interview with Voice of America, Mulla Omar, the then Taliban Chief and ruler of Afghanistan, was asked if he would give up OBL. Omar replied:

> "No. We cannot do that. If we did, it means we are not Muslims, that Islam is finished. If we were afraid of attack, we could have surrendered him the last time we were threatened."

Mulla Omar had also explained his position to high-ranking Taliban officials:

> "Islam says that when a Muslim asks for shelter, give the shelter and never hand him over to enemy. And our Afghan tradition says that,

*even if your enemy asks for shelter, forgive him and give him shelter. Osama has helped the jihad in Afghanistan, he was with us in bad days and I am not going to give him to anyone".*

[Peter Bergen at **CNN** dated 21st August 2015 is referred]

The Taliban's stance had disturbed President Bush, the mighty head of the only superpower on the globe, because the Taliban had consensus to hand him over to a third party for trial. The US had also viewed their mission as *'ending a safe haven for terror,'* so invasion was explicitly planned in that way to start attack with bombing.

Mulla Omar was adamant that bin Laden was innocent of planning the 9/11 attacks despite the accusations directed against him. Despite this, high ranking Taliban officials attempted to persuade Omar and made offers to the US through its contacts with Pakistan. The Taliban ambassador to Pakistan Abdul Salam Zaeef said at a news conference in Islamabad that:

*".....our position in this regard is that if the Americans have evidence, they should produce it. If they could prove their allegations, we are ready for a trial of Osama bin Laden."*

[Ref: *The New York Times* dated 21st September 2001;
**"Without Evidence......]**

Basically it was a follow-up of the then prevailing Afghan Civil War between the [ruling] Taliban and the Northern Alliance groups; the Alliance was holding about 10% area of Afghanistan then and was long backed by the US & the UK.

No one, even in the US had felt that the said invasion would become the first phase of a '20-year long war in the country'; then it was simply taken as America's WAR ON TERROR [WOT] and most of the world celebrated it.

Referring to *'The Washington Post-ABC News Poll'* published in the paper dated 8th September 2021; the fact remained that more number of the US citizens held that the events of 9/11 2001 had more negative than positive impact on their country. Ahead of the 20th anniversary of the attacks on the World Trade Centre and Pentagon, more than 8 in 10 Americans said those events changed their country in a lasting way. Nearly half [46%] said the events of 9/11 changed the country for the worse, while 33% only held the change better for the US.

**The Washington Post's** said polls told about a shift from 10 years ago when Americans were roughly divided on this question, and it marked even larger swing from the first anniversary of the attacks in 2002; when 55% said the country had aspired change for the better.

In this polls conducted during <u>29<sup>th</sup> August - 1<sup>st</sup> September 2021</u> by *The WP's* Director Polling, Mr Scott Clement, wrote:

> *"The Americans' perceptions of safety from terrorist attacks are also at low ebb, with 49% saying the country is safer from terrorism today than before 9/11 — one% point from the record low of 48% reached in 2010, and down from 64% percent in September 2011, four months after Osama bin Laden was killed.*
>
> *..... [Interestingly] with 57% of Democrats saying it is [safer today], while 54% of Republicans say it's less safe; independents are closer to Democrats on this question."*

Director Polling also held that the ideological split was reversed in 2021 polls for 9/11 attacks, with nearly 6 in 10 liberals saying the events changed the country for the worse [59%], compared with 44% of moderates and 45% of conservatives.

The said polls also made clear that the citizens were not happy with US military withdrawal from Afghanistan along with the evacuation of more than 120,000 Americans and allies in just over two weeks; although the Afghan war was NOT worth fighting near 54% people. Those who say the war was not worth fighting were those 53% who opined that 9/11 changed the US for the worse. The Post-ABC poll was conducted with a margin of error +/- 3.5%.]

**...but what compelled the US for attacks on Afghanistan in 2001?** The main justification was to go after OBL. When the Taliban collapsed, the ruling US officials pretended saying that the Taliban urged to: *'....stop bombing we'll hand over OBL'* [clearly it was not the whole truth]; immediately President Bush came up with new justification – the US need to nation-build – *'we need to build Afghanistan up'*. Former Defence Secretary Rumsfeld, former Vice President Cheney and former President George W Bush wanted to create a pro-American government as foothold in the region.

*'Building up Afghanistan was an open lie'* by the American leadership then in 2001; see the following words of the US President Biden in 2021.

On 8<sup>th</sup> July 2021; President Joe Biden, in his national address, reiterated the US commitment to fulfilling the Doha Agreement, guaranteeing a complete withdrawal of troops by 31<sup>st</sup> August; announcing further that:

> *"We did not go to Afghanistan for nation build. It's the right and the responsibility of Afghan people alone to decide their future and how they want to run their country. It is not inevitable the Taliban would seize control of the government and that he trusts the ability of the Afghan National and Defense Security Forces, who is 'better trained, better equipped and more competent' in terms of conducting war.*
>
> *I will not send another generation of Americans to war in Afghanistan with no reasonable expectation of achieving a different outcome."*

The subsequent events, however, proved that the US aims were not at all to destroy the terror bases in Afghanistan – the whole game was a pre-determined plan to get established bases near Iraq, Libya and Syria etc for attacks thereupon in 2003. It's a separate topic that whether they succeeded in getting this facility ripened or not.

Some historians still hold that the *'Competing motives in the Bush administration – amongst President Bush, Secretary of Defence Rumsfeld, Vice President Dick Cheney, Secretary of State Condoleezza Rice, and Secretary of State Colin Powell'* had derailed the US mission in Afghanistan.

> *"Technically, the US could have accepted the surrender, accepted Osama bin Laden, and that's it. Justice is served, right? Put Osama bin Laden on trial or execute him or whatever. But going further by invading was an attempt to extend American influence in that region (for future).*
>
> *That's where the United States got involved in ...... but more importantly, it flooded Afghanistan with money that often went into the hands of military contractors and advisers.*
>
> *.....yeah, you develop Kabul with new skyscrapers, and a couple of KFCs there, but the rural parts of Afghanistan remain neglected. And that, in many ways, is the great failure of the United States' invasion."*

[Referring to *Emily Stewart*'s analysis
at **www.vox.com** dated 21<sup>st</sup> August 2021]

## THE REAL WAR AFTER 9/11 ATTACKS:

As said in detail earlier; after 9/11 [2001] attacks on Pentagon and Twin Towers, the American government asked the then ruling Taliban in Afghanistan to hand over Osama Bin Laden [OBL] and his companion militants to Washington but the Taliban flatly refused. Pakistan tried to strike a negotiation deal with Taliban and al Qaeda members to facilitate and return OBL to American authorities.

When negotiations failed, Pakistan allowed American forces to use its military bases for launching attacks on Afghanistan; it was a military ruler's decision, the Pakistani populace didn't approve it. Rather there were public rallies in the whole country against Gen Musharraf's singular decision; world poles told that 84% populace voted against America on Afghan cause.

Gen Musharraf later confessed that the country had no option but to support the US as its Secretary Powel had threatened Pakistan of *'bombing it into stone age'* if it did not join the fight against al Qaeda. Simultaneously in 2001, US officials introduced a bill to lift all the sanctions, previously imposed on Pakistan under *Pressler and Glenn amendments.*

On 7th October 2001; the US launched its first attack on Afghan soils naming it as **Operation Enduring Freedom** in association with the UK as partner. The two were later joined by other forces, including the Northern Alliance local warriors present there. The Taliban government didn't have any air force to retaliate thus soon got knocked down. The leadership started disappearing one by one and they had no other choice except to take refuge in Pakistani border areas.

In the months that followed, the US & allied forces and their partners in the Northern Alliance, an Afghan faction, chased al Qaeda and upended the Taliban regime. Bin Laden took refuge in Tora Bora Mountains; the leader of the Taliban, Mullah Omar, went to the southern mountains. Taliban commanders and fighters returned to their homes, mostly in Helmand & Kandahar provinces. Skillful diplomatic efforts spearheaded by a US special envoy, Zalmay Khalilzad, established a process that created a new Afghan government led by the conciliatory Hamid Karzai.

**Hamid Karzai,** later the president of Afghanistan, and his group were then in Quetta, Pakistan, where they began a covert operation against the Taliban regime in Kabul. Before entering Afghanistan, he warned his fighters:

> *"We might be captured the moment we enter Afghanistan and be killed. We have 60% chance of death and 40% chance to survive. Winning was no consideration. We got on two motorbikes - and drove into Afghanistan";* —Hamid Karzai himself told later.

Karzai gathered several hundred fighters from his tribe, but were attacked by the Taliban. Karzai barely survived, and used his contacts with the CIA to call for an airlift. On 4th November 2001, American special operation forces rescued Karzai out of Afghanistan for protection.

**On 13th November 2001;** the Northern Alliance forces launched their attack on the Kabul city, on instructions of the US war planners, they made swift progress against Taliban forces. Till then the Taliban were significantly weakened by American and British air strikes since 7th October 2001. The Alliance moved ahead of plans, and the next day the Northern Alliance forces, supported by US Special Forces Unit ODA 595, entered Kabul and met no resistance inside the city. Taliban rulers and men retreated to *Kandahar* in the south.

Coupled with the fall of **Mazar e Sharif** five days earlier, the capture of Kabul was a significant blow to Taliban control in Afghanistan. The other cities quickly fell in the hands of Coalition forces writing a new chapter of history in Afghanistan.

> *[Just to remember that Ahmed Shah Masoud, Chief of Northern Alliance and a legendary anti-Taliban guerrilla commander was assassinated in the first week of September 2001, two days before the 9/11 attacks.]*

**On 5th December 2001,** Karzai and his group of fighters survived a friendly fire missile attack by US Air Force pilots in southern Afghanistan. The group suffered injuries and was treated in America; Karzai received injuries to his facial nerves.

**On 17th December 2001;** the US and its allies officially drove out the Taliban from power and established military bases near major cities across the country; most al-Qaeda and Taliban members escaped. However, few Taliban leaders moved to Tora Bora Mountains; the training base of the Taliban fighters also.

Besides above; some of them escaped into hiding in Pakistan, some of them ended up in *Kandahar*, some of them were picked and sent to the 'safe houses'. But they were no longer a sort of organized and unified group. During that decade the Taliban re-organised themselves. In mid-2010s, they appeared on the horizon once more; appeared to have received more money than they ever had. The US estimated that the ISI of Pakistan might have passed the US Aid to the Taliban with some internal planning – and surely after that the whole political scenario started changing. However, the question remained that if the US had really given 'aid' to Pakistan in those days; President Obama was more near to India then.

On 22nd December 2001; as was decided in the Bonn Conference held in those days, Hamid Karzai took over the Afghan Administration as the 'Interim Authority', which after a 2002 *loya jirga* [Afghan Grand Assembly] in Kabul named as Afghan Transitional Administration.

[HAMID KARZAI; is an Afghan politician who served as President of Afghanistan from 22nd December 2001 to 29th September 2014. Born in *Kandahar*, graduated from Kabul and later received a master's degree from India in the 1980s. He moved to Quetta city of Pakistan, where he was active as a fundraiser for the Afghan rebels during the Soviet–Afghan War [1979–89] and after. He briefly served as Deputy Foreign Minister in the Taliban's 1st stint of the government [1996-2001].

In October 2001, with the US invasion of Afghanistan, Karzai led the *Pashtun* tribes in and around Kandahar in an uprising against the Taliban; he became a dominant political figure after the removal of the Taliban regime in late 2001. During the December 2001 International Conference on Afghanistan in Germany, Karzai was selected to serve as Chairman of the Interim Administration.

In 2002, he was chosen for a 2-year term as interim president by the *Loya Jirga* [grand assembly] held in Kabul. In the 2004 presidential election, Karzai was declared the President of Afghanistan. He won a second five-year term in the 2009 presidential election which term ended in September 2014.

In later years, his relationship with NATO and the US went increasingly strained, and he was accused of corruption several times. Following the take over by the Taliban on 15th August 2021, Mr Karzai along with other former leaders met the Taliban leaders for National

Reconciliation and seeking to form an interim government – but the Taliban flatly refused to accept these oldies.]

During the same month of **December 2001,** the United Nations Security Council established the **International Security Assistance Force [ISAF] to** oversee military operations in Afghanistan including training of the Afghan National Security Forces.

From year 2002 till 2021 there were normal war activities in Afghanistan; sometimes hard days for some groups and some times diplomatic conversations. Going into details of each event may need another voluminous book – so only important events are given below in brief.

**On 17th April 2002:** US President George Bush called for billions of dollars in US aid in the name of reconstruction of Afghanistan. New American ledger was opened then and the rogues and warlords started offering their services to help the American forces to trace out Taliban & Al-Qaeda members and also for ensuring peace in their respective areas.

One USAID official told in private [later on 24ᵗʰ August 2015] that:

> *"We used the bad guys to get the badder guys. We thought we could circle back and get the bad guys later – [but] we never did."*

A Tajik militia commander, **Qasim Fahim Khan,** was also among those. As leader of the Northern Alliance, Fahim Khan played a critical role in helping the US topple the Taliban in ending 2001. He served as Afghanistan's defence minister during 2001-04 and later as the country's first vice president — despite having a stinking reputation for corruption. Even so, the Bush administration treated Fahim Khan as a VIP and once welcomed him to the Pentagon with unnecessary honour and protocol.

Details of exactly how much money Qasim Fahim and other warlords pocketed from the US remain secret but confidential documents showed the **payouts were discussed at the highest levels of government.**

**In April 2002,** Defence Secretary Rumsfeld ordered two senior officers, in a top-secret memo:

> *".....devise a plan for how we are going to deal with each of these warlords — who is going to get money from whom, on what basis, in exchange for what, what is the quid pro quo, etc - Let's get on it...."*

A follow-up memo of two months later, from Rumsfeld to Doug Feith, was also available on record asking: *'Is the DoD giving any food, weapons or money to any of the warlords or to Karzai? Is the CIA doing that? Is State doing it? We need to get a sense of that balance.'* The said memo was a part of top-secret record-files called **SNOWFLAKES** that Rumsfeld had dictated about the Afghan war during 2001-05.

President Bush maintained a light US military footprint in Afghanistan [around 8,000 troops in 2002, increasing to about 20,000 by the end of 2005] aimed at completing the defeat of al Qaeda and the Taliban and helping set up a new democracy. The idea was to withdraw eventually, but there was no clear plan for how to make that happen, other than killing or capturing the innocent villagers labeling them as al Qaeda members.

On 16th April 2003; NATO agreed to take command of the INTERNATIONAL SECURITY ASSISTANCE FORCE [ISAF], which included troops from 42 countries. The decision came at the request of Germany and the Netherlands, the two nations leading ISAF at that time, and all nineteen NATO ambassadors approved it unanimously.

In June 2003; the CIA published a report titled, *'11 September: THE PLOT & THE PLOTTERS.'* This document analyzed the 9/11 attack and also included CIA's intelligence notes on al-Qaeda and the attack, including detailed biographical pages on each of the hijackers. As per report, the CIA found that most of the attackers had traveled back and forth to Afghanistan to pledge their loyalty to bin Laden. However, this report was also turned down by the world media because it contained no reference of cogent evidence for involvement of Al-Qaeda like other numerous government sponsored reports.

On 11th August 2003; NATO formally took over charge of the ISAF operations and became involved as an alliance. Taliban leader Mullah Omar had started reorganizing his group and launched an insurgency against the Hamid Karzai government and ISAF. NATO was initially charged with securing Kabul and surrounding areas from Taliban, al Qaeda and factional warlords, so as to allow for the establishment of the Afghan government.

On 8th September 2003; Donald Rumsfeld, the US Defence Secretary, drafted a secret memo stating that:

*"I have no visibility into who the bad guys are in Afghanistan or Iraq. I read all the intel from the [intelligence] community and it sounds as*

*though we know a great deal but in fact, when you push at it, you find out we haven't got anything … We are woefully deficient in human intelligence."*

Rumsfeld was correct; ever since 9/11, the West's understanding of the tribal communities and family networks that decide war and peace in Afghanistan, was shabby, ragged and tattered.

On the other side, the Taliban were rebuilding themselves. In early 2003, Mullah Omar, though still was in hiding, sent a voice recording to his subordinates calling on them to reorganize the movement and prepare for a major offensive within a few years. Key Taliban figures founded a leadership council known as the **Quetta Shura**, after the Pakistani city where they assembled clandestinely. Recruitment was allegedly done from Afghan refugees settled in and around Quetta and after little training at camping grounds, were sent back into Afghanistan. In Washington, however, the narrative of success continued to hold sway loudly.

**In October 2003,** the UN Security Council authorized the expansion of the ISAF mission throughout Afghanistan, and ISAF subsequently expanded its mission over the whole country.

**On 22ⁿᵈ March 2004;** During his visit to Islamabad, Gen Colin Powell, US Secretary of State, announced the decision of the Bush Administration to designate Pakistan as a **Major Non-NATO Ally [MNNA]** of America - granting it the authority to purchase strategic and advanced military equipments from the US and the West. But immediately after, the US army launched countless drone strikes in FATA [*Federally Administered Tribal Areas*] of Pakistan near Pak-Afghan border. The drone strikes aimed to target supporters of al Qaeda; however, the strikes resulted in large civilian deaths and caused much opposition from the Pakistani populace.

## THE TALIBAN's RESURGENCE:

During early months of year 2005, violence started hiking up in the rural southern Afghanistan as the Taliban reasserted their presence with new tactics modelled on insurgent activity in Iraq. During the preceding four years, the Taliban had focused on retaliating the US and NATO forces in open combat—an approach that largely failed and the group suffered with significant damage—their suicide bombings and buried bombs, known as IEDs [*improvised explosive devices*], had caused more losses to their own warriors at most places.

Between January 2005 and August 2006, Afghanistan endured 64 suicide attacks—a tactic that had been virtually unknown in the country's history before then.

The US repeatedly threatened Pakistan to expand its drone strikes beyond Pakistan's tribal areas and into regions such as Balochistan but certain commanders of the Pak-Army and the general populace strictly warned the US to refrain otherwise the incoming drones would be intercepted and would be shot down on entrance into their territory. *The US thus had to drop this idea despite the fact that political leadership and President Zardari had given them the green signal.*

**ON 23ʳᵈ MAY 2005:** Elected Afghan President Hamid Karzai signed an agreement with President Bush, giving US forces access to Afghan military facilities. For doing so, Karzai charged full price to the White House; he expanded his extortions by looting the American funds through his favourite warlords and some cabinet members.

Referring to SIGAR's one interview dated <u>11ᵗʰ December 2015</u> in which a senior US official said:

> *"We were giving out contracts to pretty nasty people, empowering people we shouldn't have empowered, in order to achieve our own goals."*

In fact, the warlords were cruel tyrants whose misrule destroyed the country so how could be they considered helpful for the Americans – they were responsible for creating hatred and distance between Afghan villagers and the US military. Most senior US officials acknowledged in their interviews that the warlords were odious and corrupt.

One warlord who was both loved and hated by US officials was **Sher Mohammad Akhundzada** [a.k.a SMA], the Governor of Helmand during 2001-05. In 2005, the US and Afghan Narcotics raided Akhundzada's offices and found an enormous stash — nine tons — of opium. He denied wrongdoing - but under international pressure, he was removed from governorship after a short while.

With the absence of Akhundzada's iron hand, the province quickly became a magnet for insurgents, and its drug-trafficking problem exploded. Some US officials regretted his departure. Gen Dan McNeill later described that:

> *"Akhundzada was 'a simple-minded tyrant but effective as governor because he kept other bad guys at bay – **Akhundzada's removal was a**</u>*

*huge mistake. He was dirty but he kept stability because people were afraid of him. It's not good and I'm not advocating dancing with the devil, but maybe one of his disciples.....*"

Akhundzada became a provincial senator later but remained unapologetic about his ruthless tactics. In an interview with UK's daily 'the **Telegraph**', [later, in 2009] he said that *after he was fired as governor, 3,000 of his followers switched sides and joined the Taliban* because they had lost respect for the government.

**In February 2006;** violence from the Taliban increased on slow pace but then they pounced. Thousands of insurgents overran entire districts and surrounded provincial capitals. The **Quetta Shura** built up as a rival regime to Karzai's national forces. Over the course of the next three years, the Taliban captured most of the country's south and much of its east. The US forces and their NATO allies were sucked into heavy fighting.

**In May 2006;** a US military vehicle crashed and killed several Afghans, an event that sparked violent anti-American riots in Kabul—the worst since the war began. Later that year NATO's ISAF took command of the war across the country; the war in Afghanistan was still being painted in Washington as huge success. For commanders on the ground, however, believed that the Taliban had escalated their campaign and launching more frequent attacks on US forces.

The Taliban then opted to intensify its fund-raising from wealthy individuals and groups in the Persian Gulf. Another source of money was Afghanistan's resurgent opium industry. It was a comeback from 2001's complete ban. Western-backed campaigns to eliminate poppy cultivation or to encourage farmers to grow other crops had little discernible impact; Afghanistan soon became the supplier of over 90% percent of the world's opium – of course, for survival of the general population in villages.

**On 31 July 2006;** the ISAF additionally took over military operations in the south of Afghanistan from a US-led anti-terrorism coalition. Later France allowed a squadron of Mirage 2000 fighter aircrafts to be moved into the area, to *Kandahar*, in order to reinforce the alliance's efforts because fighting in the south was gradually gaining intensity.

**In early 2007,** Mullah Dadullah—one of the Taliban's top military commanders—was killed in fighting with US forces. Earlier, Mullah

Obaidullah Akhund—the Taliban's number three leader—was also captured in Pakistan but those were the exceptions. Top Taliban or Al-Qaeda leadership remained at large.

The US and NATO alleged that many of the Taliban Leaders were taking refuge in the Pakistani tribal regions at Pak-Afghan border. This prompted the US to target insurgent leaders with missiles fired from remotely piloted drones. The CIA program of targeted killings was publicly denied by US officials but was widely acknowledged in private.

In November 2007; in an attack, at least 70 people—many of them children—were killed as a parliamentary delegation visited the northern town of *Baghlan*. Less than a year later, a bombing at the Indian embassy in Kabul killed more than 50; the Afghan government accused elements of Pakistan's intelligence service [ISI] of complicity in the attack; a charge Pakistan denied vehemently.

The Taliban's resurgence corresponded with a rise in anti-American and anti-Western sentiments among Afghans. Those feelings were nurtured by the sluggish pace of reconstruction, allegations of prisoner abuse at US detention centres, widespread corruption in the Afghan government, and civilian casualties caused by US and NATO bombings.

In 2008; Pakistan's then ruling [PPP] leadership, especially the President Zardari in turn denounced the strikes in public but privately approved the drone-attacks, allegedly after gaining personal favours, but the American intelligence was totally flopped there; most casualties were of civilians while no significant leader of the Taliban could be harmed. By the end of the year, the US troop levels had risen to over 30,000 yet the overall strategy did not change. Bush remained determined to defeat the Taliban and Al Qaeda which were not visible in fact.

# Scenario 225

## THE TALIBAN: WHO ARE THEY?

Taliban group emerged in 1994-95 during the continuing civil war since after the **withdrawal of Soviet troops in 1989,** predominantly in the south-west of Afghanistan and the adjoining border areas of Pakistan. They vowed to fight corruption and improve security, but also followed a scrupulous and rigorous form of Islam.

During 1996-98, they had taken control of almost all of Afghanistan except some pockets of *Panjsher* valley which remained under the command of Commander Ahmad Shah Masoud – as the US and UK were backing the later with needed finances and required arsenal.

The Taliban enforced their own hard-line version of Islamic *Shariah* and introduced brutal punishments. Men were made to grow beards and women had to wear the all-covering *burka*. TV, music and cinema were banned. After their overthrow in ending 2001, they regrouped themselves in Pakistani border areas. In year 2021 there were about 85,000 full-time fighters – much stronger than at any point since 2001 – that's why they were able to defeat regular Afghan army, NATO forces and, of course, the America too.

Although the US cannot be fully blamed for crafting the Taliban, then also called Afghan Arab community; nevertheless, by distributing arms through Pakistan's ISI, the US developed an atmosphere in which radical Islam could flourish rapidly. This factor also brought thrilling optimism. In Afghanistan, teachers, merchants and many medical professionals started believing them as saviours of their Islamic values because the Taliban promised two things: Security and an end to the conflict between rival *mujahedeen* groups that continued to ravage their country through the 1990s and they continued to deliver the said two virtues until ending 2001.

### AFTER THE SOVIETS LEFT:

After withdrawal of the Soviet troops from Afghan soils, a communist ruler Najibullah, in 1989, governed Afghanistan for three years without any foreign sponsorship. In 1992, Tajik faction of *mujahedeen,* under the command of Ahmad Shah Masoud, captured Kabul, dethroned the president Rabbani [*a scholar and head of Jamiat e Islami*]. However, Shah Masoud [*head of the Northern Alliance*] and Rashid Dostum [*an Uzbek commander in Afghan Army*] could not rein the control of the capital because another Commander Hekmatyar had immediately challenged their rule. Soon Dostum defected from his troika alliance with Rabbani and Masoud, and joined Hekmatyar *Mujahedeen* Group.

The new alliance of two groups of Hekmetyar and Rashid Dostum, devastated the whole Kabul city with their ruthless and brutal bombarding from the hills surrounding the city and left the rival *Mujahedeen* groups miserably bleeding.

**On 28th June 1992;** Burhanuddin Rabbani officially became president of the Islamic State of Afghanistan, but had to battle other warlords for control of Kabul.

[In early 1994 [perhaps] in Kandahar, *Mulla Omar* led 30 men armed with 16 rifles to free two young girls who had been kidnapped and raped by a warlord. After armed scuffle, Mulla Omar caught that warlord and hanged him at a tank gun barrel; **National Geographic Documentary** (2007) *'Inside the Taliban'* is referred.

Another instance of the same year 1994: - two militia commanders confronted each other over a young boy whom they both wanted to sodomize first. In the ensuing fight, Omar's group got freed the boy. Appeals soon flooded in for Omar to intercede in other disputes of the surrounding villages.

Mulla Omar's Taliban movement gained momentum through the year and he quickly gathered recruits from Islamic schools totalling 12,000 by the year's end *with some Pakistani volunteers.* By November 1994, Omar's movement managed to capture the whole of the Kandahar Province and then captured the Herat Province in September 1995; some writers estimated that he had already taken 12 of the 31 provinces in Southern Afghanistan by that time.]

The *Daily Telegraph* dated 31st July 2015 is referred.

As mentioned earlier, Hekmatyar's forces had taken up their positions in the mountains around Kabul and bombarded the city ruthlessly. Meanwhile, one Ismail Khan controlled Herat and its surroundings; and several *Pashtun* commanders held *Kandahar, Helmand* and the south.

In short, there was chaos all over the country. A Pakistani journalist argued then that:

> "…..the internecine fighting, especially in Kandahar, had virtually eliminated the traditional leadership, leaving the door open for the Taliban.
>
> The southern Pashtun warlords and bandits continued to fight each other for territory, while continuing to sell off state machinery, property and factories to the foreign traders. Kidnappings, murders, rapes, and robberies were frequent as Afghan civilians found themselves in the crossfire."

The above situation gave rise to the Taliban movement; Afghan Arabs, members of *mujahedeen,* students of Islamic seminaries [*madarasa*] in Pakistan joined them promptly. Initial objectives of the Taliban movement included restoration of peace, disarmament of the population, strict enforcement of the *shari'a*, and defence of the Islamic values in country. Mullah Omar, their organizer, used to teach at a Pakistani *madrassa*, who had been injured during clashes with the Soviet army, returned to Kandahar and surfaced as the new leader of the Taliban then.

By December 1994, in addition to earlier 12000+ recruits, the Taliban's each victory resulted in thousands of new recruits and local warlords' influx into the Taliban movement.

**What they believed?** The Taliban are often portrayed as employing a narrow interpretation of Islamic **Shariah law** inspired by the *Deobandi* school of thought. However, by 1998 – during their first period in power, ended with the US attack after 9/11 – the Taliban issued their own harsh interpretation of Islamic life equally inspired by the *Pashtun* tribal code, called the **Pashtunwali** in local language and culture.

This pushed away women from public life, mostly barred them from working or studying and confined them to their homes unless accompanied by a male guardian [called *MEHRAM*]. Public executions and floggings were common, western films and books were banned and cultural artefacts seen as blasphemous under Islam - so were destroyed.

Some have suggested that the latest interaction of the Taliban in 2021 – has the potential to be more moderate than during the period from 1996-2001, but yet to see once they got established. In the immediate aftermath of their astonishing conquest of Afghanistan, including Kabul, there were mixed worrying indications.

Referring to **Michael Robin**'s analysis captioned as *Who Is Responsible for the Taliban;* appeared at www.Washingtoninstitute.org on 1ˢᵗ March 2002:

> *"Territorial conquest began on October 12, 1994, when 200 Taliban seized the Afghan border post of Spin Baldak. Less than a month later, on November 3, the Taliban attacked Kandahar, the second-largest city in Afghanistan. Within 48 hours, the city was theirs. Each conquest brought the Taliban new equipment and munitions -- from rifles and bullets to tanks and MiG fighters, for their continued advance.*
>
> *The Taliban maintained their momentum and quickly seized large swathes of Afghanistan. By February 11, 1995, they controlled 9 of Afghanistan's 30 provinces. On September 5, 1995, the Taliban seized Herat, sending Ismail Khan into an Iranian exile. Just over one year later, Jalalabad fell, and just 15 days later, the Taliban took Kabul."*

## TALIBAN'S 1ˢᵀ GOVERNMENT 1996:

On 27ᵗʰ **September 1996**; the Taliban, with military support of Pakistan and financial support from Saudi Arabia, seized Kabul and founded the Islamic Emirate of Afghanistan. They imposed selected Islamic injunctions in areas under their control. Researchers estimated that:

> *"....between 1994 and 1999, an estimated 80,000 to 100,000 Pakistanis trained [students from Islamic schools and madrassas] fought in Afghanistan on the side of the Taliban".*
> [p 288 of **William Maley**'s book *The Afghanistan wars,* 2009;
> Palgrave Macmillan, is referred]

This was the time when Ahmad Masoud and Commander Dostum, two former arch-enemies, had created a united front against the Taliban, later named as the Northern Alliance [NA]. In addition to Masoud's Tajik force and Dostum's Uzbeks, the Alliance included *Hazara* factions, *Pashtun* forces and some defected *Pashtun* Taliban. Both had agreed to work together under the exiled Afghan King Zahir Shah. The NA received all sorts of support from Russia, Iran, Tajikistan and India.

On 24ᵗʰ **May 1997**; the Taliban seized *Mazar-e-Sharif* town, however, after just 18 hours; a rebellion forced the Taliban to leave the city. When the Taliban again raided that town in August 1998, they took no chances and brutally massacred thousands of opponents there. The Taliban's re-capture of *Mazar-e-Sharif* drove Dostum into exile while the conflict had gone extremely brutal. As per UN reports:

> *"...there had been 15 massacres between 1996 and 2001. The Taliban especially targeted the Shiite Hazaras in retaliation for the killing of 3,000 Taliban prisoners by Uzbek Gen Abdul Malik Pahlawan in 1997, the Taliban killed about 4,000 civilians after taking Mazar-e-Sharif in 1998".*
> <u>Afghanistan: The Massacre in Mazar-E-Sharif</u>
> **Human Rights Watch** of November 1998 is referred.

Pakistan was backing the Taliban to conquer the whole of Afghanistan. With the fall of Kandahar, thousands of Afghan refugees, *madrasa* students, and Pakistani *Jamiat Ulama-e Islam* [JUI] supporters had rushed to join the movement. Upon the capture of their areas, other *mujaheden* commanders in Kandahar got angry with Pakistan, too.

The only exception was that the Taliban were unable to gain complete victory against Ahmad Shah Masoud, who retained control of his 5% territory in and around Punjsher valley in the north of Kabul. There was difference in fighting ability of the Taliban versus Shah Masoud who had received US support and training in the 1980s. Masoud remained undefeated against the Russian Army, too and [later] he held back the Taliban from ruling his territory of Afghanistan. Masoud's secret was superior training and loyal cadre of his fighters; whereas the Taliban's ranks mostly talked *jihad*. Moreover, unlike Masoud's men, the Taliban were incapable of fighting during night hours.

Another factor, that about 5,000 new *'Punjabis'* were seen by foreign media on their way into Afghanistan to supplement the fight against Ahmed Masoud. The American Defence Intelligence Agency [DIA] analyst also reported that amongst [Taliban] prisoners held by Masoud there were several Punjabi *madrassa* student fighters also.

The US State Department communiqués and analysis, drafted on the basis of Human Rights Watch reports, alleged that some Pakistani nationals fighting in Afghanistan were from the Frontier Corps of Pakistan. *Harakat-ul-Mujahedeen*, allegedly a Pakistan-supported warrior group in Afghanistan, had hijacked an Air India flight from Nepal to Kandahar in December 1999, eventually releasing the hostages after negotiations with the Taliban.

Pakistan has about 2500+ miles long border with Afghanistan thus most of the food supplies and livelihood items for the adjoining areas travel through its cities like Peshawar and Quetta. However, some Taliban trade occurred with Turkmenistan and Iran too. Pakistan remained the effective diplomatic and economic lifeline for the Taliban leadership, elite and the general populace. Pakistan also provided crucial technical infrastructure support to allow the Taliban state to function smoothly.

Pakistan's support of the Taliban was a continuation of support for Islamist rather than nationalist factions inside Afghanistan. Nor was the ISI the only supporter of the Taliban within the Pakistan government; the then PM Benazir Bhutto's interior minister, Gen Nasirullah Babar also supported Taliban warriors actively. Some media reports also suggested that *'Bhutto and Babar conceived of the Taliban as the solution to Pakistan's problems'*.

Referring to an article titled *'Pakistan Ripe for Taliban-style revolution'* published in **The Hindu** dated 24<u>th</u> February 2000:

> *"The Taliban were not beholden to any single Pakistani lobby such as the ISI. In contrast the Taliban had access to more influential lobbies and groups in Pakistan than most Pakistanis."*

Citizens of Kabul used to comment about *'Punjabi volunteers'* from Pakistan; guarding ministries in Kabul in March 2000 were Taliban officials who could only speak Urdu and not any Afghan language. The Pakistani government never disputed the reports that thousands of trained Pakistani volunteers were serving with the Taliban in those days; nor was considered it a sin or crime by worldly standards because Pakistan army used to serve in so many other countries of Africa and Europe under the commanding arrangements of the UN – then why not to help a neighbouring state when needed.

Authentic media reports like *'Pakistan under Musharraf'* in **Defence and Foreign Affairs' Strategic Policy** of <u>January 2000</u> told the facts:

> *".... In 1971, there were only 900 madaris (religious seminaries) in Pakistan; by the end of President Zia ul Haq's regime in 1988, there were over 8,000 officially funded madaris, and more than 25,000 unregistered religious schools. The most prominent of the seminaries -- the Dar al-Ulum Haqqania [Akora Khatak] from which the Taliban leadership was excessively drawn -- had 15,000 applications for only 400 spots in 1999."*

In fact, the Taliban have never been a movement that came to power by support from the society [*though they claimed so*] but they were the one faction that the US chose to support in 1996 to stabilize the country ravaged by warlords after the Soviets' withdrawal.

What happened just recently in 2021 was the worst case, of course. The world think-tanks got worried if Afghanistan would become the showcase of an Islamic statehood following the template of the IS caliphate; no one knows in fact.

## TALIBAN SUPPORT FOR OBL:

The Taliban and Osama bin Ladin [OBL]'s **al-Qaeda network** were distinct identities though inter-woven. In 1996, OBL left Sudan due to his differences with Sudanese government and re-settled with the Taliban in Afghanistan. Those were days when the Taliban were officially recognized as the government of Afghanistan by Pakistan, Saudi Arabia, and the United Arab Emirates [UAE] only.

On the other hand, the Taliban continued to shelter OBL, even after knowing about his involvement in the 1998's bombings of the US embassies in Kenya and Tanzania. The Taliban continued to harbour OBL, despite the international anger - because of Afghan traditions of hospitality – quite contrary to the fact that the Afghans had killed nearly 17,000 British men, women, and children when they were evacuating Kabul under a treaty after the First Afghan War in 1842.

Osama bin Laden was not a *'medieval barbarian'*, but a wealthy Saudi national and student before joining the Mujahedeen in Afghanistan. He regarded Western secularism as an affront to the *Sharia* Law, basis of the whole social fabric in Saudi Arabia. The West considered other religious beliefs like *Wahhabism* [one Islamic school of thought widely prevalent in Saudi Arabia] as 'medieval barbarity'. By OBL's dictionary, it looks like an ancient horror to common Western people, but its pure religious culture is only a little different from some Christian fundamentalist sects.

Many Europeans knew that OBL was not a medieval primitive barbarian but a highly sophisticated, intelligent individual, just seeking shelter and protection in Afghanistan. How the 9/11 attack was planned and perpetrated stood very widely documented later. One can read all versions that how was it planned and who financed what. Doesn't matter who did it. The only relevant truth remained that the US created this mess itself and also suffered at the end – that's Americans' hard luck that the logical end took two decades to come.

OBL had brought with him to Afghanistan a well-equipped and loyal group of 2000 fighters, called 055 brigade; many of them trained in al-Qaeda's camps for terrorism abroad. OBL had made available several hundred to fight for the Taliban at frontline against Shah Masoud. However, the Taliban suffered a high international cost for hosting OBL alone. At least 1,000 more Arabs arrived in Afghanistan following the 9/11 Attacks, crossing over from Pakistan and Iran; many got based at Jalalabad, Khost, Kandahar and Mazar-e-Sharif districts / provinces.

The US didn't adopt a consistent line on the Taliban. During 1990s, the US pressured Saudi Arabia to cut ties with OBL and Sudan to expel him, but when the Taliban took control of Afghanistan and Bin Laden moved there; *the Taliban were hosted at Camp David and treated like a legitimate government.*

At Camp David, there was a press conference after the said TREAT where the spokesperson was asked about the Taliban's human rights record and he made remarks about how sorry he felt for the reporter's husband. Both the Clinton and Bush administrations made threats they didn't back up, bribed with no conditions and made requests without considering why the Taliban would ever comply.

As per UN regulations, a unilateral attack on another country could have been considered to be a violation of international law so the NATO minions were roped in to provide plausible deniability of this war crime of 2001. Also that Bin laden was known to have been on the payroll of the same *'coalition'* that invaded Afghanistan to get him; details of the *Operation Cyclone* are referred. It was then perceived or known by the whole world - Bin Laden to be a CIA asset.

[**Operation Cyclone:** A code name for the CIA's program to arm and finance the Afghan *mujahedeen* and supporting militant Islamic groups in Afghanistan from 1979 to 1989, prior to and during the military intervention by the USSR in support of the Democratic Republic of Afghanistan. The *mujahedeen* were also supported by Britain's MI6 in conducting separate covert actions. The program had heavily supported groups with *jihadist* ties that were favoured by Pakistan's Gen Ziaul Haq, the then military ruler.

In May 1979, US officials secretly began meeting with Afghan rebel leaders through Pakistan's ISI contacts. Additional meetings were held on 6th April and 3rd July 1979 [and then off and on]. The same day, President Carter signed a *'presidential finding'* that authorized the

CIA to spend $500,000 aid to the *mujahedeen*; and the patronisation started.

The said operation was one of the longest and most expensive covert CIA operations ever undertaken. Funding officially began with $695,000 help in 1979, was increased dramatically to $20–30 million per year for 1980s, and rose to $630 million per year in 1987. The first consignment of weapons comprised of discarded **British Lee–Enfield rifles** shipped out in December 1979, but by September 1986 the program included US made hi-weaponry like **FIM-92 Stinger missiles**, c2300 in numbers. Funding continued after the 1989 Soviet withdrawal also as the *mujahedeen* continued to battle the forces of President Najibullah's army during the Afghan Civil War 1989–92).]

Peter Bergen's *Holy War Inc*, [2001],
& Steve Coll's *Ghost Wars:*
*The Secret History of the CIA, Afghanistan,*
*and Bin Laden*... [2004] are referred.

All of this Al Qaeda rubbish was a direct result of America's megalomania. Starting in the Kissinger years, the US had weaponized Islam as a tool to draw the USSR into a quagmire, which backfired on them. More details are available in **www.independent.co.uk**/news/terror-blowback-burns-cia-11820

**Terror 'blowback' burns CIA?** America's spies paid and trained their nation's worst enemies; revealed *Andrew Marshall* in Washington on 1st November 1998.

[*The Central Intelligence Agency (CIA) has its own jargon for describing the hallucinatory world within which its employees move. None of its mysterious terms are more euphemistic than 'blowback', the term coined to describe operations which end up rebounding against their creators.*]

We have to continually remind ourselves what happened after an actual terrorist attack on the twin towers on 9/11, most of the terrorists were Saudi nationals. The alleged mastermind, Osama bin Laden was a Saudi national. Money trails led to Saudi Arabia. What was the US response to airlift Saudi nationals - including relatives of Osama bin Laden - out of the country whatsoever?

The attacks on Afghanistan and subsequently on Iraq using the false pretexts that OBL or Al-Qaeda had attacked on Twin Towers in

New York and President Saddam Hussein had weapons of mass destruction [WMD] respectively – were *all statements of persistent lies and deceit by the West* which ultimately back-fired in the two devastated countries.

[*It was, perhaps, all about oil and taking the opportunity to divert hundreds of billions of dollars of taxpayer money to the privately owned defence industry - yes thinking about Dick Cheney as major beneficiary. All was done in partnership of hi-military officials in the US and Afghanistan both.*]

A 100 million dollar question from the intelligentsia that: **WHO IS RESPONSIBLE FOR TALIBAN THEN.** In 1980s, America had a very desolate choice: Either the US could support an Afghan opposition, or they could simply cede Afghanistan to Soviet domination, an option that might result in an extension of Soviet influence into Pakistan, India & Iran. Those were the days the US wanted to dictate [in routine] its desires to its foreign allies but could not afford to do so in the given Afghan situation.

*Washington needed Pakistan's cooperation;* but Pakistan ought to be mindful of its own interests, too. The most alarming was the nationalist threat to Pakistani integrity developed after the creation of Bangladesh in 1971; *Pashtunistan* claims were catching air. Accordingly, Islamabad allowed religious groups to operate on Pakistani territory and the American policymakers had to bow their heads for Pakistani interests.

After the Soviet Union's collapse in Afghanistan, Washington could have withdrawn itself from the Afghan arena and could have left sufficient home-work to do by Pakistan while passing remote instructions from the Pentagon – however, the US policy makers preferred to stay at the Afghan soils – thus faced humiliation and un-ceremonial trounce to move out suddenly after two decades' futile war.

**How the Taliban govern?** Historians, however, noted that a fundamental problem of the Taliban during their rule during 1996-2001 remained that they were *"essentially caught between a tribal society which they tried to ignore and the need for a state structure which they refused to establish"*.

When the Taliban took power in 1996, they had no funds and no plan or programme for governance beyond a vague and generalised idea of a government based on the *Sharia system.*

## HAVE TALIBAN CHANGED IN 2021?

That was the key question. The intelligentsia suggested in a paper that:

> *"During their resurgence [post-2003], and particularly their expansion into non-Pashtun areas, the Taliban increasingly proved that they were a learning organisation.*
>
> *Awareness grew within their movement that their own repressive policies had resulted in global isolation as well as opposition from many Afghans, including those who had initially welcomed the Taliban when they almost ended the inter-factional wars of the 1990s."*

Also a point to consider that the Taliban – unlike other armed insurgent groups elsewhere – never developed a political wing distinct from their military arm, with the closest to a political structure being a negotiations office in Doha. The Taliban didn't indicate what form of government they envisage, although remarks by some officials indicated that *'they plan to return to an Islamic emirate model'*.

The UK had very good relations with Saudi Arabia for decades regardless of its treatment of women. Indeed UK still sells arms en masse to help the Saudis fight their proxy and real wars throughout the Middle East. Thus paroxysms of moral outrage about the status of women in Afghanistan should not have been relevant for crafting a coherent and rational foreign policy. The same Western liberal interventionists drove Afghanistan back into the arms of the Taliban, after another generation of devastating conflict and destruction.

The Afghan Taliban is very different tribal community that occupy mountainous space left over when one takes away surrounding real countries. The US made deal at Doha with the Taliban which were [still are] an association of conservative rural *Pashtuns* from the south, to get rid of the corrupt westernized *Pashtun* elite like Hamid Karzai and Ashraf Ghani in Kabul. The strategy didn't pay – couldn't go viable - after their foreign sponsors [the US, UK & NATO] finally gave up, like Soviet invaders before them.

The intelligentsia had given thought to the issue and opined that with the passage of time, things would settle down after a conservative Taliban's reaction, and things would be far less bad for urban women and progressives like in Saudi Arabia of 2020-21.

In 1970s, when the Russians were building roads, schools and hospitals, and training female teachers and doctors, most women were wearing *'burkas'* back then; in those times the West used to give the *jihadis* money and ammunition to sabotage the Socialist plans. Now the West finally lost the Great Game – so all gimmicks to cover their follies.

The crucial point to remember is that the Taliban had taken over 'the country'; cities and capital, within in a fortnight in 1996, with a similar former alliance of convenience.

Fact also remains that the then Taliban rulers had actually sent their foreign minister to Quetta to negotiate the arrest and trial of OBL under *Sharia law* in November 2001 - but instead, the CIA wanted to have *him* arrested and get transferred to one of their prisons.

The US military and political elite since 2001 should admit that 20-years' partial occupation was a political and military strategic disaster from even before it started.

However, - THE AFGHAN WAR has been the most successful US business plan in the history of warfare whosoever drafted it.

# Scenario 226

## ISI – CIA: FRIENDS & FOES [?] AT TIMES

The **Inter-Services Intelligence** [ISI], the prime intelligence agency of Pakistan, was [and still is] accused of being heavily involved in covertly running military intelligence programs in Afghanistan.

For quite a long time, the same ISI has been the most preferred organization for the Americans.

See a historical page from the Jimmy Carter's presidential finding; an interesting description to tell the whole back-ground facts about America's dependence on Pakistan and its ISI those days:

> *"In any event, policymakers back in Washington did not believe the Soviets could be defeated militarily by the [Islamist] rebels. **The CIA's mission was spelled out** in an amended **Top Secret presidential finding** signed by President Carter in late December 1979 and reauthorized by President Reagan in 1981.*
>
> *The finding permitted the CIA to ship weapons secretly to the mujahedeen. The CIA's covert action was to raise the cost of Soviet intervention in Afghanistan. It might also deter the Soviets from undertaking other Third World invasions. But **this was not a war the CIA expected to win** outright on the battlefield.*
>
> *The finding made clear that **the agency was to work through Pakistan and defer to Pakistani priorities.** The CIA's Afghan program would not be 'underlateral' as the agency called operations it ran in secret on its own. Instead the CIA would emphasize 'liaison with Pakistani intelligence'. The first guns shipped in were single-shot, bolt-action 303 rifles, British infantry weapon until the 1950s.*
>
> *In the aftermath of [Soviet] invasion, Carter was determined to respond vigorously to what he considered a dangerous provocation. In a televised speech, he announced sanctions on the USSR, promised **renewed aid to Pakistan,** and committed ....... British Prime Minister Margaret Thatcher enthusiastically backed Carter's tough stance.*

.....*The thrust of US policy for the duration of the war was determined by Carter in early 1980:* **Carter initiated a program to arm the mujahedeen through Pakistan's ISI** *and secured a pledge from Saudi Arabia to match US funding for this purpose.*

*US support for the mujahedeen accelerated under Carter's successor, Ronald Reagan, at a final cost to US taxpayers of some $3 billion.....*

*The Soviets were unable to quell the insurgency and withdrew from Afghanistan in Feb 1989, precipitating the dissolution of the Soviet Union itself. Of the* **seven mujahedeen groups** *supported by Gen Zia's government, (there were) four espoused Islamic fundamentalist beliefs—and these fundamentalists received most of the funding.*

*By 1992, the combined US, Saudi, and Chinese aid to the mujahedeen was estimated at $6–12 billion, whereas* <u>Soviet military aid to Afghanistan was valued at $36–48 billion</u>*. The result was a heavily-armed, militarized Afghan society; thus Afghanistan was the world's top destination for personal weapons during the 1980s. Some 1.5 million Afghans died as a result of warfare between 1979 and 1996."*

.....[The writer (Mr Coll) also documented that] *"OBL informally cooperated with the ISI and with Saudi intelligence during the 1980s and had intimate connections to* **CIA-backed mujahedeen commander Jalaluddin Haqqani;** *the CIA's Islamabad Station Chief from mid-1986 until mid-1989, took an admiring view of bin Laden at the time."*
**Steve Coll**'s book **Ghost Wars:** The Secret History of the CIA, Afghanistan, and Bin Laden; [2004] p-58 {ISBN 9781594200076} is referred for more details.

## ISI IN AFGHANISTAN (1970s):

In 1974, the then Pakistani PM, Zulfiqar Ali Bhutto, said that:

*"Two can play this game. We know where their weak points are just as they know ours. The Non-Pashtuns there hate the Pashtun domination. So we have our ways of persuading Daoud [the then ruler of Afghanistan] not to aggravate our problems."*

A leading Afghan Arab, **Abdullah Anas,** in his memoirs said that:

*"ISI supported the Tajik insurgents with the blessing of Pakistan's president Zulfikar Ali Bhutto who hoped to use this uprising as a means*

> *to pressurise the Afghan government to resolve the border disputes over Balochistan and Pashtunistan".*
>
> **Abdullah Anas:** *My Life in Jihad - from Algeria to Afghanistan,* [2019] is referred.

The first ISI operation in Afghanistan took place in 1975. It was in *'retaliation to Republic of Afghanistan's proxy war and support to the militants against Pakistan'*; **Peter Tomsen**'s **"the Wars of Afghanistan: Messianic Terrorism"** [2013] is referred.

Before 1975, ISI did not conduct any operation in Afghanistan and it was only after decade of Republic of Afghanistan's proxy war against Pakistan, support to militants and two armed invasions in *Bajaur* Agency in FATA that Pakistan retaliated. Later on, in 1980s, the ISI in **Operation Cyclone** systematically coordinated the distribution of arms and financial means provided by the US Central Intelligence Agency [CIA] to factions of the Afghan *mujahedeen* of Gulbuddin Hekmatyar and the forces of Ahmad Shah Masoud, later known as the Northern Alliance.

History stands witness as **Hein Kiessling** claimed that, the Soviet backed Republic of Afghanistan support to anti-Pakistani militants had forced the then prime minister of Pakistan Zulfiqar Ali Bhutto and Naseerullah Babar, the then Inspector General of the Frontier Corps in NWFP [now Khyber PK], to adopt a more aggressive approach towards Afghanistan.

As a result, the ISI, under the command of Maj Gen Ghulam Jilani Khan set up a 5,000-strong Afghan guerrilla troops, including influential future leaders like *Gulbuddin Hekmatyar* and *Ahmed Shah Masoud*, to target the then sitting Afghan government. The first large operation, in 1975, a sponsored armed rebellion in the *Panjshir* valley was launched in which the mayor 'of their home city' was assassinated; **Hein Kiessling's Faith, Unity, Discipline: The ISI of Pakistan,** [2016] is referred.

In 1979 the Soviet Union intervened in the Afghan Civil War. *The ISI and the CIA worked together* to recruit Muslims throughout the world to take part in *Jihad* against the Soviet forces. However the CIA had little direct contact with the *Mujahedeen* as the ISI was the main contact and handler and they favoured the most radical group, namely the *Hezb e Islami* of Gulbuddin Hekmatyar.

The Pakistani backed rebellion, though unsuccessful, had shaken Afghan President Daoud Khan and made him realise the gravity of situation. He started softening his stance against Pakistan and started considering to improve relations with his neighbouring country. He realized that a *'friendly Pakistan was in his interest'*. He also accepted Shah of Iran's offer to normalize relations between Pakistan and Afghanistan. In August 1976, Daoud Khan also recognised Durand Line as international border between Pakistan and Afghanistan.

[The Afghanistan conflict *began in 1978 and had coincided with several notable operations by the American CIA. The first operation, code-named* Operation Cyclone, *began in mid-1979, during the Presidency of Jimmy Carter. It financed and eventually supplied weapons to the anti-communist mujahedeen guerrillas in Afghanistan following a 1978 Marxist coup and throughout the ten-year military occupation of Afghanistan by the Soviet Union.*

*Carter's successor, Ronald Reagan, supported an expansion under* the Reagan Doctrine, *which aided the mujahedeen along with several other anti-Soviet resistance movements around the world.*]

In 1990s, after the Soviet retreat [in 1989], the different *Mujahedeen* factions turned on each other and were unable to come to a power sharing deal which resulted in a civil war. The US, along with the ISI and the Pakistani government of PM Benazir Bhutto became the primary source of support for *Hekmatyar* in his 1992–1994 bombardment campaign against the Islamic State of Afghanistan especially its capital Kabul.

When *Hekmatyar* failed to take over power in Afghanistan, more energetic people from them got separated and made another new group called the Afghan Taliban. The ISI and the Pak-military started providing financial, logistical, military and direct combat support to the Taliban which continued till the 9/11 event of 2001. The Western media alleged that the ISI supported the Taliban's resurgence in Afghanistan after 9/11 but Pakistani officials denied this accusation. Allegations were also raised by the American Lobbies that the ISI provided support and refuge to al-Qaeda, too. Such allegations caught momentum when Al-Qaeda leader Osama Bin Laden [OBL] was killed in May 2011 in Abbottabad [Pakistan].

## AFTER THE SOVIETs LEFT AFGHANISTAN:

In 1991, after-effects of the Soviets departure from Afghanistan started showing its true colours; it was widespread civil war amongst various Afghan militant groups. The Islamists tried to install a government under

*Hekmatyar* with Jalalabad as their provisional capital, but the idea didn't work. The proposed Afghan Interim Government *[allegedly the ISI wanted to install it]* had *Hekmatyar* as Prime Minister and Abdul Rasul Sayyaf as Foreign Minister. Allegedly the scheme was a brain-child of Lt Gen Hamid Gul, the then DG ISI. The Jalalabad operation was seen as a mistake by other *mujahedeen* leaders like Ahmad Shah Masoud; as he was not informed of the plans before-hand, and nor had he participated. Both commanders were planning independently.

After operations by the Masoud's group, the defection of the communist Gen Abdul Rashid Dostum, and the subsequent fall of another communist Najibullah-regime in 1992, the Afghan political parties agreed on a peace and power-sharing agreement, called the **Peshawar Accords**. The Accords created the **Islamic State of Afghanistan** and appointed an interim government for a transitional period to be followed by general elections. According to the then media reports:

> *"The sovereignty of Afghanistan was vested formally in the Islamic State of Afghanistan; after the fall of the Soviet-backed Najibullah government.... with the exception of Hekmatyar's **Hezb e Islami**, all the parties... were ostensibly unified under this government in April 1992. ...*
>
> *Gulbuddin Hekmatyar received operational, financial and military support from Pakistan.... Had it not been for the ISI's logistic support and supply of a large number of rockets, Hekmatyar's forces would not have been able to target and destroy the Kabul city."*

Till 1994 at least, *Hekmatyar* was unable to conquer any territory from the Islamic State; in this respect he felt bitter disappointment to his patrons. The fighter sub-groups within *Hekmatyar's Hezb e Islami* got frustrated and made up their own group called the Taliban – which later held the reigns of Afghanistan during 1996-2001 and later in August 2021.

The Western media believed that the Taliban were largely founded by Pakistan's Interior Ministry under Gen Naseerullah Babar and the ISI in 1994. William Maley, Professor at the Australian National University and Director of the Asia-Pacific College, writes on the emergence of the Taliban in Afghanistan:

> *"In 1994, with the failure of Hekmatyar's attempt to oust the Afghan President Rabbani's administration, Pakistan found itself in an awkward*

*position. Hekmatyar had proved incapable of seizing and controlling defended territory. In October 1994, Pakistani interior minister Babar took a group of Western ambassadors, including the US Ambassador to Pakistan John C. Monjo to Kandahar, without even bothering to inform the Kabul government or its embassy in Islamabad."*

Once it was also alleged that the ISI had trained 80,000 fighters against the Soviet Union in Afghanistan; and until 9/11 of 2001, Pakistan military and ISI officers deployed thousands of regular Pakistani armed forces personnel and had been involved in the fighting in Afghanistan – which was not true. One can see how resourceful the Western Media was while giving so irresponsible statement because in those days, the CIA and the ISI had been performing most military activities and operations jointly.

In 1998, Russia said, Pakistan was responsible for the *'military expansion of the Taliban in northern Afghanistan'* by sending large numbers of Pakistani troops, including ISI personnel, some of whom had subsequently been taken as prisoners by the anti-Taliban group - Masoud's Northern Alliance; it was a baseless and concocted story which was published in the *Express India* dated 12ᵗʰ August 1998.

*Human Rights Watch* wrote in its year 2000's report:

> *"Of all the foreign powers involved in efforts to sustain and manipulate the ongoing fighting [in Afghanistan], Pakistan is distinguished both by the sweep of its objectives and the scale of its efforts, which include soliciting funding for the Taliban, bankrolling Taliban operations, providing diplomatic support as the Taliban's virtual emissaries abroad, arranging training for Taliban fighters, recruiting skilled and unskilled manpower to serve in Taliban armies, planning and directing offensives, providing and facilitating shipments of ammunition and fuel, and ... sometimes directly providing combat support."*

In year 2000, the UN Security Council explicitly criticized Pakistan for its military support for the Taliban; the Security Council stated that:

> *"It was deeply distressed over reports of involvement in the fighting, on the Taliban side, of thousands of non-Afghan nationals."*

Might be the Security Council had made the reference pointing out towards the Saudi and Egyptian warriors generally known as Afghan

Arabs. In July 2001, several countries including the United States, accused Pakistan of being in violation of UN sanctions because of its military aid to the Taliban. Earlier in 1996, after the capture of Kabul by the Taliban, Pakistan gave $30 million in aid and a further $10 million for servants' wages.

However, it was astonished that why the US needed to control Pakistan through UN and other allied forums because the Taliban was an off-shoot of the same *Mujahedeen* bodies and groups which were nurtured by the two countries jointly through American arsenal and finance.

More explicitly, the fact remained that Pakistan was a poor country and was not in a position to supply finances and ammunition from its own kitty; all the equipment and financial aids were supplied by the US and Pakistan's role was only of a carrier or distributor. The policies of distribution as to whom, which quality and in what quantities were issued by the US admin and the CIA - then why cries. One can simply term it the *'double face of the American Establishment'*.

Referring to a report published by the British Defence Ministry think tank in ending 2006, titled as *'The ISI and Terrorism: Behind the Accusations,* still available at **Cfr.org** which leveled baseless accusations to please its American companions stating:

> *"Indirectly Pakistan [through the ISI] has been supporting terrorism and extremism--whether in London on 7/7 [the 7<sup>th</sup> July 2005 attacks on London's transit system killing 52 people], or in Afghanistan, or Iraq."*

The US Defence Secretary Robert Gates had added *'to a certain extent, they play both sides.'*

Since the Afghan Presidential Elections in late 2009 Afghan President Hamid Karzai increasingly become isolated, surrounding himself with members of Hekmatyar's *Hezb e Islami*. The *Associated Press* reported once:

> *"Several of Karzai's close friends and advisers now speak of a president whose doors have been closed to all but one narrow faction and who refuses to listen to dissenting opinions."*

In 2010, a report by the *London School of Economics*, titled as *'The Discussion Papers'* - made public on 12<sup>th</sup> December 2010, said that:

*"Pakistan's ISI has an official policy of support for the Taliban. The ISI provides funding and training for the Taliban, and that the agency has representatives on the so-called Quetta Shura, the Taliban's leadership council.*

*Pakistan appears to be playing a double-game of astonishing magnitude; Asif Ali Zardari, the Pakistani president, met with senior Taliban prisoners in 2010 and promised to release them. Zardari told the detainees they were only arrested because of American pressure."*

In 2011, the US Chairman of the Joint Chiefs of Staff Admiral Mike Mullen called the *Haqqani* network [the Afghan Taliban's armed element] a *'veritable arm of Pakistan's ISI'* – further that the Extremist organizations serving as proxies of the government of Pakistan were attacking Afghan national troops and civilians as well as US soldiers.

The compiler of the said report, Mr Waldman, had openly warned the US and the UK that:

*".....without a change in Pakistan's behaviour it will be difficult if not impossible for international forces and the Afghan government to make progress against insurgency."*

*Al-Jazeera* wrote in early 2012 that:

*"Presidential Chief of Staff, Karim Khoram from Hekmatyar's Hezb e Islami, besides controlling the Government Media and Information Centre, enjoys a tight grip over President Karzai. Former co-workers of Khoram have accused him of acting divisive internally and having isolated Hamid Karzai's non-Pashtuns allies.*

*The damage that Khoram has inflicted on President Karzai's image in one year - his enemies could not have done the same {in full tenure}. Senior non-Hezb e Islami Pashtun officials in the Afghan government have accused Khoram of acting as a spy for Pakistan's Inter-Services Intelligence [ISI]".*

In March 2012, the Commander of NATO forces in Afghanistan, Gen John Allen, told the US Senate that there was no change in Pakistan's policy of support for the Taliban and its *Haqqani* network. The General also alleged that Pak-Army through ISI remained constantly involved in recruiting fighters and suicide bombers for the Afghan Taliban among the 1.7 million registered and 1-2 million unregistered *Pashtun* Afghan refugees living in refugee camps and settlements along the Pak-Afghan border in Pakistan.

However, Gen Allen forgot the fact that most of those *Pashtun* refugees had lived there since the Soviet–Afghan War during 1979-89 – and they were installed, nurtured, fed and equipped by the CIA then.

## CIA ACTIVITY IN AFGHANISTAN:

America's **Operation Cyclone** primarily supported militant Islamist grow- ups; and in deference to the priorities of Pakistan's ISI, CIA funding un-evenly benefited Afghan *mujahideen* commanders, most notably *Gulbuddin Hekmatyar* and *Jalaluddin Haqqani*, although the CIA developed a limited unilateral relationship with the Northern Afghan commander Ahmad Shah Masoud [*a favorite figure of British intelligence*] beginning in late 1984.

**Operation Cyclone** was one of the longest and most expensive CIA operations ever undertaken; costing over $20–$30 million per year in 1980, and peaking at $630 million during the fiscal year ending in October 1987. The program began modestly with provisions of antique British Lee–Enfield rifles but by 1986 included US-origin state of the art weaponry, such as thousands of FIM-92 Stinger missiles.

The CIA's Islamabad Station Chief Milton Bearden, among others, was one of the architects of the ambitious escalation of CIA activities in Afghanistan from 1985 on, as the Reagan administration had rejected compromise with reformist Soviet leader Mikhail Gorbachev in favour of a total *mujahedeen* victory. Funding continued as the *mujahedeen* battled the forces of Najibullah's PDPA during the civil war in Afghanistan [1989–92].

After the February 1989 withdrawal of Soviet troops, the CIA's objective was to topple the Najibullah government, which was formed under Soviet instructions. By 1990, under instructions of the CIA, the ISI and *Hekmatyar* worked to violently eliminate their Afghan rivals, including Ahmad Masoud, anticipating fall of the Afghan capital, Kabul.

> {*The historical facts are that amidst those days of Afghan Civil War, **the ISI and CIA jointly formulated** a plan to capture Jalalabad and Kabul during 1989-1990, marking a high point in cooperation between the two spy agencies. As part of the offensive, the CIA paid Masoud to close the Salang Pass, which Masoud failed to do.*

*The Najibullah government finally collapsed in April 1992, several months after the December 1991 dissolution of the Soviet Union and the end of US aid to the mujahedeen, **leaving Afghanistan a failed state** in the grip of a multifaceted civil war marked by horrific atrocities and the destruction of Kabul in mass-casualty rocket attacks.*

*THAT WAS THE TIME when the US initially welcomed the emergence of **the Taliban militia** as it sought to restore its vision of Islamic order to the Pashtuns heartland of Kandahar and then to the rest of Afghanistan.}*

The CIA's Islamabad Station Chief from May 1981 to mid-1984, Howard Hart, had called for a Pakistani bounty on killed or captured Soviet troops. Gust Avrakotos, serving as the head of the CIA's task force on Afghan operations, also praised a Pakistani program that provided incentives to *mujahedeen* commanders. The CIA & ISI jointly organized repeated unsuccessful assassination attempts on Mohammad Najibullah, then in charge of Afghanistan's secret police and later the President of Afghanistan, using CIA funds and CIA-supplied long-range rockets.

As a side note, the **CIA started funding Masoud** in late 1984 *without Pakistani involvement,* but its officers remained prohibited from interacting with him directly. British and French intelligence officers, however, did not operate under those restrictions as their CIA counterparts used to speak with Masoud in person. The British role was resented by the Pakistanis in routine and some CIA officers found the French to be 'grating,' but the CIA came to **rely on MI6** for intelligence regarding Masoud during those years.

[*Even much later, in response to the 9/11 attacks, the CIA personnel coordinated closely with Masoud's anti-Taliban Northern Alliance militia during the 2001 US invasion of Afghanistan.*]

In March 1985 President Reagan signed a draft of a National Security Decision Directive [NSDD], which formalized and provided a legal rationale for the changes that were already taking place with regard to CIA activities in Afghanistan. The resulting **NSDD–166** reportedly included a highly classified supplement signed by NSA Robert McFarlane that detailed expanded forms of US assistance to the *mujahedeen*, such as the provision of satellite intelligence, 'burst communication devices', advanced weapons systems, and additional training to the Afghan rebels through the ISI.

Furthermore, the document allowed the *CIA to unilaterally support certain Afghan assets without the ISI's participation or knowledge.* In sum, NSDD–166 defined the Reagan administration's policy as aiding the *mujahedeen* by *'all available means'*. In one [30th April] meeting, Iklé communicated the general thrust of this policy to ISI Director Akhtar Abdur Rahman; Pages-125 - 129 of the above referred book of *Steve Coll* are referred.

As a result, more Americans landed in Pakistan to train ISI handlers on the new weapons systems. In turn, the ISI developed a complex infrastructure to impart training 16,000 to 18,000 Afghan *mujahedeen* annually by early 1986; furthermore 6,000 to 7,000 rebels [*including a number of Arab volunteers*] were additionally trained every year by those *mujahedeen* that were previously trained by the ISI. Despite many congressional concerns and reservations, the ISI remained the main conduit for US support to the *mujahedeen* and the bulk of the Reagan-era aid championed by conservatives went to *Muslim Brotherhood-inspired commanders* favoured by the most notably *Gulbuddin Hekmatyar*.

In those days of early 1985, in retaliation for KGB-sponsored bombings that had killed hundreds in Pakistan, the ISI also organized *mujahedeen* teams to carry out violent raids inside Soviet territory, which the CIA had in fact approved. Soon after, a State Department message to Gen Akhtar of ISI was conveyed to the effect that the ISI should not encourage Afghans to cross the Soviet border. [*Previously Casey had approved such acts of sabotage in late 1984 during an ambivalent reception by Gen Akhtar DG ISI, stating that 'You should take the books ... and you can think of sending arms and ammunition if possible'.*]

[For media, the version was different – *'No one but President Reagan possessed the authority to foment attacks inside the Soviet Union.'*]

In late September 1986, roughly two months after Bearden replaced Piekney as Islamabad Station Chief, the CIA started delivering US-made state of the art FIM-92 Stinger surface-to-air missiles to the *mujahedeen;* the Stingers were to be used to destroy Soviet aircraft from a distance of roughly 12,500 feet, seriously targeting low-flying helicopters by the Soviet Special Forces - the Soviets eventually had to decide that it was no longer safe to use helicopters for attacks and rescue.

In April 1987, three separate teams of Afghan rebels were directed by the ISI to launch coordinated violent raids on multiple targets across the Soviet border and extending to over 10 miles into Soviet territory.

In response, the Soviets issued a thinly-veiled threat to invade Pakistan to stop the cross-border attacks: Casey was forced to resign his DCI post; the cross border fighting was also stopped by the ISI.

Bearden, CIA's Chief in Islamabad Station, endorsed supplying the Stingers as a turning point in the Soviet–Afghan war. In total, the CIA sent nearly 2,300 Stingers to Afghanistan, *creating a substantial black market for such weapons throughout the Middle East, Central Asia, and even parts of Africa* that persisted well into the 1990s. Perhaps 100 Stingers were acquired by Iran. The CIA later operated a program to recover the Stingers through cash buy-backs. Despite Masoud's reputation as one of the most effective *mujahedeen* commanders, Pakistan's ISI was instructed to give only 8 Stingers to Commander Masoud—a fraction of 1% of the total supply for *Mujahedeen*.

Mikhail Gorbachev emerged as the reformist leader of the Soviet Union in 1985 and by November 1986 the decision to withdraw Soviet troops had been made; Najibullah was informed of the *fait accompli* in December. Around the same time, the CIA rejected out of hand Soviet entreaties to work together to prevent civil war or the rise of what KGB head Vladimir Kryuchkov had told Gates that there would be a *'fundamentalist Islamic state'* in Afghanistan.

The US negotiators initially signaled a willingness to suspend CIA support to the *mujahedeen* in exchange for a Soviet withdrawal, but *President Reagan personally intervened* to declare an aid cut-off unacceptable as long as the Soviets assisted Najibullah's regime. Nevertheless, Soviet withdrawal from Afghanistan began in May 1988 pursuant to the terms of the **Geneva Accords** and was completed in February 1989. These events produced much elevation for Pakistan and its ISI in the US government.

Meanwhile, reports appeared that *Hekmatyar* was planning to install an *Islamist regime* in Afghanistan by killing or intimidating his opponents. President Gen Zia left a formidable legacy including a roughly ten-fold increase in the number of madrassas in Pakistan and the transformation of the ISI into a powerful state-within-a-state. Many of these madrassas introduced a new generation of Afghan religious students, or *'taliban'* from Kandahar to a severe, Deobandi-influenced interpretation of Islam that had not previously played a significant role in Afghan history.

Najibullah's government, backed by hundreds of millions in Soviet aid every month, demonstrated more staying power than any CIA analyst could have anticipated, successfully fending off a disastrous 1989 attempt by the *mujahedeen* to take Jalalabad. Despite such like setbacks, the *mujahedeen* scored a major victory by capturing *Khost* in early 1991. The US felt nothing objectionable in Najubullah participating in Afghan elections as part of a peaceful settlement. Nevertheless, the CIA and the ISI both continued to claim, for years, their historical victory amidst the joyful celebrations for **Fall of the Berlin Wall** and the **end of Cold War**.

## AFTER THE COLD WAR ENDING:

Shortly after taking office in 1989, President George W Bush signed a presidential summary renewing the CIA's legal authority to conduct covert operations in Afghanistan; but the country was placed low in priority list. Congress was losing interest in Afghanistan as well, slashing the CIA's Afghan budget to $280 million for fiscal year 1990 with additional cuts in fiscal 1991 – because of the end of Cold War.

In late 1990, the US suspended most aid to Pakistan – then blaming for the **Pakistan's continued progress in nuclear field**. Finally, President Bush's Secretary of State James Baker reached an agreement with his Soviet counterpart Boris Pankin for both sides to cease sending weapons to either the *mujahedeen* or Najibullah. This agreement came into force on 1st January 1992. The cessation of external assistance was more devastating to Najibullah than to the *mujahedeen*; combined with Najibullah's ally Abdul Rashid Dostum's defection.

Following Dostum's defection, Masoud's militia captured Kabul Airport from the north, while Hekmatyar and other *mujahedeen* commanders advanced closer to Kabul from the south. In a TV speech, Najibullah stated that he planned to resign as part of a peaceful transition organized by the United Nations [UN]. After a tense exchange, *Hekmatyar* rejected Masoud's pleas for compromise and reconciliation. Then forces allied with Masoud entered Kabul, took over the city and an interim government was established with Burhanuddin Rabbani [a religious scholar who had taught both Masoud and Hekmatyar during their times at Kabul University] serving as president while Masoud took reins of the defense ministry.

Despite being offered the role of prime minister which he declined astonishingly, *Hekmatyar* bombarded Kabul with rockets, inflicting mass casualties. The fighting in and around the capital plunged Afghanistan into a multifaceted civil war that continued for several years, with all sides committing substantial atrocities.

Eventually the Taliban, controlled by an obscure, soft-spoken, and insular former participant in Yunus Khalis's *mujahedeen* faction named *Mulla Omar emerged from the Pashtuns heartland of Kandahar,* taking control of all of southern Afghanistan and Herat by September 1995 before driving Masoud and the Afghan interim government from Kabul in September 1996. Extensive Pakistani and Saudi support played a key role in these Taliban victories. Masoud retreated to his native Panjshir Valley, forming the United Front [also known as the *'Northern Alliance'*], which was backed by India, Iran, and Russia.

The US originally sought to work with the Taliban and its leader Mulla Omar as a legitimate Afghan political faction. Meanwhile, Bin Laden returned to Afghanistan earlier in 1996 after being expelled from Sudan by President Omar al-Bashir under heavy American pressure, initially settling in Jalalabad, which was then controlled by former *mujahideen* whom bin Laden knew from the 1980s—*not by the Taliban.* Jalalabad fell to the Taliban in August that year; soon bin Laden moved to Kandahar, where he was merely *'a guest of the previous regime'.*

Soon, OBL established a close relationship with Mullah Omar, who repeatedly praised bin Laden as a hero of Muslims. The US became increasingly concerned with the relationship between Pakistan and the Taliban. The Taliban pursued their own interests rather than acting as a proxy for external forces. Pakistan's alleged support of the Taliban led to increasing tensions with the US – apparently without any cause.

On 7th August 1998; two massive bomb blasts occurred at the US embassies in two different East African capital cities: Dar es Salaam, Tanzania, and Nairobi, Kenya. These explosions killed 224 people, wounded more than 4,500, and caused a substantial amount of property damage. Twelve Americans were killed in these attacks while vast majority of the casualties were Kenyan civilians. Immediately the blame was placed on a faction of al-Qaeda. Western media went too far rather relatively notorious levels - consequently bin Laden was placed on the Federal Bureau of Investigation [FBI]'s *most wanted fugitives list.*

In the aftermath of those bombings, US President Bill Clinton ordered cruise missiles strikes at 'targets in Sudan and Afghanistan affirming they had clear evidence of Bin Laden's activities for the planning and execution ... of the bombings. In addition, seven suspected members of al-Qaeda were arrested.

[**On 4th November 1998;** the US moved to *'indict Osama bin Laden and al-Qaeda military Chief Muhammad Atef on 224 counts of murder for the embassy bombings.*]

In a declassified CIA document, the CIA emphasized that the international community should share this concern about OBL's planning and activity against the humanity especially against Americans; *'US Engagement with the Taliban on Osama Bin Laden'* the CIA document retrieved by the *National Security Archives* on 20th April 2017 is referred.

In February 1999, the Memoranda of Notification was signed by the president that oversaw covert action in Afghanistan, *'authorized the CIA to work with the Afghan Northern Alliance ... against [bin Laden].'* In October 1999, the Taliban proposed solutions including a trial of bin Laden by a panel of Islamic scholars or monitoring of bin Laden by the OIC (Organization of Islamic Cooperation) or the UN. The US however refused to be bound by the panel's decisions.

The CIA started reporting with increasing frequency, like a propaganda campaign, about the danger that bin Laden posed to the United States. A Senior Executive's *Intelligence Brief dated 6th February 2001 stated that the threat of Sunni terrorism was growing.*

Before the 11th September 2001 terrorist attacks on twin-towers and the Pentagon HQ, the US intelligence had determined that Afghanistan had been a training ground for bin Laden's terrorist network. These warnings were not enough to stop the attacks from occurring, resulting in the US declaring war on Afghanistan.

In 2001, the CIA's Special Activities Division [SAD] units were the first US forces to enter Afghanistan. Their efforts organized the Afghan Northern Alliance for the subsequent arrival of American forces. *The plan for the invasion of Afghanistan had been, in fact, developed by the CIA much earlier than 9/11 attacks on the Twin Towers.* SAD, the US Army Special Forces and the Northern Alliance combined to overthrow the Taliban in Afghanistan with minimal loss of US lives. They did this without the need for US military conventional ground forces.

# Scenario 227

**DURING 2007:** AMERICA STARTED ACCUSING PAKISTAN when it issued and perhaps published a report in which Pakistan was alleged of using US-aid money for strengthening its *defence against India.* It was all baseless because Pakistan had no immediate threat over Pak-Indian border then; how could a poor country like Pakistan open another war-front when it was already pulling on at 2500+ km long western Pak-Afghan border. Even otherwise, what was the aid being given to Pakistan for being a **Major Non-NATO Ally** [MNNA] – just peanuts - and that too as payment of expense-bills of military operations done in Afghanistan by the Pak-Army on the explicit directions of the American commanders there.

During the same year, a resurgence of violence broke over across Afghanistan, including a rise of suicide attacks and remotely detonated bombings; the historians said it was perhaps amongst the various warlords on issues of *'haves & haves NOT of the US funding'.*

In Afghanistan, patronage has traditionally been at the core of how government and society function. For example, **Gul Agha Sherzai,** a warlord who reportedly amassed a fortune by skimming taxes and contracts while serving as a provincial governor, had been, and was being continuously admired by the American high-ups.

During a 2006 visit to the eastern city of *Jalalabad,* Mr **Boucher,** the then Assistant Secretary of state, asked Sherzai whether he needed help with any construction projects; the reply was:

> *"I need five schools, five colleges, five dams, and five highways [Boucher asked - but why five? He said] I got this tribe, this tribe, this tribe, this tribe, and one for everybody else.' I thought that was one of the funniest things I ever heard and now I think it is one of the smartest things I ever heard."*

**Boucher** swiftly [and correctly] added:

> *"....it was better to funnel contracts to Afghans who would probably take 20 percent for personal use or for their extended families and friends than **giving money to a bunch of expensive American experts who would waste 80 to 90 percent of the funds on overhead and profit.***
>
> *I want it to disappear in Afghanistan, rather than in the Beltway. Probably in the end it is going to make sure that more of the money gets to some villager, maybe through five layers of corrupt officials, but still gets to some villager."*

**Sherzai,** nicknamed as *'the Bulldozer'*, remained active in Afghan politics. He repeatedly denied allegations of wrongdoing when he ran, unsuccessfully, for presidential seat in 2014. He asserted while speaking to the NBC News: *'There is no evidence against me. If I was involved in corruption, I would have high-rise buildings in Dubai and would have millions of dollars in foreign banks!'*

- Again; there was likelihood that the 'extra money' had gone in the pockets of the US Financial Managers / Contractors / Advisors on the Pentagon or DOD lists.

A Former National Security Council staffer confided in his interview with SIGAR on 2ⁿᵈ April 2015:

> *"In the beginning, the military kept saying that corruption was an unfortunate short-term side effect then toward the end the feeling was - Oh, my God, this could derail the whole thing.*
>
> *Yet warlords were hardly the only ones the United States targeted with bribes."*

## OBAMA OPTED TO PAY MORE PRICE:

**During 2008;** the trust, on both sides [the US and Pakistan], was seen increasingly missing since the war on terror had taken start - the US on several occasions accused Pak-Army for taking interest in pro-Taliban activities – which was, till then, the allegation without facts or evidence.

**On 11ᵗʰ June 2008;** on the Afghan-Pak border, in an American air-strike through drone attack, 11 members of the Pakistani paramilitary Frontier Corps were killed. The Pak-Army condemned that strike as **an act of**

**aggression,** souring the relations between the two countries. The strike and deaths instigated a fierce reaction from Pakistani command calling the act to have shaken the foundations of mutual trust and cooperation.

After the 11-soldiers killing episode, when Pak-Army raised its high agitation, President Bush repeated again that *'Pakistan is our strong ally.* But at the same time, the other US officials were also instigated to raise the issue that nearly 70% [roughly $3.4 billion] of the aid given to the Pakistani military had been misspent during 2002–07. Also that the ISI was tipping off *jehadists* so that they could escape in advance of American attacks against them – the world media termed it 'eye-wash'.

However US-Pak relationship turned as transactional based and **US military aids and sales to Pakistan were stayed without any cogent reason.** Gary Ackerman, member of the US House of Representatives told:

> *"...a significant proportion of US economic aid for Pakistan ended up back in the US as funds were channelled through large US contractors. Also said a large sum of US economic aid had not left the US as it spent on consulting fees and overhead costs etc"*; <u>Reuters</u> dated <u>14th April 2010</u> on media pages is referred.

In the November 2008 **Mumbai Attacks,** the US, while taking sides with India, unnecessarily pressed Pakistan that it expected full cooperation in the hunt for the plotters of the attacks. As mentioned before, the US kept on repeating that the billions of dollars of aid that Pakistan received for being a partner in war against terror were diverted and channeled in order to build better defense mechanism against India.

**On 17th February 2009:** President Obama, promising to turn around what his advisers saw as *'the good war' in Afghanistan* [as opposed to *'the bad war' in Iraq* - a lost cause], opted to send 21,000 troops more in March and then, more reluctantly, another 30,000 in December, putting the total number of US troops in Afghanistan nearly 100,000. Wary of over-investing, he limited the goals of this surge recalling ending bad months of the US war in Iraq.

Gone was Bush's intent to defeat the Taliban no matter what, even though the Taliban group could not be stopped for their attacks using their own country as a refuge. The US plan was to begin a drawdown of the surge forces in mid-2011 and eventually hand off full responsibility for the country's security to the Afghan government – but every plan fizzled out. Pentagon had persuaded the President to expand the war and to adopt a counter-insurgency strategy.

The US objective was to choke off popular support for the Taliban by protecting civilians and building trust in the Afghan government. But many saw the Afghan government as incompetent and malicious. Judges, police and most office-holders routinely subjected Afghan people to extortion. In contrast, the general populace often viewed the Taliban as brutal but efficient and devout. Belatedly, the US military commanders started a campaign to root out corruption and clean up the Afghan government. This awakening frustrated many US civilian officials who felt the uniformed brass had downplayed the problem. A White House staffer told the SIGAR later:

> *"It was like they just discovered something new about the pernicious effects of corruption. For years, the people in the field would be moaning and groaning over the compromises made by the military on working with corrupt actors but they were shut down."*

**In March 2009;** President Obama declared: '*I want to be clear: We cannot turn a blind eye to the corruption that causes Afghans to lose faith in their own leaders.*'

A few days later, the US Secretary of State Hillary Clinton said: "*Corruption is a cancer as dangerous to long-term success as the Taliban or al-Qaeda.*"

**In August 2009;** Gen Stanley McChrystal, the top US commander in Afghanistan at that time, warned about: '*Malign actions of power brokers, widespread corruption and abuse of power... have given Afghans little reason to support their government.*'

To reinforce the message, Washington mobilized a small army of anti-corruption lawyers, advisers, investigators and accountants to go to Kabul and assist the Afghan government. However, despite all that, the rot went worse.

*Barnett Rubin,* senior adviser to Richard Holbrooke, the US special envoy to Afghanistan and Pakistan during 2009-10, in his interview with SIGAR said on 20<sup>th</sup> January 2015: '*Holbrooke hated Hamid Karzai. He thought he was corrupt as hell.*'

**On 20<sup>th</sup> August 2009;** Afghans went to the polls to choose their president. It was a critical moment. Presidential elections were held peacefully and resulted in victory for incumbent Hamid Karzai, who won 49.67% of the vote, while his main rival Abdullah Abdullah finished second with 30.59% of the vote. Karzai won this re-election after cronies stuffed thousands of ballot boxes. He later admitted that **CIA had delivered bags of cash to his office, calling it *'nothing unusual.'***

Obama was contemplating whether to send additional US troops to the war zone. He needed a reliable and credible ally in Kabul. Right away, reports surfaced of electoral fraud on an epic scale — ghost voting, official miscounting, ballot-box stuffing, plus violence and intimidation at the polls. Initial results showed Karzai had won. But his opponents, and many independent observers, accused his side of trying to steal the election. A UN-backed panel investigated and determined Karzai had received about 1 million illegal votes, a quarter of all those cast. The outcome had pushed the White House in quagmire.

In public also, President Obama had escalated the war and Congress approved billions of additional dollars in support of Afghanistan.

In SIGAR interviews, key figures in the war said Washington tolerated the worst offenders — warlords, drug traffickers, defence contractors — because they were allies of the US. However, American government failed to confront a more distressing reality — that it was responsible for fuelling the corruption, by doling out vast sums of money with limited foresight. An unnamed State Department official told later that:

> *"The US officials were ....desperate to feed them [the warlords & contractors] the alcoholics at the table; we kept pouring drinks, not considering we were killing them."*

There was so much excess, financed by American taxpayers, that opportunities for bribery and fraud became almost limitless. While buying loyalty and information, the CIA gave cash to warlords, governors, parliamentarians, even religious leaders, according to the interviews. The US military and other agencies also abetted corruption by doling out payments or contracts to unsavoury Afghan power brokers in a misguided quest for stability. The US civil and military officials had partnerships with all the wrong players; the media was calling their shots openly – their palms were not being greased perhaps.

**Gert Berthold,** a forensic accountant during 2010-12, said he helped analyze 3000 Defence Department contracts worth $106 billion to see who was benefiting. The conclusion was that about 40% of the money ended up in the pockets of insurgents, criminal syndicates or corrupt Afghan officials; while Americans remained either silent partners in contracts or they were not conscious enough. The evidences were so damning but the US officials kept their eyes shut. Berthold concluded that:

> *"No one wanted accountability. If you're going to do anti-corruption, someone has got to own it. From what I've seen, no one is willing to own it."*

The White House officers urged that corruption was intolerable but also resolved to respect Afghan sovereignty and not interfere with the election. Moreover, they did not want to completely alienate Karzai. Finally the White House brokered a deal in which Karzai was declared the winner after he agreed to share some power with his main rival. The said deal had in fact ruined the US trustworthiness and integrity. Sarah Chayes, the then civilian adviser to the US military said:

> *"That was profoundly destructive to a rule-of-law principle. It was devastating that we were willing to patch up the elections.... While we had the opportunity to say that corruption is important – [contrarily] explicit instructions were given that it is not."*

Peter Galbraith, a deputy UN envoy to Afghanistan in 2009, was removed from his post after he complained that the UN was helping cover up the election fraud. He told government interviewers of SIGAR that:

> *"The US government also stood by when Karzai appointed cronies to election boards and anti-corruption posts. There was a broader impact, because of the culture of dishonesty. You cannot separate administrative fraud from the corruption of the system."*

## KERRY-LUGAR BILL;
## AN UTTER HUMILIATION FOR PAKISTAN:

On 30th September 2009; the US Congress approved a non-military aid to Pakistan. The legislation authorised $1.5 billion a year for the next five years as part of a bid to build a new relationship with Pakistan. The bill also stipulated that US military aid would cease if Pakistan would not help fight 'terrorists' including Taliban and Al Qaeda. The bill's sponsor, Howard Berman said that:

> *"..... Nor can we permit the Pakistani state – and its nuclear arsenal – to be taken over by the Taliban. To keep military aid flowing, Pakistan*

*must also cooperate to dismantle nuclear supplier networks by offering relevant information from or direct access to Pakistani nationals associated with such networks".*

The bill had originally been under discussion in the Congress since 2008. That bill [no: S3263], also known as **'Enhanced Partnership with Pakistan Act 2008'** had in fact recognized the role of Pakistan as US ally and the frontline state in combating terrorism. However, the bill died before it could be tabled before the Senate for debate following the upcoming presidential elections in December 2008.

The said bill was reintroduced in the 111th Congress session in 2009 as the Kerry-Lugar Bill. It was told to the Congress that [till that moment] Pakistan had lost more than $35 billion in economic activity in US-Afghan War since 9/11of 2001 and more Pakistani soldiers and security personnel had laid down their lives than the combined losses of the US and Afghanistan together.

**PAK-ARMY GOT ANGRY:** It is on record that the then US envoy to Pakistan, Anne Patterson, heard a hot criticism [over the Kerry-Lugar bill] from Gen Kayani and DG ISI Gen Pasha in a two-hour meeting on 6 th October 2009. Gen Kayani had made clear to the Ambassador and accompanying Gen McCrystal, during an urgent meeting at GHQ, about his concerns. Gen Crystal understood the viewpoint of Pak-Army and was not at all happy when he left the GHQ. Gen Kayani told them that there were elements in the bill that would set back the bilateral relationship. The reported remarks of the American envoy were that rejection of the bill would be taken as an insult and smack of arrogant attitude of Pak-Army.

The 'TIME' magazine of 8th October 2009 told that:

> *"Unlike previous no-strings aid packages, Kerry-Lugar makes support conditional on Pakistan's military being subordinated to its elected government, and taking action against militants sheltering on its soil.*

> *[In Pakistan] the opposition parties unite against its humiliating conditions, with even the junior partners in Zardari's ruling coalition expressing misgivings. Public opinion ranges from suspicion to hostility.*

> *Following a meeting of its corps commanders, the army expressed serious concern over the national security implications of the aid package. It's a kind of political move on the part of the military."*

Ayaz Amir, an opposition legislator, labelled the 'conditional ties' as grossly demeaning. In daily **'the News'** feature published in the <u>first week of October 2009,</u> under **'Kerry-Lugar: bill or document of surrender'**, he opined that:

> *"A convicted rapist out on parole would be required to give fewer assurances of good conduct.*
>
> *Turning Pakistan into a client state: ..... reduced to insignificant status with the acceptance of the aid bill, and the humiliation of Pakistan as it emerges as an American satellite...puppet...neo-colony".*

The Obama Administration was really caught in dilemma; the Pak-Army had categorically declined to accept the US dictations – and the US-AID was rejected; for more details see:

JUDGES & GENERALS IN PAKISTAN: VOL-III by
*Inam R Sehri* [2013]; Scenario 67; pps 942-959,
<u>GHP Surry</u> [UK]

## OBAMA INCREASED TROOPS 3-FOLD:

**On 1st December 2009:** President Obama announced another surge of US troops to Afghanistan, tripling the number to nearly 100,000. In the meantime, another scandal blew up in Kabul when the dissident voices raised from the election started subsiding; details are given else where on these pages.

After 2006, the sands of Afghan War had started slipping out of American hands; the Taliban influence was seen visibly expanding and resistance to US and NATO troops had increased. The US air-strikes and night raids heightened a sense of oppression among Afghan villagers and triggered an obligation to resist. After the Taliban offensive that year, it was hard to see how any strategy could bring victory for the US and the puppet Afghan government; the surge was one of them.

In retrospect, the US would have been better off had it never surged at all; Obama still had option to deploy fewer troops than he did—but Gen Stanley McChrystal, the top US commander in Afghanistan, and Gen Petraeus, the commander of US Central Command, had not advised the president with such kind of option. All their proposals involved further increases in the number of US military personnel deployments. Both Generals believed that escalation was warranted owing to the threat posed by the Taliban's strong moves and becoming the country a safe haven for terrorists. Both generals had witnessed that how the US counter-insurgency strategy had miserably failed in Iraq.

Had Obama done less, the US casualties and expenses would have been far lower. But Obama did err when it came to placing restrictions on the US forces. Prior to 2014, the US air-strikes were used when necessary to strike enemy targets, and commanders took steps to avoid civilian casualties. The idea was to disentangle US forces from combat and, to a lesser extent, to reduce civilian casualties. As a result, there was a pronounced reduction in the number of US strikes.

In 2016, the US forces carried out an average of 80 air-strikes per month, less than a quarter of the monthly average for 2012. Meanwhile, over 500 air-strikes per month were being conducted in Iraq and Syria against a comparable adversary. One frontline Afghan Commander in Helmand, Omar Jan, pleaded in 2016:

> "If America just helps with air-strikes and . . . supplies, we can win. My weapons are worn from shooting. My ammunition stocks are low. I do not need advisors. I just need someone to call when things are really bad."

The decision to use air-strikes only in extreme warfare virtually ensured defeat. When the unexpected happened, Obama was unprepared. Facing far greater constraints, Obama had to play the cards he was given. The Afghan government was formed and violence had returned, and a spirit of resistance had arisen in the rural Afghan people. Obama's error was mostly based on oversights and miscalculations.

On 30th December 2009; a suicide attack occurred at Forward Operating Base Chapman, a major CIA base in the province of Khost, Afghanistan. **Seven CIA officers, including the chief of the base, were killed and six others seriously wounded** in the attack. The attack was the second deadliest carried out against CIA, after the 1983 US Embassy bombing in Beirut, and was a major setback for the intelligence agency's operations.

On 27th January 2011; Raymond Davis, a former US Army soldier, a private security firm [PMC]'s employee, and contractor with the CIA, shot and killed two passer-by in Lahore, Pakistan - claiming that they came to rob him. Immediately after the shooting, a car coming to aid Davis killed a third Pakistani person, in a hit and run while speeding on wrong side of the road. In the aftermath of the incident, the US government contended that Davis was protected by diplomatic immunity, which was factually NOT. Thus, he was jailed and criminally charged by Pakistani courts on two counts of murder and the illegal possession of a firearm.

On 16th March 2011; Raymond Davis was released after the families of the two killed men were paid US$2.4 million in *diyya* [a form of blood money compensation in Islamic law]. Judges then acquitted him on all charges, Davis immediately left Pakistan but leaving behind a bitter taste in the Pak-US relationship. For more details see:

JUDGES & GENERALS IN PAKISTAN: VOL-IV
by *Inam R Sehri* [2013]; Scenario 84; pps 1308-23,
*GHP Surrey* UK

On 1st May 2011; The White House announced that Osama Bin Laden was killed by the US SEALs in Abbot Abad [Pakistan]; there it was 2nd of May morning. President Obama claimed that the information pertaining to the operation conducted in Abbott Abad was not shared with Pakistan Army. However, ISI claimed that the operation was conducted jointly, a claim which was blatantly denied by Pakistan's President Asif Ali Zardari.

However, Secretary of State Hillary Clinton stated that '*cooperation with Pakistan helped lead us to bin Laden and the compound in which he was hiding*'. Since the war on terror started in 2001, Pakistan received an estimated amount of $20 billion from the US under '**Joint Operations**' head; however, in the wake of OBL's raid, the US withheld $800 million of their due bills on this account and had refused the payment to Pakistan.

On 26th November 2011; the NATO launched an air-attack in Pakistan [called the **Salala incident**]. This criminal activity occurred when the US-led NATO forces engaged Pakistani security forces at two Pakistani military check-posts along the Afghan–Pakistan border. With two NATO Apache helicopters, an AC-130 gunship and two F-15E Eagle fighter jets, killed 28 Pakistani soldiers and wounding 12. This attack resulted in a deterioration of relations between Pakistan and the US. The Pakistani public reacted with protests all over the country and the government had to take measures adversely affecting the American exit strategy from Afghanistan, including the **evacuation of Shamsi Airfield and closure of the NATO supply line** through Pakistan – much later re-opened.

However, the re-opening of the NATO-supply routs through Pakistan was a rogue decision by the then Pakistani President Zardari alone through PM Gilani – but against their personal monetary bargains that was why Pakistan was not invited to the crucial 25th NATO summit held in May 2012 in Chicago.

> [**PRESIDENT ZARDARI DISGRACED:** *In a sudden shift in events, NATO, on <u>15<sup>th</sup> May 2012</u>, said that it would invite President Zardari to the alliance's summit in Chicago, after Pakistan proposed reopening its Afghan border to NATO military supplies. President Zardari accepted the invitation and decided to attend the summit.*
>
> *On 18<sup>th</sup> May, the US lawmakers in the House of Representatives debating the National Defense Authorization Act voted 412-1 for an amendment **that blocked $650 million proposed payments to** Pakistan unless Islamabad lets coalition forces resume shipment of war supplies across its territory.*
>
> *President Zardari arrived in Washington on 19<sup>th</sup> May to attend the NATO summit in Chicago – but was denied access to attend the conference.*]

## PAKISTAN IGNORED ON CHICAGO SUMMIT:

During **NATO's Chicago Summit [20-21 May 2012]**; NATO endorsed a plan to end the Afghanistan war and to remove the NATO-led ISAF Forces by the end of December 2014. ISAF was disestablished in the given time frame and was replaced by **Resolute Support Mission**, a follow-on training [cover-up] program.

The summit principally focussed on three main themes:

- The Alliance's commitment to Afghanistan through transition and beyond;

- Ensuring the Alliance had the capabilities it needed to defend its population and territory and to deal with challenges of the 21st century;

- Strengthening NATO's network of partners across the globe.

In order to maintain its capacity to safeguard the security and values of its members, NATO needed to continue developing the means to do so and building partnerships beyond the North Atlantic region.

During NATO's Lisbon summit held on <u>19-20<sup>th</sup> November 2010</u>, it was resolved to publish a new Strategic Concept – *'Active Engagement, Modern Defence'* – emphasizing on gradual transition process to full Afghan security responsibility to start in 2011, backed by Allied agreement on a long-term partnership with Afghanistan.

NATO was committed to support Afghanistan beyond 2014. The gradual transition of security responsibility from ISAF troops to Afghan National Security Forces [ANSF] was to be fully implemented with high spirits as the ISAF mission's closure was on cards. In 2013, when the last trance of transition was expected to be announced, the ANSF was expected to claim victory over insurgency. ISAF was increasingly shifting to training and advisory role, but continued to support combat operations alongside Afghan forces, as necessary. At Chicago, the leaders drafted out how NATO would complete the transition process by ending 2014.

**On 23<sup>rd</sup> May 2012;** after Chicago's NATO Summit, a Senate panel approved a foreign aid budget for next year that **slashed US assistance to Islamabad** by more than half and threatened further reductions if Pakistan failed to open supply routes to NATO forces in Afghanistan. The said money for **Pakistan was cut by 58%** in the backdrop of Islamabad's commitment to fight against terrorism.

**On 24<sup>th</sup> May 2012;** the Senate Appropriations Committee voted to cut aid to Pakistan by a symbolic $33 million – $1 million for each year of jail time handed to Shakil Afridi, a Pakistani doctor who allegedly assisted the CIA in finding Osama bin Laden. However, the US had agreed to reimburse $1.18 billion or almost 75% of the claims Pakistan had submitted for the expenses incurred in the fight against militants along the Afghan border.

**On 7<sup>th</sup> June 2012;** Secretary of Defense Leon Panetta said that the US was running out of patience with Pakistan over safe havens of insurgents who used to attack US troops across the Pak-Afghan borders. Panetta had spoken after talks with Afghan Defense Minister Rahim Wardak on the latest leg of an Asian tour that took him **to India, but not Islamabad** in a sign of how tense US-Pakistan relations were – but actually it was a display of hate-sentiments.

**On 8<sup>th</sup> June 2012,** US Assistant Defense Secretary Peter Lavoy arrived in Islamabad, in a fresh attempt to bring an end to a six-month blockade on NATO supplies crossing into Afghanistan – but was met with cold reception and fruitless negotiations because of his Secretary Panetta's given importance to India as against his WOT ally Pakistan, as explained in above paragraph; thus the US had to withdraw negotiators from Pakistan on **14<sup>th</sup> June** instant.

Another reason was that Secretary Panetta had ruled out an apology over SALALA air strike a year earlier that had killed 28 Pakistani soldiers - saying it was *'time to move on'*. Two days later, Gen John Allen, the top commander of American and NATO forces in Afghanistan, visited Pakistan amidst heightened tensions between the two countries. The agenda of the talks remained to restore NATO supply routes and cross-border attacks launched on Pakistani soil from Afghanistan.

**On 3<sup>rd</sup> July 2012;** Pakistan agreed to reopen key supply routes into Afghanistan ending a bitter stand-off **after US Secretary of State Hillary Clinton apologized over the SALALA Air-Attack disaster.** Next day, Washington released about $1.1 billion to the Pak-Army from a US *'coalition support fund'* designed to reimburse Pakistan for the cost of counter-insurgency operations. It was the first installment since December 2010 in connection with US-Afghan War.

**On 5<sup>th</sup> August 2012;** discussions held in a series of meetings between the US and Pakistan military commanders over multiple issues of cross-border attacks by the *Haqqani* network on Afghanistan and by the TTP on Pakistani soils - but ended without any cogent results.

**On 23<sup>rd</sup> August 2012;** an American diplomat held a meeting with Pakistani officials at the Ministry of Foreign Affairs in Islamabad as Pakistan had lodged **its first formal protest** with the US over continued drone strikes in the Pakistani areas near Pak-Afghan border.

**By 2013,** more than 350,000 Afghan soldiers and police had been trained, armed, and deployed. Their performance was mixed, marred by corruption and by *'insider attacks'* carried out on American and allied advisers. Many units depended on US advisers and air support to defeat [?] the Taliban in their offensive attacks.

**On 27<sup>th</sup> MAY 2014:** President Obama announced a timetable for withdrawing most US forces from Afghanistan by the end of 2016; he said:

> *"We have to recognize that Afghanistan will not be a perfect place, and it is not America's responsibility to make it one."*

Under his plan, leaving behind 9,800 US troops the rest were to be withdrawn from Afghanistan within almost 3 years. By the end of 2015, that number was to be reduced by roughly half. By the end of 2016, the US presence was cut to a normal embassy presence with a security assistance office in Kabul, as was done in Iraq. The 9,800 troops were meant to take an advisory role backing up Afghan forces. They were to train Afghan troops and help guide missions to rout out remaining al Qaeda targets.

**In November 2014;** the two countries, the US and Pakistan, re-started to cooperate more closely – particularly following the US's use of drone missiles to strike at Pakistan's most-wanted militants. The US later used drone missiles to kill several of Pakistan's most wanted militants who were hiding in a remote region close to the Afghan border.

## OPERATION *ZARB E AZB* IN PAKITAN:

Pakistani Army Chief Gen Raheel Sharif's *Zarb-e-Azb* **Operation** against militants in North Waziristan also 'fractured' the Haqqani Network—long accused by the US of having a safe harbour in Pakistan. The US then captured and transferred a senior Taliban commander, Latif Mehsud, to Pakistan, which had been seeking his arrest. Following an unprecedented two-week-long visit by Pakistan's Army Chief Gen Raheel Sharif, the **US-Pakistani relations were on the upswing again** following several tense years of dysfunction. In the meantime, Pakistan had killed senior Al-Qaeda leader *Adnan el Shukrijumah*—long wanted by the US, leaving a positive note for better mutual relations among the two countries.

**On 7th May 2015;** Pakistan made full payment from its national budget towards the purchase of 18 new F-16C/D Fighting Falcon Block 52 combat aircraft worth US$1.43 billion. Pakistan also paid for the F-16 armaments including 500 AMRAAM air-to-air missiles; 1,450 pieces of 2,000-pound bombs; 500 JDAM Tail Kits for gravity bombs and 1,600 Enhanced Pave-way laser-guided kits. All this had additionally cost Pakistan US$629 million. Pakistan also paid US$298 million for 100 harpoon anti-ship missiles, US$95 million for 500 sidewinder air-to-air missiles; and US$80 million paid for seven Phalanx Close-in Weapons System naval guns.

**By ending 2015,** just 9,800 US troops were left in Afghanistan. As the withdrawal continued, they focused on counter-terrorism and on advising and training the Afghans. Near the ending 2015, the Taliban mounted a series of well-planned offensives that became one of the most decisive events of the war. In the province of Kunduz, 500 Taliban fighters killed some 3000 Afghan soldiers & police and captured a provincial capital for the first time. In Helmand Province, around 1,800 Taliban fighters defeated some 4,500 Afghan soldiers & police and recaptured almost all the ground lost in the surge – but couldn't take over the provincial capital because of last-minute reinforcements from the US.

In battle after battle, numerically superior and well-supplied soldiers in defensive positions made a collective decision to throw in the towel rather than go another round against the Taliban. Those who did stay to fight often paid dearly for their courage.

**Some 14000 Afghan soldiers were killed during 2015-16 alone.** The Afghan government, then headed by Ashraf Ghani, was weaker than ever before. The Taliban held more ground than at any time since 2001. In July of that year, Obama suspended the drawdown of the US troops.

**On 11th February 2016;** the US government proposed US$860 million in aid for Pakistan during the 2016–17 fiscal year, including $265 million for military hardware in counter-insurgency funding – but till then the relationship between the two countries had again gone tense on various counts.

**On 13th April 2017;** The US dropped the most powerful non-nuclear weapon, dubbed the *'Mother of all Bombs'* [MOAB] on suspected ISIS -Khorasan militants at a cave complex in Achin District, Nangarhar Province in eastern Afghanistan. The bomb — called the GBU-43/B Massive Ordnance Air Blast — could obliterate everything within a 1,000-yard radius. Unleashing that weapon was so massive that it had to be dropped from the rear of a cargo plane.

In President Trump's initial months in office, the military had argued that the use of that heavy bomb would help it defeat the Islamic State more speedily. Mr Trump said after a meeting with emergency workers at the White House that *'it was another very, very successful mission.'* The Pentagon had given no casualty totals for the said bombing.

**On 21st August 2017;** US President Trump increased the number of troops in Afghanistan to 14000 from 8500. But on the same day the President announced his new strategy for Afghan War **and accused Pakistan** of providing safe havens to terrorists. Trump said:

> *"The Pakistani people had suffered greatly from terrorism and extremism. We recognize those contributions and those sacrifices, but Pakistan has also sheltered the same organizations that try every single day to kill our people."*

Moreover, Trump also urged India for its role in the war. Trump's speech led to rise of anti-American sentiments in Pakistan and protests against Trump were held across the country. Two months later, Trump ONCE AGAIN tweeted with an urge to develop better relations with Pakistan.

**On 1st January 2018;** President Trump again criticized Pakistan, saying *'they have given us nothing but lies and deceit'*. Mr Trump also announced cancelling a $300 million disbursement to Pakistan, citing the country's failure to take strong actions against Afghan Taliban militants and their safe havens in Pakistan. However, the relations between the two countries improved after Pakistani PM Imran Khan visited the US. Many experts viewed Khan's visit to US as *'reset in the bilateral relationship between the two countries'*.

President Trump called for dramatically strengthening trade ties between Pakistan and the US as it was a top export destination for Pakistan. Trump had also offered to mediate between India and Pakistan on Kashmir but the proposal was immediately rejected by Indian foreign office.

**On 4th September 2018;** US diplomat Zalmay Khalilzad appointed as US special adviser tasked with assisting an Afghan peace process. However, the American activities in Afghanistan touched the lowest margins of humanity and war-courtesies. **As of 2018,** the CIA was engaged in a program to kill or capture militant leaders, **code-named ANSOF,** previously **Omega.** CIA manpower was supplemented with personnel assigned from US Army Special Operations Command.

**In mid–2019,** the Human Rights Watch stated that: *'CIA-backed Afghan strike forces have committed serious abuses, some amounting to war crimes since late 2017'*.

**7th September 2019:** President Trump announced via Twitter that he cancelled plans for Taliban leaders and Afghan president to travel to Camp David to finalize a peace agreement. The peace-negotiations at Doha Qatar were also called off because of an attack that killed a US soldier and 11 others. During the same month, amidst a joint rally at Houston, Trump refused to endorse India's repeated allegations against

Pakistan. After the joint rally, Trump called himself a **'friend of Pakistan'** and termed Imran Khan as **'great leader'.**

**In January 2020;** President Trump once again held a meeting with Prime minister Khan in Davos, on the sidelines of the World Economic Forum. President Trump hailed the growing relationship between the US and Pakistan. He said that:

> *"United States has never been closer with Pakistan than it is currently under his [PM IMRAN KHAN]'s administration."*

This was the third meeting between the two countries and Trump once again offered to mediate on Kashmir issue. His remarks were welcomed by PM Khan but again refuted by India.

**On 29ᵗʰ February 2020;** The US and the Taliban signed a deal in Doha [Qatar], setting a timetable for the withdrawal of 13,000 US troops in Afghanistan and the Taliban committed to halt attacks on Americans.

During **SEPTEMBER 2020 - FEBRUARY 2021;** Afghan government-Taliban negotiations in Qatar were attempted several times but stalled with no progress. Afghan President Ashraf Ghani refused unity government proposals, while the Taliban also hesitated to agree a cease-fire.

## 2021 – YEAR OF AMERICAN SURRENDER:

**ON 14ᵀᴴ APRIL 2021:** US President Joe Biden said the remaining US troops in Afghanistan, roughly 3500 then, would be withdrawn by 11ᵗʰ September that year to end America's 'forever war'. On the same day, NATO Secretary General Jens Stoltenberg announced that the alliance agreed to start **withdrawing its troops from Afghanistan within 15 days** by all means. Soon after the withdrawal of NATO troops started, the Taliban launched offensives against the Afghan government all over, quickly advancing in front of collapsing Afghan Armed Forces.

During **MAY 2021 – 31ˢᵀ AUGUST 2021:** REGULAR WITHDRAWAL PROCESS STARTED AND CONTINUED. Taliban expanded their territorial control; their fighters made rapid territorial advances across Afghanistan, taking control about half of Afghanistan - more than 400 districts.

**In May 2021;** former President Karzai spoke with German newspaper *Der Spiegel*, where he expressed his sympathy with the Taliban, criticized the role of the US in Afghanistan - at the same time, saying that the future of Afghanistan relies heavily on neighbouring Pakistan. He also considered the Taliban *'victims of foreign forces'* and said that Afghans were being used to be each against the other.

**On 2nd July 2021**: US handed over **Bagram Airfield** to Afghan military control after the last troops in the base left. US military's withdrawal was nearly 90% complete, with the entire process to be completed by **31st August 2021**. The Taliban said they would present a written peace proposal to the Afghan government very soon.

**ON 6TH AUGUST 2021**; First provincial capital fell in the Taliban's feet. *Zaranj*, in south of the country became the first provincial capital to fall to the Taliban in years. Many more were to follow in the ensuing days, including the prized city of *Kunduz* in the north.

**ON 13TH AUGUST 2021**: Four more provincial capitals fell down in a day, including *Kandahar*, the country's second-largest city and the spiritual home of the Taliban.

**ON 14TH AUGUST 2021**: The Taliban took over the major northern city of *Mazar-e-Sharif*. The US sent more troops to help evacuate its civilians from Kabul as the Afghan President Ghani said he was consulting with local and international partners on next steps.

**ON 15TH AUGUST 2021**: The Taliban took control of the key eastern city of Jalalabad without a fight. Also the Taliban entered Kabul; the US evacuated diplomats from its embassy by helicopter in that day's early hours.

That day the Taliban controlled nearly the whole of Afghanistan and encircled the capital city of Kabul. Some politicians in NATO member states described this chaotic withdrawal of Western troops from Afghan soils and the collapse of the Afghan government as *the greatest debacle that NATO ever suffered since its founding*.

**On 17th August 2021**: The Taliban consolidated their control over the whole country; they vowed to respect women's rights 'within Islamic law'.

Through the above lines; can any sane person interpret that
the Americans had taken care of Pakistan as an ally or associate –
even the slave nations are not treated like that.

# Scenario 228

## DOHA AGREEMENT FEB 2020

When President Donald Trump took office in January 2017, the Afghan war was on. He initially approved an increase of the US forces in Afghanistan to roughly 14K. Trump, as a person, disliked wars and especially bloody war in Afghanistan, and was looking for an exit. He started fresh negotiations with the Taliban in 2018 which ended in Doha Accord of 29ᵗʰ February 2020 though the level of violence and Afghan casualties' rates in 2019 were at par with those of earlier recent years.

## QATAR HOSTED THE TALIBAN EARLIER:

IN 2010-12 the US missed a golden opportunity for peace in Afghanistan.

After nearly a decade's bloodshed in Afghanistan, the Taliban representatives secretly arrived in Qatar in 2010 to talk to Western officials; the Americans were eager to secure a peace deal that would allow NATO a dignified exit from Afghanistan and leave the country stable and peaceful.

In March 2012, the Taliban suspended initial talks with the US on issue of prisoner exchanges. They wanted the release of five Taliban figures held at Guantanamo Bay in exchange for the freedom of US soldier Sgt Bowe Bergdahl who had been held by the Taliban since 2009.

> [*There were more than 20 high-ranking Taliban members who had been living in Qatar with their families. Within those two years, Taliban had sent their representatives from Qatar in Japan, France, Germany and Iran to explain the 'cause of Taliban vision' about Afghanistan. Nearly all Taliban high-members had come to Qatar through Pakistan; thus in Doha, they were careful about their activities and movements.*]

Doha, capital city of Qatar, was not a big city and there were about 6,000 Afghan labourers and businessmen who had been living here since long. They lived in Doha in comfortable homes all paid by the Qataris; they had seen war and fighting for 30 years but then wanted to live in peaceful environment. As a confidence-building measure, providing protection to those Taliban leaders participating in peace talks and finding solution of Afghan problem became a priority for the US and the Afghan High Peace Council.

*The Afghan government was keen on opening an office for the Taliban in Turkey or Saudi Arabia, because those countries were more influential and had a closer working relationship with Kabul but the Taliban's preferred venue was Qatar because they considered it a neutral location. The US was also happy with this option.*

President Hamid Karzai finally gave the green light to the office after receiving guarantees that it would work only as a venue for peace talks and on low profile. The president did not want Doha Office to be used for other activities, such as the expansion of Taliban ties with the rest of the world, recruitment or fundraising.

Referring to *Dawood Azami's* essay at the **BBC World Service** website appeared on 22nd June 2013:

> *"In addition to the prisoners exchange task, there were other compelling reasons too; mainly to reduce Taliban's dependence on Pakistan. The Afghan government wanted to create distance between the Taliban and Pakistan, and for Taliban members to be able to participate in talks without risking arrests by Pakistan. The Pakistani government also wanted to show that it did not control the Taliban and they were based in Qatar not in Pakistan."*

The fact remained that Qatar was not one of the three countries - Pakistan, Saudi Arabia and United Arab Emirates - which recognised the Taliban regime in Afghanistan during 1996-2001 – rather it had 'cordial' relations with the militants. After the Taliban regime was toppled in 2001, some of its high-ranking figures sought asylum in Qatar, but their requests were quietly declined or ignored for a number of reasons, including because their names were on the UN / US sanction list, or they were wanted by the US. Thus the opening of the Taliban office brought Qatar in the international limelight it always aspired.

There stands a long US-history behind such US-Taliban talking chances in Doha or elsewhere. Imagine a question:

*Why hasn't the US left Afghanistan earlier?* The answer is the combination of terrorism threats and the US electoral politics. In the post-9/11 world, US presidents had to choose between spending resources at very low geo-strategic value and accepting some unknown risk of a $2^{nd}$ terrorist attack like of 9/11; nowhere had that dynamic been more evident than in Afghanistan.

In the early years after the 9/11 attacks, the political atmosphere in the US was charged with fears of another assault. That was one reason why Bush, after seeing the initial defeat of al Qaeda and the Taliban, never considered calling back the troops home. Only after the surge and the death of bin Laden did withdrawal from Afghanistan became conceivable.

The terrorist threat receded during the first half of Obama's presidency, yet he, too, could not ignore the possibility. NO high-level Obama admin-official advocated such a move; intense criticism was seen all around. Only after the surge and the death of bin Laden a *'zero option'* could be considered. Days after bin Laden was captured and killed in May 2011, a Gallup poll showed that 59% of Americans believed the US mission in Afghanistan had been accomplished.

In 2014, the rise of the Islamic State in Iraq & Syria [ISIS] and subsequent string of high-profile terrorist attacks in the West made even modest drawdown schedule less feasible strategically and politically. After the setbacks of 2015, the US intelligence assessed that terrorist groups could once again establish safe havens in Afghanistan. Confronted with that finding, President Obama had accepted the advice of his top Generals to keep the US forces there in Afghanistan.

Same thing happened with President Trump; he had the least patience for the mission in Afghanistan. With Trump agitating for an exit, substantive talks between the Taliban and the US commenced in 2018. Earlier efforts between 2010 and 2013 had failed because the conditions were not ripe: the White House was occupied with other issues, negotiating teams were not in place, and Mullah Omar, the Taliban's leader, was in seclusion—and then died in 2013. By 2019, those obstacles no longer stood in the way, and Trump was uniquely determined to go ahead.

## US-TALIBAN TALKS – DOHA DECLARATION:

In October 2018; the US officials and Taliban representatives held their first meeting in Doha, Qatar. The talks continued into the next year for eight rounds.

Zalmay Khalilzad, the US special representative for Afghanistan, stood for Washington in the talks, while co-founder Mullah Abdul Ghani

Baradar and Sher Mohammad Abbas Stanikzai, the head of the Taliban's political office in Doha, represented the Taliban group.

> [*As the talks were under way, violence spiked with 1,174 deaths and 3,139 injuries between July and end-September 2019, showing a 42% increase over the same period compared with the year before. According to the data provided by the US Central Command Combined Air Operations Centre, **the US air force dropped a record 7,423 bombs on Afghanistan – more than at any time in the last 10 years.**]*

More than 100,000 Afghans were killed or wounded since 2009 when the UN Assistance Mission in Afghanistan started documenting casualties.

**On 3rd September 2019**, the US Secretary of State was presented the US-Taliban Pact, which was mutually agreed and drafted after detailed talks in numerous meetings between the two, but he declined to sign the pact. On one side America was expecting a deal with the Taliban that was designed to wind down its 18-year war in Afghanistan – BUT on the other hand the said final pact was termed a *'risky affair'* by the US government.

The Defence Secretary Mark Esper discussed that Afghan deal with President Trump. Had the said deal approved, it could begin a withdrawal of 5,400 US troops, roughly a third of the then present force, from five bases within 135 days. The 'agreement in principle' was proposed by former US envoy Zalmay Khalilzad after nine rounds of talks with Taliban representatives in Qatar and was the first tentative step towards peace since US attack on Afghanistan in 2001.

The US re-treat from Afghanistan had come on cards much earlier than this Doha Agreement of February 2020 or the actual withdrawal of the American forces ending on 31st August 2021. The end game had actually been started when the *'Secret Papers about Afghan War'* appeared in limelight in which *the whole American nation got astonished knowing that total lies were told, spoken or released by the respective leaderships during their tenures about the actual happening on Afghan soils.*

> See *'Documents Reveal US Officials Misled Public on War in Afghanistan'* By Thomas Gibbons-Neff; appeared in media on 9th December 2019:

The US special envoy Kalilzad, made quick progress by offering Taliban a timeline for the complete withdrawal of the US forces. The two sides worked towards a comprehensive cease-fire, and not aiding al Qaeda or other terrorist groups. As said above, over the course of nine rounds of talks, the two sides developed that draft agreement. The Taliban representatives in the talks and the group's senior leaders had earlier refused to meet all of Khalilzad's conditions - but then **'Give & Take'** bargain prevailed to reach the final agreement.

It fell apart. Although Trump toyed with the idea of holding a dramatic summit to announce a deal at Camp David in September 2019, he was torn between his campaign promise *'to end endless war'* and the possibility of a resurgent terrorist threat, which could harm him politically. During an interview with **Fox News on 1ˢᵗ August 2019**, he was distinctly non-committal about fully withdrawing. He said:

> *"We're going down to 8,600 [troops], and then we'll make a determination from there; a high intelligence presence would stay in the country."*

So when the Taliban escalated their attacks in the backdrop of this announcement, killing one American soldier and wounding many, Trump concluded that he was getting a bad deal and **called off negotiations** - thus another chance to end the war slipped away.

A popular conception prevailed that the US should have just left Afghanistan; President Trump was free to pull the plug as he pleased. In reality, getting out was nearly as difficult as staying. It was quite a different scenario when the moment arrived, see the uncertainties, weigh the political fallout of a terrorist attack, and still taking edge.

The proposed Afghan deal missed several crucial things; it didn't guarantee the continued presence of US counter-terrorism forces on Afghan soils and the survival of the pro-US government in Kabul, or even an end to the fighting in Afghanistan. No one spoke with certainty that war in Afghanistan would end with the signing of the said pact. A widespread notion, referring to the **TIME** magazine of **4ᵗʰ September 2019**, was:

> *"It is all based on hope. There is no trust. There is no history of trust. There is no evidence of honesty and sincerity from the Taliban. Some intercepted communications show that they think they have fooled the US while the US believes that should the Taliban cheat, they will pay a hefty price."*

That explained why the then US Secretary of State, Mr Pompeo, had declined to put his name on the deal. The Taliban asked for Pompeo to sign an agreement with the Islamic Emirate of Afghanistan, the official name of the government founded by the Taliban in Afghanistan in 1996. The US didn't want that de facto recognition of the Taliban as a legitimate political entity thus they refused.

However, Pompeo's spokesperson told the media that '.....he [Mr Pompeo] might sign if Trump and all parties struck a deal'.

There were two alternatives; Khalilzad himself could sign it. Or the US and Taliban could issue a joint statement, supported in turn by the pro-US Kabul government with some countries like Japan, Russia and China's approval or guarantees. But who could guarantee the peace in Afghanistan after four decades of war. The stage was then being set for the withdrawal of most American forces by the end of November 2020. As usual, the US tied strings with the deal document; to open negotiations with the US-backed President Ghani; reduce violence near areas under US forces control; and keep foreign militants out of the areas they control.

The US military, intelligence officers and diplomats were worried that once a withdrawal agreed, it would be irreversible. Most bureaucrats termed it as Trump's stunt for 2020 US elections. Most of them were optimistic about their 'hard-won progress towards building a stable country over nearly two decades of war [?]'. Some officers thought the result would be far worse than the status quo - a return to the total civil war that consumed nearly forty years of Afghanistan; which started with Soviet's occupation in 1979.

Days before, a deadly Taliban car bomb exploded in Kabul, just as Khalilzad was concluding an hour-long interview promoting the tentative peace deal to an Afghan news outlet. It was enough to remind the US that the proposed pact didn't require the Taliban to reject terrorism or stop attacking Afghan forces. The Taliban were sure that the US would withdraw all foreign troops within a year; Taliban officials also took the US strings [conditions] very casual. Bill Roggio, a simple soldier of the US army, correctly estimated that:

> "The Taliban's goals for Afghanistan have not changed. It seeks to eject the US, reestablish its Islamic Emirate of Afghanistan and impose its Islamic government."

In fact, the said Doha agreement draft was the best deal; say 50:50. The US and its allies could get to head off a pre-emptive pullout of US troops in time for the 2020 US elections. Military officials had long known they needed to reduce the number of troops to a smaller, cheaper footprint to mollify US policymakers tired of writing cheques after 18 years of war, and the US public in general.

Publicly, President Ghani had, though not officially, embraced the deal; but privately there was an exchange of shouting between him and Khalilzad in Kabul – the later telling Ghani that he got to accept this deal because Afghanistan was losing the war. Afghan-born Khalilzad, the American king-pin didn't show draft of the Taliban agreement to Ghani, the elected Afghan president, and a university classmate of Khalilzad's. Even though President Ghani had agreed to send a delegation to Oslo to start talks with the Taliban in the last week of September. The 15-person delegation included three women, but the names were not announced until just before the talks – Taliban were likely to attack the 3-ladies as per their philosophy.

BUT it seemed that the White House was ready to accept the deal because they knew that they were not in a position to counter attack the Taliban – thus inclined to decide for 'leave', but the American bureaucracy didn't. However, no one wanted to take ugly decisions.

Following the suspension of the talks [*Trump had abruptly suspended the talks with the Taliban following the killing of a US soldier in Sep 2019*], the Taliban intensified attacks, with the last quarter of 2019 becoming one of the bloodiest since the US invasion in 2001. Taliban spokesman *Zabihullah Mujahid* told the media openly that Washington would regret turning its back on the talks – and so it did.

In ending week of November 2019, during a trip to Bagram Air Field in Afghanistan over the Thanksgiving holiday, President Trump said the US would stay in Afghanistan '*until such time as we have a deal, or we have total victory, [though] they want to make a deal very badly.*' Trump had also reaffirmed that he wanted to reduce the American military presence in the country to 8,600 troops, down from about 13,000.

However, the bilateral talks resumed in December same year [2019]. The secret war-papers and its report had also appeared in Dec 2019 in media just as talks between the US and the Taliban had restarted for another round of peace negotiations in Doha, Qatar.

## DOHA AGREEMENT *VERBATIM*:

**Agreement for Bringing Peace to Afghanistan**
between the Islamic Emirate of Afghanistan
which is not recognized by the United States as a state and is
known as the Taliban and the United States of America

**February 29, 2020**

which corresponds to Rajab 5, 1441 on the Hijri Lunar calendar and
Hoot 10, 1398 on the Hijri Solar calendar

A comprehensive peace agreement is made of four parts:

1. Guarantees and enforcement mechanisms that will prevent the use of the soil of Afghanistan by any group or individual against the security of the United States and its allies.

2. Guarantees, enforcement mechanisms, and announcement of a timeline for the withdrawal of all foreign forces from Afghanistan.

3. After the announcement of guarantees for a complete withdrawal of foreign forces and timeline in the presence of international witnesses, and guarantees and the announcement in the presence of international witnesses that Afghan soil will not be used against the security of the United States and its allies, the Islamic Emirate of Afghanistan which is not recognized by the United States as a state and is known as the Taliban will start intra-Afghan negotiations with Afghan sides on March 10, 2020, which corresponds to Rajab 15, 1441 on the Hijri Lunar calendar and Hoot 20, 1398 on the Hijri Solar calendar.

4. A permanent and comprehensive ceasefire will be an item on the agenda of the intra-Afghan dialogue and negotiations. The participants of intra-Afghan negotiations will discuss the date and modalities of a permanent and comprehensive ceasefire, including joint implementation mechanisms, which will be announced along with the completion and agreement over the future political roadmap of Afghanistan.

The four parts above are interrelated and each will be implemented in accordance with its own agreed timeline and agreed terms. Agreement on the first two parts paves the way for the last two parts.

Following is the text of the agreement for the implementation of parts one and two of the above. Both sides agree that these two parts are interconnected. The obligations of the Islamic Emirate of Afghanistan which is not recognized by the United States as a state and is known as the Taliban in this agreement apply in areas under their control until the formation of the new post-settlement Afghan Islamic government as determined by the intra-Afghan dialogue and negotiations.

## PART ONE

The United States is committed to withdraw from Afghanistan all military forces of the United States, its allies, and Coalition partners, including all non-diplomatic civilian personnel, private security contractors, trainers, advisors, and supporting services personnel within fourteen (14) months following announcement of this agreement, and will take the following measures in this regard:

A. The United States, its allies, and the Coalition will take the following measures in the first one hundred thirty-five (135) days:

1) They will reduce the number of U.S. forces in Afghanistan to eight thousand six hundred (8,600) and proportionally bring reduction in the number of its allies and Coalition forces.

2) The United States, its allies, and the Coalition will withdraw all their forces from five (5) military bases.

B. With the commitment and action on the obligations of the Islamic Emirate of Afghanistan which is not recognized by the United States as a state and is known as the Taliban in Part Two of this agreement, the United States, its allies, and the Coalition will execute the following:

1) The United States, its allies, and the Coalition will complete withdrawal of all remaining forces from Afghanistan within the remaining nine and a half (9.5) months.

2) The United States, its allies, and the Coalition will withdraw all their forces from remaining bases.

C. The United States is committed to start immediately to work with all relevant sides on a plan to expeditiously release combat and political prisoners as a confidence building measure with the coordination and approval of all relevant sides. Up to five thousand (5,000) prisoners of the Islamic Emirate of Afghanistan which is not recognized by the United States as a state and is known as the Taliban and up to one thousand (1,000) prisoners of the other side will be released by March 10, 2020, the first day of intra-Afghan negotiations, which corresponds to Rajab 15, 1441 on the Hijri Lunar calendar and Hoot 20, 1398 on the Hijri Solar calendar. The relevant sides have the goal of releasing all the remaining prisoners over the course of the subsequent three months. The United States commits to completing this goal. The Islamic Emirate of Afghanistan which is not recognized by the United States as a state and is known as the Taliban commits that its released prisoners will be committed to the responsibilities mentioned in this agreement so that they will not pose a threat to the security of the United States and its allies.

D. With the start of intra-Afghan negotiations, the United States will initiate an administrative review of current U.S. sanctions and the rewards list against members of the Islamic Emirate of Afghanistan which is not recognized by the United States as a state and is known as the Taliban with the goal of removing these sanctions by August 27, 2020, which corresponds to Muharram 8, 1442 on the Hijri Lunar calendar and Saunbola 6, 1399 on the Hijri Solar calendar.

E. With the start of intra-Afghan negotiations, the United States will start diplomatic engagement with other members of the United Nations Security Council and Afghanistan to remove members of the Islamic Emirate of Afghanistan which is not recognized by the United States as a state and is known as the Taliban from the sanctions list with the aim of achieving this objective by May 29, 2020, which corresponds to Shawwal 6, 1441 on the Hijri Lunar calendar and Jawza 9, 1399 on the Hijri Solar calendar.

F. The United States and its allies will refrain from the threat or the use of force against the territorial integrity or political independence of Afghanistan or intervening in its domestic affairs.

### PART TWO

In conjunction with the announcement of this agreement, the Islamic Emirate of Afghanistan which is not recognized by the United States as a state and is known as the Taliban will take the following steps to prevent any group or individual, including al-Qa'ida, from using the soil of Afghanistan to threaten the security of the United States and its allies:

1.  The Islamic Emirate of Afghanistan which is not recognized by the United States as a state and is known as the Taliban will not allow any of its members, other individuals or groups, including al-Qa'ida, to use the soil of Afghanistan to threaten the security of the United States and its allies.

2.  The Islamic Emirate of Afghanistan which is not recognized by the United States as a state and is known as the Taliban will send a clear message that those who pose a threat to the security of the United States and its allies have no place in Afghanistan, and will instruct members of the Islamic Emirate of Afghanistan which is not recognized by the United States as a state and is known as the Taliban not to cooperate with groups or individuals threatening the security of the United States and its allies.

3.  The Islamic Emirate of Afghanistan which is not recognized by the United States as a state and is known as the Taliban will prevent any group or individual in Afghanistan from threatening the security of the United States and its allies, and will prevent them from recruiting, training, and fundraising and will not host them in accordance with the commitments in this agreement.

4.  The Islamic Emirate of Afghanistan which is not recognized by the United States as a state and is known as the Taliban is committed to deal with those seeking asylum or residence in Afghanistan according to international migration law and the commitments of this agreement, so that such persons do not pose a threat to the security of the United States and its allies.

5.  The Islamic Emirate of Afghanistan which is not recognized by the United States as a state and is known as the Taliban will not provide visas, passports, travel permits, or other legal documents to those who pose a threat to the security of the United States and its allies to enter Afghanistan.

## PART THREE

1.  The United States will request the recognition and endorsement of the United Nations Security Council for this agreement.

2. The United States and the Islamic Emirate of Afghanistan which is not recognized by the United States as a state and is known as the Taliban seek positive relations with each other and expect that the relations between the United States and the new post-settlement Afghan Islamic government as determined by the intra-Afghan dialogue and negotiations will be positive.

3. The United States will seek economic cooperation for reconstruction with the new post-settlement Afghan Islamic government as determined by the intra-Afghan dialogue and negotiations, and will not intervene in its internal affairs.

Signed in Doha,
Qatar on February 29, 2020,
which corresponds to Rajab 5, 1441 on the Hijri Lunar calendar and
Hoot 10, 1398 on the Hijri Solar calendar,
in duplicate, in Pashto, Dari, and English languages,
each text being equally authentic.

## AFTER-EFFECTS OF DOHA ACCORD:

In 'The Financial Times' dated 13ᵗʰ August 2021, a columnist *Gideon Rachman* had correctly predicted that:

> *"It is true that Trump set the US on the path out of Afghanistan and began the delusional peace talks with the Taliban that have gone nowhere. But rather than reverse the withdrawal of troops, Biden accelerated it.*
>
> *The horrific results are unfolding on the ground in Afghanistan, as the Taliban take city after city. The final collapse of the government (in Afghanistan) looks inevitable."*

The hasty withdrawal decision of President Biden's administration gave the Taliban a green light to move quick – as long as they did not attack the US and NATO forces. *Lost in the bargain were the Afghan people* who feared the breaking out of yet another extended but deadlier period of intra-Afghan fighting. Confronted with all-round criticism over the manner his admin cut loose from the Afghan mess, Mr Biden shifted the blame to his predecessor, Mr Trump.

If the manner of reaching the *Doha deal* with the Taliban's political *Shura* served as a dampener for the increasingly worried Afghan government, the hurried withdrawal plan made the Ghani regime a sitting duck, only counting the days towards its collapse. All of his pleas, including a visit to Washington, could not make the Biden Admin move from its intended goal. Afghan President Ghani spent the in between go-time not for its country but in planning for his own future and shifting his wealth and investment docs to safe places like Dubai.

Some political experts held that President Trump should own this debacle. He and his Secretary of State Mike Pompeo started negotiating a *'peace deal'* with the Taliban; making concessions on behalf of the Afghan government [including releasing 5,000 prisoners] without any participation from the Afghan government. Trump gave the Taliban legitimacy, and even, at one point, wanted to invite Taliban leaders to Camp David.

And as is typical of Republican presidents - *Trump signed that peace deal with a withdrawal date after he wouldn't be in office.* Bush did the same in Iraq, signed a deal calling for the withdrawal of all US troops in Iraq with a withdrawal date he knew would be after he was out of office.

**How the US created a disaster in Afghanistan** - And what the US military was actually doing in Afghanistan all this time? To get answers to the above questions one can find a video by an investigative reporter Azmat Khan and former US ambassador to Afghanistan Michael McKinley who explains what the US military was actually doing in Afghanistan, what it got wrong, and why America's long intervention there was considered a failure; see it at:

https://www.youtube.com/channel/UCLXo7UDZvByw2ixzpQCufnA

How did the Afghan government collapse so quickly in August 2021? It was primarily born out of uncertainty created by talks held in Doha, Qatar, concluded on 29th February 2020 between the US and the Taliban, confirming a full American and allied forces withdrawal from Afghan soils. US and Afghan military officials got demoralized, and described the deal as the government's guaranteed defeat against the Taliban. Said an Afghan Military Commander:

> *"The forces saw that document as the end. The day the deal was signed we saw the change. Everyone was just looking out for himself. It was like [the United States] left us to fail."*

Conditions within the Afghan military quickly deteriorated thereafter, marked by a *combination of corruption and ill-discipline in all ranks.*

The Americans were ready to leave Afghanistan just as the Soviets did; civil war was ahead with the Taliban eventually getting the upper hand and that the sitting Afghan government was to flee sooner; as it happened. The historians could foresee that there would be no compromise by the Taliban in accepting the *Islamic Shariah & Islamic Law* and that they would insist on calling their State as '**The Islamic Emirates of Afghanistan**'.

No surprise that the US Withdrawal was inevitable: Intelligentsia was ready to confront with this expected development; though most were actually surrounded by the most ill-informed gentry who were clueless and confused about the whole Afghan Spectacle. Headlines in papers started screaming that '*if the US withdraws, Afghanistan faces civil war*' – but was a bare fact; an unconcealed statement of the very obvious.

Pakistan's *Gen [R] Tariq Khan,* in his article on media pages of 4<sup>th</sup> July 2021, titled as **AFGHAN END GAME,** had predicted [*it was 41 days earlier to the actual fall of Kabul on 15<sup>th</sup> August 2021*] America's humiliating defeat; also before President Biden's speech of 8<sup>th</sup> July 2021. He wrote:

> "*This was bound to happen and when Pakistan eagerly put its best foot forward and facilitated US-Taliban dialogue the possible implication should have been clearly understood then by everyone.*
>
> *First, that if there was no agreement [at Doha] a status quo would remain in Afghanistan and that the Americans would have to choose between continuing to stay till stability was achieved or to leave despite the violence it would be subjected to.*
>
> *….as an agreement was arrived at, the implications were very obvious: Given the clearly stated Taliban position on their aversion to the new Constitution, their own perception on a power sharing formula, the name of the State, Islamic Law and system of governance etc., there was very little to negotiate or discuss.*"

However, an agreement was arrived at despite the Taliban's inflexible position on their principal points. Such an agreement was predictably limited to a ceasefire arrangement between the Taliban and the US [*not the Taliban and the Afghan Government*] and that the US would be allowed and facilitated to withdraw unhindered from Afghanistan.

Thus the civil war on Afghan soils was also on tips; the Taliban were not to reconcile with a Government that they felt had facilitated foreign occupation – the US, UK and the NATO. The Taliban wanted to wrest total control and there was no one to stop them; there was also an element of vindication in an ethnic as well as ideological conflict. The collapse of the Afghan National Army and the US framed security apparatus that was constructed almost overnight was bound to fail. The Taliban had seen the NATO combined forces and the US with eye-to-eye – they had seen their hollowness and thus planned their total defeat. They knew their enemy since the better part of 20 years. Gen Tariq correctly narrated that:

> *"This was a conflict waiting to happen in the wake of the US attempt at fiddling with the very essence of the Afghan National character and nature that was based on history, tradition, culture and geography. These elements the US ignored as they patched together an unrealistic 'Afghan Unity Government' and gave them a Westernised Constitution to put into practice which was obviously neither acceptable to the Afghan people nor did it have any place in the Afghan ethos."*

A fact that Ashraf Ghani's government had always demonstrated through its deep-seated hatred; with the [then] latest insult passed on by the Afghan National Security Advisor, Hamdullah Mohib, stating that *'Pakistan was a brothel'*. Ghani got nothing by such attitudes but lost his own honour and Pakistani mass's sympathy. Why would Pakistan assume that having ousted the US, it would interfere in the Taliban's governance? Since two decades the two Afghan regimes and the US made successive and hefty deals with India at the cost of Pakistan's integrity and security. Thus hopefully, even if there would be civil war in Afghanistan, the Pakistan would extend support to the Taliban none else.

Immediately after President Biden's speech of 8ᵗʰ July 2021, the Taliban started sending their fighter groups to government-controlled rural outposts, striking deals with low-level officials through bribes or safety guarantees. The country's elite military units remained committed to safeguarding the government holdouts, but the local leaders and lower military personnel didn't stand by them - thus their efforts to defend the country failed.

After all, no one asked the US to withdraw from Afghanistan so hurriedly; it was their decision to do so having concluded that this was a *never-ending war that was not winnable*. In their haste to withdraw they abandoned their allies: the sitting government of Afghanistan as well as let down their strategic partner - India.

In their eagerness to negotiate some settlement with the Taliban, Pakistan was again pressed to convince the Taliban to talk to the US. Finally, the US secured a ceasefire between themselves and the Taliban BUT leaving Afghanistan at its own mercy.

.....AND thus the story of extending constant torture to
Pakistan in the name of 'TERROR STATE' at the cost of
pleasing the governments of Afghanistan and
India ended with most horrific humiliation for America.

# Scenario 229

## TALIBAN RE-CAPTURED AFGHANISTAN - 1

**EARLIER WAR ACTIVITY IN 2021:** <u>On 23<sup>rd</sup> July 2021</u>; in the last call between US President Joe Biden and his Afghan counterpart before the Taliban seized control of nearly the whole rural districts of the country, the leaders discussed military aid, political strategy and messaging tactics, but neither Biden nor Ashraf Ghani appeared aware of or prepared for the immediate danger of the entire country falling to the Taliban, a transcript reviewed by **Reuters** dated <u>1<sup>st</sup> September 2021</u> showed; they both talked for roughly 14 minutes.

**On 9<sup>th</sup> August 2021;** the US Embassy in Kabul posed a question to its 400K followers on Twitter:

> *"This #PeaceMonday, we want to hear from you. What do you wish to tell the negotiating parties in Doha about your hopes for a political settlement? #PeaceForAfghanistan."*

The phrase divulged all about the changed American mind and trends in Afghan policy. Within 3 days, Ghani's Afghan government was reduced to only three major cities. President Biden, the leader of the world's most powerful nation, announced to dispatch 3,000 US troops to Afghanistan to bring back its diplomats and staff but within next two days the game was over. The US diplomats had to evacuate their fortress-like US Embassy the same day; two-decade-long misadventure ended in one day and with a trillion-dollar throwaway. Most think, Afghan citizens were left to live back in stone-age; but the time decided it much earlier than the US had planned.

For the US, it was not at all a heroic defeat – the comeback of Taliban also brought an end for supremacy myth of a global power. In history it would be captioned as the **Great Defeat** from **one of the poorest countries** on globe. The [15<sup>th</sup> Aug] Sunday's episode was even more embarrassing than of Saigon in 1975; even more humiliating than a rogue re-treat of 1984's Reagan Administration from Beirut when a suicide bomber of Hezbollah had killed 240+ US military personnel—the largest loss for the Marines in a single incident since the World War-II.

**On 11ᵗʰ August 2021;** the US intelligence reports indicated Taliban fighters could isolate Afghanistan's capital in 30 days and possibly take it over within 90. Instead, the fall happened in less than a week.

The Biden-Ghani call also underscored persistent political infighting that plagued the Afghan government. When Biden asked him [Mr Ghani] to include former Afghan President Hamid Karzai in a press conference, Ghani pushed back and said:

> *"Karzai would not be helpful. He is contrary, and time is of the essence, we cannot bring every single individual … We have tried for months with President Karzai. Last time we met for 110 minutes; he was cursing me and he was accusing me of being a US lackey."*

> Biden paused before responding: ***"I'm going to reserve judgment on that."***

In a follow-up call later that day; Gen Mark Milley and US Central Command commander Gen Frank McKenzie spoke to Ghani. Reuters also obtained a transcript of that call. In this call, too, an area of focus was the global perception of events on the ground in Afghanistan. Gen Milley told Ghani:

> *"…..the perception in the US, in Europe and the media sort of thing is a narrative of Taliban momentum, and a narrative of Taliban victory. And we need to collectively demonstrate and try to turn that perception, that narrative around."*

> *"I do not believe – the time is our friend here. We need to move quickly,"* McKenzie added.

Hidden confession of defeat was prevailing on both sides; with the US and in Afghanistan.

NOW Attend a former Soviet ambassador's remarks on the situation: ***"We meddled in Afghanistan, and then we stopped paying attention."***

In 'The Financial Times' dated 13ᵗʰ August 2021, *Gideon Rachman* had correctly predicted that:

> *"If Donald Trump were presiding over the debacle in Afghanistan, the US foreign policy establishment would be loudly condemning the irresponsibility and immorality of American strategy. Since it is Joe*

*Biden in the White House there is instead, largely, an embarrassed silence.*

*The horrific results are unfolding on the ground in Afghanistan, as the Taliban take city after city. The final collapse of the government looks inevitable."*

......and suddenly Kabul falls down in the hands of its ex-rulers, the Taliban; America quits.

## JO-BIDEN URGED GHANI TO HOLD:

In the call, Biden offered aid if Ghani could publicly project he had a plan to control the spiralling situation in Afghanistan. **Biden said: 'We will continue to provide close air support, if we know what the plan is.'** Days before the call, the US had carried out air-strikes to support Afghan security forces; a move the Taliban said was in violation of the Doha Peace Agreement.

The US president also advised Ghani to get buy-in from powerful Afghans for a military strategy going forward, and then to put a 'warrior' in charge of the effort, a reference to Defence Minister Gen Bismillah Khan Mohammadi was being made. President Biden had urged:

> *"The Afghan armed forces were trained and funded by the US government. You clearly have the best military. You have 3000,000 well-armed forces versus 70-80,000 (Taliban people) and they're clearly capable of fighting well."*

Days later, the Afghan military started folding across provincial capitals in the country with very little resistance to the Taliban.

In much of the call, Biden focused on what he called the Afghan *government's 'perception problem'* adding that:

> *"I need not tell you [Mr Ghani] the perception around the world and in parts of Afghanistan, I believe, is that things are not going well in terms of the fight against the Taliban. And there is a need, whether it is true or not, there is a need to project a different picture. If Afghanistan's prominent political figures were to give a press conference together, backing a new military strategy that will change perception, and that will change an awful lot I think.*

*We are going to continue to fight hard, diplomatically, politically, economically, to make sure your government not only survives but is sustained and grows."*

After the call, the White House released a statement that focused on Biden's commitment to support Afghan security forces and seeking funds for Afghanistan from Congress. Ghani replied Biden that:

*"I believe there could be peace if we could 'rebalance the military solution' but we need to move with speed. We are facing a full-scale invasion, composed of Taliban, full Pakistani planning and logistical support, and at least 10-15,000 international terrorists, predominantly Pakistanis thrown into this."*

Afghan government officials, and US experts, have been consistently pointing to Pakistani support for the Taliban as key to the group's resurgence.

Afghan President Ghani had also blamed Pakistan earlier on 17<sup>th</sup> May 2021 in an interview to **German magazine** *Der Spiegel* alleging that:

*"Pakistan operates an organised system of support for the Taliban insurgents, who receive logistics and financial support from there, besides carrying out recruitment.*

*.....various decision-making bodies of the Taliban were named after Pakistani cities like Quetta Shura, Miranshah Shura and Peshawar Shura, where they were supposedly based."*

The Pakistani Embassy in Washington had immediately denied those allegations with full force saying that *'....it was unfortunately an excuse and an afterthought peddled by Mr Ghani to justify his failure to lead and govern.'*

Pakistan's Foreign Office had also earlier rejected the remarks from the Afghan president calling them *"irresponsible and baseless"*. PM Imran Khan had replied Mr Ghani in the same harsh tone that it was **unfair** to blame his country for the situation in Afghanistan; adding that:

*"President Ghani! Let me just say that the country that is most affected by turmoil in Afghanistan is Pakistan. Pakistan suffered 70,000 casualties+ in the last 15 years..... Pakistan wants to see the ending of the conflict at the earliest."*

By the time of the call, the US was well into its planned withdrawal from Afghanistan, which Biden had postponed from the May date set by his predecessor, Mr Trump. The US military had closed its main Afghanistan airbase, at Bagram, in early July [2021]. As the two presidents spoke, Taliban fighters had controlled about half of Afghanistan's district centres, indicating a rapidly deteriorating security situation.

Afghan government was promising a shift in its military strategy, to start focusing on protecting *'population centres'* — major cities — rather than fighting to protect rural territories. Biden referred approvingly of that strategy; he said that doing so would help not just on the ground but in the 'perception' internationally that was required to shore up world support for the Afghan government. Biden said:

> *"I'm not a military guy, so I'm not telling you what a plan should precisely look like, you're going to get not only more help, but you're going to get a perception that is going to change ...,"*

Mr Ghani, for his part, assured Biden that *"your assurance of support goes a very long way to enable us, to really mobilise us in earnest."*

Within two weeks after Biden's tele-talk with Ghani, the Taliban captured several provincial Afghan capitals and the US had to say with utter disappointment that it was up to the Afghan security forces to defend their country. Pentagon spokesman John Kirby said on 9th August 2021.

> *"These are their military forces; these are their provincial capitals, their people to defend."*

## FALL OF THE CAPITAL - KABUL:

On 15th **August 2021;** President Ghani fled the presidential palace, and the Taliban occupied it immediately. On the same day, the next generation of the Taliban successfully took over Kabul and thus the whole Afghanistan following an accelerated sweep across the country. They had planned their operations since 2020's deal between them and the US's representative in Qatar under the then US President Donald Trump's instructions - called as **DOHA DECLARATION** in which the US agreed to a complete withdrawal of US and allied military forces.

As the deadline for US-army withdrawal drew near day by day, the Taliban began rapid seizures of outposts, towns, and cities and all leading ways to Kabul. An immediate development on ground was the departure of President Ashraf Ghani, whose exit from the country was confirmed by Abdullah Abdullah, the Afghan Foreign Minister. On 15th August 2021 he announced on his FaceBook page that:

> *"The former Afghan president has left the nation in this state; [for that,] God will hold him to account."*

In a later announcement, Ghani himself said he left the country to avoid bloodshed as Taliban forces had entered the presidential palace. By midday, a Taliban official announced the group's plans to rename the state as the **Islamic Emirate of Afghanistan.**

Referring to the world's press media of that day, 15th August 2021; and to the Current Affairs programs of subsequent two weeks, the Taliban's insurgency over the last month had seen the capture of major cities; Kunduz was the first 'key city' to fall following days of negotiations led by tribal elders and resulting in its surrender. After that, it was almost like a domino effect — other major towns like Kandahar, Herat and Mazar e Sharif fell to the Taliban through negotiated deals with local officials. These deals with the Taliban typically involved surrendering control of the cities in exchange for safe passage home.

On the same Sunday morning, Taliban forces had reached city of Jalalabad, where govt forces and officials surrendered without a single shot fired. Soon, the remaining cities surrounding Kabul quickly fell into the Taliban's hands; thus the Taliban reached the capital's gates within hours.

All around Kabul there was panic. Civilian flights were unable to leave the Kabul airport because on the runway people were running after the moving planes and trying to stick around the wings, wheels and landing assemblies. No one including the US and its allied countries were expecting so quick developments and even Taliban commanders themselves. Taliban openly said in press conferences that we were planning to take over in December 2021 after holding due negotiations with President Ashraf Ghani but he fled away; so coward he was – so we had to move in.

Taliban's strategy to take control of Kabul through peaceful negotiations instead of violent offensive proved effective. An exodus of residents and foreign diplomats began as the Taliban entered the Presidential Palace and other key government buildings. Most Afghans lined up outside the local banks to retrieve cash as fears were growing; it was despite the Taliban's due assurance for peace and tranquility.

Referring to the daily 'DAWN' dated 15th August 2021: The fact remained that the US spent billions of dollars supplying the Afghan military with the tools to defeat the Taliban, but the rapid capitulation of the armed forces meant that the same armaments and guns then fuelled the Taliban's battlefield successes. President Biden, while defending his decision to withdraw American forces and leaving the fight to the local Afghans, said:

> "We (the US) provided our Afghan partners with all the tools — let me emphasise: all the tools but Afghan defence forces showed little appetite for that fight and, in their tens of thousands, have been laying down their arms — only for the Taliban to immediately pick them up."

Footage of Afghan soldiers surrendering in the northern city of *Kunduz* showed army vehicles loaded with heavy weapons and mounted with artillery guns safely in the hands of the Taliban rank and file was widely spread in the world media. In the western city of Farah, fighters patrolled in a car marked with an eagle swooping on a snake — the official insignia of the country's intelligence service. In the list of surrendered arsenal, there was *sophisticated equipment* like armoured vehicles, humvees, small arms and light weapons, as well as ammunition.

American experts were astonished over such hauls — on top of unacknowledged support from regional allies — provided the Taliban a massive boost. The weapons not only helped the Taliban's march on Kabul but also strengthened group's authority in the cities it had captured. With US troops all gone, the Taliban found themselves flush with the US-supplied tools, without having to raise a single penny. One expert Commented:

> "It is incredibly serious. It is clearly going to be a massive boon to them [Taliban]. Some of that weaponry was later brazenly paraded ahead of the US troops' 9/11 withdrawal deadline by the Taliban. This crisis was a worst-case scenario considered when making procurement decisions for that weaponry."

At Kunduz airport, a Taliban fighter on a red motorbike, head-to-toe in Taliban dress, was filmed staring at a military helicopter sitting on the tarmac. It was a picture of jubilation mirrored across the Taliban-held territory. While the Taliban continued to show off these big prizes, the aircraft at least would have no impact on the battlefield without pilots. Former CIA counter-terrorism analyst Aki Peritz said:

> *"They will be for propaganda purposes only. More useful will be the light arms and vehicles used to navigate the country's rugged terrain. Coupled with the army's dwindling morale, they will boost the threat the Taliban posed to the Western-backed governments."*

As the crisis unfolded, Biden's administration said it would still equip the Afghan military that appears on the verge of collapse.

Referring to a write-up titled as *'Unfinished problem....'* **AP | Reuters | AFP** Published on world media pages on <u>16<sup>th</sup> August 2021</u>:

> *"More than 60 countries have issued a joint statement saying Afghans and international citizens who want to leave Afghanistan must be allowed to depart."*

In fact, the Taliban's quick takeover of Afghanistan raised alarm at the global level, with world leaders clamouring for the protection of human rights and bringing an end to armed aggression in the war-torn country. Some sought introspection, terming it a collective Western failure. Yet others held out an olive branch, looking to establish relations with the new regime, whose leaders were ousted from the seat of power in 2001. Some countries put their appalling remarks on all sorts of media pages.

### 'IT'S FAILURE OF THE WORLD' - UK:

The Taliban's takeover of Afghanistan was termed as *'failure of the international community'*, Britain's Defence Secretary Ben Wallace said next day of Taliban's take over, assessing that the West's intervention was <u>*a job only half-done*</u>. He told **BBC** television:

> *"All of us know that Afghanistan is not finished. It's an unfinished problem for the world and the world needs to help it. The 20-year intervention by the US-led forces in Afghanistan wasn't a waste, it wasn't for nothing.*
>
> *If it's a failure, it's a failure of the international community to not realise that you don't fix things overnight,"*

Mr Wallace accused Western powers of being short-sighted in policy matters and devising suitable strategies.

### *Know the country's history before you attack*: Iran

Iran's **President Ebrahim Raisi** said on <u>16<sup>th</sup> August 2021</u>:

> *"I'm afraid when you deal with a country like Afghanistan that is 1,000 years of history of fighting foreign powers and civil wars, you manage its problems and you might have to manage it for 100 years at least."*

America's defeat in Afghanistan was a chance for lasting peace; the 'defeat' of the US in Afghanistan must usher in durable peace in the war-wracked country. The President added that:

> *"The military defeat and the US withdrawal from Afghanistan should offer an opportunity to restore life, security and lasting peace in that country."*

The statement came after the Taliban seized control of Kabul.

### China: *'ready for friendly relations'* with Taliban:

China was ready to deepen *friendly and cooperative relations* with Afghanistan, a government spokeswoman told on <u>16<sup>th</sup> August 2021</u>, after the Taliban seized control of the country. Foreign ministry's spokeswoman Hua Chunying told the media that:

> *"The Taliban have repeatedly expressed their hope to develop good relations with China, and that they look forward to China's participation in the reconstruction and development of Afghanistan.*
>
> *We welcome this. China respects the right of the Afghan people to independently determine their own destiny and is willing to continue to develop... friendly and cooperative relations with Afghanistan (as a neighbouring country)."*

Hua called on the Taliban to *'ensure a smooth transition'* of power and keep its promises to negotiate the establishment of an *'open and inclusive Islamic government'* and ensure the safety of Afghans and foreign citizens.

### *Taliban to uphold human rights*: New Zealand

PM Jacinda Ardern of New Zealand on <u>16<sup>th</sup> August 2012</u> pleaded the Taliban leaders to uphold human rights in Afghanistan by allowing women to continue in work and education and to let foreigners and Afghans who want to leave the country go. She added that:

> *"I would just again implore those who made these moves in recent days to acknowledge what the international community has called for — human rights and the safety of their people."*

### Takeover of Kabul was 'unexpected': Russia

Kremlin diplomat in Afghanistan, Zamir Kabulov told the *Ekho Moskvy* Radio Station that:

> *"Russia will evacuate some of its embassy staff in Kabul in order not to create too big a presence. Some of roughly 100 Russian embassy staff will be placed on leave or evacuated in some other fashion.*
>
> ***The Taliban's swift takeover of the Afghan capital was somewhat "unexpected. Russia was too optimistic in its assessment of the quality of the armed forces trained by the Americans and NATO."***

The outside perimeter of the embassy was being guarded by the Taliban.

### We must focus on rescue mission: Germany

German Chancellor Angela Merkel said Germany's focus must be on its evacuation operation in Afghanistan. After a meeting with the leaders of her CDU Party, she said:

> *"We are witnessing difficult times. Now we must focus on the rescue mission. The withdrawal of Western troops from Afghanistan was the 'biggest NATO debacle' since the founding of the alliance."*

With the Taliban sweeping to power after NATO troops withdrew, CDU party Chief Armin Laschet said:

> *"It is evident that this engagement of the international community was not successful. It is the biggest debacle that NATO has suffered since its founding, and we're standing before an epochal change."*

### Concerned over rapid developments in Afgh....: Qatar

Qatari Foreign Minister Al-Thani, in a statement on 16<sup>th</sup> August 2021, said:

*"There is international concern about the fast pace of developments and Qatar is doing its utmost to bring a peaceful transition, especially after the vacuum that happened."*

### 'Taliban must cease violence': Australia

Australian PM Scott Morrison said on 16<sup>th</sup> August 2021 that:

*"His country is working to get more than 130 of its citizens and people who have been granted humanitarian visas out of Afghanistan after the Taliban seized control of the country.*

*As a partner committed for many years to help Afghanistan build its future, we are deeply concerned at the potential for further loss of life and suffering."*

PM Morrison called for the Taliban to cease all violence against civilians, treat Afghan government officials and elected leaders with dignity and allow people to leave the country without threat or hindrance.

### 'The clock has run out': EU Commission

EU Commission Vice President Margaritis Schinas tweeted:

*"The clock has run out on how long we can wait to adopt the complete overhaul of Europe's migration and asylum rules we need."*

### 'Endless US presence in Afghanistan not acceptable': America

President Joe Biden addressed his colleagues and allies on Afghan war that:

*"One more year, or five more years, of US military presence would not have made a difference if the Afghan military cannot or will not hold its own country. And an endless American presence in the middle of another country's civil conflict was not acceptable to me."*

### 'All abuses must stop': UN

United Nations Chief António Guterres on 16<sup>th</sup> August 2021 expressed concern, saying:

*"The conflict in Afghanistan was forcing hundreds of thousands to flee amid reports of serious human rights violations."*

Later that day, the UN Secretary General Guterres told an emergency UN Security Council meeting on Afghanistan in New York that:

> "*The world should work together to suppress the global terrorist threat in Afghanistan'. The international community must unite to make sure that Afghanistan is never again used as a platform or safe haven for terrorist organisations.*
>
> *I appeal to the Security Council — and the international community as a whole — to stand together, to work together and act together (in the given situation)."*

Guterres urged all nations to use all tools at [their] disposal to suppress the global terrorist threat in Afghanistan and to guarantee that basic human rights should be respected.

The Secretary General urged the international community to '*speak with one voice to uphold human rights in Afghanistan.* **Afghans deserve our full support.** '*It was essential that the hard-won rights of Afghan women and girls are protected.*'

### '*We are heartbroken*': Canadian PM

Canadian PM Justin Trudeau, while speaking to media reporters on 15<sup>th</sup> August 2021, said:

> "*Canada is constantly monitoring the rapidly evolving situation to get the latest developments on ground in Afghanistan. We are heartbroken at the situation the Afghan people find themselves in.*
>
> *Our ongoing work to bring Afghans to safety in Canada under [the new Special Immigration Measures program] remains a top priority, and we will continue to work in close collaboration with partners and allies on this commitment."*

More than 60 countries issued a joint statement saying Afghans and international citizens who want to leave Afghanistan must be allowed to depart and added that airports and border crossings must remain open, the US State Department said late on 15<sup>th</sup> August 2021.

### AFGHANS DESERVED SAFETY & HELP:

According to **Reuters**, the US government and countries including Australia, Canada, France, Germany, Italy, Japan, Republic of Korea, Qatar and the UK said in a joint statement that:

*".....those in positions of power and authority across Afghanistan bear responsibility — and accountability — for the protection of human life and property, and for the immediate restoration of security and civil order.*

*....The Afghan people deserve to live in safety, security and dignity. We in the international community stand ready to assist them."*

The European and neighboring countries immediately stepped in to help civilians evacuate the country — the United Arab Emirates [UAE] and Pakistan started facilitating the evacuation of foreign diplomats and staff through their airports; Germany sent its military planes to evacuate German nationals and Afghan support staff – and so did the UK. The US Embassy employees and citizens scrambled to go for evacuation before the Afghan capital was taken.

One can peep back into a very rare two-party consensus in America — the leaders of both political parties decided it was time to leave Afghanistan and to leave the country with the Taliban. The only dispute remained was whether the President Trump, which had committed to withdrawal by May 2021, could have directed the retreat more competently than President Biden, who faced one of the most humiliating debacles in the American history.

Poor Americans were in a fix – who to blame for those dreadful moments; what was the purpose of the US intervention in Afghanistan. The answers would shape one's views about the lost 20 years. The intervention was to defend the US from terror attacks as well as to destroy the Taliban and al Qaeda being allegedly responsible for 9/11.

Of course, since 9/11 the US went free of notable *jihadist* attacks – but it remained a fact also that right-wing domestic terrorists killed more Americans at home than *jihadists*. The 20-year mission got accomplished at the loss of fewer American combat deaths in Afghanistan than the number of civilians killed on 9/11 itself.

Referring to **Robin Wright**'s essay titled *'Does the Great Retreat from Afghanistan mark the End of American Era'* appeared at **newyorker.com** on 15<sup>th</sup> August 2021:

*"In 2011, the United States pulled out of Iraq, opening the way for the emergence of ISIS. The repeated miscalculations challenge basic Washington policy-making as well as US military strategy and*

*intelligence capabilities. Why wasn't this looming calamity - or any of the earlier ones - anticipated? Or the exits better planned? Or the country not left in the hands of a former enemy? **It is [no doubt] a dishonourable end.***"

NOW the history would be written with truths that George W Bush's **'war on terror [WOT]'** was an ill-written drama-script; despite having mobilized NATO's 136 countries to provide various types of military assistance, and 23 countries to host US forces deployed in offensive operations; even the America's vast tools and tactics proved ill-equipped to counter the will and endurance of the Taliban and allegedly their Pakistani backers. In the long term, its missiles and warplanes were unable to subjugate a movement of about 60,000 fighters in a small devastated country, Afghanistan.

Think about the major repercussion of this American defeat. ***Shariah* won a key battle against democracy**; the US and the West's top arsenal with billions of dollars in aid could not defeat a true and sincere ideology [*West say it hard-line doctrine*] with majority local following. If the world would not accept the Taliban truly and realistically, with whatever features they keep, Afghanistan might again become a safe haven for like-minded warriors to whom they used to label as militants or *Jihadists*.

*Robin* has correctly analysed through ill-based interventions in Afghanistan and Iraq. The actions unambiguously proved that the US could neither build nations nor create armies out of scratch, especially in countries that have a limited middle class and low education rates. It takes generations. Ethnic and sectarian divisions thwart attempts to overhaul political, social, and economic life all at the same time; Pakistan is also an example to be cited here. The US spent 88 billion dollars training and arming an Afghan force of some 300,000 men, more than four times the size of the Taliban's militia, but lost once more. About a month earlier, President Biden said that:

> "....he trusted the capacity of the Afghan military, who is better trained, better equipped and more competent in terms of conducting war – (but) all gone with the wind...."

America's Great Retreat is at least as humiliating as was the Soviet Union's withdrawal in 1989 from the same country, an event that brought end to its empire and Communist rule. The Soviet Union had spent about 50 billion dollars during the first seven of its ten years stay here and the US spent much more. However, no difference; the

Americans flying out on their helicopters were no different than Soviet troops marching across the Friendship Bridge from Afghanistan on 15<sup>th</sup> February 1989.

Both of the big powers left Afghanistan as losers, with their tails between their legs, leaving behind chaos – so had left the Britain after **The First Anglo-Afghan War in 1839-42** when about 17,000 British troops and civilians were mercilessly slaughtered by the same Afghans in Kabul.

Referring to *David French* in weekly **TIME** of 16<sup>th</sup> August 2021:

> *"The jihadist military had suffered a grievous blow [in December 2001] but the extremist theology lived on. We [Americans] could not extinguish an idea, and the idea still possessed power....At every stage, the Taliban and their al Qaeda allies were the second-strongest force in the land."*

In nut shell, the Americans could not destroy the Taliban or al Qaeda - despite 20 years of military attacks, they still existed; the US took a long time to understand their capabilities. In December 2001, a small force of the US-army, supported by local allies, and American air power had out-routed the Taliban quite easily; then what went wrong later - why the US allowed them to flourish again.

In the end, the above referred weekly **TIME** correctly ended up with:

> *".....we should have pulled out long, long ago ....our leaders have misled Americans about the reality of the conflict....There is no realistic prospect of taking back Kabul, much less the rest of Afghanistan.... And, thanks to the bipartisan failure to lead, al Qaeda has won a long and critical battle against the most powerful nation in the world..... This victory [of Taliban] did not end the 'endless war'. Instead it made our enemy more dangerous."*

One blog of 16<sup>th</sup> August 2021 on the internet media held that:

> *"Yes,... If the people doing the subjugation are their own tribesmen then what is our business to intervene? The Taliban are a force of (hardly) 80,000 in a country of 38m. How have they achieved control when Afghani forces number approx 300,000? The only possible way is through the complicity of the population; some of them are women. We had no business establishing ourselves in Afghanistan in the first place."*

## THE BURDEN OF SHAME – ON BIDEN:

Referring to UK's **main-line press** dated <u>16<sup>th</sup> August 2021</u>: the US President Joe Biden has been criticised by media across the political divide; see the world's media comments below:

A **CNN** columnist *Stephen Collinson* said:

> '*The **debacle of the US defeat and chaotic retreat** in Afghanistan is a political disaster for Joe Biden, whose failure to orchestrate an urgent and orderly exit will further rock a presidency plagued by crises and stain his legacy.*'

**Wall Street Journal opinion [Editorial]:**

> '*President Biden's statement on Saturday washing his hands of Afghanistan deserves to go down as one of the **most shameful in history** by a Commander in Chief at such a moment of American retreat.*'

*George Packer* in **The Atlantic** said:

> '*The Biden administration failed to heed the warnings on Afghanistan, failed to act with urgency—and its failure has left tens of thousands of Afghans to a terrible fate. This **betrayal will live in infamy.***
>
> *There was enough blame attached for the Afghanistan crisis to fill a library of books, condemning the betrayal of the Afghan people as he placed the **burden of shame** on Biden.*'

An opinion made by *David E. Sanger* in **The New York Times** claimed:

> '*.....Biden would go down in history, fairly or unfairly, as the president who presided over a long-brewing **humiliating final act** in the American experiment in Afghanistan*'.

**New York Post editorial** said:

> '*President Biden says he inherited Trump's withdrawal plans, but that is a lie. He could have taken more time, tried to at least secure the capital, and left a small peacekeeping force. Instead, we pulled out in the dread of night, so quickly we had to send troops back just to make sure our embassy was safely evacuated. It's as humiliating an end as the **rooftop scramble in Saigon in 1975.***'

*Max Boot,* columnist for **the Washington Post** commented:

> *'Strengthened by the copious U.S. weaponry they have captured — and by the prestige that comes with having humbled a superpower — the Taliban will now be more dangerous than ever. This is on Biden, and it* **will leave an indelible stain on his presidency.'**

*Paul Brandus,* columnist in **USA Today** held:

> *'Biden is in charge now, this catastrophe is appearing on his watch, and he will have to take his lumps. That's the way it goes. Life and politics are often unfair. Yet as bad as things look for Biden today, I wonder just how much* **long-term damage** *this will actually do to him and the America.'*

*Kyle Smith* in the **New York Post:**

> *'The utterly nauseating and unnecessary abandonment of Afghanistan to its fate recalls a similar humiliation at the hands of Islamist radicals in the Jimmy Carter administration. President Biden's profligate spending policies are unleashing inflation that is sparking voter distrust so noticeable that even NPR is sounding the alarm.'*

*Trey Gowdy* on **Fox News** said:

> *'Thousands of lives taken [or] have been lost in defence of our nation. Tens of thousands of our sons and daughters have been injured. And more than a trillion dollars of our money has been spent in Afghanistan alone. And* **we are left to wonder why.'**

*Senator Joni Ernst* on **Fox News** said:

> *'.....condemn the* **slap on the face to the thousands** *of men and women who served in this war and a total abandonment of a country and its people by Biden.*
>
> *The rushed and haphazard withdrawal of US forces in Afghanistan is not* **the strategic shift** *President Biden sold to the American people. Instead, it's a total abandonment of a country and its people – and a gift to the Taliban.'*

A columnist in the **British Press** also hit at President Biden that day. Commons Foreign Affairs Committee Chair Tom Tugendhat wrote in

**The Times** that:

> 'The fall of Kabul is **the biggest foreign policy disaster** since Suez. The operation to seize the canal in 1956 symbolised the end of Britain's global ambition and refocused us on NATO and alliances. It showed conclusively that the US could limit our actions and change our policy.'

A columnist **Ian Birrell** in the 'I' wrote:

> 'The withdrawal, begun by a Republican president and speeded up by his Democratic successor, is driven by domestic concerns rather than the slightest consideration for people they are leaving to suffer. It is a **betrayal of Afghanistan's people,** of our wider strategic interests and all those troops killed or maimed fighting for its future.'

The **Financial Times'** Editorial note said:

> 'A desire in the White House to wrap up nagging foreign policy problems so it can focus on China is understandable. But the **abandonment of Afghanistan** raises doubts over the depth of US commitment to supposed allies, and its determination to see military entanglements through to the bitter end.'

**Mark Almond** wrote in the **Daily Mail** that:

> 'What makes this debacle different from the Americans' hasty retreat from Saigon in 1975 is the existence across the West of small cells of radical Islamists who will be inspired by our **humiliating retreat from Kabul.** There were no Vietcong cells in London waiting to be activated then. Today things are different. The humiliation of the West in Afghanistan has set Islamist fundamentalism back on a roll.'

**Nick Timothy** in the Daily Telegraph:

> 'It is ludicrous to think Britain – alone or in concert with all the militaries of Europe – could or should have fought a new Afghan war alone. First Donald Trump did a deal with the Taliban promising the withdrawal of troops by May this year (2021). Then President Biden declared he had **zero responsibility to Afghanistan,** insisting his sole obligation was to protect America's national self-interest. As his predecessor might have put it: **America first (?)**'

*Simon Tisdall* in the Guardian:

> '*What will it take for Joe Biden to admit he is **disastrously wrong about Afghanistan?** The US leader struck a defiant pose last week. Sounding like a slightly desperate Olympics coach, he told Afghans it was their country. If they want it, they have to fight for it. In American politics-speak, this is called tough love - without the love.*'

Leo McKinstry in the Daily Express:

> '*Over the last 20 years, Britain is estimated to have spent almost **£40 billion in Afghanistan, while 456 of our brave personnel** have lost their lives in the struggle, yet those heroic sacrifices tragically look like they were made in vain.*'

The Sun editorial:

> '*Biden **ignored repeated warnings** then withdrew crucial air support for the Afghan army it has spent billions arming over 20 years. It was an action which borders on the criminal; a total and unnecessary moral failure which left Britain powerless.*'

## TALIBAN PROMISED SECURITY FOR ALL:

The takeover of the sprawling capital city had been years in the making, but was ultimately accomplished in a single day. The Taliban had conquered nearly all provincial hubs in Afghanistan during the week earlier, faced little to no resistance as they entered the city through its major traffic arteries. By evening of 15<sup>th</sup> August 2021, the Taliban were giving TV & Media interviews in the lavish presidential palace, just hours after Ghani had departed Afghanistan.

Next day, the Pentagon was speeding in additional troops to assist with the withdrawal of US personnel after the *American flag was lowered* from their adorned embassy. The footage of Taliban fighters occupying the palace and rolling up the Afghan national flag stood as a defining image of a failed US effort to transform Afghan society at the cost of a trillion dollars and thousands of lives lost. As the Taliban encircled and then entered Kabul on 15<sup>th</sup> [it was Sunday], the US personnel at the embassy in Kabul were being shifted to the airport along with acting US ambassador Ross Wilson, with the American flag.

Asked about comparisons to the US departure from Vietnam in 1975, Secretary of State Blinken said on ABC News:

*'This Week is manifestly not Saigon.'*

Taliban co-founder, Abdul Ghani Baradar, emerged as the undisputed winner of America's longest war, issued a video statement on behalf of the Taliban's political bureau, recorded in Doha in conciliatory tone:

> *"We have reached a victory that wasn't expected - we should show humility in front of Allah. Now it's about how we serve and secure our people and ensure their future to the best of our ability."*
> **The Washington Post** of 16<sup>th</sup> August 2021 is referred.

President Biden's key-colleagues, friends and foes all blasted at this *'chaotic retreat'* following his decision to withdraw the remaining US troops, though not asked for a return to war. Foreign Secretary Blinken took defended the Biden administration's decision at various TV shows, arguing that the Taliban's current offensive would have happened even if US forces remained in Afghanistan; adding that:

> *"If the president had decided to stay, all gloves would've been off, we would've been back at war with the Taliban attacking our forces, the offensive you've seen throughout the country almost certainly would've proceeded."*

Blinken did not directly answer the question of how the US failed to anticipate the speed of the Taliban's takeover; just a week before, the US military had estimated that collapse could take 90 days. Instead, it took 10 days, with provincial capitals falling one after the next.

The Taliban sent squads of 15 armed men each to all government HQs, embassies and diplomatic missions to protect them, and had set up checkpoints along the city's entrances and main streets. On WhatsApp, the group message proclaimed that '....*we are in charge of security for Kabul.*' The messages listed telephone numbers in various areas that citizens could call if they saw problems such as looting or robbery, extortion or irresponsible behaviour on the part of armed individual Taliban. One message said:

> *"The Islamic Emirate assures you that no one should be in panic of feeling fear. Taliban is taking over the city without fighting and no one will be at risk."*

Taliban's political and military opponents pleaded them to refrain from revenge. Former Afghan president Hamid Karzai appeared in an online video and said that:

> "........he hoped that the problems of our country and our capital ... will be solved and that the Taliban will guard the safety of the people's lives and property."

**Vince Cable,** a British MP from Twickenham, while making a speech on Remembrance Sunday said:

> *"Yes, the Taliban have humiliated the west – but more importantly, did our soldiers die in vain. The narrative that the USA and its allies are in terminal decline will have been reinforced by the crisis in Afghanistan.*
>
> *After the UK commitment to a continuing NATO-led force in Afghanistan in 2006, every year mention was made of Britain's dead soldiers in Afghanistan and the many thousands wounded, some of whom also brought their physical injuries and mental scars to my advice surgeries."*
>
> Ref: Daily the '**INDEPENDENT**' dated 16<sup>th</sup> August 2021.

The fact remained that outside of Kabul, apart from minor modernisation, little changed for centuries and life continued to stagnate. *'For someone born in Afghanistan, by Western values he is unfortunate, particularly females but that does not give us the moral or legal Right to interfere by imposing other values'.*

A British Bolger opined: The narrative that the West did some good and that *'millions of women got education'* became a curse ultimately; it proved to be rubbish. Those women would never get to use their education for anything useful; they could be equally cowed and enslaved like ever – wait for a harsh misery to come. He added:

> *"The ugly truth is that 'Great Britain' does what the Americans tell us to do: no more, no less. With this week's instructions – RUN – comes a tragic, unforgivable sense that those who served and died over two decades did so in vain."*

# Scenario 230

## TALIBAN RECAPTURED AFGHANISTAN - 2

### BBC's TWO BASIC QUESTIONS:

After America's humiliating exit, *the BBC* discussed online the same very basic questions that: *Why did the US made (wrong) choice of Afghanistan & why the war lasted so long?*

The same story in short; that after 9/11 of 2001, the US asked Afghanistan to hand over Osama Bin Laden to them – but the then rulers, the Taliban, refused so the US intervened militarily, quickly removing the Taliban from government and vowed to support democracy and eliminate the terrorist threat. The militants slipped away and later re-grouped – then raised their guns to fight back.

NATO allies had joined the US and a new Afghan government was installed in Kabul in place of the Taliban in December 2001. Deadly Taliban attacks continued at their pace. President Obama's *'troop surge'* in 2009 helped push back the Taliban but it was not for a long term. Year 2014 was the bloodiest year since 2001; NATO's international forces ended their combat mission, leaving responsibility for security to the Afghan army. That gave the Taliban momentum and they seized some territory also.

Five years later, the US started peace talks with the Taliban – but keeping the puppet Afghan government away; they were not called to the meeting table till the withdrawal agreement of 29th February 2020 was signed in Doha, Qatar. However, the US-Taliban deal could not stop the Taliban attacks - they switched their focus from the US & NATO bases to Afghan army, Afghan security forces and civilians, and resolved for targeted assassinations – which lasted till the doom-day of mid August 2021.

Other figures closely associated with the American-backed government floated their recorded videos congratulating the Taliban on their victory. High Council for National Reconciliation Chair Abdullah Abdullah announced the formation of a new *'coordination council'* with Karzai and former warlord politician Gulbuddin Hekmatyar to deal directly with the Taliban in Kabul. Its purpose was to prevent chaos and to better manage the affairs related to peace and the peaceful governance. The Taliban didn't respond to the group. The US officials kept their focus on the evacuation and were seen *'not interested in the Afghan-to-Afghan talks'*.

The news of Taliban's quick advance to Kabul spread when helicopters were seen landing at the US Embassy early Sunday [15th August 2021] and armoured diplomatic vehicles were seen leaving the compound. Diplomats scrambled to destroy sensitive documents and smokes seen from some embassy's premises.

The Pentagon deployed another 1,000 troops to Afghanistan from a brigade combat team with the 82nd Airborne Division resulting in a total of 6,000 US troops on ground at Kabul International Airport which had already taken over air traffic control at the airport. Even then the US government was struggling to get real-time information. There was a big chaos at the Kabul airport and around – details are gives elsewhere on these pages.

Bagram and Sorobi districts in Kabul province also surrendered without shots being fired; the militants had made *'political deals'* with Afghan government officials and the local leaders – like in Mazar e Sharif and Jalalabad earlier. On the same day morning [15th Aug] Afghan forces handed over Bagram air base — once the US military's high-ranking important airfield in the country — to the Taliban; the air base was then holding 5,000 inmates in the prison – which were all released at once. Other prisons were also taken over by Taliban immediately and most inmates released.

*Biden's statement* **'washing hands of Afghanistan is one of the most shameful moment in US history':** *Left and right-wing media got united in condemnation of 'America's chaotic retreat' and 'betrayal' of Afghan people; some glimpses are detailed on other pages where appropriate.*

As the Taliban entered Kabul – countries like Germany, Denmark and Norway said they would suspend operations. The British ambassador was scheduled to be airlifted the next day evening. Iranian officials said its embassy in Kabul would be evacuated by next day [Monday]. Other governments, including Russia and Turkey, said their missions would continue to operate; some neighbours like UAE & Pakistan helped evacuation process.

On the very next day of Taliban's take over, the world media started approaching friends and foes of Afghanistan for its future plans. Responses from 3 neighbouring countries were hereunder.

**PAKISTAN:** In Pakistan – long accused of aiding the Afghan Taliban – PM Imran Khan said:

> "....the Taliban had broken the chains of mental slavery in Afghanistan.......the Taliban have freed their country from superpowers".

PM Khan was not alone in portraying the Taliban's victory as a triumph. Influential religious clerics and senior Pakistan military generals also celebrated publicly. Siraj ul Haq, the chief of Pakistan's *Jamaat-e-Islami* [JI], an Islamic political party, said in a speech:

> '...it was a historic win over a superpower and would create an exemplary Islamic government in Afghanistan'.

Pakistan had pushed for peace during the Doha negotiations [2019-20], but many believed the main priority for Pakistan remained keeping the Taliban onside. However, it could be a two edge-sword; the strength of the Taliban's resurgence could further embolden already powerful radical Islamist groups in Pakistan and thus make it more vulnerable.

As the Taliban swept across Afghanistan, some Pakistanis saw it as a reason to celebrate. Islamist organizations in a number of Pakistani cities doled out sweets to locals. On social media, some people crowed over the failure of the US war effort and nation-building project next door. Raoof Hasan, Special Assistant to Pakistan's PM, mocking the assessments of Western experts on South Asia, tweeted:

> "Afghanistan witnessed a virtually smooth shifting of power from the corrupt Ghani government to the Taliban. The contraption that the US had pieced together for Afghanistan has crumbled like the proverbial house of cards."

Pakistani PM Khan's government, however, refrained from recognizing the new Taliban's government in Kabul. PM Khan was a vocal opponent of the American **'WAR ON TERROR'** in the region and blamed it for stoking a parallel Pakistani Taliban insurgency, then stressed the importance of all sides working to secure an inclusive political solution. He had truly cited Pakistan as a victim of cycles of regional unrest and conflict - by the interventions of the US especially.

Pakistan's National Security Adviser Moeed Yusuf explained it more vividly in an interview [August 2021]:

> *"We under no circumstances are prepared to see protracted instability that in the past has caused spill-over into Pakistan. We suffered all of these 40 years."*

Referring to **Ishaan Tharoor**'s allegations dated 18th August 2021 at 'Today's World View' newsletter:

> *"For years, the Western media and the US bemoaned the support afforded to the Afghan Taliban by Pakistan's military establishment and through its Inter-Services Intelligence [ISI]"*

But if it was so, none of the media agency or the US State department ever bothered to go deep into the basic rout-cause that US had continuously backed Afghan Presidents KARZAI & GHANI in association with Indian government and that:

- *India's RAW & TTP had launched about 16,000 terrorist attacks on Pakistani soils after 2005.*

- *Especially hit Pakistan's Tribal areas and Balochistan killing more than 80,000 soldiers and civilians.*

- *.....Caused over $150 billion loss in Pakistan's economy.*

- *.....Also drove 3.5 million of Pakistani citizens away from their homes.*

The Western media claimed that the Taliban's long-running insurgency and its rapid takeover of Afghanistan were linked to Pakistan – **but who created Al-Qaeda and Taliban – it was the US who created them,** backed them with cash finance and military equipment during 1970-80s to oppose the Soviet intervention in Afghanistan; see the details in preceding chapters of this book.

For its allies in the Pakistani establishment, the Taliban's appeal was both political and strategic, thus Pakistan served as a major US ally during and after the 2001's invasion of Afghanistan – but the US betrayed.

The situation turned around at 180 angles when *the US started preferring India, sending them huge funding* in the name of training of Afghan

Security Forces there; total bill paid: nearly $88bn. As a result, India planted those trained Afghani groups at the Pak-Afghan border to attack Pakistani territories labelling them as Pakistani Taliban [TTP] killing about ....[*see the above lines again for details*].

With so enhanced loss of military and civilian lives, especially with the notorious pinching instructions of **DO MORE; DO MORE,** Pakistan had to react in its own way – so the world has seen the end of the LONGEST US WAR with so humiliating defeat.

> **LESSON:** *in wars, powerful partners should deal with the allies sincerely and whole-heartedly. The basic Islamic philosophy is 'Friend of your friend is friend AND the friend of your enemy is Enemy' – one can analyse these words in recent past of the troika of the US – Pakistan – India.*

## ISI's GEN HAMID GUL PREDICTION:

Now recall famous words of late Pakistani Gen Hamid Gul, known as the Godfather of Pakistani geo-strategic policies, televised in 2014 – so why crying that **the ISI defeated the Soviet Union in Afghanistan with the help of America – and then the ISI, with the help of America, defeated America.**

It's no secret that under President Trump's pressure, Pakistan had released Abdul Ghani Baradar — the political key-figure of the Taliban - from prison in 2018 so he could participate in peace negotiations held in Doha, the Qatari capital. In June [2018]'s **Washington Post:** PM Khan had argued that he and his government did the *'real diplomatic heavy lifting'* to bring the Afghan Taliban to the negotiating table and urged the US and Afghan governments to *'show more flexibility'* in the talks.

In Pakistan, new influx of Afghan refugees was [and still is] endangered on top of the more than 3 million it has hosted since the waning days of the Cold War. The Taliban takeover does not dim the threat of anti-Islamabad militancy, and it could also encourage Islamist extremist movements and ethnic *Pashtun* separatists operating within Pakistan. Meanwhile, Western frustrations with the Pakistani connection to the Afghan Taliban could only intensify in future.

These developments would probably take Pakistan further away in all developmental fields, perpetuating dysfunction at home and locking it into a foreign policy defined by more dependence on China – but the people were happy to keep the US away calling it treacherous and deceitful.

**RUSSIA:** Russia reacted to the Taliban's return to power with cool real politik. Zamir Kabulov, Russia's presidential envoy to Afghanistan, said on state television on 16th August 2021 that:

> *"If we compare the negotiability of the colleagues and the partners, I have long since decided that the Taliban is much more able to reach agreements than the puppet government in Kabul."*

Russia has long criticised the US intervention in Afghanistan. In February 1989, the Soviet Union evacuated its troops while crossing over the Friendship Bridge into Uzbekistan. This August [2021], US-allied warlords and their fighters were forced to flee over the same bridge.

In Afghanistan, the Russia's policy went different than in Syria and Iraq; Russia was seen ready to engage if the Taliban could ensure security for the diplomatis community and prevent militants from launching assaults against its neighbours such as Uzbekistan and Tajikistan.

The Russian envoy to Afghanistan, even hinted the possibility that Russia would recognise the Taliban government – but depending upon the behaviour of the new rulers. However, the Taliban promptly took the Russian embassy under protection, and its ambassador, Dmitry Zhirnov, told about the Taliban's promise that *'not a single hair will fall of Russian diplomats'*.

**CHINA:** Since long China, no doubt, was feeling uneasy about the US military engagement in Afghanistan. Then astonishingly, it also blamed the US for its *'irresponsible withdrawal'* from Afghanistan. In recent times, the continued presence of the US in Afghanistan was seen as a lesser of two evils but Beijing adopted a careful line in its policy towards the new Taliban regime. Chinese media called Afghanistan a *'graveyard of empires'* and Beijing never opted to be mired in this Great Game. China's foreign ministry spokeswoman said:

> *'.... [we're] ready to develop good-neighbourly, friendly and cooperative relations with Afghanistan but Afghanistan would not serve as a staging ground for acts detrimental to China'.*

China would, however, plan to participate in the post-war reconstruction and provide investments etc. On 16th August 2021; China's spokesperson, Hua Chunying, reiterated that:

*"Beijing welcome the Taliban's promise that they will allow no force to use the Afghan territory to engage in acts detrimental to China and its expression of hope that China will be more involved in Afghanistan's peace and reconciliation process and play a bigger role in future reconstruction and economic development".*

For many years, China remained concerned about its far-west Xinjiang Uyghur region while demanding the Taliban refrain from hosting any *Uyghur groups* on their territory.

Referring to **Simon Jenkins** in **the Guardian** dated 16<u>th</u> August 2021:

*"**The fall of Kabul** was inevitable. It marks the end of a post-imperial western fantasy. Yet the west's reaction beggars belief. Call it a catastrophe, a humiliation, a calamitous mistake, if it sounds good. All retreats from empire are messy. This one took 20 years, but the end was at least swift.*

*The US had no need to invade Afghanistan. **The country was never a 'terrorist state'**.... It was not at war with the US; indeed the US had aided its rise to power...... The Taliban had hosted Osama bin Laden in his mountain lair through his friendship with the Taliban leader, Mullah Omar.....(but not as terrorist entity)"*

After the 2001 invasion, the US Defence Secretary Donald Rumsfeld demanded that George Bush should *'punish and get out'* but neither President Bush nor UK's PM Tony Blair listened. For reasons never fully explained, Blair declared a **'doctrine of international community'** and pleaded for Britain to be in the first bombing run over Kabul.

In 2006, British army of 3,400 volunteered to suppress resurgent Taliban rebels in *Helmand*, a southern province of Afghanistan. Secretary John Reid held that only remnants of the Taliban remained there and that *'not a shot needed firing'*. Gen David Richards said it would be *'just another Malaya'* – but seven years later, **British troops had to leave defeated and wounded;** the local *Pashtuns* are masters at humiliating outside powers.

*[**The then PM Tony Blair and his cabinet could have known their history that the same Pashtuns had slaughtered nearly 17,000 British men, women, and children when they were evacuating Kabul ending the First Afghan War 1839-42 and the British Empire was defeated; had to leave the whole Afghanistan.**]*

Twenty years of dependency on lavish western taxpayers means that soldiers, interpreters, journalists, academics and aid workers were seeing friends threatened and killed. Years of assistance and training went in vain. The US wasted its trillions dollars [see details in separate chapter] and the Britain alone washed out its £37bn just to feel a fresh taste of imperialism. *'How many times must it be drummed into British heads that the British Empire is over?'* **Simon Jenkins** is referred again.

*'To make the world better....'* is an old slogan now; soldiers need not to die for it, 454 British soldiers and civilians lost their lives in Afghanistan. *'The world is not threatening Britain. Terrorism does not need state sponsors, nor will it be ended by state conquest'*, held *Simon Jenkins*, referred above, in very sincere tone.

## WAR OF BOMBS & BULLETS IS OVER:

**On 18<sup>th</sup> August 2021;** a lengthy text message became viral in the whole world from an unknown destination – interesting it was; let us share:

**"War of Bombs & Bullets is OVER; A War of Brains is Starting -**

- America has miscalculated the biggest step it took 19 years ago; the step of thinking that Afghanistan is a walk in the park to take over – pity on their knowledge.

- And it again miscalculated its withdrawal. If anyone thinks that America mistakenly has withdrawn from Afghanistan is mistaken as well – pity on their wisdom.

- America has three SELF CREATED enemies at this time: China, Iran and China's ally - Pakistan.

- America wanted a civil war to ensue in Afghanistan that will spill over into Pakistan, destabilise Chinese western border and put Iran at alert with *Sunni Taliban* taking over its western borders.

- Civil war did not start; and that made the American plans upside down – pity on their rogue planning.

- The *Shia* dominated Northern Areas [of Afghanistan] and its leaders supported Taliban and made peace with them. That created havoc for the Americans and victory for Iran. No threat at its eastern borders.

- China pre-emptively invited and started a dialogue with the Taliban and peacefully chalked out the future; NO rifts there either.

- Pakistan fenced off its border months earlier with Afghanistan and absolutely stayed away from its internal matters thus there was no conflict between the Taliban and Pakistan – thus NO Civil War.

- The Indian investment [in Afghanistan] of billions of dollars fizzled out; and the Indians fooled the US that they had a stronghold in Afghanistan. India even lost its bet in post American withdrawal from Afghanistan; they couldn't handle the situation – all their narratives went to the dogs as well.

- Americans are angry and annoyed with the Indians for misleading them - more than they are with the Afghans.

- Afghan government was a puppet to begin with and the Americans knew it because they are the ones who IMPOSED them on the Afghan people.

## NOW AFTER...?

- Now after America losing India falling on its face,...the entire war is going to be fought in the news and with narratives.

- **No bombs, No bullets, No bunkers. A war of brains......**

- India will try to delude the world with wrong narratives. They are a wounded Jackal - And a wounded jackal is more DESPERATE.

- Pakistan has won. Pakistan is Stronger than before. Pakistan is on a more solid diplomatic ground than it has been in the past 19 years of this war.

- The world should be ready for a peaceful region where China, Pakistan, Iran and access to Central Asia through Afghanistan will define a new Chapter in the future of CPEC. CPEC only had one obstacle and that was unhindered access to Central Asian countries, it is here now. And it being here is the death of INDIA. A stronger region with Pakistan leading in it is a nightmare for India.

But get ready to hear the screams of BLA, PTM and all other Afghan based Indian supported rogue elements. They will be dying along with Afghan puppet regime.

GOOD DAYS ARE HERE – and AHEAD

Historians of Afghan-US relations held that the Taliban and al-Qaeda were inseparable; their joint training sessions were known to all. Moreover; the Taliban were not a centralised and unified force; some leaders wanted to lead a peaceful life then but hardliners were reluctant to break links with al-Qaeda and other affiliated factions. There was a regional branch of the **Islamic State** group - ISKP [*Khorasan*] – used to oppose the Taliban regime but how would they behave in changed scenario – was not clear.

Like al-Qaeda, ISKP was also degraded by the US and NATO; they were able to re-group again during the post-withdrawal period. Its fighter numbers were estimated as less than 2000 but it would try to gain footholds in Kazakhstan, Kyrgyzstan and parts of Tajikistan, which could be a serious regional concern in the near future.

Let us re-visit the issue once more.

Many factors were responsible for this catastrophe, an unexpected event called fall of Kabul. Firstly; the melting of the Afghan National Security Forces [ANSF], which were well-armed as well as well-trained by the Americans themselves and having five times numerical superiority over the Taliban militia, allowed the latter a free passage across the various cities and district HQs.

Secondly; the *performance of the US intelligence remained zero* since six months at least; they fell flat, showing how detached, lazy and casual the US administration remained about the ground situation in Afghanistan. The US lost interest in Afghan affairs after the Biden Administration announced the withdrawal plan in April 2021.

The world intelligentsia failed to comprehend the rapidity of how a 20-year old multinational Afghan project led by the world's sole superpower could be wound up in few weeks – and that too forced by a militia of little more than 60,000. It would take time the world feel about the deeper implications and envisage the whole spectrum of consequences of this episode.

Among all the stakeholders, no one got affected by the disaster as profoundly as the Afghan people. The images and video clips of the then prevailing chaos and anarchy in the streets, roads, bus stops, and Kabul Airport were heartbreaking. These scenes of human helplessness and pessimism will continue to shame the world for failing the people of Afghanistan.

Referring to <u>Amanat Chaudhry</u>'s essay titled *'The fall of Kabul and beyond'* in daily 'theNews.com.pk' dated <u>19<sup>th</sup> August 2021</u>:

> *"When the history books get written, the myopic and lopsided policies pursued by the Biden Administration will characterize the legacy of the 'experienced' president for all the wrong reasons. He will not be able to shrug off the questions about the Americans leaving the people of Afghanistan to fend off for themselves.*
>
> *Worthy of equal blame is the now-deposed Ghani administration that kowtowed to its foreign masters and built up an empire of corruption, incompetence, and unpleasantness, practically alienating the Afghan people....."*

The Taliban takeover was celebrated by some people in Pakistan at full bloom – forgetting that the Taliban philosophy and democracy lie at two opposite polls – one have to make one choice.

With Kabul overtaken by the Taliban, all the previous peace deals including the Doha Agreement and regional efforts as well as the expectation from the Taliban to keep them dissociated from so-called terror outfits like Al-Qaeda had practically gone dead. That was why the Taliban-run Afghanistan needed international legitimacy and financial assistance to be viable; as noted by Mullah Baradar: *'....the Taliban's test has just begun'*.

## BLAST AT KABUL AIRPORT – 13 KILLED:

On 27<sup>th</sup> August 2021; thirteen [13] US service members and at least 60 Afghans were killed and 140 wounded in two bombing attacks outside Kabul's airport. The deadly blasts came as the US and other countries raced to complete a massive evacuation of their citizens following the Taliban takeover of Afghanistan. Eighteen US service members were also injured.

ISIS in Khorasan, known as ISIS-K, claimed that an ISIS militant carried out the suicide attack and President Biden immediately ordered US military commanders *"to develop operational plans to strike ISIS-K assets, leadership and facilities."*

US officials had warned over the past week that a threat of a terror attack at the airport was becoming more acute; the US diplomats in Kabul warned American citizens to immediately leave several gates of the airport, citing security threats. The risk of potential suicide attacks by ISIS-K had already led the US to establish alternative routes to Kabul airport before the evacuation operation started.

Thousands of Afghans gathered, in hopes of being evacuated, at the airport's gates after Taliban's take over of Kabul on 15<sup>th</sup> August 2021. The social media, after the explosions, showed chaotic scenes of crowds of people trying to help the wounded amid bodies on the ground. Pentagon held that one of the explosions happened at the airport's Abbey Gate and the other at or near the Baron Hotel, a short distance from Abbey Gate.

Abbey Gate is the main entry point to the airport and primary security there was being provided by US Marines. The area around that gate had been used for holding refugees after they passed through the Taliban check points outside the airport, and before they were allowed to go to airport.

Baron Hotel was used by British soldiers and other allies as an evacuation handling centre to process evacuees, before moving them up to the Abbey Gate. Over 95,700 people were evacuated since 15<sup>th</sup> August and over 101,300 since the end of July. Even after the attack, scores of people continued to gather at the airport - ahead of US' 31<sup>st</sup> August 2021 deadline for the final exit from a 20-year war ridden Afghanistan.

Several European countries, including Belgium, Denmark, Netherlands, Poland, New Zealand and Canada completed their evacuation missions till then. The UK continued its evacuation operation despite attack; 13,146 people -- including embassy staff, British nationals, those eligible under the Afghan Relocation and Assistance Policy program and a number of nationals from partner nations -- were evacuated by the UK.

Abdullah Abdullah, the Chairman of Afghanistan's Reconciliation Committee under the previous government condemned the said attacks; the Taliban had taken away security from the former Afghan President Hamid Karzai and Abdullah Abdullah.

**On 31<sup>st</sup> August 2021;** the Taliban practically took over the whole country except a negligible resistance in Panjsher valley but the resistance could not last more than 4 days. All of the Afghanistan was under Taliban control. It marked the end of an era: America's longest but humiliating war was over; America suffered multiple losses. It happened fast, stunning the world and leaving many in the country racing to find an exit. But even among those surprised by the way the end played out, many knew the war was destined to end in bad tone. See further:

> "......the seeds of disaster were planted back at the war's very beginning. Soon after the US landed in Afghanistan after the 9/11 attacks, the successive US governments struggled to answer exactly why the military was there. In the very beginning, the goal was relatively clear: to capture the perpetrator of the attacks, OBL, but almost immediately, the goals went blurred rather got scratched."
>
> [*Rajaa Elidrissi's* essay of 1<sup>st</sup> September 2021
> at **vox.com** is referred]

On the same day of **31<sup>st</sup> August 2021**; EU countries vowed to dole out an unspecified amount of funds to significantly beef up financial support for Afghanistan's neighbors to manage the refugee crisis at their borders. But they also pushed back discussions on the bloc's own role in accepting Afghani asylum seekers, citing various reasons.

In 5-hours long meeting in Brussels, EU interior ministers adopted a text that pledged financial support to relevant international organizations and neighboring countries of Afghanistan to reinforce their capacities to provide protection and sustainable livelihood for Afghan refugees. Exactly how much money they offered to Pakistan and Iran; no one divulged.

This financial support was in fact a broader strategy for keeping Afghan migrants away from EU countries amid fears of another surge. The Interior Ministers of the EU countries signed a statement saying:

> "Based on lessons learned, the EU and its member states stand determined to act jointly to prevent the recurrence of uncontrolled large-scale illegal migration movements faced in the past, by preparing a coordinated and orderly response - incentives to illegal migration should be avoided."

## LAST AMERICAN SOLDIER LEAVES KABUL:

On **31<sup>st</sup> August 2021**; the US Army shared an image, taken with night-vision optics, of the last US soldier to step aboard the final evacuation flight out of Kabul — Maj Gen Chris Donahue, Commander of the 82nd Airborne Division was the person in focus.

America's longest war took the lives of 2,400 plus US troops and an estimated 240,000 Afghans, and costing them more than $2 trillion: www.dawn.com/news/1643653 dated 31st August 2021 is referred.

Celebratory gunfire echoed across Kabul as Taliban fighters took control of the airport before dawn on 1ˢᵗ September 2021 following the withdrawal of the last US troops, ending 20 years of war that left the group stronger than it was in 2001. Shaky video footage distributed by the Taliban showed fighters entering the airport after the last US troops took off a minute before midnight, marking the end of a hasty and humiliating exit for Washington and its NATO allies. Taliban Qari Yusuf said at Al-Jazeera TV:

> *"The last US soldier has left Kabul airport and our country gained complete independence."*

Although the US succeeded [in 2001] in driving out the Taliban from power and stopped Afghanistan being used as a base by Al Qaeda, it ended with the Taliban group controlling more of the country than they ever did during their previous rule from 1996 to 2001. Those years are still known for the Taliban's strict interpretation of *Shariah*, and the world was aspiring to see whether the Taliban could form a more moderate and inclusive government in the months ahead.

In 2021; thousands of Afghans fled fearing Taliban reprisals. A massive but chaotic airlift by the US and its allies over the two weeks succeeded in evacuating more than 123,000 people from Kabul, but tens of thousands who helped Western states during the war were left behind. About 100 to 200 Americans wanted to leave but were unable to get on flights.

**Gen Frank McKenzie,** commander of the US Central Command, told a Pentagon briefing that the Chief US diplomat in Afghanistan, Ross Wilson, was out on the last C-17 flight. Gen McKenzie told reporters:

> *"There's a lot of heartbreak associated with this departure. We did not get everybody out that we wanted to get them out. But I think if we'd stayed another 10 days, we wouldn't have gotten everybody out of that country."*

As the US troops departed, they destroyed more than 70 aircrafts, dozens of armoured vehicles and disabled air defenses that had thwarted an attempted Islamic State rocket attack on the eve of the last US departure.

President Joe Biden, in a statement, defended his decision to stick to the given deadline for withdrawing US forces. He said:

*"The world would hold the Taliban to their commitment to allow safe passage for those who want to leave Afghanistan.*

*Now, our 20-year military presence in Afghanistan has ended."*

Biden thanked the US military for carrying out the dangerous evacuation. He added that the US long ago achieved the objectives it set in ousting the Taliban in 2001 for harbouring Al Qaeda militants who masterminded the 11th Sept 2001 attacks on America – however, he had to entertain heavy criticism from Republicans and some of his fellow Democrats for his handling of Afghanistan since collapse of the US-backed government.

Senator Ben Sasse, a Republican member of the Senate Intelligence Committee, called the **US withdrawal a national disgrace** that was the direct result of Biden's misadventure, cowardice and incompetence. However, one Democratic Senator Sheldon Whitehouse tweeted:

*"Bravo to our diplomats, military, and intelligence agencies. An airlift of 120,000 people in that dangerous and tumultuous situation is something no one else could do."*

Blinken said the US was prepared to work with the new Taliban govt if reprisals against opponents in the country would not be the Taliban's policy. He said:

*"The Taliban seek international legitimacy and support. Our position is any legitimacy and support will have to be earned. The Taliban must revive a war-shattered economy without being able to count on the billions of dollars in foreign aid that flowed to the previous ruling elite and fed systemic corruption."*

The population outside the cities was facing what the UN officials called an acute *catastrophic humanitarian situation* worsened by a severe drought. One local opinion appeared:

*"Our culture has become toxic; we see Russian and American influence everywhere, even in the food we eat. That is something people should realize and make necessary changes. This will take time but will happen."*

**On 2nd September 2021**; after the Taliban got firm footing in Kabul, there was a sudden surge at the Spin Boldak - Chaman land border crossing, which lead to the deadly stampede killing one person after the unprecedented number of people started fleeing from war-torn Afghanistan to Pakistan. Pakistan had closed its border due to excessive influx of unwanted Afghan refugees from Taliban terror. A 64-year-old man from Afghanistan named Safi Ullah died in the incident as confirmed by his son Shahid Ullah to the CNN reporter - *"Me and my father were trying to cross the border with the rest of our family, I lost my father in the stampede, later we found him dead."*

On 29th September 2021; a top US General conceded openly that the US *'lost the 20-year war in Afghanistan'*. **Gen Mark Milley,** Chairman of the US Joint Chiefs of Staff, told the House Armed Services Committee that:

> *"It is clear; it is obvious to all of us, that the war in Afghanistan did not end on the terms we wanted, with the Taliban in power in Kabul. The war was a strategic failure; it wasn't lost in the last 20 days or even 20 months. There's a cumulative effect to a series of strategic decisions that go way back; ..... We accomplished our strategic task of protecting America against Al-Qaeda, but certainly the end state is a whole lot different than what we wanted."*

**Gen Milley** was correct to mention that a lot of lessons were learned here. He listed a number of factors responsible for the US defeat going back to a missed opportunity to capture or kill Al-Qaeda leader Osama bin Laden [OBL] at *Tora Bora* soon after the October 2001 US invasion. In 2003, the US troops should not have been shifted to Iraq from Afghanistan. President Biden, in April [2021], ordered a complete pullout of US forces from Afghanistan by 31st August because an accord had already been reached with the Taliban by former president Donald Trump – called the Doha Agreement of 29th February 2020.

**Gen Milley & Gen Kenneth McKenzie,** Commander of US Central Command, had personally recommended that some 2,500 troops should remain on ground in Afghanistan but Biden had received *'split advice'* about what to do then. Ultimately, it was up to the commander-in-chief to make a decision so he announced *that it was time to end a 20-year war.*

## TALIBAN's ARMED PARADE IN KABUL:

The new Taliban ruling team held a military parade in Kabul on Sunday, the 14th November 2021, using captured American armoured vehicles and Russian helicopters in a display that showed their ongoing transformation from an insurgent force to a regular standing army.

Referring to daily 'DAWN' dated 18th November 2021:

> *"The Taliban operated as insurgent fighters for two decades but have used the large stock of weapons and equipment left behind when the former Western-backed government collapsed in August to overhaul their forces.*
>
> *The parade was linked to the graduation of 250 freshly trained soldiers of Afghan army."*

The Taliban's Defence Ministry spokesman Enayatullah Khwarazmi told that the exercise involved dozens of US-made armoured security vehicles driving slowly up and down a major Kabul road with MI-17 helicopters patrolling overhead. Many soldiers carried US made-M4 assault rifles. Most of the weapons and equipment the Taliban forces were carrying and using were those supplied by Washington to the American-backed Ghani's government in Kabul in a bid to construct an Afghan National Force capable of fighting the Taliban – but that day never appeared.

Those forces melted away with the fleeing of Afghan President Ghani from Afghanistan — leaving the Taliban to take over major military assets. Taliban officials also told that pilots, mechanics and other specialists from the former Afghan National Army would be integrated into a new force, which had already started wearing conventional military uniforms in place of the traditional Afghan dress normally worn by their fighters.

> *[According to a report of late 2020 by the Special Inspector General for Afghanistan Reconstruction [SIGAR], the US government transferred to the Afghan government more than $28 billion worth of defence articles and services, including weapons, ammunition, vehicles, night-vision devices, aircraft, and surveillance systems, from 2002 to 2017.]*

Some of the aircraft were flown into neighbouring Central Asian Countries by fleeing Afghan forces; the Taliban were on the way to get them back.

# Scenario 231

## THE NEW TALIBAN CABINET

On 7<sup>th</sup> September 2021; the Taliban announced their interim cabinet comprising of 33 members with Mohammad Hasan Akhund at the head and the groups co-founder Abdul Ghani Baradar in his deputy's role; other political, tribal and ethnic groups were not given place in the governing list.

[.... **Just Hold-On:**
On **24<sup>th</sup> August 2021;** even before the formal cabinet was announced on 7<sup>th</sup> September 2021 it was a surprise for the whole world when a former Guantanamo detainee named **Abdul Qayyum Zakir** was appointed as Afghanistan's acting Deputy Defence Minister by the Taliban high council; it was first reported by **daily Al Jazeera** next day. Pakistan's PM Imran Khan had, a week earlier, endorsed the Taliban's seizure of power in Afghanistan for breaking the *'shackles of slavery.'*

A legendary battlefield commander, Zakir was seen by the Western agencies, as an ally of the leaders of the *Haqqani* network, a Taliban sub-set. He had aligned reportedly with *Haqqani* leaders in opposing the Taliban major leadership's suggestion for peace talks with the Afghani President Ghani and his government. His motto remained waging *jihad* until victory was won by the Taliban or to become martyrs.

Zakir was well known to Pakistan's ISI, who had arranged for his quick release from custody in Quetta [Pakistan] after being arrested in 2010. Thereafter, 38-years-old Zakir, directed Taliban military operations largely in *Helmand* province, targeting NATO soldiers mostly as per Western security officials version.

Zakir's pick as Deputy Defence Minister was cited as another example of how the Taliban's seizure of power in Afghanistan accounted for Pakistan a geopolitical victory. Pakistan's biggest gain was that India ultimately lost its influence in Afghanistan.]

Nearly all of the key posts announced by the Taliban's spokesman, from the prime minister, deputy prime minister, foreign minister etc, were handed to senior Taliban clerics or leaders of all the Taliban factions. However, it was not immediately apparent whether members of the Tajik, Hazara and Uzbek communities would also be part of the ruling structure later.

Here are some facts about the main appointments.

*Mohammad Hasan Akhund, acting Prime Minister: Akhund has been the longtime head of Taliban's powerful decision-making body, Rahbari Shura, or leadership council. He was first the foreign minister and then deputy prime minister during the Taliban's last rule from 1996-2001. Like many others in the Taliban leadership, Akhund derives his prestige from his proximity to the movement's first leader. A UN report described him as a 'close associate and political adviser' to Mulla Omar.*

Akhund is highly respected within the movement, especially by its supreme leader Haibatullah Akhundzada. Akhund is believed to be more of a political than a religious figure, with his control over the leadership council also giving him a say in military affairs.

*Abdul Ghani Baradar, acting Deputy PM; Baradar was once a close friend of Mullah Omar; served as deputy defence minister during the Taliban's last rule over Afghanistan. Following fall of the Taliban government in 2001, Baradar served as a senior military commander responsible for attacks on coalition forces. He was arrested and imprisoned in Pakistan in 2010. After his release in 2018, he headed the Taliban's political office in Doha, becoming one of the most prominent figures in peace talks with America.*

*Amir Khan Muttaqi, acting Foreign Minister: Originally from Paktia but then acquired residential status from Helmand. Muttaqi served as minister of Culture & Information during the previous Taliban government, as well as minister of Education. Muttaqi was later sent to Qatar and was appointed a member of the Peace Commission and Negotiation team that held talks with the US.*

Neither militant commander nor religious leader, Muttaqi is the Chair of the Invitation and Guidance Commission, which during the insurgency had led efforts to get government officials and other key figures to defect. In statements and speeches while fighting raged for control of the country, he projected a moderate voice, calling on forces holed up in provincial capitals to talk to the Taliban to avoid fighting in urban areas.

During the days after the fall of Kabul in August 2021, Muttaqi played a similar role with the lone holdout province of Panjshir, calling for a peaceful settlement to hostilities.

> *Mullah Yaqoob, acting Defence Minister: Son of the Taliban's founder Mullah Omar, Yaqoob had originally sought to succeed his father in 2015. He stormed out of the council meeting that appointed his father's successor, Mullah Akhtar Mansour, but was eventually reconciled.*

Still in his early 30s and without the long combat experience of the Taliban's main battlefield commanders, he commands the loyalty of Taliban group in Kandahar because of the prestige of his father's name. He was named as overall head of the Taliban military commission last year, overseeing all military operations in Afghanistan and was one of the three deputy leaders, along with Baradar and Sirajuddin Haqqani.

Still considered relatively moderate by some Western analysts; Taliban commanders hold he was among the key-leaders controlling military campaigns in cities before the fall of Kabul.

> *Sirajuddin Haqqani, acting Interior Minister: Head of the influential Haqqani network, Sirajuddin Haqqani succeeded as its leader following the death of his father, Jalaluddin Haqqani, in 2018 and held respect from his tribe.*

**Initially backed by the US as one of the most effective anti-Soviet militia** in the 1980s; his semi-autonomous group was blamed for some of the deadliest attacks on coalition forces. Later he was equally disliked by the US but Taliban continued to own and back the Haqqani group. Haqqani group has been based in the lawless frontier areas between Afghanistan and Pakistan.

> *Zabihullah Mujahid, acting Deputy Information Minister: The long-time spokesman for the Taliban, Mujahid has for more than a decade been the key conduit for information on the group's activities, regularly posting details of suicide attacks through his media accounts. No photo of him existed until he gave his first press conference following the fall of Kabul in August 2021, and for years American military intelligence believed Mujahid was a persona for several individuals running the*

*group's media operations – he has appeared in live media as the best spokesman on behalf of the Taliban government.*

The key question confronting the Taliban was that of international recognition; though the Taliban said *'...they want strong and healthy relations'* with other states but no country on the globe recognized their government till ending the year 2021 at least.

**On 7th September 2021;** Afghan women convened an anti-Pakistan protest rally, near the Pakistan embassy in Kabul. The Taliban fired shots into the air to disperse the crowds; banning any demonstrations that didn't have official approval for both the gathering itself and for any slogans that might be used. It was the first decree issued by Taliban's new interior ministry, [*led by Sirajuddin Haqqani; allegedly wanted by the US on terrorism charges*]. The Taliban warned opponents that *'they must secure permission before any protests or face severe legal consequences'*.

On one pretext or the other, the protests and demonstrations started with the formal announcement of the interim Taliban's government in Afghanistan; in Herat, two people at the demonstration site were shot dead. In another indication of questionable situation for human rights, another senior Taliban figure said **on 8th September 2021** that Afghan women, including the country's women's cricket team, will be banned from playing / sports etc till a formal decision of the *SHURA* appears.

However, the Taliban needed to assure the world that things would be different this time around as compared to their previous stint; most reservations were regarding the fundamental as well as women's rights. Secondly, most countries were looking for their pledge to take action against foreign terrorists based on Afghan soil. In an interview with the **Australian broadcaster SBS,** the deputy head of the Taliban's Cultural Commission, Ahmadullah Wasiq, said:

> *"I don't think women will be allowed to play cricket because it is not necessary that women should play cricket. In cricket, they might face a situation where their face and body will not be covered. Islam does not allow women to be seen like this.*
>
> *It is the media era, and there will be photos and videos, and then people watch it. Islam and the Islamic Emirate [Afghanistan] do not allow women to play cricket or play the kind of sports where they get exposed."*

[Daily **the Guardian** dated <u>8th September 2021</u> is referred]

## US WANTED 'INCLUSIVE' CABINET:

The Taliban was cold to the US suggestion to include *'old guards'* in the **'inclusive government'** arguing that ethnic minorities were duly represented in its Cabinet announced a month earlier and that women would be added later.

On 8th October 2021; Suhail Shaheen, ambassador-designate to the UN, told **Al Jazeera** in an exclusive interview that:

> *'The international community must respect the wishes of the Afghan people....Our [Taliban's] Islamic emirate is ready for inclusively but not selectivity.'*

On 8-9th October 2021; the US officials, including intelligence and Department of State, held their first face-to-face meeting with Taliban officials in Doha since American troops pulled out from Afghanistan a month earlier. Taliban delegation was led by acting Afghan Foreign Minister Amir Khan Muttaqi, Spy Chief Mullah Abdul Haq Wasiq, Minister of Information and Culture Mullah Khairullah Khairkhwa and Sheikh Shahabuddin Delawar. On other side of the table, there were Qatari officials and representatives of a number of other countries, including the America.

The continued closure of high schools for girls and killing of *Hazara* people had drawn criticism from many states, and caused concerns among the Western nations who were hesitant to recognise the new government in Afghanistan on the said issues.

> [*Maulvi Delawar is one of the founding members of the Taliban negotiation team based in Doha. He was sent by the group's founding Chief Mullah Omar to establish the Doha political office.*]

Here one can recall *DR EJAZ AKRAM AND PEPE ESCOBAR'S* **'Letter to the Taliban'** available on all media pages of 22nd September 2021, which asked the US sponsored international community that:

*"On the demand for an 'all inclusive government'* [in Afghanistan]:

- *Imagine if the* **French revolutionaries** *were asked to retain the elements of the kingdom of Louis XVI while forming the new republic to keep it all 'inclusive'.*

- *Imagine that the **American revolutionaries** were asked to keep the British loyalists as a part of the new American republic to keep it all inclusive.*

- *Imagine that the **Bolsheviks** were asked to keep the Czarist loyalists in the government to keep it all inclusive.*

- *Imagine that **Chairman Mao** was asked to keep the Kuomintang as a part of his new set up to keep things all inclusive.*

- *Imagine that **Imam Khomeini** was asked to keep the elements of Reza Shah's puppet government to keep the new Iranian government all inclusive.*

- *Imagine that **Erdogan** was asked shortly after the coup to keep the Gulen movement intact to keep the Turkish government all inclusive.*

- *Imagine that the **Saudis** are asked to give due representation to a quarter of its Shi'ite population to keep the Kingdom all inclusive.*

- *Imagine that **India's Modi** is asked to give full citizenship rights to Muslims, Sikhs and other minorities to keep RSS-India all inclusive."*

If all of the above couldn't be, then what logic is the so-called international community practicing when asking the Taliban to keep those who aided and abetted the utterly unjustified foreign occupation as a part of their government to keep things all inclusive?

In Afghanistan it was not a mere change of government; successive puppet governments responsible for killing their own people and spreading subversion in the region were sent to exile. A state is one group that has to have a monopoly on the legitimate use of violence. All other groups have to be disarmed and disbanded.

In Afghanistan, the majority population keep Muslim beliefs and values. The Taliban's vast force is *Pashtun*, practicing *Pashtunwali* code - ***Hanafi Sunni Shariah***, but *non-Pashtun* Afghans are all Muslims too. Therefore, the Taliban would naturally build their governing structure based on Islamic values; to expect that the Afghans would subscribe to liberalism is simply an opposite fantasy.

The Taliban took control of the entire country without a fight. The Afghan Army dispersed so easily and hugged the Taliban fighters and many even joined them. Had the public opinion not behind their resistance movement, it could never succeed. AND this is the proof of Taliban's inclusion; they gave general amnesty to all. One could ponder;

*"Who had more mercy in their hearts; the progenitors of the modern republics or the Taliban? We have never seen such a spectacle in recent human history. If this is not inclusion, then what is this?"*

[In Dr Ejaz and Pepe's essay, their opinion comes up that the 'so-called rogue international community' is screaming over Islamic system for Afghanistan because of their historical prejudice against Islam and Muslims. Edward Said illustrated it quite well in his famous classic, **Orientalism**. The contemporary **Islamophobia Trade** is another proof of the West's unfounded hatred for Islam as religion.]

The Muslim intelligentsia held that the interim set up in Afghanistan must not include elements of the Ancient Regime who were on the payroll of their enemy-states; as they fought for twenty long years against the Taliban cause. Islam is neutral to the form of government; it only insists that regardless of the form of the government, the outcome must be justice.

The Qura'n, the holy book of Muslims, also suggests that justice is not equality. Equality is giving everyone the same; justice is giving whomever their due. Thus honest and competent people from all ethnic backgrounds should be chosen, then trained and then run the government. Of course, the Taliban community which struggled and sacrificed enormously to throw out the foreigners, would have more say in matters of state formation, compared to those who sided with the oppressor to kill their own people and their neighbours.

# Scenario 232

....CORRUPTION by all;
Afghan governments,
the US officers of establishment, Afghan Warlords,
the US & Afghan Contractors
– all inclusive.

What prompted the US government and the President Trump to conclude negotiations with the Taliban leadership [on their terms] in Doha on 29th February 2020? See the background factors of this hard decision in **Craig Whitlock's** article appearing in Daily 'INDEPENDENT' dated 9th December 2019, written about 80 days before signing that agreement – title being '*US officials distorted statistics to mislead [American] public about Afghan war, confidential documents reveal*'.

An 18-year [till then], trillion-dollar conflict was known to be failing from an early stage – but this was concealed from the public; what had been going on behind closed doors in Washington's power corridors. The senior US officials failed to tell the truth about the **War in Afghanistan,** making rosy proclamations they knew to be false and hiding unmistakable evidence the war had gone out of their hands.

Referring to the same essay but titled as *CONSUMED BY CORRUPTION* appearing on media channels on the same day - the US flooded Afghanistan with money — then turned a blind eye to the graft it fuelled.

The author was pointing towards **THE AFGHAN-WAR PAPERS** - a secret treasure trove of the Afghan-war spread over nearly two decades then. The salient remarks, gathered from the hundreds of state-managed interviews of the high ranking Generals, Diplomats, Advisors, Commanders, Secretaries of State, Trainers and Afghani Warlords.

The interviews were conducted during 2014-18 by the Office of the Special Inspector General for Afghanistan Reconstruction [SIGAR]. The agency was created by the US Congress to investigate fraud and waste, but it used the interviews for a special academic project, titled 'LESSONS LEARNED' to diagnose policy failures from the war.

**Lessons Learned Report** about corruption omitted the names of the vast majority of those who were interviewed, as well as the most unsparing criticisms about how Washington was seen at fault. The Washington Post sued SIGAR in federal court — twice — to force it to release the interview records under the Freedom of Information Act [FOIA] – and ultimately won the case in 2019. The documents made clear that the *seeds of runaway corruption were planted at the outset of the war.*

- *Americans used the bad guys to get the 'badder guys' - but couldn't circle back and get the bad guys later; we never did.*

**In September 2016,** SIGAR published a 164-page report that chronicled how corruption had harmed the US mission in Afghanistan. Emphasizing that *'The US government should take into account the amount of assistance a host country could absorb....'* BUT no one in White House, Pentagon or CIA bothered. Little glimpses:

- The war was intended as a short-term tactic but the practice ended up binding the United States to some of the *country's most notorious figures* for years.

- Facts remained that about halfway into the 18-year war; Afghans stopped hiding how corrupt their country had gone. Dark money sloshed all around. Afghanistan's largest bank liquefied into a cesspool of fraud. Travellers lugged suitcases loaded with millions, or more, on flights leaving Kabul.

- President Hamid Karzai won re-election after cronies stuffed thousands of ballot boxes. He later admitted the CIA used to deliver bags of cash to his office for years, calling it **'nothing unusual'**.

- In public, as President Obama escalated the war and Congress approved billions of additional dollars in support, the Commander in Chief and lawmakers promised to crack down on corruption and hold crooked Afghans accountable – but could do nothing.

- In reality, US officials backed off, looked away and let the thievery become more entrenched than ever.

- Key figures in Washington and Afghanistan tolerated the worst offenders — warlords, drug traffickers, defence contractors — because they were so-called allies of America.

- In return they blamed the US government which failed to confront a more distressing reality — that it was responsible for fuelling the corruption, by doling out vast sums of money with limited foresight or regard for the consequences.

- The US and allied officials were *"so desperate to have the alcoholics to the table, we kept pouring drinks, not knowing [or] considering we were killing them."*

- Scale of corruption was the unintended result of swamping the war zone with far more aid and defence contracts than impoverished Afghanistan could absorb. There was so much excess, financed by American taxpayers, that opportunities for bribery and fraud became almost limitless.

- The basic assumption remained that corruption was an Afghan problem and we were the solution. But there was one indispensable ingredient for corruption — money — and we [the US] were the ones who had the money.

- To purchase loyalty and information, the CIA gave cash to warlords, governors, parliamentarians, even religious leaders. The US military and other agencies also abetted corruption by doling out payments or contracts to unsavoury Afghan power brokers in a misguided quest for stability.

- We had partnerships with all the wrong players. The US kept on standing shoulder-to-shoulder with these people, even through all these years. It was a case of security trumping everything else.

- **Gert Berthold,** a forensic accountant, helped analyze 3000 Defence contracts worth $106 billion to see who was benefiting. The conclusion: About 40% of the money ended up in the pockets of insurgents, criminal syndicates or corrupt Afghan officials.

- And it was often a higher percent. We talked with many former [Afghan] ministers, and they told us: *'you're under-estimating it'*.

- No one [in US] wanted accountability. *'If you're going to do anti-corruption, someone has got to own it. From what I've seen, no one is willing to own it.'*

- The CIA, the US military, the State Department and other agencies used cash and lucrative contracts to win the allegiance of Afghan warlords in the fight against al-Qaeda and the Taliban – but entangled themselves deep into sand-grave of un-paralleled corruption.

The documents were part of a project examining the root failures of the longest armed conflict in US history. They included more than 2,000 pages of previously unpublished notes of interviews with people who played a direct role in the war, Generals and diplomats.

The interviews were managed by the **Office of the Special Inspector General for Afghanistan Reconstruction** [SIGAR]; it was created by Congress in 2008 to investigate waste and fraud in the war zone. In 2014, at Mr Sopko's direction, SIGAR departed from its usual mission of performing audits and launched a side venture titled as *'Lessons Learned'*.

The $11m project was meant to diagnose policy failures in Afghanistan so the US would not repeat the mistakes the next time it invaded a country or tried to rebuild a shattered one. More than 600 people with firsthand experience in the war were interviewed - mostly Americans, NATO allies and about 20 Afghan officials.

SIGAR published *Seven Lessons Learned* reports since 2016 that highlighted problems in Afghanistan. James Dobbins, special envoy to Afghanistan under Presidents Bush and Obama said:

> *"We don't invade poor countries to make them rich. . . We invade violent countries to make them peaceful and we clearly failed in Afghanistan".*

## RUMSFELD's 'SNOWFLAKES' MYTH:

The **Rumsfeld memos** were released by the Pentagon in response to a FOIA lawsuit filed in 2017 by the National Security Archive, a non-profit research institute at George Washington University. There are hundreds of pages of memos, known as **'SNOWFLAKES'**, which Rumsfeld dictated about the Afghan war during 2001-05.

Since 2001, more than 775,000 US troops were deployed to Afghanistan, many repeatedly. Of those, 2,300+ died there and 20,589 were wounded in action, according to Defence Department figures; see the core failings of the war that persist to this day.

How the three consecutive presidents - George Bush, Obama and Donald Trump - and their military commanders were unable to deliver on their promises to prevail in Afghanistan. The US officials acknowledged that their **war-fighting strategies were fatally flawed** and that Washington wasted enormous sums of Tax-payers' money trying to remake Afghanistan into a democratic modern nation.

The US government didn't carry out a comprehensive accounting of how much it spent on the war in Afghanistan, but the costs were staggering. Since 2001, the Defence Department [DOD], State Department and the US Agency for International Development [USAID] spent nearly $978bn. These figures didn't include money spent by other agencies such as the CIA and the Department of Veterans Affairs responsible for medical care for wounded veterans.

**Jeffrey Eggers,** a retired **Navy SEAL** and **White House** staffer for Presidents Bush and Obama, told government interviewers that:

> *"What did we get for this $1 trillion effort? Was it worth $1 trillion? After the killing of Osama bin Laden, I said that Osama was probably laughing in his watery grave considering how much we have spent on Afghanistan."*

The said secret documents also contradicted a long chorus of public statements from US presidents, military commanders and diplomats who assured Americans year after year that they were making progress in Afghanistan and the war was worth fighting. Several of those interviewed described explicit and sustained efforts by the US government to deliberately mislead the public. They said it was common at military HQ in Kabul - and at the White House - to distort statistics to make it appear the US was winning the war; while in fact they were facing cheats and defeats.

**On 11th October 2001,** four days after the US started bombing the Taliban, a reporter asked Mr Bush: *'Can you avoid being drawn into a Vietnam-like quagmire in Afghanistan?'* Mr Bush replied confidently:

> *"We learned some very important lessons in Vietnam. People often ask me, 'How long will this last?' This particular battlefront will last as long as it takes to bring al-Qaeda to justice. It may happen tomorrow, it may happen a month from now, it may take a year or two. But we will prevail."*

In those early days, other US leaders mocked the notion that the nightmare of Vietnam might repeat itself in Afghanistan. Mr Rumsfeld had rather joked at a news conference on 27th November 2001, saying: *'All together now - quagmire!'* But throughout the Afghan war, documents proved that US military officials had resorted to an old tactic from Vietnam - *manipulating public opinion.* In news conferences and other public appearances, those in charge of the war followed the same talking points for 18 years. No matter how the war was going - and especially when it was going badly - they emphasised how they were making progress.

To augment the '**Lessons Learned**' interviews, hundreds of pages of previously classified memos about the Afghan war that were dictated by the then Defence Secretary Rumsfeld during 2001-06 were also made open by the Trump administration. Those secret memos were roughly 59,000 pages, given code-named '**SNOWFLAKES**' by Mr Rumsfeld; the memos comprised of brief instructions or comments that the Pentagon boss dictated, often several times a day, to his subordinates. See a **hand-written note** of 17th April 2002, worded in Mr Rumsfeld's abrupt style:

> *"I may be impatient. In fact I know I'm a bit impatient. We are never going to get the US military out of Afghanistan unless we take care to see that there is something going on that will provide the stability that will be necessary for us to leave. - Help!"*

**On 18th April 2002;** President George W Bush, in a speech at Virginia Military Institute, said:

> *"The history of military conflict in Afghanistan [has] been one of initial success, followed by long years of floundering and ultimate failure. We're not going to repeat that mistake."*

The intelligentsia generally believed that at the outset, the US invasion of Afghanistan had a clear, stated objective: To *retaliate against al-Qaeda* and prevent a repeat of the 9/11 attacks but as the war dragged on, the goals and mission kept changing and a lack of faith in the US strategy took root inside the Pentagon, the White House and the State Department. Rumsfeld, the then Defence Secretary had to note down in 2003 that: *"I have no visibility into who the bad guys are . . . We are woefully deficient in human intelligence."*

It was year 2006 when the US officials feared that **narco-traffickers had become stronger** than the Afghan government and that money from the drug trade was powering the insurgency. No single agency or country was in charge of the Afghan drug strategy throughout the war years; so the State Department, the DEA, the US military, NATO allies and the Afghan government all felt astray in this field. Then there were also the rumours that, at later stage, the US and the NATO military officers had also joined hands with certain warlords in poppy export trade.

In October 2006; Mr Rumsfeld's speechwriters delivered a paper titled *Afghanistan: Five Years Later.* Packed with optimism, it highlighted more than 50 promising facts and figures, from 19,000+ Afghan women trained in 'improved poultry management' to the 'average speed on most roads' - up 300%. The report said:

> *"Five years on, there is a multitude of good news. While it has become fashionable in some circles to call Afghanistan a forgotten war, or to say the US has lost its focus, the facts belie the myths."*

Defence Secretary Rumsfeld thought it was brilliant, so wrote a memo under his own hand, that:

> *"This paper is an excellent piece. How do we use it? Should it be an article? An op-ed piece? A handout? A press briefing? All of the above? I think it ought to get it to a lot of people."*

Next day, the report was circulated to media reporters and also posted on Pentagon websites. Since then, US Generals always preached that the war was progressing well, no matter the reality on the battlefield. Two years later, as the casualty rate among US and NATO troops was touching another high, Lt Gen David Rodriguez held a news conference in Kabul and said that the US forces were steadily making deliberate progress.

It has been discussed in another chapter in detail, that the US flooded Afghanistan with far more aid than it could possibly absorb. During the peak years of fighting, 2009-12, the US admin and military commanders believed the more they would spend on schools, bridges, canals and other civil-works projects, the faster security would improve – but ultimately all the projects were found on drawing charts only.

However, it proved to be a colossal misjudgement – that too through corrupt mafias of Afghan warlords in connivance with the American, mostly retired, soldiers via so-called contractors. One US-AID worker guessed that 90% of what they spent was overkill:

> *"We lost objectivity. We were given money, told to spend it and we did, without reason."*

At first, Afghan poppy farmers were paid by the British to destroy their crops - which only encouraged them to grow more the next season. Later, the US government eradicated poppy fields without compensation - which only infuriated farmers and encouraged them to side with the Taliban.

After returning from a fact-finding mission to Afghanistan in June 2006, **Gen Barry McCaffrey** reported that:

> *"The Taliban had made an impressive comeback and predicted that 'we will encounter some very unpleasant surprises in the coming 24 months.' The Afghan national leadership are collectively terrified that we will tip-toe out of Afghanistan in the coming few years - leaving NATO holding the bag - and the whole thing will collapse again into mayhem."*

Two months later, **Marin Strmecki,** a civilian adviser to Mr Rumsfeld, gave the Pentagon chief a classified, 40-page report loaded with more bad news. It said that enormous popular discontent was building against the Afghan government because of its corruption and incompetence. It also said that the Taliban were growing stronger, thanks to support from Pakistan, a US ally. The Pentagon buried that report and released a very different story to the public.

No one bothered about the warnings narrated by two above officers. On 8th September 2008; Maj **Gen Jeffrey Schloesser,** in an open news briefing from Afghanistan, commented:

> *"Are we losing this war? Absolutely no way....... Can the enemy win it? Absolutely no way"*

In March 2011, during congressional hearings, cynical lawmakers pelted **Gen David Petraeus,** the then commander of US and NATO forces in Afghanistan, with doubts that the US strategy was working. The General responded that the past eight months had seen important but hard-fought progress – but not giving details of gains if any.

One year later, during a visit to Afghanistan, the then Defence Secretary Leon Panetta stuck to the same script saying to the reporters that '*...the US campaign made significant progress*'. He had to say that to save his country's honour though he had just personally dodged a suicide attack.

Some of the interviews taken by SIGAR were mysteriously short. The interview record with **John Allen**, the Marine General who commanded

US and NATO forces in Afghanistan during 2011-13, consisted of five paragraphs. In contrast, other influential figures, including former US ambassador Ryan Crocker, sat for two interviews that yielded 95 transcribed pages. However, mostly the principles of State-Security were followed. For instance, the State Department asserted that releasing portions of certain interviews could jeopardize negotiations with the Taliban to end the war. The Defence Department [DOD] and Drug Enforcement Administration [DEA] also classified some interview excerpts.

## SEE SOME MORE FACTS:

A US military officer estimated that one-third of the police recruits were *'drug addicts or Taliban from inside'*; yet another called them *'stealing fools'* who looted so much fuel from US bases that they perpetually smelt of gasoline. Thinking about and then making out a policy that the US could build the Afghan military that fast and that was insane in fact. Meanwhile, as US hoped for the Afghan security forces failed to materialise, Afghanistan became the world's leading source of a growing plague: OPIUM.

The US spent about $9bn to fight the opium problem over the past 18 years, but Afghan farmers continued with cultivating more opium poppies than ever. In 2018, Afghanistan was responsible for 82% of global opium production, according to the UN Office on Drugs and Crime. **Douglas Lute**, the White House's Afghan war advisor in 2007-13 told SIGAR:

> *"....almost everything they [the US commanders] did to constrain opium farming backfired. We stated that our goal is to establish a 'flourishing market economy,' I thought we should have specified a flourishing drug trade - this is the only part of the market that's working [here in Afghanistan]."*

**Col Bob Crowley**, who served as a senior counter-insurgency Adviser to US military commanders in 2013-14, told government interviewers that:

> *"**Every data point was altered** to present the best picture possible. Surveys, for instance, were totally unreliable but reinforced that everything we were doing was right and we became a self-licking ice cream cone."*

**Gen Douglas Lute**, who served as the White House's Afghan war kingpin during the Bush and Obama administrations, gave statement in 2015:

*"We were devoid of fundamental understanding of Afghanistan - we didn't know what we were doing. What are we trying to do here? We didn't have the foggiest notion of what we were undertaking.*

*If the American people knew the magnitude of this dysfunction . . . 2,400 lives lost. .... the deaths of US military personnel are [blamed] on bureaucratic breakdowns among Congress, the Pentagon and the State Department - Who will say this was in vain?"*

**John Sopko,** head of the federal agency [SIGAR] that conducted the interviews, acknowledged that the documents show: *"The American people have constantly been lied to."*

But the reports, written in dense bureaucratic prose and focused on an alphabet soup of government initiatives, left out the harshest and most frank criticisms from the interviews. The introduction to one report released in May 2018 reads:

*"We found the stabilisation strategy and the programmes used to achieve it were not properly tailored to the Afghan context, and successes in stabilising Afghan districts rarely lasted longer than the physical presence of coalition troops and civilians."*

The reports also omitted the names of more than 90% of the people who were interviewed for the project; it was to avoid controversy over politically sensitive matters.

## LIES & COOKED FIGURES AT HEIGHT:

With descriptions of how the US got stuck in Afghan War and the regime's resolve to conceal them from the public - broadly resembled Pentagon's top-secret history of the Vietnam War. When they were leaked in 1971, the **'Pentagon Papers'** caused a sensation by revealing the US government had long misled the public about how the US came to be entangled in Vietnam. *The 7,000 pages in 47 volumes* were based entirely on secret state dossiers, diplomatic cables, decision-making memos and intelligence reports. To preserve secrecy, the Defence Secretary McNamara had issued an order prohibiting the authors and reporters from interviewing the key figures mentioned in that luminous report.

In Afghan War too; at the admin level, deep-seated disagreements were seen unresolved. Some US officials wanted to use the war to turn Afghanistan into a democracy. Others wanted to transform Afghan culture and elevate women's rights. Still others wanted to reshape the regional balance of power among Pakistan, India, Iran and Russia; see high official's remarks:

> *"With the Pak-Afghan strategy there was a present under the Christmas tree for everyone. By the time you were finished you had so many priorities and aspirations it was like no strategy at all."*

Here in Afghanistan context; the SIGAR interviews also revealed how US military commanders struggled to articulate who they were fighting, let alone why. Was al-Qaeda the enemy, or the Taliban? Was Pakistan a friend or an enemy? What about the Islamic State and the confusing selection of foreign *jihadists,* which warlords were on the CIA's payroll? - the answers could not be settled by any US government during the two decades. As a result, in the field, US troops often couldn't differentiate between friends and foes, for and against. A former adviser to the Army Special Forces told the SIGAR in 2017:

> *"They thought I was going to come to them with a map to show them where the good guys and bad guys live. It took several conversations for them to understand that I did not have that information in my hands. At first, they just kept asking: 'But who are the bad guys, where are they?' - The view wasn't any clearer from the Pentagon even."*

President **Obama, on 1ˢᵗ December 2009,** said during his speech at the US Military Academy at West Point New York, that:

> *"The days of providing blank cheques are over. . . . It must be clear that Afghans will have to take responsibility for their security and that America has no interest in fighting an endless war in Afghanistan."*

Presidents Bush, Obama and Trump all promised the public that they would avoid falling into the trap of *'nation-building'* in Afghanistan – but all failed miserably on this score; they collectively allocated more than $133bn to build up those tribal lands. From the Secret Papers trove it appeared that the philosophy of high-flying projects were failing from the first day. The US officials tried to create a democratic government in Kabul modelled after their own in Washington. It was a foreign concept to the Afghans, who were accustomed to tribalism, monarchism and Islamic law. A former State official told in an interview [2015]:

> *"Our policy was to create a strong central government which was idiotic because Afghanistan does not have a history of strong central*

*governments. The timeframe for creating a strong central government is 100 years, which we didn't have."*

The **INDEPENDENT**, the UK's newspaper, cited an instance that:

*"...one contractor told he was expected to dole out $3m daily for projects in a single Afghan district roughly the size of an American county.'"*

The same contractor once asked a visiting congressman whether the lawmaker could responsibly spend that kind of money back home:

*"He said hell no. Well, sir, that's what you just obligated us to spend and I'm doing it for communities that live in mud huts with no windows. "*

Enough is on record that the US Generals continued to lie in public - they were making steady progress on their strategy: to train a robust Afghan army and national police force that could defend the country without foreign help – but they all collapsed like a house of cards. However, the US military trainers described the Afghan security forces as incompetent, unmotivated and rife with deserters.

[*They also accused Afghan commanders of pocketing salaries - paid by US taxpayers - for tens of thousands of 'ghost soldiers.'* Due to their un-soldier like attitudes, 50-60,000 members of Afghan forces were killed - an unsustainable casualty rate.]

**John Garofano,** a Naval War strategist in *Helmand* during 2011, said military officials in the field used to spend huge amount of resources making out colour-coded large sized charts on expensive machines – just to show heralded positive results. Nobody dared to question whether the charts and numbers were credible or meaningful. There was no willingness to answer questions like actual number of schools built. Where are strategic bridges? How many male or female students admitted and taught etc. Other senior officials said they placed great importance on one point in particular, albeit one the US government rarely likes to discuss in public.

**Col Bob Crowley,** an Advisor on counter-insurgency in Afghanistan during 2013-14, told government interviewers that:

*"....truth was rarely welcome at military HQ in Kabul. Bad news was often stifled. There was more freedom to share bad news if it*

*was small - we're running over kids with our armoured vehicles - because those things could be changed with policy directives. But when we tried to air larger strategic concerns about the willingness, capacity or corruption of the Afghan government, it was clear - it wasn't welcome."*

**In July 2016,** after a surge in Taliban attacks on major cities, **Gen John Nicholson Jr,** Commander of the US forces in Afghanistan at the time, repeated the same lie before the reporters urging that *'we are seeing some progress'.* One can recall the history that during Vietnam War, the US military commanders had relied on same-like dubious dimensions to persuade Americans that they were winning.

In Afghanistan, the tragedy remained that the Pentagon had started highlighting the **body counts or the number of enemy fighters killed;** and inflated the figures as a measurement of success. The US military had generally avoided publicising body counts but a stage came when the government opted to speak about [touted] statistics that officials knew were distorted, spurious or downright false.

Perhaps the said policy was made out due to constant pressure from President Obama and Pentagon to produce figures to show the troop surge of 2009-11 was working, despite hard evidence to the contrary. Then the Generals and officers tried using troop numbers trained, violence levels, control of territory though none of it was accurate; the metrics were always manipulated for the duration of the war.

Even when casualty counts and other figures looked bad, the White House and Pentagon turned them ridiculous. Suicide bombings in Kabul were portrayed as a sign of the Taliban's desperation; and a rise in US troop deaths was cited as proof that American forces were taking the fight seriously. A senior NSC official said:

> *"It was their explanations. For example, attacks are getting worse? 'That's because there are more targets for them to fire at, so more attacks are a false indicator of instability.' Then, three months later, attacks are still getting worse? 'It's because the Taliban are getting desperate', so it's actually an indicator that we're winning."*

And this went on and on for various reasons; and all field reports were sent up like that regardless of conditions on the ground. From the ambassadors down to the low level, they all said they were doing a great job. Upon arrival in Afghanistan, US army brigade and battalion commanders were given the same basic mission: to protect the population and defeat the enemy – but only on papers or through sermons.

So they all went in for whatever their periods of stay were and were given that mission and got executed that [rogue] mission. At the time of return each officer held that *'you know ...., we couldn't accomplish our mission.'* So the next guy got screwed up . . . coming and going.

## THE TOLL OF WAR

Since 2001, an estimated 157,000 people were killed in the war in Afghanistan.

| | |
|---|---|
| Afghan civilians | 43,074* |
| Afghan security forces | 64,124* |
| Humanitarian aid workers | 424 |
| Taliban fighters and other insurgents | 42,100 |
| U.S. contractors | 3814 |
| Journalists and media workers | 67 |
| U.S. military personnel | 2300+ |
| NATO and coalition troops | 1145 |

**Sources:** Defence Department; Costs of War Project, Brown University; UN Assistance Mission in Afghanistan; Committee to Protect Journalists

**Note-1:** US military number is current through November 2019. The other figures and estimates are current as of October 2019.

**Note-2:** The above figures do not include the 80,000+ deaths occurred in Pakistan due to the [TTP] Pakistan Taliban's suicide bombings and 450+ American DRONE assaults on civilian and Armed forces – totalling c 16,000 attacks.

## US-STOLEN ARMS DEALS

See a STORY OF ARMS DEALS IN AFGHANISTAN [Nov 2018] by *James & Jason* appeared at www.apNews.com on 16th December 2021.

This write-up, by www.ap.org, is based on extensive interviews, text messages associated with a **federal criminal case**, private FB group messages, court records and documents from military investigative proceedings.

**It was November 2018,** and the driver, Tyler Sumlin, bearded former US Army soldier, was [feeling] uncomfortable, and understandably tense: He was transporting a platoon's worth of stolen rifles, enough C4 to blow up his car and those around him, a live hand grenade – [perhaps] too late to turn around.

Riding shotgun was Sumlin's military blood brother, Sgt 1st Class Jason Jarvis, a soldier on active-duty from Fort Bragg's 18th Ordnance Company in North Carolina.

The two men, who'd been close **since they served in Afghanistan;** a few months earlier, Jarvis had reached out to ask if Sumlin had interest in making some money. Jarvis was looking to sell stolen military equipment from an armory at Bragg.

Sumlin said he might be able to find a buyer.

Then they were heading to El Paso, Texas, to sell the stolen weapons. In a **series of stories,** The Associated Press [AP New] had detailed how the US military had problems with **missing and stolen guns and explosives,** and how some weapons were used in domestic crime.

But the inside story of how two men attempted to sell stolen Army weapons revealed another threat: *an organized group of soldiers and veterans taking advantage of flaws in the military's system to make fast money.* Here are details about a case that left other soldiers appalled and enraged — betrayed, by two of their own.

In 2009 as Sumlin and Jarvis sat together on a rock in Kunar Province, Afghanistan. The two young men had become brothers amid the breakneck tempo of wartime Afghanistan. Sumlin and Jarvis **specialized in explosive ordnance disposal,** or EOD, the kind of work — with its stifling & hulking bomb suits. Their work eliminating improvised explosive devices set by the Taliban was nonstop, and gave them little time to process what they saw, heard and smelled. It was a pressure cooker of a job inside a pressure cooker, intense even in the high stakes world of the battlefield.

Like many soldiers, they found some balm in the friendship of others who'd seen what they'd seen. Like many military subcultures, the tight-knit EOD community had its own code of conduct, ethics and language. Sumlin joined a private *Facebook* group where the EOD community commiserated, argued and joked one another. They also held each other to account, debating whether a member's conduct violated the brotherhood's code.

**Sumlin left the Army in December 2017,** but deployed again to do bomb disposal with a private defense contracting company. Meanwhile, Jarvis remained in the Army. At Fort Bragg, home to some of the Army's most elite units, Jarvis worked in an armory. And that gave him access to a wealth of military firearms, parts and other equipment such as night vision goggles and explosives. Inside the Fort Bragg armory, Jarvis took photographs of weaponry — and then he stole it, and set out to sell it.

His buddy, Sumlin, sent the photos and an inventory list of the pilfered weapons and explosives to an accomplice who called himself *'Mr. Anderson.'* a former Army combat engineer who had served in both Iraq and Afghanistan; and was one of several other soldiers or veterans connected to the scheme.

**In May 2018,** Sumlin and Jarvis began mining their contacts to offload the haul through a promising person identified as *'Evan,'* who they hadn't met before. Here is an Inventory: *"NVG-13, Aimpoint-8, ACOG-18, PEQ2A-10, DD Rail-24, DD-Barrel-15, Various Troy toys,"* Anderson texted to Evan, including Jarvis' photos. The letters and numbers described a litany of arms and night vision goggles, rifle optics and lasers designed for aiming, and rifle parts. Evan texted back saying:

> *'Wow, items are good, any idea on price if I take everything?'*

> *"I'll let you know as soon as I hear back from him,"* Anderson wrote, referring to Sumlin.

Over the next few days, the conversation continued, copies of messages show. Anderson and Evan complained about the weapons' high prices. They sounded paranoid when they discussed dealing with amateur gun dealers like Sumlin and Jarvis, and feared they would attract attention from law enforcement.

After a few days, Evan said he'd found a buyer who wanted it; all of it. What Anderson didn't know was that Evan was a longtime confidential informant working with Homeland Security Investigations, an arm of the Department of Homeland Security.

In his communication with Sumlin and Anderson, Evan said, he represented a buyer who claimed to be connected to narco-traffickers. [*Sumlin denied that the weapons were meant to be sold to **drug-runners**.*]

> "*I didn't know (the buyer) was south of Texas,*" Anderson wrote.

> "*Yep he goes between Texas and Mexico all the time,*" Evan wrote back.

> "*I wouldn't sell anything to anyone down there,*" Anderson replied.

> "*Lol ... well he has always been a cash buyer without question and never any issues at all,*" Evan responded. "*It sounds like they've made a deal.*"

> "*I hope so. They still have to meet and conclude,*" wrote Anderson.

By mid-November 2018, Jarvis had rented a Chevy Tahoe SUV in North Carolina and drove the stolen cache south. He met Sumlin in Inverness, a small town in central Florida's lakes region, so they could prepare the weapons for sale, according to a federal criminal complaint.

**Sumlin and Jarvis had initially sought $250,000 for the firearms and explosives. After some back-and-forth, they settled on a much lower price: $75,000.**

According to the *Army Criminal Investigation Division's case file,* Jarvis and Sumlin later told agents about '*criminal transactions*' in Colorado, North Carolina, Florida, Georgia and Texas. **Another soldier confessed to stealing** multiple rifle optic systems and a bomb suit, which were given to Sumlin.

In Florida, Jarvis and Sumlin cleaned the firearms to remove their fingerprints. They also paid to have some parts modified to fit the rifles. With the cache assembled, cleaned, packed in storage containers and loaded for delivery, the men got into the SUV for the 24-hour drive to Texas.

**On 14th November 2018;** arriving in El Paso, they pulled into a truck stop where a man they thought was the buyers' contact, known as Andy, waited with some others. They told Sumlin and Jarvis to follow them to a nearby warehouse — [it was a real trap]. There, the agents confirmed that the two men were indeed carrying multiple firearms, military equipment and C4 plastic explosives. A SWAT team pounced, arrested them and secured the cache.

Homeland Security agents seized more than 30 firearms; several blocks of C4; a hand grenade; shaped charges; body armor; night vision devices; binoculars; ammunition; lasers and magazines. In Mexico, where drug traffickers have fought openly, the equipment could unleash carnage.

*According to the report by Army criminal investigators, the items stolen by Sumlin, Jarvis and their accomplices between 2014 and 2018 were valued at close to $180,000. But the US government only recovered roughly $26,000 worth.*

Jarvis and Sumlin were indicted on eight different federal charges, including conspiracy and gunrunning. Sumlin posted bail and returned to his Florida home to pick up the pieces; he faced a **possible 70 years in prison.**

Explosive Ordnance Disposal Technicians work on the border amid Mexican drug-related violence. What if the weapons had ended up with narcos? They might have been used against the good guys. Sumlin had crossed a line by selling items that could have killed one of their own. [In the last] the two, Sumlin and Jarvis, had faced decades in prison, but both reached deals with federal prosecutors. They pleaded guilty so the other seven counts were dropped; the term was then reduced to 10 years in prison and a $250,000 fine.

**But they didn't even get that** - each was sentenced to five years' probation, and Jarvis was ordered to mental health counseling and required to take prescribed medication.

To Evan, Sumlin and Jarvis are terrorists. If they were Muslim or Black, he said, they wouldn't have gotten off so easily. Evan wrote a Homeland Security that:

*"It was very frustrating. There were other guys who got much worse for much less."*

-------------------------------------------------

Now see another article of the recent times but based on the same investigative file of November 2018 – an extension of the Stolen Arms deals. Referring to an article by JAMES LAPORTA appearing at **www.apNews.com** dated 15<sup>th</sup> June 2021:

> **"A guide to US military stolen arms:** *An Associated Press [AP] investigation found that at least 1,900 US military firearms were lost or stolen during the 2010s. Civilians later used some of the missing weapons in violent crimes.*
>
> *To reach its total, AP culled criminal investigations, court records and property loss forms, and analyzed data from military registries of small arms. AP's analysis shows that alarming number of guns was missing."*

Referring to a fact-story published at **www.apnews.com** [dated 16<sup>th</sup> June 2021] next day in the same that weapon theft or loss spanned the military's global footprint, touching installations from coast to coast, as well as overseas. In Afghanistan, someone cut the padlock on an Army container and stole 65 Beretta M9s. The theft went undetected. After two weeks, empty pistol boxes were discovered in the parking compound; the weapons were not recovered.

> [*Even elite units were not immune. A former member of a Marines special operations unit was busted with two stolen guns; a Navy SEAL lost his pistol during a fight in a restaurant in Lebanon.*]

The American Police caught hold of a gun from within a street fight; it was a 9mm Beretta which was later found to be linked with four shootings in Albany, New York.

And there was something else; the pistol was US Army property, a weapon intended for use against America's enemies, not on its streets.

The Army couldn't say how its Beretta M9 got to New York's capital. In June 2018 police realized that someone had stolen from a safe inside Fort Bragg, North Carolina - 600 miles away. *'It's incredibly alarming. It raises the other question as to what else is seeping into a community;'* Albany County District Attorney held.

An Associated Press investigation had found that at least 1,900 US military firearms were lost or stolen during the 2010s, with some resurfacing in violent crimes. The fact remained that AP's total was a certain undercount because Pentagon was not eager to release the true figures. Government records had vanished from armories, supply warehouses, Navy warships, firing ranges and other places where they were used, stored or transported.

The Pentagon used to share annual updates about stolen weapons with Congress, but the requirement to do so ended years ago and public accountability has slipped. The members floated their opinions:

*'There must be full accountability in Congress with regular reporting of missing or stolen weapons;'* one senator roared. The Army and Air Force couldn't readily tell the AP News how many weapons were lost or stolen from 2010 through 2019. Sometimes, weapons disappeared without a paper trail. Military investigators regularly close cases without finding the firearms or person responsible because shoddy records lead to dead ends.

[*As a general principle, the military's weapons are especially vulnerable to corrupt insiders responsible for securing them. They know how to exploit weak points within armories or the military's enormous supply chains. Often from lower ranks, they may see a chance to make a buck from a military that can afford it. It's all about the money in which all related offices could be involved.*]

During the Afghan War especially, theft or loss happened more than the US Army had publicly acknowledged. During an initial interview, Miller significantly understated the extent to which weapons disappeared citing records that only a few hundred missing rifles and handguns. But an internal analysis done by the Army's Office of the Provost Marshal General tallied 1,303 firearms.

The AP's investigation began a decade ago. From the start, the Army gave conflicting information on a subject with the potential to embarrass -- and that's when it provided information at all. Top officials within the Army, Marines and Secretary of Defense's office said that weapon accountability remained a high priority, and *'when the military knows a weapon is missing it does trigger a concerted response to recover it.'* But for the Pentagon, the missing weapons were not a widespread problem and that the number was a tiny fraction of the military's stockpile – US Army always has a very large inventory of several million weapons.

In the recent past [mid 2021], an Army trainee, who fled Fort Jackson in South Carolina with an M4 rifle, hijacked a school bus full of children, pointing his unloaded assault weapon at the driver before eventually letting everyone go.

In October 2019, police in San Diego were startled to find a military grenade launcher on the front seat of a car they pulled over for expired license plates. The driver and his passenger were middle-aged men with criminal records. Alarming side is that the stolen military guns from Afghanistan were sold or passed on to street gangs and cartels involved in violent crimes. The AP identified eight instances in which five different stolen military firearms were used in a civilian shooting. The Pentagon does not track crime guns, and its spokesman Kirby said his office was unaware of any stolen firearms used in civilian crimes.

In a case the police recovered a stolen service pistol before troops at Fort Bragg realized it was missing. AP News found a second instance, involving a pistol that was among 21 M9s stolen from an arms room. Another steady North Carolina source of weapons had been Marine Corps Base Camp *Lejeune*. Detectives in Baltimore found a Beretta M9 stolen from a Lejeune armory during a cocaine bust. The Naval Criminal Investigative Service found in the 2011 case that three guns were stolen; no one was charged.

Investigators found sensitive and restricted parts for military weapons on sites including eBay, which normally adhere to the statement it has *'zero tolerance'* for stolen military gear on its site. At Fort Campbell, Kentucky, soldiers stole machine gun parts and other items that ended up with online buyers in Russia, China, Mexico and elsewhere. The civilian ringleader, who was found with a warehouse of items, was convicted. Authorities said he made hundreds of thousands of dollars.

When an M203 grenade launcher couldn't be found during a 2019 inventory at a Marine Corps supply base in Albany, Georgia, investigators sought surveillance camera footage. It didn't exist. The warehouse manager said the system couldn't be played back at the time.

An analysis of 45 firearms-only investigations in the Navy and Marines found that in 55% of cases, no suspect could be found and weapons remained missing. In unresolved cases, relevant records were destroyed or falsified. Numerous security lapses in the 2012 case were unearthed, including that missing pistols weren't properly logged in the ship's inventory when they were received and what day they disappeared because sailors' gun-decked inventory reports by not doing actual counts.

Seems like in Afghanistan, the armed services, were responsible for about 3.1 million small arms. Across all four branches, the US military had an estimated 4.5 million firearms, according to an organization Small Arms Survey. The Marines and Navy were able to produce data covering the 2010s - the Navy showed that 211 firearms were reported lost or stolen.

In addition, 63 firearms previously considered missing were recovered. The Marines showed that 204 firearms were lost or stolen, with 14 later recovered. *For missing weapons, the Pentagon relies on incident reports from the services, which it keeps for only three years.*

Pentagon officials told the AP News that nearly 100 firearms were unaccounted during 2018-19 – the figures were higher than what the services reported to the Pentagon. However, the number of missing weapons was down significantly in 2020, when the pandemic curtailed many military operations – and in Afghanistan the army operations were stalled after signing of Doha Accord in February 2020.

The AP News asked the Army for details on missing weapons in 2011 and filed a formal request a year later for records of guns listed as missing, lost, stolen or recovered in the Department of Defense Small Arms and Light Weapons Registry. In 2013, the flow of information over this subject was blocked on the pre-text that 'they' were dealing with millions of weapons......there's so much room for discrepancy. However, the reports guided that there were 230 lost or stolen rifles or handguns between 2010 and 2019.

AP News obtained two memos covering 2013 through 2019 in which the Army tallied 1,303 stolen or lost rifles and handguns though the in-charge army offices didn't agree with figures.

# Scenario 233

## SECRET PAPERS ON US-AFGHAN WAR PROUDNESS & OTHER DEFEAT FACTORS

### IMPORTANT NOTE:

*Americans, at their own, analysed real causes of
the US defeat in Afghanistan.
Here are briefs of some of those posts and comments;
picked from ONLY the AMERICAN MEDIA with reference to
the Secret Papers of and interviews by
SIGAR - later compiled by WP's Craig Whitlock*

The Americans now admit that the US left Afghanistan after a blatant defeat; leave aside the trillions of dollars wasted in corruption and mismanagement. Every participant amongst the soldiers, administrators, and politicians stands equally responsible for this tarnished retreat. Since ending 2001, the records gathered from known archives described 20 years of error, misconception, and deceit throughout the US military, State Department, White House, CIA and the Pentagon.

The America's decision makers, who had planned to land in Afghanistan, couldn't study their early histories of war. They fought to uphold its self-coined myth that the US is supreme. They should have recalled:

- The **KOREAN WAR** [June 1950 – July 1953] in which almost **40K Americans** were killed and more than **100K wounded.**

- Also the **VIETNAM WAR** [March 1965 – April 1975] in which **58,220 US military** fatal casualties occurred; Pentagon's *'Defence Casualty Analysis System [DCAS] Extract'* is referred.

The American experience in Afghanistan appeared virtually identical to the Russian experience in Afghanistan during 1979-89 which the Americans had avowed to avoid.

[*However, the journalists like* Craig Whitlock *would be very few in America who unearthed the whole truth while pin-pointing that - who screwed up, who was responsible for collecting and processing false information, who caused strategic and tactical confusion and who were responsible for despatching dead bodies of soldiers and civilians, in most parts of the world and who decided to throw the US tax-payers money away in vain.*]

**Why do Americans did this - and so consistently?** There is no answer with the Americans even; except that it could be some in-built or manufacturing defect in its *'cultural genes'*. One can have an idea by analysing certain really global disasters imposed by the US over the rest of the world – in fact *Americans are idealists*.

**The Curse of American Idealism:** One learned Blogger explained this phenomenon in very factual way. He wrote on media pages that Idealists are taught to ignore the details of the current situation as these interfere with a vision for the future. Ignorance of other cultures, possible constraints on action, and determination in the face of resistance are idealists' virtues - they love power – and to achieve it by any means including usages of military, economic and political resources until these are entirely depleted. And that's why it's America – they [may] lie and believe themselves justified in doing so; that's how the achievements are exaggerated and setbacks minimised.

The US leaderships mostly hated the political process of discussion and compromise; see their history. Values like honesty, integrity, and solidarity were found often jeopardised thus fairly diagnosed as the causes of failure.

> *"Whether on the Left or Right, among the Believers or the Atheists,* **optimism is the name of the game in America'**; even most American think-tanks held it so.*"

**On 9ᵗʰ August 2021;** a week before the Taliban's taking over Kabul, **Courtney Tychinski,** the Special Projects Editor at **PentaVision** [Pennsylvania], wrote:

> *".....[fantastic] candid interviews recorded with high-serving US officials both in White House and the military, attained through the Freedom of Information Act. They provide an overview on **how no one truly knew what the US's goals were in the war in Afghanistan.** Just diminishing al-Qaeda following 9/11? Punishing Afghanistan for harbouring 9/11 conspirators? Nation-building? And when no one knows what the goals are, how do we measure 'success and effectiveness' of US & NATO troops there?*

*.....it left me questioning more and more the rationale behind a war that never seemed fully logical."*

On **24**[th] **August 2021;** one US citizen **Murtaza** rated it amazing and added that the failure of the war in Afghanistan, an immensely costly and brutal two-decade long project of the American elite, revealed much about the way that the US government functions today. A jaw-dropping account of the North Korea-level lying engaged in by the US officials at the highest ranks, telling stories they knew to be completely false about the progress of the war, concealing massive financial corruption, and killing huge numbers of Afghan civilians while denying it till the last possible moment.

This **'Secret Papers'** [SIGAR] compilation speaks that the US attempted to impose a political and security order on Afghanistan without even the most basic understanding of the country and its people. In the end the endeavour just became about throwing gigantic amounts of money down a black hole, much of it funnelled to *'connected* [?]' Afghan insiders were the unsavoury allies of America on the ground, and the lion's share to American & Afghan contractors who made fortunes out of the war.

On **11**[th] **September 2021;** *Wick Welker* – an American Doctor, writer and author of many books, wrote on media sheets - it was amazing.

See an article titled **US 'LOST' the 20-year war in Afghanistan: top US General;** published on **FRANCE24** dated <u>29</u>[th] <u>September 2021</u>:

Gen Mark Milley, Chairman of the US Joint Chiefs of Staff, conceded before the House Armed Services Committee in a stark admission [on the same day of 29th Sep] that:

> *"The US 'lost the 20-year war in Afghanistan'. It is clear; it is obvious to all of us, that the war in Afghanistan did not end on the terms we wanted, with the Taliban in power in Kabul (again). The war was a strategic failure. It wasn't lost in the last 20 days or even 20 months.*

> *There's a cumulative effect to a series of strategic decisions that go way back. Whenever you get some phenomenon like a war that is lost -- and it has been, in the sense of we accomplished our strategic task of protecting America against Al-Qaeda, but certainly the end state is a whole lot different than what we wanted.*

*So whenever a phenomenon like that happens, there's an awful lot of causal factors. And we're going to have to figure that out. A lot of lessons learned here."*

## THE US GENERALS ADMITTED DEFEAT....

Gen Milley listed a number of factors responsible for the US defeat going back to a missed opportunity to capture or kill Al-Qaeda leader Osama bin Laden [OBL] at *Tora Bora* soon after the 2001 US invasion of Afghanistan.

The General also cited the 2003 decision to invade Iraq, which shifted US troops away from Afghanistan; not effectively dealing with Pakistan; and pulling advisers out of Afghanistan a few years ago.

Gen Milley and Gen Kenneth McKenzie, commander of US Central Command, told a Senate committee a day earlier [on 28<u>th September 2021</u>] that they had personally recommended that some 2,500 troops should remain on the ground in Afghanistan.

White House press secretary Jen Psaki said Biden had received *'split advice'* about what to do in Afghanistan, which the US invaded following the 9/11 event of 2001. *'Ultimately, it's up to the commander-in-chief to make a decision,'* Psaki said. *"He made a decision that it was time to end a 20-year war."*

'Secret Papers' was a timely publication about the release of candid interviews with many military personnel of various ranks and influence in the Afghanistan war. The people being interviewed thought they were giving an account for historical purposes not journalistic. And what was the general gestalt of the longest running war in American history - **unmitigated disaster.**

Craig Whitlock, by releasing the war-documents in open, gave the world a beautiful chronology of the **misinformed decisions to start the war up until the recent disastrous withdrawal** from Afghanistan. Under the garb of fighting with Al Qaeda, the US made war only to be **utterly confused about who their enemies actually were.** The Americans couldn't tell the difference between different factions of the Taliban; AND between the Taliban and Afghani civilians. Right from the first day, the US policy was to have zero diplomacy with the Taliban - something that proved to be an enormous mistake in the last.

**President Bush had no exit strategy.** He started a reckless war as a knee jerk reaction and everyone at the time supported him. Later, the US spent more on *'nation building* in Afghanistan than ever before. They created **a puppet Afghan government, mired by incompetence and corruption, which was wholly dependent on the US military to even survive.** The US tried to install the US like culture for those who didn't know how to behave with women in their own families, use a urinal, know the difference between left and right shoes etc etc. The US tried to force a way of life and government onto the people that were entirely unaccustomed and unmanageable.

> *You can't just walk into a country and make a government within 18 months, or 5 years of whatever ridiculous terms were set by Bush, Obama and Trump.*

The US tried diplomacy with a host of warlords who had zero allegiance to anyone. So then the US just threw heavy bags of money at the problem, spending billions of dollars building roads, bridges and schools in a nation that had no means of maintaining such infrastructure.

In the year 2000, the Taliban banned growing poppy in Afghanistan and it worked. As soon as the US came, it was seen widely as a legitimate way to have an income. **Once the Taliban were gone, Afghan farmers supplied about one third of the world's opium.** The US & the UK then paid farmers to destroy their crops which resulted in them growing even more poppy to sell and then make money off of destroying the crops, playing on both sides of the wicket.

**Bush, Obama and Trump oversaw a culture of fabricating metrics, downplaying military involvement and continually propping up a failed puppet government** that they created. After 20 years, these leaders destroyed a nation and left it in the very hands of those they fought - the Taliban. President **Trump literally wanted Taliban leaders to come to White House for a photo op.**

The bottom line is that the US has been doing this since 80 years, destabilizing countries and leaving them to rot.

> Next question should be that: **who profited from the war?** Who was sub-contracted? What companies were hired and **who the civil and military officials had financial interests in those companies –** AND contractors – AND choosing warlords to get hefty amounts of Dollars.

Most people know the answer; *no doubt that few Americans too made a tremendous amount of money off of the Afghanistan war.*

## AMERICAN INTELLIGENTSIA BLOGS:

**Brandon Westlake** – an artist by profession wrote that:

Wow, what an eye-opening **'Secret Documents'** treat. The Americans do have feelings of what happened in Afghanistan and why, **and who the key players were.** The humiliating defeat shows what an outright tragedy it remained. A military escapade built on blunder and ignorance, mismanagement and stupidity. It has been a comedy of errors in fact, and one on a massive deadly scale - hard to miss the connection to Vietnam.

**Umar Lee** - an American writer and political activist from Missouri, wrote:

This is like watching a 20 years long movie when you already know the multiple heroes would suddenly disappear gutted with shame at the ending. Short and corruptive numerous missteps highlighted from successive American admin and the US military; missteps of the US military and often contradictory directives from the Pentagon. The retreat speaks about false beliefs of American idealism, ignorance of Islam as religion, criminal alliance with warlords, creating a class of corrupt Afghan millionaires, and a poorly choreographed counter-insurgency strategy. *Twenty years were enough for unveiling cruel face of the American imperialism* – Secret Papers were just some of the factors.

**Secret Papers unearthed some untold facts** that lot of Afghans liked and supported the Taliban as the deliverers of peace and order. The Taliban ended the opium trade and the US couldn't do so even in twenty years after spending billion of dollars [$9bn exactly] on that menace.

**Secret Papers** told first time that Americans often neglected to avail the opportunity to negotiate with the Taliban and integrate them into the Afghan political system in 2002 and failed to do so thus unnecessarily extending conflict; consider US leaderships' own vested interests. Then the Taliban were in power again, and appear to be stronger, wiser, and more competent. Think Iraq; it's now politically-run by a sectarian government with strong ties to Iran – so whoever won the *'War on Terror',* most certainly went against America's philosophy and plans.

President Bush got us all into this mess; Obama knew this was a war that couldn't be won and so did Donald Trump; Joe Biden showed courage to finally pull the plug.

Hold on! The US was [once more] mistaken – but it'll repeat it again; the Americans believe. Let there be some problem at some place on the globe, America will be there with its mercenaries and ample Tax-Payers' money. It'll translate their issue with its own liking – and war would start – Korea, Vietnam, Iraq and later Afghanistan were in fact not America's babies.

> *Yeah, Americans know – as the Northern Virginia defence contractors and counter-terrorism strategists need to build more vacation homes; Tysons and Halliburtons need more expansion.*

One **Alex Anderson,** an American television series host, and author of 30+ books, wrote with distress that:

> *"….Conceit, cultural arrogance, blinkered worldview, lack of empathy, power without accountability, lack of empathy [artistic and otherwise], the inability to take others suffering as significant, form without substance-each new manifestation of the eternal devil turns another countenance...this arguably seems to have been the legacy of the United States since WWII as far as its military forays into other regions of the world are concerned."*

Very painful but fact remains that *'winning'* is no longer the prime consideration for the American military commanders. However, the dark and conspiratorial thoughts do beg more that why the US wanted to change other regimes without understanding much about them; and repeated the same errors over and over again? Americans question themselves that:

- *What is the basis of our standing and refusal to learn from history [our own and more about other nations']?*

- *Why do we keep making these attempts at nation building only to succeed in creating failed states?*

- *Why do we persist in dedicating our massive wealth to cause unimaginable destruction, devastation & deaths – in unknown poor communities?*

The **'Secret Papers'** made an average American surprising, about the world's wealthiest nation waging futile war against one of the poorest country on the globe – and availed dishonourable defeat after 20 years engagement there.

[Afghanistan has been called *'The Graveyard of Nations'* for a reason. The British were in there twice and lost. The Russians were in there for ten years and failed. America was there for 20 years...and what? What did it accomplish?]

The credentials of the Taliban have now been well established. With 20 years of fighting the world's premier military power, their credibility stands enhanced now; AND in magnitude, too. As an extra-added bonus, an unexpected bonanza, they have now replaced their outdated weapon caches with the state of the art military hardware weapon systems, courtesy of the American Taxpayer coupled with the successive US leadership.

But there comes more. This Defeat has put the US in an unenviable position where no other country would trust it or its loyalty be believed. Any promises of support, guarantees to be there when the going gets tough, or claims of kinship on ethical, moral or humanitarian grounds would be responded to with a laugh at best, bitter scepticism at the worst – **PAKISTAN is one example to be immediately quoted here.** Referring to Alex Anderson again:

*"A blanket of cynicism has been tossed over any pretension to even the most naive moral high ground. This attitude will be well-grounded on previous experience and contains interminable long-term consequence."*

The Afghan-war defeat is a chronicle of misconduct, corruption, malfeasance, dishonesty on the part of America. It is the cataloguing of criminal complacency, ignorance, stupidity, pointless death, waste, and a hydra's head of other evils of America's longest-standing war.

- This is the story of an astounding lack of planning, leadership, vision, discipline, responsibility and moral ownership.

- It is [Secret Papers] a document offering up to Americans dark chaos, a chronology of the bloody ignorance, monumental stupidity, cynical dishonesty, blind foolishness & arbitrary emptiness of it all.

But there is no answer to any question arising from this compendium of misfortune; Why? Wait for the time.

## AMERICA's SLOW MOTION FAILURE:

An article titled as 'America's Slow-Motion Failure in Afghanistan' By **Carter Malkasian** available at **FOREIGN AFFAIRS** of <u>March/April 2020</u> had timely warned the American government by saying that:

> "The United States has been fighting a war in Afghanistan for over 18 years. More than 2,300 U.S. military personnel have lost their lives there; more than 20,000 others have been wounded. At least half a million Afghans—government forces, Taliban fighters, and civilians—have been killed or wounded. Washington has spent close to $1 trillion on the war. No attack on the US homeland was seen since 9/11.....
>
> Numerous US officials conceded that they had long seen the **war as un-winnable.** Polls have found that a majority of Americans now view the war as a failure. Whatever the future brings, for 18 years the United States has been unable to prevail.
>
> The obstacles to success in Afghanistan were daunting: widespread corruption, intense grievances, [alleged] Pakistani meddling, and deep-rooted resistance to foreign occupation. Yet there were also fleeting opportunities to find peace, or at least a more sustainable, less costly, and less violent stalemate. American leaders failed to grasp those chances."

On 8<sup>th</sup> September 2021; another American Steve started his comments by quoting saying of Gen John Allen, Commander of NATO forces in Afghanistan: *'This is what winning looks like.* – [Feb. 2013]'.

Variations of the same hollow rhetoric, from virtually every major American military figure associated with Afghanistan, expressed for infinite times. And it isn't just the military, both Republican and Democratic administrations also chewed the same like phrases amidst deteriorating situations in Afghanistan.

From the very beginning, with the US invasion in 2001, no one knew what to do with the country after it fell. *Bush insisted that they were not there to nation build, but that's exactly what we were doing.* Obama continued many of the same policies; also pumped oceans of money into that country but with no meaningful plans. In the Vietnam conflict, the US had done the same mistakes – but the policy makers didn't learn a single thing from that earlier war.

Interestingly, at the very end, one political figure that had grown sceptical of the Afghan war back in 2009 was the then Senator Joe Biden - and finally came in a position to do something about the prolonged American wastage – AND he did in his 1st available opportunity.

On 6th September 2021; Ryan, who was in Afghanistan for a couple of years, and had compulsively, read almost everything, gave written opinion

> "…..nothing in this was particularly surprising to me, but it's [Secret Papers Report] is an excellent presentation and, to my experience, the accurate".

On 10th Sep 2021; Steven Zeitchik - a celebrity reporter of the Washington Post held: The whole American intelligentsia agree - that the debate of President Biden's sermon regarding abrupt exit from Afghanistan should be taken through a thorough and objective analysis of the past 20 years' events since 9/11 – and it should be a serious demand, too.

There are number of books on the Afghan War in American market; readers can choose from:

- Carter Malkasian's THE AMERICAN WAR IN AFGHANISTAN: A HISTORY;
- David Loyn's THE LONG WAR;
- Peter Bergen's THE RISE AND FALL OF OSAMA BIN-LADIN; and
- Spencer Ackerman's REIGN OF TERROR.

There are also a number of researches done and written over the last decade like:

- Steve Coll's GHOST WARS and DIRECTORATE S;
- Dexter Filkins' THE FOREVER WAR;
- Anand Gopal's NO GOOD MEN AMONG THE LIVING; and
- Lawrence Wright's THE LOOMING TOWER.

In most of the above books and works, the contents, material, observations and conclusions are the same or similar, according to their time frames, as later revealed in the Secret Papers. However, the successive US governments didn't seize them seriously. One more factor could be that the previous authors had no direct access to the narratives, analysis, and insights based on those documentation and interviews of key commanders, soldiers, government officials who played significant roles; as described in Whitlock's monograph since first day of the said war.

**Secret Papers** judiciously pointed out that a military strategist is always told and trained to never start a war without having a plan to end it. Here in Afghan War, the Bush administration never articulated how the war would be ended. For years, the American people were always told that the US was winning; but Presidents Bush, Obama, and lastly the Trump cronies never measured up their so called success factually on the Afghan soils.

It was Americans' hard luck that the swift and early American success in 2002 turned out to be a curse when the Bush administration changed his war policy from hunting terrorists to nation building. Despite the arrogance of Secretary of Defence Rumsfeld, the war turned against the Americans while changing strategies and commanders on a regular basis.

Another major problem the US troops faced was that they could not distinguish between the good guys and the bad guys. *For American troops Taliban and al-Qaeda were the same,* a gross error in that the Taliban followed an extremist ideology and were Afghans especially the *Pashtuns*, while al-Qaeda was made up of Arabs with a global presence who wanted to overthrow Middle Eastern autocrats allied with the US. By 2002, the Americans were fighting an enemy that had nothing to do with 9/11 which was the stated purpose of the war by President and their policy makers.

America's early success also got deteriorated as the Bush administration shifted its focus to Iraq for the removal of Saddam Hussein from power. Troops, supplies, and funding dissipated quickly; numerous commanders got frustrated with Pentagon for their lack of interest and refusal to provide the necessary equipment, troops, and funding to continue with the war in Afghanistan so effectively.

Such American errors, coupled with mass corruption of the Afghan government, and the refusal of the successive US leadership to face the facts on the battlefield had promptly enhanced the mess; obvious lack of goals and benchmarks added more fuel to the fire.

Nation-building strategy in Afghanistan, together with idea of imposing an American style democracy, on a country where the people are accustomed of living in tribal cages since centuries, with nearly zero education in rural areas, having no foundation or history of such notions – thrusting US-like governmental system on them was idiotic from the outset. Yet to unearth which advisor had guided President Bush to think so – the White House team and their strategists were bound to re-write their failure in the coming times – thus the humiliating retreat in August 2021.

The Americans tried to handle an uphill task – *task of constructing Afghan army from scratch.* The entire episode heralded the results witnessed in August 2021 when 300,000+ Afghan army collapsed and faded away when confronted by the Taliban. The US strategists had zero knowledge of the Afghan culture and their living priorities otherwise they could have saved trillions of dollars, twenty years and an embarrassing defeat.

*Steven Zeitchik* of the WP – once more commented:

> *"Another key issue was the role of Pakistan which had its own agenda visa vie the Taliban and indirectly its fears of India. By creating a sanctuary for the insurgency, it made the American task very difficult."*

Steven raised fingers on the ISI but the fact remained that the Islamabad government knew how to play in changing situations in an un-necessary prolonged war – that too without sincerity of purpose – that too to eat the tax-payers' billions dollars by keeping the *'warlords and contractors'* on the front for face-saving. Pak-Army played well as per their **'national strategy'** – not to become part of the collective and the highest corruption in the history of mankind.

*Steven Z* himself admitted in the same article that:

> *"American errors are numerous......Flooding the country with money for projects that were not needed or absorbable was very detrimental to the American mission.*
>
> *Support for Hamid Karzai and his corrupt regime, along with alliances with murderous warlords were self-defeating.*
>
> *Trying to eradicate the opium trade was high minded, but with no alternate source of income.*
>
> *Afghan farmers and warlords learned to manipulate the American strategy to reduce the drug trade was very problematical."*

## AN OBJECTIVE ANALYSIS OF US FOLLIES:

*Craig Whitlock,* in his compilation of the '**Secret Papers**', unearthed and introduced the major players in the war from Rumsfeld, Cheney, McChrystal, Petraeus, Obama, and Trump with all of the flaws exhibited by their thinking that led to failure. Whether implementing counter-insurgency, huge infrastructure projects, building inside enemy territory, and *Petraeus' strategy of being 'hell-bent at throwing money at problems'* was doomed to failure.

The bottom line as Lt Gen Douglas Lute, a Director of Operations for the Joint Staff at the Pentagon stated:

> *"....we were devoid of a fundamental understanding of Afghanistan - we didn't know what we were doing...What were we doing there? We didn't have the foggiest notion of what we were undertaking...There is a fundamental gap of understanding on the front end, overstated objectives, an over-reliance on the military, and a lack of understanding of the resources necessary."*

The Trump administration ran into the same roadblocks. His tough talk about 'winning', increased bombing that resulted in higher death counts for civilians; and did not accomplish much. It's on record that:

> *"President Trump's promises to deliver **clear cut victory** had failed he ordered the state Department and Pentagon to engage in formal, face to face negotiations with the Taliban to find a way to extricate US troops from Afghanistan without making it seem like a humiliating defeat."*

For over a decade American policy makers and commanders knew that lasting military defeat of the Taliban was not possible at all as they were a *Pashtun*-led mass movement that continued to gain strength. However, the Bush and Obama made no attempt to engage the Taliban in the diplomatic process. They should have done it much earlier – after gaining victory in 2002 – but they couldn't understand the nature of that soil. In 2009, President Obama took a hard-line approach and sent more troops to Afghanistan instead of opening dialogues with the Taliban; thus dooming any hope to end the war.

Finally, President Trump negotiated a deal whereby all US troops would be withdrawn from Afghanistan by 1ˢᵗ May 2021. However, he left an inheritance to Joe Biden who chose to oblige Trump's settlement with the Taliban to avoid further warfare. Many had chosen to blame President

Biden for an abrupt ending of the longest war and the Taliban's victory - however it was because of two decades of confusion and suffocation and a war strategy that was doomed to failure based on multiple factors enumerated above.

Now the Americans know what successes were repeatedly announced by Bush, Obama, and Trump and their buddies, in private they knew that Afghan security forces showed nil progress every where, the Taliban continuously marched at their pace, and corruption pervaded Afghan ruling puppets alienating the masses. The dominating theme, as Whitlock suggested, remained that:

> *"U.S. leaders knew their war strategy was dysfunctional and privately doubted they could attain their objectives. Yet they confidently told the public year after year that they were making progress and that victory—winning was over the horizon.*
>
> *It was impossible to square negative trends with the optimistic public messaging about progress, so US officials kept the complete datasets confidential."*

One contributor, *Chris Barsanti*, wrote in the WP dated 7th September 2021 with an interesting caption: **THE AFGHAN PAPERS REVEAL 'HOW NOT TO FIGHT A WAR'.**

> "Everyone *had opinions about how the longest war in American history had been lost and who lost it.*
>
> *It was Joe Biden. It was Donald Trump. It was Barack Obama. It was George W. Bush. It was corruption. It was opium. It was Pakistan. It was imperialism. It was too many troops. It was not enough troops..... one pinned the war's loss on* **critical race theory.** *Like the parable of the blind men and the elephant, many arguments [just] grasped a fragment of the truth; very few saw the whole....."*

The details of *Secret Papers on Afghanistan War* opened a big Pandora Box of the US supremacy and showed how three presidents in succession ignored all the evidence, avoided making tough decisions, and instead chose to bury their mistakes and let the war go with the wind. An interview with a Special Operations planner of the first bombing campaigns in October 2001 told that they had received some general guidance like, *'Hey, we want to go fight the Taliban and al-Qaeda in Afghanistan.'*

In fact, in the original plan, Taliban's regime change wasn't an objective. Feeling confident after the Taliban's quick collapse, President Bush *'jumped into the war with only a hazy idea of whom it was fighting'* and blurred the line between al-Qaeda [*who had allegedly attacked America*] and the Taliban who had a mutual support agreement with al-Qaeda but not an enemy.

In fact, the Taliban were more interested in negotiating than fighting. Several diplomats described the American decision to hunt down the Taliban unnecessarily as start of the grinding guerrilla war. They definitely did not appear to understand that they were about to try and build a whole new Afghanistan; but in those days the policies were taking turn over nights. After the Taliban defeat, the US got possession of a largely rural nation – already devastated by the Soviets. The US diplomats and State Department officials argued that leaving Afghanistan in that shape was unwise, leaving a strategic vacuum.

It was a task which Pentagon never wanted. The plan – to build an US-style government in Kabul under the control of an English-speaking tribal leader Hamid Karzai – made no sense in a tribal nation like Afghanistan; it was one hundred years job. It was not what Afghan masses needed; given the level of cultural ignorance the US policy makers had at that time. Americans did nothing to win hearts and minds of their subjects – the rural tribal masses.

Thus in the absence of a cohesive counter-insurgency strategy, the Taliban continued to gain strength in the 2000s, aided by the rampant corruption and ineffectualness of the Karzai government and aided by Pakistan's tribal border-areas where their own *Pashtun* part-families were residing and providing them safe sanctuaries. Even Islamabad had no control over that TRIBAL BELT – it never remained so since the English-rule times.

In 2009, President Obama approved the pointless military 'surge' that also failed to shatter the Taliban's determination. During 2008-10, billions in American aid flooded in without an organized spending plan; virtually the white elephants. One advisor said: *'We were building schools next to empty schools.'*

With that little strategic intelligence, one can see how the US held on to Afghanistan as long as it did. *The Afghanistan Secret Papers* made the Americans uncomfortable. Like the Pentagon Papers, the secrets contained here were not really secrets to the people running the war. One

Army colonel said '.....*the war was started in confusion, erratically pursued, and concluded in chaos'*.

---------------------------

**POST-SCRIPT:**

From the historical facts narrated above, one can understand that the relationship between the CIA and ISI was long established on firm footing during 1970s and 1980s. Then the USSR broke into pieces in 1989 – after the Soviet exit from Afghanistan – the decades old COLD WAR ended. The US lost its interest in the region especially in Afghanistan. The civil war amongst the various factions of *Mujahedeen* started because the America had pulled out itself leaving all those fighting factions at their own denying all the financial and other aids to them.

When the afghan tribal *Mujahedeen* groups were left astray without their bread and butter, they concentrated their attentions towards ISI alone. ISI was not in a position to withdraw itself all of a sudden like the US because they could jointly attack northern areas of Pakistan to snatch food from the poor villagers in border areas for themselves and their families. However, Pakistan and ISI stood by Afghans with their own meager resources.

Americans played the same game again while attacking Afghanistan after 9/11 event. He used the ISI in the same like manner as they did in 1980s – even then the ISI stood by them. But when the US felt during the on-going war that they were self sufficient – they again shun their relations with the ISI and Pakistan – and tilted towards India suddenly.

President Obama went too far into US-INDIA new relationship; he signed numerous pacts with India; had agreed for training of the Afghan Security Forces in India against an hefty payment of $88 billion (approximately) – visited India to sign pacts and agreements without even discussing an iota of its war strategy with Pakistan which keeps 2500km long border with Afghanistan whereas India had not even a single inch to share.

Obama's that childish behaviour made a clear line drawn between the American friends and foes in its longest war of the US history – thus got a shameful and humiliating defeat at last – making CIA & Pentagon to walk back with their wet pants.

# Scenario 234

## COLLAPSE OF A SUPER POWER

### FIRST FACTOR – CORRUPTION:

The world media legitimately pondered and commented that why, despite spending $1+ trillion and building an army and police force at the cost of $88 billion, the US was forced to exit so unceremoniously. The ongoing popular discourse about the collapse of the Afghan state apparatus — the national unity government, provincial governors, the Afghan National Army, Afghan police etc — had rightly focused on the chaotic departure of the US forces and the peaceful takeover by the Taliban. How come the only superpower with its military might and economic prowess could not overcome allegedly a disorganised group of the Taliban?

Various explanations ranging from Afghanistan being the *'graveyard of superpowers'* to the ideological commitment of the Taliban to the poor strategic choices made by US presidents were discussed at various august debating forums. The alternative hypothesis remained that it was *an issue regarding the collapse of an elitist state* artificially nurtured and pumped up by external stimuli. Once those incentives were withdrawn the artificial superstructure went dismantled within days whatsoever.

**Main question:** Why the soldiers and police force *surrendered so easily* to the Taliban? A possible explanation was that in the case of Afghanistan, a new elite class was popped up by an artificial respiratory system and administered injections of huge doses of the US money. The country did not have the capacity to absorb roughly $100bn annually — five times its 2020 GDP [the 2001 GDP was only $4bn]. A new class of contractors, suppliers, transporters, importers, experts, bankers and military commanders was added to the traditional elites such as warlords, government officials, clergy leaders, drug traffickers etc. *The US companies and intermediaries, got lions shares of their contracted amounts for providing safe passage of dollars to all concerned including Americans.*

*Ishrat Husain* in his article published in **daily DAWN** dated 29<u>th</u> September 2021 provided a plausible explanation to the above important query:

> *"The said enlarged elite class was the main beneficiary of the continued occupation of Afghanistan by external forces; incomes, rent-seeking opportunities, businesses, jobs and corruption swelled the elite's wealth. Having transferred this wealth abroad they were the first ones to take flights out of Kabul helped by the US forces.*
>
> ***SIGAR Report, Afghanistan Papers** and **Carnegie Fund** reports have amply documented the leakages, misappropriations and capital flight - [back to America and Dubai].*
>
> *For almost two decades, billions of dollars in corruption proceeds were funnelled from Afghanistan, a country devastated by four decades of conflicts, to abroad. These outflows played a part in stunting Afghanistan's economic and political development, facilitating resurgence of the Taliban and worsening regional instability."*

Compare this scenario with the plight of the common citizen of Afghanistan where 90% of the population was living below the poverty line; SIGAR found enough evidence of embezzlement and diversion of donor funds.

Another big question: *why corruption is being equated with the Taliban's rise;* - because the ordinary Afghan villagers had lost trust in successive US and Afghan governments both. They welcomed the Taliban not only because they were fed up with continuing violence and insecurity for the last four decades but also because they felt the Taliban would not indulge in such like corruption at least – so rampant since 2001. **Trust was the glue that kept the population attached to the Taliban.**

Ishrat Hussain further divulged that successive Afghan governments were popularly seen as having been imposed by outsiders, taking orders from the US and NATO. The army and police were recruited, trained, equipped and paid by the same outsiders not to protect the citizens or Afghanistan's territorial integrity but as a counter-insurgency force. Almost all institutions of the state had become dysfunctional and the erosion of their capacity diverted the population's attention and support towards the Taliban who could fill the vacuum.

**The Economist** reported in its <u>November 2020</u> issue that security actually improved in the areas the Taliban controlled. Local Taliban leaders solved most disputes and decisions were taken immediately and enforced effectively. The teachers actually turned up at work. *'Boys at least can still get an education and the sick can receive healthcare in areas occupied by the Taliban'*; **the Economist noted.** It was this expectation of corruption-free good governance, expeditious and inexpensive justice and access to basic services that led residents to pave the way for the Taliban.

Coming back to the same - Why soldiers and policemen surrendered so easily to the Taliban? Simply because –

> *'a soldier won't risk his life when he hasn't been paid his salary for months, his family is on the brink of starvation and he knows that his commanders have amassed huge wealth by diverting his dues and that they don't care about forces' welfare'.*

A sense of uncertainty and de-motivation prevailed because they knew their paymasters [the US] would no longer fund them. *It was the survival instinct that overwhelmed them and resulted in their surrender, incompetence and ineptness.*

The lesson from Afghanistan's story was that miss-governance and corruption by elites at the expense of the majority's welfare caused popular estrangement, alienation, disregard and allowed non-state but nationalist actors to run the state. And the US high command Generals had also accepted this reality; see the speech of the US military chiefs before the American Lawmakers about the Afghanistan debacle - *cumulative effect of 20 years of mistakes:*

WASHINGTON: [The latest testimony before the House Armed Services Committee]

> *".....major strategic issue that we are going to have to really unpack today - we need to **fully examine the role of Pakistan but the focus should be on finding the root cause of the US loss** - a whole series of decisions that took place over 20 years, not on a single-source.*
>
> *My assessment is, this is a 20-year war, and it wasn't lost in the last 20 days or even 20 months. There's a cumulative effect to a series of decisions that go way back.*
>
> *Whenever you get some phenomenon like a war that is lost — and it has been ... (because) certainly the end state is a whole lot different*

*than what we wanted. So, whenever a phenomenon like that happens, there's an awful lot of causal factors. And we have to figure that out. A lot of lessons learned here."*

**Gen Miley** also cited some major decisions, by successive US administrations, which he believed contributed to the loss. Those included *'letting Osama bin Laden escape from* **Tora Bora'**.

Another mistake, according to him, was shifting focus from Afghanistan to Iraq in the early stage of the war.

> *".....Pulling all the troops out of Afghanistan with the exception of a few others, was a major strategic decision. Pulling off intelligence advisers ... we blinded ourselves to our ability to see how the war was going."*

**On 29ᵗʰ September 2021;** throughout that day's hearing, Republicans and Democrats sparred over who to blame for America's failures in Afghanistan. **Gen Frank McKenzie,** the head of Central Command, linked Kabul's collapse in August to former President Trump's deal with the Taliban, which promised a complete withdrawal of US troops.

Gen McKenzie argued that once the US troop presence was pushed below 2,500 to meet the deal's deadline, the disentanglement of the US-backed Afghan government accelerated. He added that:

> *"The signing of the Doha agreement had a really pernicious effect on the government of Afghanistan and on its military — psychological more than anything else, but we set a date — certain for when we were going to leave and when they could expect all assistance to end."*

In the US-Taliban accord, signed in Doha, Qatar <u>on 29ᵗʰ Feb 2020</u>, the Trump administration had pledged to fully withdraw its troops from Afghanistan by May 2021 and the Taliban committed to stop attacking US and coalition forces. Some lawmakers, however, defended the withdrawal. Committee's Chairman Adam Smith said:

> *"The decision the president TRUMP made was to stop fighting a war that after 20 years it was proven we could not win. There was no easy way to do that."*

## US-PAK REMAINED APART TILL END:

See the diplomatic activity between two countries during the last days of Afghan-War in 2021:

*"President Joe Biden couldn't find time to call PM Khan — somewhat without explanation — but US-Pakistan engagement on Afghanistan continued. Secretary of State Antony Blinken and Pakistani FM Mr Qureshi spoke multiple times. US Special Rep for Afghan Reconciliation Zalmay Khalilzad continued his visits to Islamabad and Rawalpindi, last one in July [2021].*

*CIA Director Bill Burns visited Pakistan in a secret trip though was made public later. COAS Gen Bajwa received multiple calls from officials in Washington, including from Secretary of Defence Lloyd Austin. The National Security Advisors of the two countries met twice in person, and the ISI chief visited Washington just in last week of July [2021]. A new quadrilateral relationship was announced between America, Pakistan, Afghanistan, and Uzbekistan."*

Yet despite all this, there was seen no movement on intra-Afghan peace talks beyond a set of inconclusive meetings in Doha in July [2021] — because the Taliban had gained extra-ordinary momentum and advances in Afghanistan those days and the Afghan government's position was worsening rapidly; the Taliban leadership was not ready to listen any advice or even comment from outside including Pakistan. The US took it that Pakistan was not helping them being in good relations – so the distance enhanced bit by bit; till the total US defeat.

However, Pakistan repeatedly indicated earlier, covertly and openly, that it wanted the mutual relationship to be defined more broadly than with regard to Afghanistan — especially based on *'geo-economics,'* its favoured current catch-all for trade, investment, and connectivity. Pakistan could never approve that the US failures in Afghanistan be blamed on Pakistan. During the recent past, the US mostly expected Pakistan to 'DO MORE' on Afghanistan issues. Referring to '**The Future of Pakistan**' by *Stephen P. Cohen* in ***Brookings.edu*** [2011]:

*"The sticking points from the US side, however, remain: wariness about trusting Pakistan, and a desire for Islamabad to put pressure on the Taliban. Pakistan argues the requests to* **'do more'** *from the US side are never-ending."*

This mantra of **DO MORE** was repeatedly read over in terms of pushing the Taliban toward a peace agreement with the corrupt Afghan governments of Karzai and Ghani which the Taliban always and openly refused. Pakistan told the US about its inability because both the Afghan presidents were in hi-profile association with India, Pakistan's rival state who had launched about 16000 terrorist attacks in Pakistan with the aid of these two stooge rulers – and that the US had been ignoring all that activity knowingly – rather tolerated Afghan-Indian strategy with smiles.

The result was obvious – a humiliating defeat for the US and India both.

*Madiha Afzal* wrote in her article published in the '**Foreign Policy**' dated 6<u>th</u> August 2021; much earlier than the Taliban's taking over Kabul:

> *"Pakistan's official stance is that it would prefer a peaceful outcome in Afghanistan, some sort of a power-sharing arrangement reached after an intra-Afghan peace deal.*
>
> *Many are sceptical of this given Pakistan's support of the Taliban regime in Afghanistan in the 1990s* [basically it was the US support delivered to them via Pakistan]. *But Pakistan argues that a protracted civil war in Afghanistan would be disastrous for it, on three dimensions:*
>
> - *First, insecurity from Afghanistan would spill over into Pakistan.*
>
> - *Second, Pakistan fears that this would set up space for the resurgence of the Tehrik-e-Taliban Pakistan [TTP], a group responsible for killing tens of thousands of Pakistani civilians and attacking the country's army, security forces, and politicians.*
>
> - *Third, this would increase the amount of refugee flows to Pakistan [which has hosted millions of Afghan refugees since the 1990s, including 3 million at present], which it can't afford."*

Of course, these were well-founded and documented fears.

The Western media and the US power corridors were aware about what a Taliban victory would mean for Pakistan. Also the implication, that the road to a comprehensive Taliban military win would be violent or at least un-predictable. What Pakistan didn't discuss openly was: Pakistan had long preferred the Afghan Taliban to local *Pashtun* nationalists, which it viewed as threatening, and to the successive two Afghan governments of Karzai & Ghani; also which it viewed friendly with India. And the Afghan Taliban's ideological twin, the TTP, had posed an existential threat to Pakistan which had killed c80,000 Pakistanis during two decades of the recent war.

This tension was clearly making Pakistan nervous. Pakistan encountered the TTP in military operations since 2008 onwards, but many of them sought refuge across the border in Afghanistan, and regrouped themselves as a continuous process since then. The Afghan Taliban's rule over Afghanistan would almost certainly embolden the TTP, engulfing Pakistan in violence it experienced between 2007 and 2016. PM Khan's government had to negotiate a deal with the Afghan Taliban to constrain the TTP, but there was a real question of deal's effectiveness in the coming times.

The above explained tension was not perceptible to Pakistan's public; thus Pakistanis being supportive of the Afghan Taliban were against the TTP. However, the top civilian and army officials admitted to these facts then; was also alleged that the army chief and the DG ISI called the Afghan Taliban and the TTP *'two faces of the same coin.'*

During mid-year [2021], when the Taliban marched ahead in rural Afghanistan, with fingers being pointed at Pakistan's relationship with Taliban, Pakistan distanced itself from the group. PM Khan openly said that:

> *"Pakistan doesn't speak for the Taliban, nor is it responsible for it; .....that a 'rushed' US withdrawal before peace talks has set the stage for the current situation. ..... the Taliban's battlefield victories render moot any leverage Pakistan could have over it. ....that the TTP faction could be hiding among Afghan refugees in Pakistan."*
>
> [Daily **DAWN** dated 29ᵗʰ July 2021 is referred.]

Yet the world remained sceptical, amid reports of purported Taliban fighters being treated across the border in Pakistan.

In her article *Madiha Afzal,* cited above, pointed out that from America's perspective, the main task was for Pakistan to exercise its leverage in pushing the Taliban to reduce violence and toward an intra-Afghan peace deal. The second was the potential for counter-terrorism cooperation in the post-withdrawal landscape; but a chequered past marred the relationship. For Washington, part of the reason it lost the war against the Taliban was because the Taliban found support in Pakistan, including sanctuary for the Haqqani network and the *Quetta Shura.*

That Osama bin Laden [OBL] was found in Abbott Abad in 2011 eroded any remaining trust from the US side. Yet America needed Pakistan's help in the region, especially amidst withdrawals from Afghanistan.

And Pakistan largely delivered on the Trump administration's main request, to bring the Taliban to the table for talks with the US – that's why the Doha Declaration and this ending of 20 years long war.

The US Secretary of State Antony Blinken's statement after their exit from Afghan soils that *the US will re-assess its ties with Pakistan after the Taliban takeover* confirmed the US would continue to see Pakistan through the Indian prism of doubts and distrust, and would always expect Pakistan to **do more** despite its loss of human lives more than any war partner state.

During the last week of September 2021, Pakistan's Foreign Minister Mr Qureshi emphasised the need for cooperation between the two countries beyond counter-terrorism and Afghanistan. He reiterated:

> *"Our engagement has often been narrowly framed, dictated either by short-term security interests or the imperative to deal with a common challenge, and we want to break out of this pattern.*
>
> *This approach may not be viable for the US and would be a strategic mistake in the current international environment which is moving fast towards a multi-polar world. Asia is most reflective of this change as China advances in continents across the world via geo-economics through its Belt and Road Initiative [BRI]."*

Pakistan was a most favoured US-ally in and after 2001 and was instrumental in fighting the War on Terror that claimed the lives of c80,000 Pakistani civilian and forces; nevertheless, the relationship between the two remained multifaceted. The situation gone changed after the Afghan war ended; the rising multipolar world started posing challenges to the US and its status as the sole superpower. President Joe Biden admitted that:

> *"We're engaged in a serious competition with China. We are dealing with the challenges on the multiple fronts with Russia."*

Competing with Russia and China was certainly a challenge; the US-India strategic partnership faced a serious setback in the wake of the US withdrawal from Afghanistan. India's relations with China were of adversarial nature. Pakistan on the other hand had played a pivotal role in the US-China relations in the past. Former Secretary of State Henry Kissinger's first secret visit to China in the 70s was an event to note in the same context. Pakistan could help connect the US and China again in areas of converging interests and cooperation – but the US never aspired to move this way.

Pakistan emphasized that in the world of increased connectivity and interdependency, the US needed to work in this direction, particularly after its withdrawal from the Trans-Pacific Partnership [TPP] in 2017. Had the US wanted to maintain presence in this Asian region, Pakistan's involvement could be vital. Pakistan, having a unique strategic location, deserve more economic participation from Washington through developing trade, transit links, and business-to-business ties; and should consider *'peace and stability in Afghanistan'* critical.

The fact remains that America was not happy with CPEC, although Pakistan's security establishment had stressed multiple times that **'seeing Pakistan through CPEC prism only was misleading.'** Moreover, any inter-camp politics was not in the interest of any country. However, the US didn't see eye to eye with this and didn't buy the argument of geo-economics due to its hostile relations with China. The US was not ready to develop a policy towards Pakistan on a broader context; it continued to see Pakistan through specific prism of **DO MORE.**

Pakistan successfully conveyed its views and asserted that it would not compromise its national interest anymore. PM Imran Khan's stance of **ABSOLUTELY NOT** provided basis to the US to be a *'partner in peace and not in war'*; these were pillars of the policy Pakistan intended to pursue; and the approach Pakistan sought for relationship with its counterpart — a relationship based on understanding, mutual respect and diplomatic reciprocity. In a rapidly changing international environment, it was a mistake to abandon Afghanistan like in the 90s. Pakistan's FM Mr Qureshi re-asserted:

> *"It would not be in the interest of the US to repeat such a mistake of distancing itself from Pakistan and not have a continued working relationship with a country which has been an ally for over seven decades."*
>
> **Nasim Rizvi**'s analysis appeared in daily **THE EXPRESS TRIBUNE** dated 30th September 2021 is referred.

## ROLE OF INDIA IN AFGHAN WAR:

India was the only South Asian country to recognize the Soviet-backed Democratic Republic of Afghanistan in the 1980s after the Soviet's entry and occupation.

India aided America for the overthrow of the Taliban and became the largest regional provider of humanitarian and reconstruction aid to Afghanistan during Karzai & Ghani's governments. Indians were working in various rebuilding projects in Afghanistan – but in fact India's foreign intelligence agency R&AW was working in cover to malign Pakistan and train and support TTP insurgents. During 2006 there were 600 Balochi separatists who were receiving military training in Indian camps which later launched thousands terrorist attacks in Pakistan; *Mariana Baabar's* essay in **OUTLOOK INDIA** dated 24th April 2006, titled as *"RAW is Training 600 Balochis in Afghanistan"* is referred.

Relations between Afghanistan and India received a major boost in 2011 with the signing of a *Strategic Partnership Agreement,* Afghanistan's first accord with the US since the Soviet invasion of 1979.

A major shift in India's position on Afghan Taliban was reported by a top Qatar official in June 2021, revealing that an Indian delegation quietly visited Doha to meet Taliban's leadership. The agenda had taken several weeks in the making in the first half of 2021, and likely involved Qatari mediation between India and the Taliban, too; *Geeta Mohan's* essay in **INDIA TODAY** dated 22nd June 2021 is referred

After 9/11 event and the US-led invasion of Afghanistan in 2001, India offered intelligence and other forms of support for the Coalition forces. After the overthrow of the Taliban, India established diplomatic relations with the newly established Afghan national government of Karzai. India also provided $650 million to Afghanistan in humanitarian and economic aid. India's more emphasis on training of Afghan civil servants, diplomats and police gave it a strategic insight.

In 2005, India sponsored Afghanistan's membership in the South Asian Association for Regional Cooperation [SAARC]; which matured in 2007 and Afghanistan finally became the eighth member of SAARC. It was basically to develop strategic and military cooperation against the Taliban because an Indian national [a spy of RAW] was killed by the Taliban in November 2005. India filtered its own benefits out of this killing and deployed 200 Indian soldiers in the garb of providing security for Indian nationals. In fact those were the so-called soldiers who targeted Pakistan's Balochistan province and the Pak-Afghan border tribal villages inside Pakistan.

India also pursued a policy of close collaboration with Afghanistan and Iran in order to bolster its standing as a REGIONAL POWER to launch attacks inside Pakistan. It signed three memorandums of understanding [MOUs] with Afghanistan on various disciplines to keep and increase Indian security personnel on Afghan soils. During Hamid Karzai's visit to India in April 2006, an agreement providing $50 million to promote bilateral businesses was also signed; that initial amount was then revised to $150 million, then to $750 million.

The Indian Army's Border Roads Organisation constructed a road in 2009 in the remote Afghan province of Nimroz, connecting Delaram to Zaranj providing a viable alternative route for the duty-free movement of goods through the Chabahar port in Iran to Afghanistan. It was a key strategy to build up transportation links bypassing land routs through Pakistan, helping reduce the Afghan economy's dependence on Pakistan.

On 7th July 2008; the Indian embassy in Kabul was attacked by a suicide car bomber – killing 58 people and leaving 141 wounded. Senior Indian Army officer Brig Ravi Mehta was entering the embassy gates in a car when the attack took place; he and another hi official were killed at the spot. India alleged that the blast was sponsored by the Pakistan's ISI which was immediately refuted. Next month, Afghan President Karzai visited New Delhi for official condolence to that human loss.

On 18th October 2009; the Indian embassy in Kabul was attacked again by a car bomb killing about 17 people and leaving tens wounded.

On 26th February 2010; another attack took place at the Arya Guest House [state hotel] resulting in the death of 17 Indian doctors and a civilian. It was a combined suicide car bombing and shooting attack by two militants allegedly belonging to the Taliban.

According to 2010 Gallup poll, which interviewed 1,000 adults, 50% Afghans approved of the job performance of India's leadership and 44% disapproved with 6% refusing to answer. According to the survey, Afghan adults approved of India's leadership more than of US leadership.

On 20th September 2011; former Afghan president Burhanuddin Rabbani was assassinated with several other people in a bomb attack in Kabul. After the Taliban government was toppled in NOVEMBER 2001, Rabbani had returned to Kabul and served briefly as President from 13TH November to 22ND December 2001, till Hamid Karzai was chosen as his successor at the **Bonn International Conference**. Mr Rabbani was killed at his home by a suicide bomber who, officials believed, had concealed a bomb in his turban. He was meeting members of the Taliban at that time. The council leaders were there in negotiations with the Taliban.

On 4th October 2011; Afghanistan signed a strategic pact with India; calling it a Strategic Partnership Agreement during a visit of President Karzai to Delhi. Indian PM Man Mohan Singh said violence in Afghanistan was undermining security in South Asia so *India would 'stand by Afghanistan'* when foreign troops withdraw from the country in 2014.

Mr Karzai's visit followed a series of attacks which had damaged ties between Kabul and Pakistan as the increasingly close relationship between Kabul and Delhi was viewed with suspicion. The pact was believed to include an Indian commitment to increase its training of Afghan security forces and police. Both sides were to launch Partnership Council, topmost body to implement the **Strategic Partnership Pact** in May 2012.

This strategic partnership agreement between India and Afghanistan could have evoked howls of protest from Pakistan as it had long been regarded its western neighbour as part of its sphere of influence – but Pakistan remained cool. Pakistan, however, noted New Delhi's way to expand influence and to become Regional Leader in Southern Asia.

Instead, Pakistan's PM Mr Gilani said:

> *"India and Afghanistan are both sovereign countries and they have the right to do whatever they want to but regional stability should be preserved."*

Soon after, PM Gilani met his Indian counterpart Man Mohan Singh on the margins of a regional summit in the Maldives; both PMs promised a new chapter in ties. It was resolved that the next round of talks between officials as part of an engagement on various issues would produce definite results. Afghanistan or the pact was scarcely mentioned in public or media.

In those days, Pakistan was battling multiple calamities, including soar ties with the US; even looking worse than those with India. It was also struggling to tackle the militant groups like TTP and *Sapah e Sahaba* that had posed mortal dangers for Pakistan itself and additionally a deep economic downturn generally. While Pakistan continued to invest time and energy in Afghanistan, a large part of the war had come home too and it was struggling to enforce its writ on the northern border areas adjoining Afghanistan. A lessening tension with India could help at this point but it didn't happen.

**Disappointed with the US behaviour;** hostile Pakistan balked at trade and transit through Pakistan though unnecessarily. Sajjad Ashraf, a professor at the Lee Kuan Yew School of Public Policy, said:

> *"If the three countries can reach an understanding and let India develop Afghan capacity leading to regional economic integration, Pakistan too becomes a winner. In the age of globalisation, following any other course will result in Pakistan lagging behind."*

For India, peace in Afghanistan was important to be able to exploit the vast economic potential of the Central Asian states. It shared Afghanistan's concerns about the security of the nation after the western withdrawal from a combat role in 2014. In the meantime, Afghanistan, India and Iran signed the **Chabahar Agreement** as against the Gwadar project of the CPEC.

**On 22nd May 2014;** the Indian consulate in Herat was attacked by 3 militants equipped with AK-47s, RPGs, hand grenades and suicide vests.

**On 24th December 2015;** India donated three Mi-25 attack helicopters to Afghanistan as part of the bilateral strategic partnership to counter the Taliban groups. The next day, on **25th December,** Indian PM Narendra Modi visited Kabul to open the newly constructed Afghan parliament opposite the ruins of the Darul Aman Palace, which had been built by India for $90 million. PM Modi and President Ghani held that:

> *"Though, India and Afghanistan need no introduction, we are bound by a thousand ties… We have stood by each other in the best and worst of times"*

**On 4th June 2016;** PM Modi and Afghan President Ghani formally inaugurated the $290-million Salma Dam with a capacity of 42 MW power generation. The dam was expected to help Afghanistan capitalize on opportunities that would open up once the India backed Chabahar project completed; hoping to link the port in Iran to Central Asia's road and railway networks.

**In August 2021;** After Taliban's take over, Dozens of refugees from Afghanistan arrived in India following the new government established; India hosted hundreds but no details yet.

## NEW COLD WAR – NOW US vs CHINA:

**On 21ˢᵗ September 2021;** the US President Joe Biden, while addressing the UN General Assembly, said:

> *"We've ended 20 years of conflict in Afghanistan, and as we close this period of relentless war, we're opening a new era of relentless diplomacy of using the power of our development aid to invest in new ways of lifting people up around the world."*

After the US withdrawal from Afghanistan, Biden's administration shifted their attention and energy towards persistent peace-keeping policy. However, the growing Sino-US wedge was alarming because of the impact it could have on the world-order and the possibility of a rift in US-Russian relations. Today's emerging realities require re-adjustments, which negate what President Biden narrated in his speech. The main issue for the whole Western block and the US was, in fact, the China's economic expansion.

A new grouping of Australia, UK and US [AUKUS] remained under discussion and finally agreed upon and signed as a new initiative to deal with growing Chinese engagements in the Indo-Pacific region. Already a four-member group of Australia, India, Japan and the US known as QUAD was there for the same purposes – a manifestation of what Beijing termed **COLD WAR MENTALITY**. The first summit of QUAD held in Washington on 24ᵗʰ September 2021 was a mature effort to further consolidate the security alliance aimed at containing China. Both QUAD and AUKUS could be termed as an eastern NATO that focused on the Indo-Pacific region.

After spending 2-3 trillion dollars during its 20 years of futile war in Afghanistan, the US shifted its focus on two major threats to its influence in Europe and the Asia-Pacific — Russia and China. In military power, China was far behind the US but then came on par with the US in the economic arena. It has also tried to bridge the gap in military and technological power. Even Russia recovered itself from the 1990's fall syndrome of the USSR and its rise challenged America's so-called unbeatable power-myth.

America's new policy was based on new main objective in Asia. Priority was given to isolate and contain China in the Asia-Pacific region by utilising AUKUS and QUAD relationships along with South Korea, Taiwan, the Philippines and Vietnam. Exploiting grey areas like unrest in

Xinjiang, Tibet, Hong Kong mounted its strategic priority. Over the years, China got consolidated its soft power by diplomacy, aid, trade and investments under its Belt and Road Initiative [BRI]. Yet to see how President Biden would transform his claims and plans into reality - given shaken US confidence amidst its humiliation in Afghanistan.

Since the Taliban's takeover of Kabul on 15th August 2021, the US and India missed no opportunity to hurt and damage Pakistan. Despite serious human rights violations by the Indian security forces in Occupied Jammu & Kashmir and violence against minorities particularly Muslims in Assam, *President Biden warmly welcomed PM Modi to the White House.* Biden's message to Pakistan was loud and clear that India would remain a priority despite BJP's communal persecution and grave violation of human rights. Biden-Modi duo would shape things to contain China and Pakistan.

After withdrawing from Afghanistan, the US was in no need of any assistance and support from Pakistan. It started using its advantageous position to reformulate a new strategy aiming at Beijing and Islamabad. The US opted to tame Pakistan by using its clout in IMF, World Bank, Asian Development Bank and other multilateral financial institutions to exert maximum pressure on Islamabad. It was difficult to determine how Pakistan would cope with the Indo-US nexus in future.

Lastly, the US and India started playing diplomatic tactics to create a wedge in Sino-Russian relations. In the last 30 years, Russia and China have strengthened relations through their fundamental role in the **Shanghai Cooperation Organization,** which led to a deepening of strategic, security, economic and political ties between the two; but yet to see how India and the US would cause a rift in Sino-Russian relations. So far, both Russian President Vladimir Putin and Chinese President Xi Jinping remained firm on maintaining their deep-rooted ties. However, one can expect rupture in their relations when China would announce and show an aggressive and offensive stance against AUKUS and QUAD.

Russia would also like to maintain its age-old friendship with India; meaning thereby that a loose agreement over tolerance and cooperation was likely. The famous dictum that *'in global politics, there are no permanent enemies and no permanent allies but only interests'* would matter in Sino-Russian relations and Pak-US ties both. Following its humiliating withdrawal from Afghanistan, the US was confronted with several foreign policy challenges.

# Scenario 235

## COST OF THE AFGHAN WAR

### SPENING $290m DAILY ON AFGHAN WAR:

America spent $290 million every day for 7,300 days [more than 2.1 trillion] on its war efforts and nation-building projects in Afghanistan; Brown University's data report disclosed. For more details daily 'DAWN' dated 14th November 2021 is referred.

That's how the United States ended up spending more than $2 trillion in the last 20 years in Afghanistan, the University's report titled as **Costs of War Project** said. The report also pointed out that the money helped *'create a tiny class of young, ultra-rich Afghans,'* many of whom started as interpreters for the US army and became millionaires. The contracts helped fuel a system of mass corruption that engulfed the country and, eventually, doomed its fragile democracy. **The CNBC** commented:

> *"The US made all these efforts to rebuild Afghanistan, yet it took just nine days for the Taliban to seize every provincial capital, dissolve the army and overthrow the US-backed government."*

In an interview with the Pentagon watchdog SIGAR, **Ryan Crocker,** a two-time US ambassador to Afghanistan, *blamed this post-9/11 corruption for America's failure.* The Ambassador remarked:

> *"The ultimate point of failure for our efforts, you know, wasn't an INSURGENCY. It was the weight of ENDEMIC CORRUPTION."*

Ambassador Crocker believes that the US bears responsibility for much of the corruption in Afghanistan because it flooded the country with billions of dollars more than its economy could absorb. Yet, in the early years of the Afghan-war, awarding government contracts to Afghan nationals was seen as a key part of the overall US counter-insurgency strategy. Several of these Afghan millionaires started their careers as interpreters for the US military and often their loyalty was the only criterion for getting the hefty defence contracts.

As has been mentioned earlier; as per Pentagon analysis, 40% of the $108 billion that the US Defence Department paid to contractors in Afghanistan between 2010 and 2012 ended up in the hands of either the Taliban, the Haqqani network, organised crime rings, drug traffickers or corrupt Afghan officials – more speaking about President Obama's inherent deficiencies in command, ability, capacity & control.

## COSTS OF AFGHAN WAR: DOD'S FIGURES:

Referring to **Robin Wright**'s essay titled *'Does the Great Retreat from Afghanistan Mark the End of American Era'* appeared at **newyorker. com** on 15th **August 2021:**

> *"For the US, the costs didn't end with its withdrawal from either Afghanistan or Iraq. It could cost another two trillion dollars just to* **pay for the health care and disability of veterans** *from those wars. And those costs may not peak until 2048.*
>
> *America's longest war will be a lot longer than anyone anticipated two decades ago—or even as it ends. In all, forty-seven thousand civilians have died, according to Brown University's Costs of War Project. More than twenty-four hundred were US military personnel, and almost four thousand were US contractors.*
>
> *The cost of the post-9/11 wars in Iraq, Afghanistan, Pakistan, Syria, and elsewhere totals* **about $8 trillion.** *"*

However, one can go into more details here. As per figures released, after the exit-date of 31st **August 2021**, by *the US Department of Veterans Affairs [DOD]*, the American journey of war remained the longest in Afghanistan as compared to other wars taken from the beginning till today. The details are:

> *Revolutionary: 8.4 years [1775 – 1783];* **Civil War:** *4 years [1861 – 1865];* **World War I:** *1.6 years [1917 – 1918];* **World War II:** *3.7 years [1941 – 1945];* **Korean War:** *3.1 years [1950 – 1953];* **Vietnam:** *10.75 years [1964 – 1975];* **Iraq War** *8.75 years [2003 – 2012];* **Afghanistan:** *19.8 years [2001 – 2021].*

The US had mounted an invasion of Afghanistan following the alleged foreign attacks on Twin Tower and Pentagon - in New York, Washington DC and Pennsylvania on 11th **September 2001** [popularly known as 9/11] in which nearly 3,000 people were allegedly killed.

The war in Afghanistan caused high costs for the US in terms of lives lost, troops deployed and dollars spent. During the height of the conflict, America had a deployment of nearly 100,000 people in Afghanistan – including US Armed Forces and Department of Defence [DOD] Funded Contracted Personnel. Referring to the **Congressional Research Service [DOD]**; after FY2017, the Department had started withholding US Armed Forces levels from public release.

Quoting the details collected by *Megan Duzor* of the **VOA News:**

> *"In this longest US War since 2001,* **2442 US troops have died** *in the conflict in Afghanistan. American researchers at Brown University estimate that in total about 70 times number of people has been killed in Afghanistan during that period, including over* **47,000 civilians.**
>
> *The breakdown of the TOTAL DEATHS - 171,336 comes as under:*
>
> **US Troops - 2,442; US Contractors - 3,846; Other allied troops - 1,144; Humanitarian aid workers – 444; Journalists and media workers – 72; Afghan National military and police - 75,314; Civilians - 47,245; AND Taliban fighters - 51,191.**
>
> *As per Pentagon's record, US military operations in Afghanistan have cost $824.9 billion since 2001. Brown University's researchers put the* **total cost of operations in both Afghanistan and Pakistan** *at nearly $2.3 trillion."*

**BBC's research** issued its own figures in this regard; see its concise report released on media during the first week of September 2021.

US forces landed in Afghanistan on 7<sup>th</sup> October 2001. With the withdrawal of foreign forces from Afghanistan and the takeover by the Taliban; look below - how much the US and its NATO allies spent in that country in 20 years of military occupation. US troop numbers grew as Washington poured in billions of dollars to fight a Taliban insurgency and fund reconstruction, peaking at about 110,000 in 2011; official data didn't **include special operations forces, and other temporary units.** In 2020, they were reduced to only 4,000.

NATO member countries were also part of the foreign troop presence in the country. However, they formally ended their combat mission in December 2014, but kept a 13,000-strong force there to help train Afghan forces and support counter-terrorism operations. There were significant numbers of private security contractors in Afghanistan. This included [till ending 2020] more than about 8,000 US citizens on various assignments; the **US Congress** held all concerned records.

Following the final withdrawal of the US troops, Biden quoted two figures for the total cost of the war. He said:

> *"After more than $2 trillion spent in Afghanistan... [or] you could take the number of $1tn, as many say. However, the vast majority of spending in Afghanistan came from the US."*

NOW see another analysis on the **COSTS OF AFGHAN WAR....**

The American military had achieved a quick victory over the Taliban and Al Qaeda in early 2002 but soon the focus was shifted towards Iraq; the Afghan conflict became a secondary effort and the mission went blurred. The Taliban also got consolidated, in the meantime gathered their scattered groups while remained hidden in border-tribal areas. Senior American officials almost always briefed about the on-paper progress and stories.

**Thomas Gibbons-Neff** wrote in *'Washington Post'* dated 29th August 2021 about the lies spoken by the American elite and asked that: *'What Did the US Get for $2 Trillion in Afghanistan'*?

Thomas gave a little brief that the US spent as the details:

- $1.5 trillion    on WAR
- $500 billion    on INTEREST
- $87+ billion    on training of Afghan Forces
- $24 billion    on Economic Development
- $9+ billion    on Counter-Narcotics

SIGAR released reports which determined that an assessment of above spending on the said war found very little accounts to show for it.

A senior National Security Council official said that:

> *"....the Obama's White House, along with the Pentagon, pushed for data that showed President Obama announced surge in 2009 was succeeding. [However,] It was impossible to create good metrics. We tried using troop numbers trained, violence levels, control of territory, and none of it painted an accurate picture. **The metrics were always manipulated for the duration of war.**"*

Since 2014, after the Pentagon officially and euphemistically 'ended combat operations' putting the Afghan military in the lead, more than 50,000 Afghan security forces died. Of the $133 billion that the US spent on reconstruction programs in Afghanistan, about $88 billion went toward training the Afghan Army and police forces. **Robert Finn,** the US ambassador to Afghanistan in 2002-03, told investigators that:

> *"If you look at the overall amount of money spent in Afghanistan, you see a tiny %age of it went to help the people of the country. It almost all went to the military and even most of that money went for local militia and police training..... That tribal leaders and patronage* **networks engendered a new form of corruption."**

Quoting the **BBC** dated **3rd September 2021:**

> *"In 2010-12 when the US had more than 100,000 soldiers in Afghanistan, the cost of the war grew to more than $100bn a year, **according to US government figures.** As the US military shifted its focus away from offensive operations and concentrated more on training up Afghan forces, costs fell sharply to about $45bn in recent years."*

The $2 trillion figure referenced by President Biden was based on **a study by Brown University,** which included interest on debt used to finance the war and expenses such as veterans' care. This study also included spending in Pakistan, which the US used as a base for Afghan-related operations. It found that costs of the war and future commitments, including the amounts America owed to Pakistan for tasked solo operations by the Pak-Army in Afghanistan from 2001 to 2020, amount to $2.3tn.

The UK and Germany - who had the largest numbers of troops in Afghanistan after the US - spent an estimated $30bn and $19bn respectively over the course of the war.

Despite pulling out nearly all their troops, the US and NATO promised a total of $4bn a year until 2024 to fund Afghanistan's own forces; but of course had to discontinue in the wake of Afghan Army's zero performance. The fact remained that the bulk of the money spent in Afghanistan had gone to counter-insurgency operations, and on the needs of troops such as food, clothing, medical care, special pay and benefits; separate heads like lost to waste, fraud and abuse over the years are also to be considered.

In a quarterly report to the US Congress in <u>October 2020,</u> the watchdog responsible for the oversight of reconstruction efforts in Afghanistan [SIGAR] estimated that: *'....about $19bn were lost in 'waste, fraud and abuse' during May 2009 - December 2019'.*

***Nongovernmental Estimate*** of US costs for the 20-year war in Afghanistan is more than double the calculation made by the US Department of Defence (DOD); Anwar Iqbal's essay in daily **'DAWN'** dated <u>8th November 2021</u> is referred.

The Special Inspector General for Afghanistan Reconstruction [**SIGAR**], released its latest findings in the first week of November 2021, focusing on how the ever-soaring costs of war forced Washington to reconsider its Afghan strategy. The report noted that the Brown University's Costs of War Project in its latest estimates put total costs of the war at $2.26 trillion.

This **Watson Report** builds on Department of Defence [DOD]'s $933 billion Overseas Contingency Operations [OCO] budgets and State's $59 billion OCO budgets for Afghanistan and Pakistan. Unlike the DOD Cost of War Report, the Watson report adds what it considers to be Afghanistan-related costs of $433 billion above DOD baseline costs, $296 billion in medical and disability costs for veterans, and $530 billion in interest costs on related Treasury borrowing.

> [*DOD's latest Cost of War Report, dated <u>30<sup>th</sup> June 2021</u>, said its cumulative obligations for Afghanistan, including US war fighting and reconstruction, had reached $839.8 billion. Cumulative reconstruction and related obligations reported by State, USAID, and other civilian agencies reached $49.7 billion.*]

The SIGAR report notes that since 2002, Congress appropriated more than $145.96 billion for reconstruction and related activities in Afghanistan, of which nearly $110.26 billion was for six of the seven largest active reconstruction accounts.

The **International Narcotics Control & Law Enforcement** [INCLE] reported cumulative appropriations of $5.50 billion and $0.57 billion in funds remaining for possible disbursement on <u>30<sup>th</sup> June 2021</u>. The fall of Kabul in August 2021, delayed all the disbursements. The Congress created the **Afghanistan Security Forces Fund** [ASFF] to provide the **Afghan National Defence Forces** [ANDSF] with equipment, supplies, services, training, and funding for salaries, as well as facility and infrastructure repair, renovation, and construction.

President Trump signed the **Consolidated Appropriations Act 2021,** into law on 27<sup>th</sup> December 2020, which provided an appropriation of $3.05 billion for ASFF for fiscal year 2021 and a revocation of $1.10 billion for ASFF for fiscal year 2020, reducing the original appropriation from $4.20 billion to an adjusted appropriation of $3.10 billion.

As of 30<sup>th</sup> September 2021, cumulative appropriations for ASFF stood at more than $81.44 billion, with nearly $76.39 billion having been obligated, and nearly $75.72 billion disbursed.

The SIGAR report also included a joint statement issued after 8<sup>th</sup> Sept 2021's virtual meeting of the foreign ministers of Pakistan, China, Iran, Tajikistan, Turkmenistan, and Uzbekistan. The statement affirmed *'the importance of sustained international engagement on Afghanistan, especially in supporting its humanitarian and development needs.'*

The SIGAR report noted that in 2019, Afghanistan imported goods totalling $7.33 billion while exporting only $975 million worth according to World Trade Organization data. This produced a negative merchandise trade balance of $6.36 billion, equivalent to 30.1% of Afghanistan's GDP.

Since the war against the Taliban began in 2001, **about 456 UK troops died.** President Ghani said in 2019 that more than 45,000 members of the Afghan security forces had been killed since he became president five years earlier. Brown University's research in 2019 estimated the loss of life amongst the national military and police in Afghanistan to be more than 64,100 since October 2001. **According to the UN Assistance Mission in Afghanistan [UNAMA],** nearly 111,000 civilians were killed or injured since it started recording civilian casualties in 2009.

Not only the Afghan War caused losses to the US, INDIA's $3b investment in Afghanistan went in vain too. Referring to the *APP's Article no:2822* dated 11<sup>th</sup> September 2021 on media pages:

> *"India had been using Afghan soil against Pakistan since 2001 by investing about $3 billion on infrastructure, training of Afghan forces and other projects to establish a network for its permanent foothold and to achieve its overt and covert designs - by sponsoring terrorism against Pakistan from Afghan territory."*

**India invested $3b** in Afghanistan to destabilise Pakistan; it violated various Articles of the UN Charter including Article 2(4), Article 41(3) of the Vienna Convention, and Paras 2 & 5 of UN Security Council Resolution 1373 of 2001. However, when the Taliban re-captured Afghanistan in August 2021, Indian designs turned into total loss and chaos; the Modi's government had acted as top spoiler of regional peace. It's already on record that India had supported and trained *Dai'sh & TTP* elements to use as proxy tools for its nefarious designs against Pakistan, Afghanistan and the region.

## US MONEY – LOOTED: YOU TOO BRUTUS....

In January 2010, Afghan anti-corruption agents trained by the US, raided **New Ansari Money Exchange** HQ in Kabul, one of the country's largest financial outlets, and carted away tens of thousands of documents. US officials suspected the politically connected firm was laundering money for narcotics traffickers and insurgents by moving billions of dollars to Dubai and other foreign destinations.

*Michael Flynn*, the then military intelligence chief in Afghanistan and later President Trump's national security adviser, told that the US forces played a pivotal role in the operation and examined the seized documents and data. He also added:

> *"It was a huge success. We conducted that raid and in three days, we did a lot of exploitation. We brought in (rope) about 45 people from around the country very quietly. New Ansari was just incredibly corrupt. It had double books and people were just stealing us blind - Was anyone held accountable? No, no one was held accountable."*

Why not held accountable - they turned out to be men from Afghanistan's presidential palace. Months after the raid, investigators wire-tapped a conversation in which a senior aide to Karzai, named **Zia Salehi** allegedly agreed to block the New Ansari probe in exchange for a bribe. He was arrested in July 2010. Within hours, however, Karzai personally intervened and ordered Salehi's release from jail, declaring that investigators had over-stepped their authority. The Afghan government later dropped all charges against all.

- *The fact prevailed that Karzai's aide, Zia Salehi, had been on the CIA's payroll for years, too.*

Obama admin bogged down again, and the US-inspired anti-corruption drive lost even more steam. The Salehi case was a spinning point as his arrest had provoked a *'hornet reaction'* by the presidential palace, which ordered Afghan law enforcement agents to stop cooperating with the US officials. In real terms, the interest and enthusiasm lost after Salehi Case.

> *"The American money was empowering a lot of bad people. There was massive resentment among the common people. Americans were considered the most corrupt here so had no credibility on the corruption issue'.* [SIGAR's Interviews referred]

Less than two months after Salehi's catch and release, an even bigger scandal arose to test the White House's credibility. **KABUL BANK,** the country's biggest, nearly collapsed under the weight of $1 billion in fraudulent loans — an amount equal to one-twelfth of the country's entire economic output the year before. The Afghan government engineered an emergency bailout to stem a run on the bank as angry crowds lined up to withdraw their savings.

Investigators soon determined that Kabul Bank had falsified its books to hide hundreds of millions of dollars in unsecured loans to politically connected business executives, including the president's brother Mahmoud Karzai and the family of Fahim Khan, the warlord then serving as the country's first vice president. An American officer of the US Treasury Department posted in Kabul as Afghan Government Adviser told the interviewers:

> *"On a scale of one to 10, it was a 20 here. It had elements that you could put into a spy novel, and the connections between people who owned Kabul Bank and those who run the country."*

Much of the looted money had originated from the US treasury, which subsidized the salaries of Afghan soldiers, police and civil servants who had made up the bulk of Kabul Bank's deposits. At first, the Obama admin loudly announced to fully investigate the Kabul Bank scandal — not only to recover the stolen money but also to demonstrate to the Afghan people that no one was above the law.

The US officials were upset because there were a million things to do, and all of it depended on the Karzai regime as an effective partner but if this [**Kabul Bank Scandal**] was allowed to continue, every move would become debateable. There was a lot of personal anger and disgust. Especially embarrassing as the US had deployed tens of financial advisers and watchdogs to Kabul yet had somehow missed a giant FRAUD scheme under their so-called direct supervision.

Another American, former consultant to Afghanistan's Central Bank for three years, asked the said US Advisor about Kabul Bank's fall; see reply:

> *"We had an hour-long conversation. I asked him, do you think this is a financially sound bank? He said, 'Yes.' And literally 30 days afterward, the whole house of cards came down. This was one of the biggest misses in my career. A $1 billion bank collapsed, and the US adviser swore to me it was financially sound."*

However, the insider US military officers and spy agencies had known about troubles inside Kabul Bank a year before its meltdown. The US intelligence officials were tracking *illicit money flows from the bank to the Taliban* and other insurgents and had shared the information with their counterparts in Afghan intelligence. But none of the intelligence agencies bothered more *'because it wasn't in their mandate'*.

A year after the scandal became public, the US Ambassador in Kabul, **Karl Eikenberry,** made the case a top priority and pressed Karzai to take action. But once more, the embassy backed off after Eikenberry was replaced by Ryan Crocker in July 2011. *Aah; how fragile and precarious US policy was* then; literally overnight the entire policy changed. Crocker was instructed to make the issue go away; bury it as deep as possible, and to make silent all voices within the embassy.

The **US Ambassador Crocker,** as well as US military commanders and others in Washington, didn't want to risk alienating Karzai, because they needed his support as thousands of additional American soldiers had arrived in the war zone. Crocker and his colleagues didn't want Congress or international donors to use that bank scandal as an excuse to cut off aid to Kabul. The US got eased after changing its Ambassador.

Later, for his part, Crocker told SIGAR that he agreed corruption was an enormous problem that had sabotaged the war effort but by the time the Kabul Bank scandal struck, it was too late. The Ambassador maintained:

> *"I was struck by something Karzai said and repeated a number of times during my tenure, which is that the West, led by the US, in his clear view, had a significant responsibility to bear for the whole corruption issue.*
>
> *I always thought Karzai had a point, that you just cannot put those amounts of money into a very fragile state and society, and not have it fuel corruption –* **NO you just can't.**"

America spent $290 million every day for 7,300 days; but when Taliban fighters seized Kabul without firing a single shot, President Biden blamed Afghans for failing to defend their country; the Afghan political leaders fled the country and the Afghan military gave up without fighting – what an awesome defeat of a super power.

Referring to *Christina Wilkie's* essay Dated 10<sup>th</sup> September 2021 at **CNBC.Com:**

> *"America's fault began when they invaded Afghanistan seeking revenge against al-Qaeda for the twin-towers terrorist attacks that allegedly killed 2,977 people on 11<sup>th</sup> Sept 2001 [9/11].*
>
> *The US Embassy in Kabul was closed on the first day of the Taliban's entry in Kabul and the American soldiers left the soils two weeks later. Abandoned air bases, half-finished construction projects and tens of thousands of untraceable guns litter the countryside, all purchased with American money."*

Christina, like many others, wrote correctly that the US dollars also created the '*9/11 millionaires and caused mass corruption* in Afghanistan' - a new class of ultra-wealthy Afghans who made their fortunes working as contractors for the US and NATO. A few of these millionaires became role models for a new generation of Afghan entrepreneurs and philanthropists. Many more exploited their family ties to government officials or provincial warlords in order to secure lucrative contracts. Over the time, the US government contracts became the fuel for a system of mass corruption that engulfed the country and, eventually, doomed its fragile democracy.

In the eyes of **Ryan Crocker,** a two-time **US ambassador** to Afghanistan, the US bears responsibility for much of the corruption in Afghanistan because it flooded the country with billions of dollars more than its economy could absorb; but no one bothered then.

In the early years of the war in Afghanistan, when American soldiers were still hunting al-Qaeda terrorists and battling Taliban fighters, the idea of using local *Afghan contractors* to supply US military bases seemed like a good one. By contrast, in Iraq most of the supply and logistics work for US troops was performed by non-Iraqis, typically through contracts with huge multinational firms. But in Afghanistan, awarding government contracts to Afghan nationals was a key part of the US counter-insurgency approach and thus the whole scheme. Later it became an *official Pentagon procurement policy* – duly approved by Congress in 2008. A 2011 congressional report on military contracting held:

> "*Employing local nationals injects money into the local economy, provides job training, builds support among local nationals, and can give the US a more sophisticated understanding of the local landscape.*"

But what happened at last - several Afghans who though became millionaires working as US contractors had become interpreters for American soldiers, accompanying service members on dangerous missions during some of the deadliest years of the war. The loyalty they earned as interpreters later served them well in the defence contracting business.

One Hekmatullah Shadman's story is known in Pentagon. As troop levels were increased in Afghanistan after President Obama's announcement, so did Shadman's revenue that was already on role of a US military base in Kandahar since 2005. He had started contracting with one truck but then grew up so sharply that in 2009, Shadman's company billed the Department of Defence for $45 million. During 2007-12, Shadman's trucking company collected $167 million from US government contracts; all proved by his bank statements. But who were his unofficial American partners – Pentagon never got moved purposefully!

That's why, Shadman's success was tainted. In 2012, the Department of Justice accused Shadman of fraud. The US government admitted that he had paid kickbacks to American soldiers and Afghan government officials in exchange for his contracts and that he grossly inflated his costs and billed the Defence Department for work that was never done.

There were also allegations that he transferred funds to a known Taliban *money-person.* When Shadman was asked, he denied all the allegations against him, and *several of the US officers who worked with Shadman in Kandahar publicly came to his defence.* A protracted legal battle ensued, and when the case was finally settled in 2019 the US could recover only $25 million in shape of his assets.

Attempts to locate Shadman were unsuccessful. But it wasn't just Afghans who abused the American lucrative contracting business in Afghanistan. One of the top suppliers of fresh food to US forces in Afghanistan was Netherlands based Supreme Group BV, founded by an American Stephen Orenstein. The company's revenue increased

50-fold in a decade; **Bloomberg** placed Orenstein on Billionaire's Index in 2013.

In 2009, Supreme Group hired the outgoing director of the federal agency that awarded its contracts, the Defence Logistics Agency, to be the company's CEO. A year later, Supreme Group was handed a multibillion-dollar, no-bid contract extension by the Defence Logistics Agency. In 2014, Supreme Group pleaded guilty to fraud charges that included creating a fake subcontractor and billing the government for the subcontractor's fees.

> 'The company agreed to pay $389 million in fines and damages, one of the largest penalties ever imposed on a defence contractor at the time.'

In the overall context of the US war in Afghanistan, however, the federal cases brought against Orenstein and Shadman were not the exception. The vast majority of the contracting fraud and corruption in Afghanistan went unreported and unpunished; as normally happen in such situations. According to a Pentagon analysis:

> *"40% of the $108 billion that the Defence Department paid to contractors in Afghanistan between 2010 and 2012 ended up in the hands of either the Taliban, the violent Islamist Haqqani terror network, organized crime rings, trans-national drug traffickers or corrupt Afghan officials."*

Veterans of the conflict say statistics like above can obscure what was in reality a more complicated and ethically murky situation. In a country where roads are often controlled by tribal warlords, transporting necessary and lifesaving supplies overland to American soldiers often required paying fees for safe passage to whichever group controlled the roads. In areas controlled by the Taliban, these amounts, of course, went in the Taliban's kitty. Refusing to pay the warlords who controlled the roads could have harmed the soldiers and contractors gravely.

> *"You could be hardcore about stuff and say, We're not going to pay anybody, but, I'm telling you, you were going to get hit on the road,"* Rodney Castleman, an American employee of an Afghan trucking company told; **The New Yorker** dated 3rd July 2016 is referred.

Security trumped everything else, and the contractors who delivered goods intact and on time needed safety. To some American officials, paying off a local strongman to guarantee safe passage seemed more reasonable than paying an American defence contractor to bomb their way across the country. **Richard Boucher,** who served as Assistant Secretary of State for South and Central Asia during President Bush's administration, described two different levels of corruption in an interview in 2015 with SIGAR:

> *"There is corruption that spreads the wealth and takes care of everybody, that gets to the widows and orphans. And there is the corruption that goes to my house in the Riviera."*

**Col [R] Chris Kolenda,** in a 2016 SIGAR interview, said:

> *"By 2006, just five years into the US war, the elected government in Kabul had self-organized into a **kleptocracy.** The kleptocracy got stronger over the time, to the point that it became priority of the Afghan government - not good governance.....*
>
> *It wasn't just Americans who saw this happening. High-ranking Afghan government officials did, too."*

In 2010, **Dr Rangin Spanta,** then President Hamid Karzai's National Security Advisor, told the US officials that Corruption was not just a problem for the governance in Afghanistan; but a new system of governance in itself. Despite all the pathways along which American money travelled through Afghanistan, there was *one place it never reached: the pockets of the country's poorest citizens.* After two decades of so-called nation-building with $2.1 trillion, the economic status of ordinary Afghans had barely changed at all. According to the World Bank, Afghanistan was the sixth-poorest nation on Earth in 2020 — a ranking essentially unchanged since 2002; Income per capita was just $500.

Crocker had correctly told SIGAR in 2016 that: *"Our biggest single project, sadly and inadvertently of course, may have been the **development of mass corruption.**"*

## AMERICA ROBBED BY THE AMERICANS:

The famous SIGAR report and the other studies openly pointed out that the US funds for Afghanistan were most probably robbed by the American security officials posted there during different times in various capacities – but the whole **corruption-game was played in the name of Afghan Contractors.** Of course the later class of Afghans also made huge fortunes out of the US-AFGHAN WAR but it was not possible without the connivance and share-holdings of the officers and men who used to dole out the contracts and tenders to them for a choice of services.

Daily **Independent** dated <u>13<sup>th</sup> September 2021</u>, however, jolted the whole world by quoting a figure of $14 trillion as America's spending on Afghan War, whereas President Biden cited figures of 1 trillion and the Brown University Study mentioned 2 trillion; see the said newspaper-essay's opening paragraph:

> *"Up to half of the $14 trillion spent by the Pentagon since 9/11 went to for-profit defence contractors, a study released Monday found. While much of this money went to weapons suppliers, the research is the latest to point to the dependence on contractors for war-zone duties as contributing to mission failures in Afghanistan in particular."*

In the post-9/11 wars, the US corporations contracted by the Defence Department not only handled war-zone logistics like running fuel & food convoys but performed other 'missions' like training and equipping Afghan security forces — the forces that collapsed without firing a single bullet in August 2021 as the Taliban swept the country. President Biden placed blame squarely on the Afghans themselves. *"We gave them every chance - what we could not provide them was the will to fight."*

In Afghanistan, Afghan contractors allegedly were paying protection money to warlords and the Taliban themselves, and the Defence Department insisting on equipping the **Afghan air force with complex Black-hawk** helicopters and other aircrafts that only the US contractors knew how to maintain. **Hartung,** the Director of the Arms and Security Program at the Centre for International Policy, said:

> *"If it were only the money - that would be outrageous enough. Instances are there where the Pentagon's reliance on contractors backfired. But the fact - it undermined the mission and put troops at risk is even more outrageous."*

The truth remains that before President Biden began the final American withdrawal from Afghanistan in earlier months of the year [2021], **there were far more contractors in Afghanistan than the US troops.** The US saw about 2300 military members die in all post-9/11 conflicts, but nearly 3800+ contractors had succumbed to their lives; it's estimated.

The contracting practices started with the then-**Vice President Dick Cheney, the former CEO of Halliburton;** the company which had received more than $30 billion to help set up and run bases, feed troops and carry out other work in Iraq and Afghanistan. Cheney and defence contractors argued that relying on private contractors for work that service members did in previous wars would allow for less military troops, and be more efficient and cost effective. By 2010, Pentagon spending had surged by more than one-third, as the US fought dual wars in Iraq and Afghanistan. Harry Stonecipher, then the *vice president of Boeing*, told **The Wall Street Journal**, a month after the surging attacks:

> *"Any member of Congress who doesn't vote for the funds we need to defend this country will be looking for a new job after next November."*

And it remains a reality that a third of the Pentagon contracts went to just five weapons suppliers. In one fiscal year, the money *Lockheed Martin* alone got from Pentagon contracts was one and a half times the entire budgets of the State Department and the US Agency for International Development [USAID]. **Jodi Vittori,** a former Air Force colonel, pointed to the US insistence that the Afghan air force should have used US-made helicopters while the Afghans preferred Russian helicopters, which were easier to fly, could be maintained by Afghans, and were suited to rugged Afghanistan. When US contractors pulled out with US troops taking their knowledge of how to maintain US-provided aircraft with them, top Afghan leaders bitterly complained.

**Hillary Clinton,** Secretary of State under President Obama, had also accused defence contractors at risk in war zones of resorting to payoffs to armed groups, making protection money to the Taliban groups. The US relied, in part, on defence contractors to carry out one of the tasks most central to its hopes of success in Afghanistan — helping to set up and train an Afghan military and other security forces – but ultimately fell like feathers when the Taliban started moving. Some American intelligentsia held the opinion that:

> *"....relying less on private contractors, and more on the US military, might have given the US better chances of victory in Afghanistan. Using contractors allowed America to fight a war that a lot of Americans forgot we were fighting."*

### INDIA's COLOSSAL LOSS:

Referring to an essay appeared in 'AL-JAZEERA' dated 29th August 2021; it remained a hard fact that the Taliban takeover was a *'body blow to Indian interests* in Afghanistan.

Analysts said the Taliban's return to power was a major diplomatic and financial setback for India, which had cultivated close relations with the puppet Ghani's government. Afghanistan was vital to India's strategic interests in the region and a close partner for almost two decades. At the end this South Asian giant became the region's *'most disadvantaged'* player.

Afghan President Ashraf Ghani, with whom New Delhi had cultivated a close relationship, fled the country in mid-August as the Taliban surrounded the capital, Kabul. The sudden collapse of the Western-backed government in Kabul on August 15 precipitated an unprecedented exodus of diplomats, foreign aid workers and Afghans who worked for Western countries and feared reprisals from the Taliban. India was perhaps the first nation that closed their missions in Afghanistan after the Taliban's take-over.

India, under **Operation Devi Shakti**, had already evacuated more than 800 people from Afghanistan before the formal take-over of Kabul by the Taliban. On 26ᵗʰ August 2021, India could evacuate only 24 of its citizens along with 11 Nepalese nationals in a military aircraft. More than 180 it had planned – but others could not reach the airport to board the aircraft.

New Delhi invested $3bn in development projects, offered scholarships to Afghan students, and helped construct the Afghan Parliament building at a cost of $90m, earning huge goodwill in the country of 38 million. During the 2020 Afghanistan Conference, India's External Affairs Minister S Jai Shankar said no part of Afghanistan was *'untouched by the 400-plus projects'* that India had undertaken in all 34 provinces of the country. Bilateral trade between the two countries had also increased significantly over the years and reached $1.5bn in 2019-20.

India, which considered the Taliban as a proxy of its archrival Pakistan, had maintained close ties with the Northern Alliance instead, which had defeated the Afghan armed group in 2001 with the help of US-led NATO forces. India had gone from being Kabul's closest regional partner to one of the region's most destitute player in Afghanistan context, said **Michael Kugelman**, Deputy Director of the Asia Programme at the US-based Wilson Centre. India was out of the game in Afghanistan, in fact.

Foreign policy gurus held that India was too late in reaching out to the Taliban to secure its interests, as reports emerged that Indian officials met the Taliban in the Qatari capital, Doha, in June 2021. One expert opined:

> "*Two factors went against New Delhi; India's reluctance to reach out to the Taliban until it was too late, and an Afghan reconciliation process with a deep Pakistani footprint, owing to its ties to the Taliban.*
>
> *One deprived India of potential leverage, and the other put New Delhi at a geopolitical disadvantage.*"

The Afghan reconciliation process was an outcome of Doha Agreement between the Taliban and the US signed on <u>29<sup>th</sup> February 2020</u> *[the details are given in an earlier chapter]*. India remained wary of the Taliban, given its proximity to Pakistan's military spy agency the Inter-Services Intelligence [ISI], while Islamabad had lodged formal complaints against New Delhi for using Afghan soil to '*carrying out terror activities in Balochistan and around Pak-Afghan borders*'.

Afghanistan at last availed a pro-Pakistan government, and this would give Pakistan and India's other key rival, China – Pakistan's close friend – an opportunity to play more of a role in Afghanistan. There could also be security risks, because already there were numerous dissident roaring and separatist voices in many Indian provinces.

During its first stint in power, from 1996-2001, the Taliban faced international isolation as it was recognised by only three countries – Pakistan, Saudi Arabia and the United Arab Emirates [UAE]. But things were different this time as regional powers such as China, Russia, and Iran indicated they might work with the Taliban to secure their interests.

India's former External Affairs Minister Kunwar Natwar Singh, in an interview of mid 2021 suggested '*New Delhi should establish diplomatic ties with the Taliban* if it functioned as a responsible government. However, India's former ambassador to Afghanistan, Gautam Mukhopadhaya, said:

> "*The situation has not crystallised yet. We don't even have a transitional administration yet [in Afghanistan]. I think for the time being we have to wait and watch.*"

At a minimum, establishing informal links with the Taliban government could put New Delhi in a stronger position to ensure that its assets and investments in Afghanistan shouldn't be imperilled – it was a sane advice from the Indian think-tanks.

## GHANI's CORRUPTION & COSTS:

Also worth consideration the *Pak-media's assessment about real costs of the Afghan-War;* once more referring to Anwar Iqbal's assessment about Afghan War Published in daily **DAWN** dated 8<u>th</u> November 2021:

> *"A non-governmental estimate of US costs for the 20-year war in Afghanistan is more than double the calculation made by the US Department of Defence [DOD].*
>
> *The Special Inspector General for Afghanistan Reconstruction [SIGAR], an official agency that reports directly to Congress, released its latest findings this week, focusing on how the ever-soaring costs of war forced Washington to reconsider its Afghan strategy."*

A US government agency started probing into claims that former Afghan president Ashraf Ghani took with him $169 million while fleeing Kabul, a senior member of his security staff had video proof of the alleged theft; **daily DAWN** of dated 11<u>th</u> October 2021 is referred.

Brig Gen Piraz Ata Sharifi, who headed Mr Ghani's bodyguard squad, said in an interview that he not only saw huge bags of cash being transferred but also acquired a video clip from a CCTV camera. Mr Sharifi told the **Daily Mail Online** from a hideout in Afghanistan:

> *"One of my jobs was to disarm the soldiers on guard at the ministry before the president arrived, for his security."*

Mr Sharifi, wanted by the Taliban for interrogation, was hiding at an undisclosed location in Afghanistan. The Taliban announced a reward of one million Afghanis for his arrest. From hiding he however, told that:

> *"We were waiting for the president there. But then I got a call to say that instead of coming to the defence ministry, the president went to the airport. The defence minister had also fled; so had my boss - so had all of Mr Ghani's close family and entourage."*

Sharifi claimed ex-Afghan president stole hundreds of millions, perhaps billions of dollars before fleeing. He added:

> *"I have a [CCTV] recording [from the palace] which shows that an individual at the Afghan Bank brought a lot of money to Mr Ghani before he left - Hundreds of millions, perhaps billions of dollars. There were many big bags, and they were heavy."*

Sharifi said he was disappointed as he liked Mr Ghani - this money was for the currency exchange market. Each Thursday, the dollars were brought for that purpose. This time it was taken by the president. Mr Ghani knew in the end what would happen. So, he took all the money and escaped. Mr Ghani, however, denied the allegation that he left Kabul with four cars and a chopper full of $169 million, adding that he left Afghanistan un-ceremoniously to avoid bloodshed. His abrupt departure allowed the Taliban to take Kabul two weeks before the US troop pullout.

Earlier that week, the US government's Inspector General in-charge of investigating misuse of aid money, John Sopko, told Congress he's looking into claims that Mr Ghani and his subordinates stole millions of dollars before fleeing. Sopko told the Congress that:

> *"There are allegations, but not only with President Ghani. There are allegations with senior officials in their finance ministry, their central bank and a number of other ministries walking off with millions of dollars. But again, those are just allegations. We have not confirmed any of those yet."*

**In September 2021,** White House Press Secretary **Jen Psaki** told reporters that so far, they had no evidence of Mr Ghani's involvement in this theft, but the Biden administration would let the UN probe the allegations.

**On 31st October 2021;** the US Secretary of State Antony Blinken said that former Afghan President Ashraf Ghani had pledged to fight till death but fled Kabul when the Taliban appeared around.

Also, a conservative US think-tank, **Hudson Institute,** rated the reported US-Pakistan talks on a formal agreement for using Pakistani airspace for operations in Afghanistan as a major development. However, *Pakistan's Foreign Office had declared the news as FALSE* a week earlier. The Foreign Office [FO] on 23rd October 2021 issued a formal statement on a CNN report claiming that a formal agreement for the use of Pakistan's airspace by the US to conduct strikes in Afghanistan was close; clarifying that there was *'no such understanding between the two countries'*.

In an interview to **'CBS - Face the Nation'** talk-show, former US special envoy for Afghanistan *Zalmay Khalilzad* said that the Biden administration could have done more to prevent the collapse of the government in Kabul. At Sunday's show, the interviewer asked Secretary Blinken if he had personally tried to persuade Mr Ghani to stay in Kabul. Mr Blinken said he was on the phone with Mr Ghani on Saturday, the 14th August night, pressing him to accept a plan for transferring power to a new government in Kabul, This government would have been *'led by the Taliban but would have included all aspects of the Afghan society'* - he said.

Mr Ghani told him that *'he was prepared to do that, but if the Taliban wouldn't go along, he was ready to fight to the death.'* - And the very next day, he fled Afghanistan. The Taliban captured Kabul the same day then. In fact, Blinken was engaged with President Ghani over many weeks, many months – but of no avail.

Asked if he did everything he could, the top US diplomat said the State Department was reviewing everything that the US did, starting from 2020 when the Trump administration made an agreement with the Taliban.

The review included *'the actions we took during our administration, because we had to learn every possible lesson from the last couple of years'* - and also from the last 20 years, he said.

Pointing out that this was America's longest war, Secretary Blinken said President Biden ended the longest war to ensure that another generation of Americans would not have to fight and die in Afghanistan he also added:

> *"And I think when all of this settles, that's profoundly what the American people want and is in our interest. Meanwhile, we are doing everything to make good on our ongoing commitments."*

Another Hudson report, distributed with the review, noted that several US commentators had voiced their desire to disengage with Pakistan – however ended with:

> *"That would be a mistake... Pakistan remains important for the US policy."*

Earlier this week, US Under-Secretary of Defence for Policy **Colin Kahl** told Congress that Pakistan has continued to give the US access to its airspace and the two sides were also talking about keeping that access open. The intelligentsia of the world and media were unable to understand that there was no accord at all between the two nations nor it was possible in the given situation. Dr Kahl told the Senate Armed Services Committee that:

> *"Pakistan is a challenging actor, but they don't want Afghanistan to be a safe haven for terrorist attacks, external attacks, not just against Pakistan but against others as well.*
>
> *They [Pakistan authorities] continue to give us access to Pakistani airspace and we are in conversation about keeping that access open."*

However, those American efforts went futile – Pakistan straightaway refused to allow its bases or airspace by any foreign state; friend or foe.

# Scenario 236

## OPIUM FACTOR IN AFGHAN WAR:

### UNODC's SURVEY 2018:

As per UNODC records, opium accounted for around a third of Afghanistan's GDP. It has been the country's biggest cash crop which also provided almost 0.6 million full-time jobs. This, despite the fact that the US military spent $1.5m a day on counter-narcotics measures since their presence there in October 2001; the US spent almost $9bn. It was on top of the trillions dollars spent fighting the war itself. *'To put it bluntly, these numbers spell about total failure of Americans in this field, too'.*

In March 2000; Abdul Hameed Akhunzada, Head of the Taliban's anti-drug Commission, said in an interview with The **Washington Post:**

> *"We are 100 percent determined to control drugs, but we cannot do it alone. This problem existed long before the Taliban, and we need much more help from the outside world to solve it.*
>
> *Ironically, the only power that demonstrated an ability to cripple the Afghan drug industry was the Taliban."*

In July 2000, when the Taliban controlled most of the country, Afghan leader, Mullah Omar, had declared that opium was un-Islamic and imposed a ban on growing poppies. Much to the surprise of the world, the ban worked. Afraid to cross the Taliban, Afghan farmers immediately ceased planting poppies. The UN estimated that poppy cultivation plunged by 90% in 2000-01. There were uproar in global heroin markets and the Afghan economy got disrupted as well; but even today, Afghans recall the moment with awe and wonder. Tooryalai Wesa, a former governor of *Kandahar* province, told SIGAR in an interview:

> *"When [the] Taliban ordered to stop poppy cultivation, Mullah Omar enforced it with ....... No one cultivated poppy after the order was passed. Now, billions of dollars came and were given to the Ministry of Counter-narcotics. It actually didn't decrease [anything]. The poppy [cultivation] even increased."*

<u>Despite spending so enormous amounts, why is business still booming?</u>
Let us start from the day Afghanistan was attacked after 9/11.

**On 11<sup>th</sup> October 2001;** President George W. Bush, in a televised news
conference, four days after he launched the war in Afghanistan, said:

> *"It'd be helpful, of course, to eradicate narco-trafficking out of
> Afghanistan as well."*

Afghan farmers ploughed more soil to grow poppies and the British
struggled to cope with the opium problem. The Bush administration
debated whether and how to get involved in eradication of poppy
cultivation. Yet the bureaucratic dysfunction was just as bad in
Washington as it was in London or elsewhere.

The State Department's Bureau of International Narcotics and Law
Enforcement Affairs were supposed to take charge of US policy but
Pentagon was unsure about what to do with President's announcement and
wish. However, in a confidential **October 2004** memo, Rumsfeld wrote:

> *"She [?] thinks it is important to act soon, to avoid having a situation
> where drug money elects the Afghan Parliament, and the Afghan
> Parliament then opposes Karzai and corrupts the government."*

**One month later,** Rumsfeld sent another confidential memo to Doug
Feith, the Pentagon's Policy Chief, to complain about the Bush
administration's aimless approach.

> *"With respect to the drug strategy for Afghanistan, it appears not to
> be synchronized — no one's in-charge. Department of State has to
> develop a strategy. Other countries in the region want to get involved
> — Pakistan, Uzbekistan, Turkmenistan, Tajikistan, along with
> Afghanistan. Why don't you see what you can do about that?"*

As soon as America invaded and toppled the Taliban regime in 2001,
Afghan farmers were sowing their poppy seeds as usual. The officials were
concerned about a rebound in opium production but focused on other
priorities, such as hunting for Osama bin Laden and other al-Qaeda leaders.
President Bush had asked the UN and NATO allies to tackle the problems
of opium production and trafficking; only Britain agreed to take charge.

In the spring of 2002, British officials floated an irresistible offer. They
agreed to pay Afghan poppy farmers $700 an acre — a fortune in the

impoverished, war-ravaged country — to destroy their crops. However, details of the $30 million program ignited a poppy-growing passion. Farmers planted as many poppies as they could, offering part of their yield to the British while selling the rest in the open market. Others harvested the opium sap right before destroying their plants and got paid anyway. See an interesting comment:

> *"Afghans, like most other people, are quite willing to accept large sums of money and promise anything knowing that you will go away. The British would come and hand out sums of money and the Afghans would say, 'Yes, yes, yes, we're going to burn it right now,' and the Brits would leave. They would then get two sources of income from the same crop."*

**On 9th December 2004;** Afghan President Karzai, in a speech said:

> *"Opium cultivation, heroin production is more dangerous than the invasion and the attack of the Soviets on our country. It is more dangerous than the factional fighting in Afghanistan. It is more dangerous than terrorism...."*

Karzai had declared the efforts to eradicate poppy cultivation as a 'holy war' which was also pushed by American Congress *to do something.* In 2004 - the INL took a hard line on it. The agency hired a small army of 1,200 security contractors to crack down against poppy farming, including mercenaries from South Africa, veterans of the Balkan wars and Gurkha soldiers from Nepal. **Ronald McMullen** took charge as Director of the Agency's office in 2006 to fulfil the mission. In his interview later he told:

> *"I was baffled by some of the tactics the contractors and Afghan counter-narcotics police were using. I was shocked to learn that the American-funded anti-poppy police unit was eradicating Afghan poppies by hand. We'd send a truck of counter-narcotics police out to a field of blossoming opium poppies, the police would hop out of the truck, pick up sticks and walk through the field whacking poppies with their sticks."*

The fact remained that the US, British and UN officials exaggerated data to make it appear that they had destroyed far more poppy fields than they really had during McMullen's **tenure of 2005-07.** There was systematic over-reporting and intimidation but no one wanted to hear it; thus they had to end up with absurd numbers. Also that those flawed eradication programs were driven by Congress wanting to see something tangible, even though it was clear there was no simple solution.

In a **September 2005** diplomatic cable, the then US Ambassador **Ronald Neumann** warned the White House and the State Department that:

> "...narcotics could be the factor that causes corruption to consume Afghanistan's fledgling democracy. Many of our contacts correctly fear that the burgeoning narcotics sector could spin Afghan corruption out of anyone's control. They fear that the sheer mass of illegal money from growing, processing, and trafficking opium could strangle the legitimate Afghan state in its cradle."

But Bush administration officials could not agree on a course of action. The policy makers at White House generally held the opinion:

> "......that these are just poor peasant farmers; if we treat them like enemies then we are just making enemies. If we are trying to stabilize the country we don't want to turn the populace against us. They've been growing poppies for thousand years here and if we rip out their fields we are impoverishing them."

In fact, the Pentagon and the British government were slow to recognize that narcotics were fuelling the insurgency. The military didn't want to deal with the drugs issue — better to be an ostrich — had to take them kicking and screaming. It created a whole new problem that the military didn't know how to deal with.

Washington couldn't understand that a successful counter-narcotics effort was going to be a function of a massive rural development effort in Afghanistan; it was very different situation than of Operation Plan-Colombia. INL Director McMullen, cited above, held:

> "Urging Karzai to mount an effective counter-narcotics campaign was like asking an American president to halt all US economic activity west of the Mississippi - that was the magnitude of what we were asking the Afghans to do."

In 2007, the UN published a report titled '**Afghanistan Opium Survey.**' The report detailed the extent of drug trafficking in the area, a reality that underpinned the Taliban's ability to sustain its insurgency. The report found that 53% of the country's GDP increased as a result of revenue from the heroin trade. 8,200 tons of *heroin* was being shipped in and out of Afghanistan annually. Intelligence asserting the Taliban's involvement confirmed that the guerrillas were using the revenue to buy arms and resources; **McCoy, Alfred**'s book titled as '**The Rise and Decline of US Global Power**' [2017] Chicago, IL: Haymarket Books, p99 is referred.

## OBAMA FAILED TO TACKLE OPIUM, TOO:

**On 19th November 2009;** the US Secretary of State Hillary Clinton said at a news conference in Kabul that:

> *"We are starting to see results. Farmers are beginning to switch from poppies to pomegranates. Girls are attending schools."*

After President Obama took office in 2009, the US policy for Afghan War changed altogether and with immediate effect. The State Department's new special representative for Afghanistan and Pakistan, *Richard Holbrooke,* wrote an op-ed in **The Washington Post** in 2018 blasting the Bush administration's poppy eradication efforts as:

> '*.....the single most ineffective program in the history of American foreign policy.*'

Upon taking office, Mr Holbrooke brought eradication to a standstill. The US government shifted its focus to programs that tried to persuade Afghan poppy farmers to *switch to other crops* or *adopt other livelihoods altogether*.

The above two efforts also proved wastage of time and money. In *Helmand* province, USAID and the US military paid Afghans to dig or renovate miles of canals and ditches to irrigate fruit trees and other crops but the canals worked just to irrigate poppies only — which were much more profitable to grow. Similarly, USAID invested millions of dollars to entice *Helmand* farmers to start wheat-growing. While wheat production increased, farmers relocated their poppy fields to other parts of the province. According to UN estimates, during 2010-14, poppy cultivation across the country nearly doubled; in Afghanistan, poppy is not just another crop – it's something special for farmers.

The American military commanders were relieved by the Obama's decision to abandon poppy eradication programs because Afghanistan was not an agricultural country. Their largest industry was war, then drugs, then services; Agriculture was their fourth or fifth priority. At the same time, military officials were seen more concerned because the opium trade was providing a major revenue stream to the Taliban who had imposed taxes on farmers and traffickers.

The commanders were not sure how to control or to curtail at least that regular income of the Taliban sitting in *Helmand*'s mountains. There was no civilian effort on record that told the military to perform in counter-narcotics field. No coherent strategy was there because of contradictions between counter-narcotics and counter-insurgency.

Counter-insurgency operations mostly relied on support of the population and those were often disrupted by counter-narcotics manoeuvres that were intended to eradicate opium. The commanders were always seen debating and discussing the issue but at the level of policy, it was an inconsistency that was left in doldrums and despair.

## OPERATION IRON TEMPEST:

In November 2017, the US military commanders in Afghanistan launched **Operation Iron Tempest,** a storm of air strikes by B-52 bombers, F-22 Raptors and other warplanes; the US planes did nine strikes in total, each one taking out an individual building in a series of almost simultaneous explosions - a jaw-dropping view of the precision bombing. The main target was a network of clandestine opium production labs which was helping to generate $200 million a year in drug money for the Taliban. **Air Force Brig Gen Lance Bunch** said during a press conference in Kabul that the war changed its shade and it was their new strategy to move forward, and it would definitely be a game-changer.

> [*The F-22 has been the most advanced stealth fighter in the world. Each aircraft costs $140m dollars and it costs at least $35,000 an hour to fly.* **Lt Gen Jeffrey Harrigian,** *of the US Air Forces, was anxious that the policy of attacking revenue sources in Afghanistan was not working as well as in Syria.*]

Result: a big media caption that air-strikes killed eight civilians; videos were also released 'with honour'. But, according to new research from **the London School of Economics,** Operation Iron Tempest was not what it seemed. The study found that, *'despite excellent intelligence [?]'*, the multi-million-dollar campaign could not gain a negligible effect even.

**UK's Dr Mansfield** studied the Afghan opium industry for 2-decades plus. He jumped over his seat when he saw the video clips of air-strikes, saying – '*what is the target here?*' Yet American Forces were claiming the attacks were a success. Dr Mansfield's conclusion was surprising. Despite the incredible resources the American military were pouring in, Dr and his team were convinced that *the US Air Force was using 21st century fighter jets to bomb little more than mud huts.*

Opium is woven deeply into the fabric of conflict in Afghanistan which turned into the longest war in American history. Allegedly, the profits from the heroin were used to fund the Taliban – but the history tells otherwise. The Taliban in their 1st stint of rule had banned poppy-cultivation by law. In 2016 when a BBC reporter travelled through some poppy farms, that institutionalised poppy cultivation was in a government-controlled area; and then there was President Ghani's rule – a paid puppet of the US.

The farmers didn't feel any need to disguise what they were growing, as thousands of swollen opium poppy heads nodded cheerfully in a field just half an hour from *Mazar-e-Sharif* airport, and right at the main road. The 5-6 farmers were at ease under the protection of an ominous looking man with an AK47 slung over his shoulder – he was the local policeman.

[*Growing opium is a very serious crime in Afghanistan, punishable with death, yet here was a policeman welcoming a BBC reporter to a poppy field at the height of the harvest.*]

By 2017, the evidence of the Allied failure to contain opium production had become impossible to ignore. Four days before *Operation Iron Tempest* began in November, the UNODC had announced that poppy cultivation had risen multiple times. When US and British forces invaded Afghanistan in October 2001 poppies were grown over c74,000 hectares - 285 square miles. The new figures showed production had increased more than four-fold in 15 years: *the opium was being grown on 328,000 hectares - 1,266 square miles in Afghanistan.*

And there had been another change too. In the past the opium latex would be dried and smuggled out of Afghanistan as a sticky paste to be refined elsewhere. In 2017-18, Afghan and western officials were estimating that half, possibly more, of Afghan opium was being processed either into morphine or heroin within Afghanistan. It made smuggling easier and also massively increased the profits for drug traffickers while the Afghan government used to take **tax @ 20%** of profits.

This spike in heroin production was deeply felt when America was struggling to contain its own *opioid crisis*. The White House declared it a national public health emergency in October 2017; as about two million Americans were found addicted.

- **November 2017's sudden <u>Operation Iron Tempest</u> became understandable because Afghanistan was the biggest producer of opium in the world then – taking 90% share.**

   *It makes up 95% of the market in Europe; 90% of the Canadian market – and only 1% of US supply is from Afghanistan. Virtually all the heroin used in America comes from Mexico and South America.*

The logic of **Operation Iron Tempest** was simple – to hit the Taliban where it could hurt i.e. their finances. The US commanders then estimated that around 60% of the Taliban's finances come from the narcotics trade so attacking the drug trafficking networks would reduce the insurgents' revenues. The campaign was highly celebrated for its success but, as had been so often in the history of conflicts in Afghanistan, this *campaign miserably failed within one year.*

Heroin production in Afghanistan was not an industrial process, says Dr Mansfield. The makeshift workshops where Afghans used to refine opium should not really be described as 'laboratories' either; no white coats, Bunsen burners or sterile rooms. Heroin is usually made in an ordinary Afghan housing compound - a mud outer wall with up to six, usually mud-built, buildings inside. And, because it involves poisonous fumes, it usually takes place in the open. That makes the process hard to hide because it leaves a distinctive pattern of fire-pits, usually in rows.

An active site would also have piles of oil drums, a press to extract the morphine, fuel - gas canisters, coal or wood - for the fires, and barrels containing chemicals, as well as people and vehicles coming and going.

*The US military released 23 videos showing attacks on supposed heroin labs.* Dr Mansfield said it was clear just from looking at them that there was no heroin production in any premises of them.

However, *within a year it was Thuss...* <u>Operation Iron Tempest</u> had fizzled out. Many of the suspected labs turned out to be empty, mud-walled compounds. After more than 200 air-strikes, the US military concluded it was a waste of resources to keep blowing up primitive targets with advanced aircraft and laser-guided munitions. *What a rogue and bogus intelligence collection it was;* the tax payer Americans asked; as of all the failures in Afghanistan, the war on drugs was perhaps the most useless. The key players in anti-narcotics campaigns acknowledged that none of the measures had worked and, in many cases, they made things worse. Ehsan Zia, a former Afghan cabinet minister, told SIGAR that:

> *"The US and other NATO countries never settled on an effective strategy; they just threw money at the opium problem. They constantly changed policies and relied on consultants who were [totally] ignorant about Afghanistan. The only thing they are experts in is bureaucracy."*

Negating the US efforts to restrict opium cultivation in Afghanistan, the opium production skyrocketed over the course of 20-year war. In 2018, Afghan farmers grew poppies on four times as much land as they did in 2002. With business booming, the opium industry has tightened its stranglehold on the Afghan economy, corrupted large sectors of the Afghan government and provided the Taliban a rising source of revenue; US, European and Afghan officials were on the same page.

The biggest problem was corruption in Afghanistan and drugs remained part of it – factually inseparable. The US and Britain tried all sorts of strategies to shrink opium production; they bribed farmers to stop cultivating poppies, hired mercenaries to invade poppy fields and drew up plans to spray defoliants from the sky - but the poppies spread anyway. For most of the war, the US military kept on struggling but had to discontinue on various counts – mainly perhaps got alarmed if its force could become the poppy-farmers' friends or business partners. During President Bush times, most US Generals didn't approve battle over opium - they saw it as a distraction to their primary mission of dealing with Al-Qaeda.

It was after 2009, during the Obama era, when the US military collected evidence that drug money was financing the insurgency – so felt it as a military threat. Even then they were seen reluctant to take action that could alienate poppy farmers — a large chunk of the population — or US-friendly warlords had earned huge profits from opium trafficking. **Andre Hollis,** Pentagon's top official in 2001-03 and later an Adviser to the Afghan Counter-narcotics Ministry said:

> *"The US Defence Department fundamentally didn't understand what getting involved in counter-narcotics entailed. Everyone was focusing*

*on traditional roles. They would only talk to those in their battle space. From a DOD perspective, it was tactical and about finding and killing al-Qaeda. Everyone had his own agenda and counter-narcotics were way down the list."*

## SIGAR's 270-PAGES REPORT ON OPIUM:

In June 2018, SIGAR published a 270-page report that documented the failure of the war on Afghan opium and made policy recommendations. The report concluded that:

*"A whole-of-government US counter-narcotics strategy should be developed to coordinate various agencies around shared, long-term goals. The strategy should be aligned with and integrated into the larger security, development, and government objectives of the United States and the host nation."*

Together, the Pentagon documents revealed that many people involved in the war on opium thought the policies they were carrying out made no sense. Till June 2016 at least, the outcome was a legacy showing what the US military did in OPIUM WAR was harmful; partly because most people were stupid and partly because they deliberately chose not to listen. Some officials gave similar accounts of foolishness and blamed bureaucratic infighting for many of the problems. There remained a violent competition in Washington not only within Congress, between the Pentagon, Capitol Hill and the administration - also between different parts of the administration. It was sad to see so many people behaving so stupidly.

Referring to the **BBC-Reality Check** dated 25<u>th</u> August 2021:

**The Taliban claimed opium poppy cultivation was stopped and the flow of illegal drugs halted when it was last in power in Afghanistan;** yes, there was a sharp drop in 2001 - when it was last in control. The poppy cultivation had risen in subsequent years.

*Afghanistan has been the world's largest producer of opium and still it is. Its opium harvest accounts for more than 80-90% of the world's supply. In 2018 the UNODC estimated opium production contributed about one third of the country's economy; but that was President Ghani, the American puppet's government not of Taliban. After the Taliban took control of Afghanistan in August 2021, spokesman Zabihullah Mujahid said:*

"When we were in power before, there was no production of drugs. We will bring opium cultivation to zero again and that there would be no smuggling".

At first, opium poppy cultivation rose substantially under Taliban rule - from around 41,000 hectares in 1998, to more than 64,000 in 2000. This was largely in Taliban-controlled *Helmand* province, which accounted for 39% of the world's illicit opium production. Following the Taliban's ban on opium poppy farming, there was a noticeable dip in opium and heroin seizures globally in 2001 and 2002; then things changed after 9/11 event.

Referring to an APP Report appeared in daily **THE EXPRESS TRIBUNE** dated 22nd September 2021 on the subject of PM Modi's involvement in *Drug Trafficking Network*:

> *"The pin-drop silence of Indian PM Narendra Modi is in question after the seizure of 3000 kg of heroin worth INRs:210 billion [$3 billion] at the Mundra Port in Gujarat, operated by his friend and financier Gautam Adani.*
>
> *In the biggest-ever single drug haul in India, the heroin was shipped via two containers from Afghanistan to the port operated by the Adani Ports and Special Economic Zone Limited."*

The daily *Hindustan Times* dated 20th September 2021 is referred.

The consignment, originating from Afghanistan was shipped to Gujarat, India, on September 13-14 via Iran's Bandar Abbas Port and was hidden inside two containers of semi-processed Afghan talc, imported by a firm based in Andhra Pradesh. Gautam Adani, who hails from the Modi's constituency Gujarat, owns nearly one-fourth of the cargo movement in INDIA and manages 13 domestic ports in seven maritime states of Gujarat, Maharashtra, Goa, Kerala, Andhra Pradesh, Tamil Nadu and Odessa.

Also, the information regarding the 25% share of PM Modi in the port raised many eyebrows, with fingers pointed at him for promoting drug smuggling in the country.

The topic dominated social media conversations as politicians, civil society and journalists targeted Adani Group and the Modi government over the confiscation of so much 'powder' from the Mundra port.

The Congress attacked PM Modi asking how such a drug syndicate was operating in India *'under the nose of the government'* as well as the Narcotics Control Bureau [NCB]. Adani, as all knew, was chief financier of Modi in 2014 elections. Congress spokesperson Pawan Khera said at a press conference:

> *"Why are Prime Minister Narendra Modi and Home Minister Amit Shah, who are from Gujarat, unable to break this drug syndicate? The smuggling of drugs into India had increased substantially in the last few years. This will not only destroy the future of the youth of India, but it is the potential funding route for the terrorist organizations globally."*

BJP's Rajya Sabha MP Subramanian Swamy offered to file a Public Interest Litigation after the capture of heroin of *'very high quality'*. Leader of Telugu Desam Party, Dhulipalla Narendra Kumar said:

> *"It was a 'shame for India' to emerging as the epicenter of the contraband mafia. How is it possible for the international drug and uranium mafia to operate in Andhra Pradesh [Indian State] without the support of the government and top police officers?"*

## INDIA IN AFGHAN-DRUG TRADE:

Referring to an analysis appeared in daily **THE EXPRESS TRIBUNE** dated <u>22<sup>nd</sup> October 2021</u> on the subject of India's *Drug Trafficking Network*:

> *"The sudden exit of the United States and its allied forces from Afghanistan has caught the Indian drug trafficking network in a highly compromising situation as New Delhi is currently trying to destroy evidence of its links to drug money.*
>
> *Ignoring its disastrous impacts on Indian society and pouring of illicit money in the national kitty, India indulged in the drug trade ......[so deep]."*

India seemed to be the major beneficiary of the 20 years long war in Afghanistan. India invested $3bn in Afghanistan during the longest war from 2001-21, New Delhi claimed. However, the estimates showed that it might have reclaimed this spending in multiple times through the Afghan-opium trafficking and that too in multiple amounts.

The narcotics were headed to Delhi, the Mundra Port shipload of heroin originated from Kandahar and was loaded into two containers at Iran's Bandar Abbas Port.

An earlier seizure in Mumbai had also originated from Iran's Chabahar Port, owned by an Indian company and managed by India business tycoon Adani. This raised serious questions as to how the Mundra Adani Prot benefited from the consignments landing there. It also raised questions whether the drug cartels were aware of the coming of the Taliban so they wanted to clean up the fields as they had earlier banned opium cultivation.

India's illegal drug business swelled to Rs:300 billion and the state-seizures made roughly around 10% of the trade. The exponential increase in the size of Indian domestic drug consumption owing to cheap and uninterrupted supply could be judged by a 2019 report by the Indian Union Ministry of Social Justice and Empowerment pegged *opioid* use in India at 2.6% of total drug use, thrice the global average of 0.7%.

After the Taliban ouster in 2001, poppy and its derivatives' (un-official) trade in Afghanistan jumped to 3,400 tonnes in just a period of two years from 180 tonnes because the Taliban had banned opium cultivation.

According to the UNODC, by 2003 the Afghan drugs were raking in $2.3 billion from growing poppies to trafficking its derivatives. Amidst the presence of international forces in Afghanistan, the poppy trade had reached astronomical levels of around 9,000 tonnes.

The drug mafia was rescuing this bountiful crop of 2020-21 from the Taliban, who ironically were being accused by India and the West for living off drug proceeds.

An estimated 1 million cocaine users in India can afford to pay upwards of Rs:5,000 a gram. A 2019 study by two JN University professors, based on the National Family Health Survey 2015-2016, found that, at 70.8%, the prevalence of substance abuse among north-eastern men was 20% higher than the rest of India.

The two major seizures of drugs, mentioned above, in India within a month raised alarm bells and serious concerns regarding the credibility of Indian security agencies in international drug regulatory bodies.

But strangely, what never gets traction is the complicity of Western powers in the expansion of poppy plantations in the war-ravaged country. The western media, which monopolised the coverage of Afghanistan, never seriously blamed the occupiers as they went about perpetuating a myth of the country being a *'graveyard of empires.'*

The acclaimed analysts and mainstream international media were inclined to draw solid conclusions based on the above quoted events and past facts regarding the Indian state's involvement in a worldwide sophisticated drug peddling network. In the recent past, the world witnessed how India became an international market for radioactive material.

Indian state's patronage sponsored *dangerous business of sale* and purchase of weapon grade radioactive material further supported the flourishing India's radioactive market; radioactive material taken out from Afghanistan in clandestine way. This indicated towards Indian governments' greed for easy money to further speed up its regional power ambitions.

The analysts believed that the Indian intelligence network managed and completely controlled the supply chain of poppy products starting from the plantation, processing, smuggling and sale in the international drug market. They urged the world not to turn a blind eye towards the Indian involvement in the illegal highly dangerous business of drug trafficking.

The UNODC should have inquired about the issue to unearth the ground realities and that the international community must fulfil its combined responsibility to demand immediate control measures to safeguard the future of human generations.

# Scenario 237

## THE $88 BILLION GAMBLE

### GHOST AFGHAN ARMY & POLICE:

See an article by **Bryan Bender** *& **Paul Mcleary** in 'FOREIN POLICY' dated 13th August 2021 – which gives an insight vision of the writers who had foresightedness and courage to pen down their analysis BEFORE the fall of Kabul in the feet of the Taliban. Its opening paragraph was:

> *"The United States spent more than $88 billion to train and equip Afghanistan's army and police, nearly two-thirds of all of its foreign aid to the country since 2002. So why are they crumbling in the face of the Taliban onslaught?"*
>
> *The breathtaking failure to mold a cohesive and independent Afghan fighting force can be traced to years of overly optimistic assessments from US officials that obscured — and in some cases, purposely hid — evidence of deep-rooted corruption, low morale, and even **ghost soldiers and police** who existed merely on the payrolls of the Afghan Defense and Interior Ministries.....*"

However, in the last the Afghan commanders came out with an excuse that how could they operate without high-tech air and ground support from foreign allies. In fact, the special operations were really doing quite well but that was always when they had Americans advising and assisting them. When Afghanistan's second and third-largest cities, *Ghazni* and *Herat*, had fallen to the Taliban and next day *Lashkar Gah*, the capital of *Helmand* province, was also taken over by the Taliban; there appeared growing doubts among military officials and Washington that the Taliban could soon be at the gates of the capital and Afghan units would fizzle away. And two days later it happened exactly as had been anticipated.

When 3,000 American troops were flowing into Kabul to evacuate US diplomats, who were instructed a day before to destroy sensitive govt documents before fleeing for their safety, Pentagon still had hopes for Afghan regiments' performance. Pentagon's *Press Secretary John Kirby* was telling media reporters that:

> *"We want to see the will and the political leadership, the military leadership, that's required in the field. We still want to see that, and we hope to see that, but whether it happens or not, whether it pans out or not, that's really for the Afghans to decide.*
>
> *The Afghan forces' advantages are their numerical superiority and that the Taliban lacks an air force - you have to use it."*

...but Kabul collapsed in a short while.

The facts remained that the Afghan security forces had expanded substantially over the past two decades — from just 6,000 under the Ministry of Defense and no national police at all in 2003, to 182,071 and 118,628, respectively, as of April 2021, according to the latest Pentagon figures. As the forces had ballooned, they had always claimed about their increased skills or expertise. One US commander boasted a decade ago:

> *"Afghanistan's army fought with skill and courage - they had 'proven themselves to be increasingly capable.'"*

In July 2021, the Pentagon's chief spokesperson insisted that the Afghan forces *'know how to defend their country.'* But the counter-evidence was coming up that government forces were ill-prepared to take on any sustained conflict - was often left out of public testimony or simply classified as secret.

Documents revealed that in 2015, the Pentagon started shielding actual data on the Afghan forces from the public, in a move that the Special Inspector General for Afghanistan Reconstruction [SIGAR] was assigned a special task to unearth real facts. The independent watchdog concluded:

> *"....it was unable to publicly report on most of the US-taxpayer-funded efforts to build, train, equip, and sustain the Afghan forces."*

The Pentagon loosened some restrictions on data but since 2017, much of the previously available information about the size, strength and casualty rates of Afghan military units remained mysterious – especially about the *'operational performance of the Afghan forces'*.

Hiding the core facts by the Pentagon itself was a warning sign – showing the organization's incompetence but the signs had been mounting since years that the rosier assessments didn't reflect the reality on the ground. In army establishments, a loss to desertion is the most deplorable factor; the high rate of fleeing leads to a lack of cohesion. **Mike Jason,** a retired Army colonel who commanded training units in Afghanistan, said:

> *"If you don't pump new energy and professionalism into the force constantly, it disintegrates pretty quickly and you won't recognize it two years later, much less often.*
>
> *That caused huge losses for the Afghan army and they've had to start from scratch with a lot of recruits. Almost every year they are having 20-30% strength either from casualties or desertion."*

The poor performance of the Afghan Air Force also spurred ground troops to flee. A former senior US military commander in Afghanistan divulged:

> *'They realized after fighting two to three days, being hit in various locations all around the country, that the Afghan air force would not deliver reinforcements, re-supplies, air medics, or air support'.*

Some also viewed the original conception of the training program as faulty. **Mark Jacobson,** a former Pentagon official held that:

> *".....too much focus was given to preparing the Afghan military to repel a foreign army rather than a home-grown insurgency like the Taliban. We failed in trying to make the Afghan army in our own image; we tried to create regiments and brigades when we needed to create an army and police force that was basically special forces designed specifically to beat back an insurgency, not to defend the Afghan borders against outside conventional attacks.*
>
> *Another factor - the most effective Afghan units, which could only be engaged in one battle at a time, were in heavy demand."*

## CORROSIVE EFFECTS OF CORRUPTION:

*Bryan Bender & Paul Mcleary* in their essay referred above also discuss about the Corrosive Effects of Corruption within the ranks, as well as questionable accuracy of data on the actual strength of the force and an inability to assess intangible factors such as *the will to fight.* Problems such as fake personnel records that corrupt actors used to pocket salaries for both **'ghost soldiers and police'** were common. The fact remained:

> 'The (feelings about) abandonment of Afghanistan by the US and its allies caused the dramatic change in the ability of the Taliban to accelerate its campaign to take territory and in the process, destroyed the confidence of the Afghan security forces.'

**O'Hanlon,** a former Adviser to the US commanders, sadly told that:

> "One problem is just that we never expected an abrupt departure. We always assumed there would be a 12- to 24-month notification of a drawdown or a departure and that would have allowed for some adjustments.
>
> The speedy US and NATO withdrawal had a huge effect on rank and file of Afghan troops (he believes). Anybody who was a fence sitter on how hard they were going to fight in defense of the government has decided not to be a fence sitter anymore, but to go ahead and lay down their arms and either do a deal with the Taliban or blend in."

However the end result remained that the Afghan force had been there but with low degree of control, poor leadership, and lack of adequate recruitment, desertion and weak battlefield performances. While the Afghan security force boasted of sophisticated and advanced weapons, it suffered from lack of cohesiveness, corruption and mismanagement. The Taliban, on the other hand, also lacked high technology weapons but were financially stable with a binding force of their Islamic ideology in philosophy and practice.

Referring to **Reuters / daily DAWN** dated 15th August 2021:

> "Despite about $88 billion budgeted for training the Afghan army; it took the Taliban little more than a month to brush it aside.
>
> The rout of Afghan forces as Taliban fighters seized one provincial city after another provides a stark answer to anyone wondering about the success of two decades of America-led efforts to build a local army."

Over the few days prior to reach Kabul, the Taliban had seized every major city in Afghanistan — from *Kandahar* in the south to *Mazar-i-Sharif* in the north, *Herat* in the west to *Jalalabad* in the east – then they knocked at the gates of Kabul without any fear of reprisal or retaliation.

Afghan President Ashraf Ghani praised Afghan security and defence forces in a brief televised address a day before, saying *'they had a strong spirit to defend their people and country.'* But the world got shocked at the lack of resistance put up by any Afghan army units. Some abandoned their posts and others reached agreements with the Taliban to stop fighting and hand over their weapons and equipment.

The US officials held, that in some instances, provincial governors asked security forces to surrender or escape, perhaps in order to avoid further bloodshed because they believed defeat was unavoidable. Where deals were not cut, Afghan forces still melted away. One US official correctly explained: *'Once morale goes, it spreads very quickly, and that is at least partly to blame.'*

The US commanders were long worried that:

> *"Rampant corruption, well documented in parts of Afghanistan's military and political leadership, would undermine the resolve of badly paid, ill-fed and erratically supplied front-line soldiers — some of whom had left for months or even years on end in isolated outposts, where they could be picked off by the Taliban."*

**AFP** [*French International News Agency*] had published series of images in the world press and social media in which Taliban fighters were seen driving Afghan National Army vehicles through the streets of *Laghman* province, Afghanistan on 15^th August 2021.

Over many years, hundreds of Afghan soldiers were killed each month – un-official figures: c60000. But the army fought on, without any of the airborne evacuations of casualties and expert surgical care standard in Western armies, as long as international backing was there. Once that went, their resolve evaporated. Another US official asked: *"Would you give your life for leaders who don't pay you on time and are more interested in their own future?"*

The same was the analysis shared by some in the Taliban movement itself. One Taliban commander in Ghazni said:

> *"....the government forces' collapse started as soon as the US forces started withdrawing as they didn't have any ideology except fleecing the Americans.*

> *The only reason for this unexpected fall of provinces was our commitment and the withdrawal of US troops."*

The defeat highlighted the failure of the US to create a fighting force in the image of its own highly professional military with a motivated, well-trained leadership, high-tech weaponry and seamless logistical support.

On paper, Afghan security forces numbered around 300,000+ soldiers. In reality, the numbers were never that high. Dependent on a small number of elite Special Forces units that were shunted from province to province as more cities fell to the Taliban, the already high rate of desertion in the regular army soared.

As government forces started to fall apart, hastily recruited local militias, loyal to prominent regional warlords also rushed in to fight. Western countries had long been wary of such militias. Though more in line with the realities of traditional Afghan politics where personal, local or ethnic ties outweigh loyalty to the state, they were also open to corruption and abuse and ultimately proved no more effective than conventional forces.

Leaders like Rashid Dostum fled to Uzbekistan as the Taliban advanced and warlords surrendered to them being docile and obedient.

Question however, arises whether it was ever a realistic goal to create a Western-style army in one of the world's poorest countries, with a literacy rate of 40% [*that too in cities only*] and a social and political culture far from the developed sense of nationhood underpinning the US military. US army trainers who worked with Afghan forces struggled to teach the basic lessons of military organisation but even those were blown in air by illiterate Afghanis.

**Jonathan Schroden,** an expert at the CNA Policy Institute, who served as an adviser to US Central Command [**Centcom**] and the US-led international force in Afghanistan, opined:

> *"The Afghan army functioned as much as a 'jobs programme' only. But the chronic failure of logistical, hardware and manpower support to many units, meant that even if they want to fight, they run out of the ability to fight in relatively short order."*

Afghan forces were forced to give up repeatedly after pleas for '**supplies and reinforcements**' went un-answered, either because of incompetence or the simple incapacity of the system to deliver. Even the elite Special Forces units that had borne the brunt of the fighting in recent years suffered most. Within a month, at least a dozen commandos were executed by Taliban fighters in the northern province of Faryab after running out of ammunition and being forced to surrender.

**Richard Armitage,** the former US diplomat who organised a fleet of South Vietnamese Navy ships to carry some 30,000 refugees out of Saigon before it fell in April 1975, watched the situation as the threat of a similar disaster unfolded in Kabul.

As Deputy Secretary of State under former President Bush when the US invaded in 2001, was deeply involved in Afghanistan diplomacy. He said:

> *"The Afghan army's collapse pointed to the wider failures of two decades of international efforts.*
>
> *I hear people expressing frustration in the press that the Afghan army can't fight a long fight. I can assure you the Afghan army has fought, can fight if it's got something to come out of their barrels.*
>
> **The question is; is this government worth fighting for?"**

## AMERICA MOVED TOO SLOWLY:

Since 2002, the US allocated about $88 billion in security assistance to Afghanistan, a sum that dwarfed the defence budgets of other developing nations. In 2011 alone, at the peak of the war, Afghanistan received $11 billion in security aid from Washington. Yet after almost two decades of help, the Afghan army and police were still too weak to fend off the Taliban, the Islamic State and other 'FREEDOM FIGHTERS'.

SIGAR, the US government watchdog, chronicled severe shortcomings with the Afghan security forces over the years. The interview records obtained by them contain new insights into what went wrong and exposed gaping contradictions between real facts and lies at all levels; administrative, military, diplomatic and political – showing up an utter shameless image of one and the only super power.

Almost always, the Afghan commanders inflated the numbers so they could pocket salaries – paid by the US – for ghost personnel, according to the US state-audits. On paper, the Afghan security forces looked robust, with 352,000 soldiers and police officers but on ground there were only 254,000 serving in the ranks. As a result, When Washington asked the Afghans to produce biometric data, fingerprints and face scans, to verify the real presence – it had gone too late till then.

The fact remained that the US moved too slowly to build up the Afghan forces during the first few years of the war when the Taliban presented a minimal threat. Then, after the Taliban rebounded, they rushed and tried to train too many Afghans too quickly. **Marin Strmecki,** a former adviser to Rumsfeld, told SIGAR in 2015 that:

> *"The poor timing and inept planning are mortal setbacks. These are strategic consequences to this. This is not just doing well or it would be nice to be able to operate better. You succeed or fail on whether you can do these things in a timely manner."*.....
> Ref: **The Washington Post** dated 9th December 2019

Drawing partly on the interviews but largely on other government documents, SIGAR published two '**Lessons Learned**' reports in **2017 and 2019** that highlighted an array of problems with the Afghan security forces. The reports followed several SIGAR audits and investigations that had pinpointed similar troubles with the Afghan forces.

From a base in **Khost Province**, the CIA used to support a militia contingent since early 2001 continuously and constantly. It was called the **Khost Protection Force** [KPF]; the organization was reported to have 4,000 members in 2015 and 8,000–10,000 in 2018. In August 2021, 6,000 KPF soldiers / fighters surrendered to the Taliban – a sharp blow to the US.

**Lt Gen Douglas Lute,** White House's Afghan war Czar with Presidents Bush and Obama, told government interviewers that:

> *"We got [the Afghan forces - what] we deserved. If the US government had ramped up training between 2002 and 2006, when the Taliban was weak and disorganized, things could have been different. Instead, we went to Iraq. If we committed money deliberately and sooner, we could have a different outcome definitely."*

In **October 2004,** the Pentagon had talked high about the Afghan army and police; it praised the 15,000 soldiers in the promising Afghan army as *'a highly professional, multi-ethnic force, which is rapidly becoming a pillar of the country's security.'* It also touted how the Afghan national police – partly under the tutelage of Germany – had 25,000 newly trained officers - but internally, Bush admin officials shared anxieties and sounded alarms.

In **February 2005,** the then Defence Secretary Rumsfeld forwarded a confidential report to Secretary of State Condoleezza Rice about the Afghan National Police [ANP]. The report was titled, '**ANP Horror**

**Stories'** and described how most of the police were illiterate, under-equipped and barely trained. Rumsfeld wrote in a memo, accompanying the report, saying:

> *"Please take a look. This is the Afghan National Police situation. It is a serious problem. My impression is that these two pages were written in as graceful and non-inflammatory a way as is possible (and appropriate)."*

One month later, Rumsfeld sent another confidential memo to National Security Adviser **Stephen Hadley**, complaining about a tangled arrangement between the Pentagon and the State Department to train Afghan police that was going nowhere; saying that:

> *"He was ready to toss in the towel. I don't think it is responsible to the American taxpayers to leave it like it is. We need a way forward. I've worked on it and worked on it. I am about to conclude that it is not possible for the US Government bureaucracy to do the only sensible thing."....*
>
> Ref: **Rumsfeld's published memoirs [2011].**

The above details show that Rumsfeld pushed to train the Afghan forces quickly yet wanted to keep them small to avoid massive expenses but Bush admin said <u>Rumsfeld was stingy and short-sighted.</u> Bush White House insisted that Washington would have saved money in the long run – *if it had built a bigger Afghan army and police force sooner.*

## DISORGANISED & RIDICULOUS APPROACH:

The initial war-years were marked by a '<u>disorganized, unprepared, ridiculous US approach</u>' to train the Afghan security forces. At first, the Bush admin insisted on a cap of 50,000 Afghan soldiers and police – but the fact that they were 'totally irrelevant for security needs'; and it was known to all in White House and the Pentagon.

**Zalmay Khalilzad,** the US ambassador in Kabul during 2003-04, later confirmed in an interview that:

> *"The Afghan government wanted Washington to pay for security forces of 100-120K Rumsfeld drew a hard line and held the training program 'hostage' until the Afghans agreed to the 50,000 cap, which led to long delays.*

*So we were fighting in 2002-03 about those sorts of numbers - it was apparent [that] more Afghan forces were required. **Now we're talking about** God knows what, 300,000...."*

Thus that internal dispute dragged on till 2004-05 and the situation became extremely tense in war-areas and the need was felt that the Afghan forces should be expanded quickly to fight the re-emerging Taliban. See a comment then appeared in media:

*"The way it gets resolved is the way everything gets resolved in Washington – by not getting resolved".*

However, another problem was that the US government lacked the capacity to train and equip large foreign armies from scratch. They were not to invent how to launch infantry operations or how to do artillery at the start of a war. All was being done on ad hoc. There was no doctrine and no science to it. It got done very unevenly - creating security forces for another society remained the most important political act for the states – which requires more enhanced wisdom and funds.

**In January 2009**, the war was going bad and at top speed. President Obama took over and immediately unveiled a new counter-insurgency strategy and nearly tripled the number of US troops in Afghanistan. Obama told the American people that surge in the US troops was temporary. He later promised to bring home all the native soldiers back till ending 2016. His war strategy also caused huge expansion of the Afghan security forces; more than 350,000. The idea was not bad – that the Afghans could take over the fight onwards.

The number of US troops in Afghanistan decreased from 100,000 in 2010-11 to 13,000 in 2019; the Trump administration had escalated air-strikes to win the war from the Taliban with three times as many bombs and missiles on average each month; US Air Force statistics are on record. In view of withdrawing more US troops from Afghan soils, he and his diplomats got engaged in peace talks with the Taliban.

The American military commanders assured the public time and again that the Afghan security forces were constantly improving and that the US troops would eventually be relieved but it could never. A Marine **Gen Mattis,** who later served as Trump's Defence Secretary, told a Senate panel in July 2010:

*"This is the worst nightmare for the Taliban, that the Afghan army is increasingly effective, partnered with our forces and moving against*

*an enemy that they know better than anyone - I think this is very heartening."*

In ending 2010, at a White House news conference, the then **Defence Secretary Robert Gates** said:

*"The Afghan security forces are progressing ahead of schedule. They are performing well in partnership with coalition troops and will continue to improve with the right training, equipment and support."*

Members of Congress from both parties also lavished praise on the Afghans; though it was all blatant lie.

In March 2011; **Sen Carl Levin**, the Chairman of the Armed Services Committee, said in a hearing.

*"The growth in the size and capability of the Afghan security forces and control of territory by those forces is robbing the Taliban of their propaganda target and bringing us closer to the success of the mission."*

**Sen John McCain** had added then:

*"We are turning around the war. Afghan security forces are growing in quantity and improving in quality even faster than it was planned."*

On 22nd June 2011; President Obama, in a televised statement to the nation declared success against al-Qaeda and the Taliban and the withdrawal of 33,000 troops, about a third of US forces, by next year. He said the troops would be back by the summer of 2012 or by September at the latest. The first 5,000 would return next month and another 5,000 by the end of the year. Also adding that *'Tonight, I can tell you that we are fulfilling that commitment - we are meeting our goals.'*

**Lt Gen Mark Milley** during a **2013 press briefing** from Kabul said:

*"Everything is going according to plan. This [Afghan] army and this police force have been very, very effective in combat against the insurgents every single day. Have there been one or two outposts that have been overrun? Yes. But you're talking about 3-4,000 outposts that are in the country."*

Just after about two years, Pentagon officials started to revise their assessments. They still held that the security forces were making progress but acknowledged that maybe they had overstated the Afghans' abilities in the past. The then Defence Secretary **Ashton Carter,** during a visit to *Kandahar* in **February 2015** said:

> *"It's not that the Afghans aren't good at fighting. They are; but just a few years ago there really was no Afghan national security force at all."*

10 months later, during another visit to the war zone Carter said:

> *"The Afghan security forces are getting there. . . . If you'd have asked me to bet on it five years ago, I don't know. I'd may be give you even odds on it or something. But it's coming together."*

## ODD CONDUCT OF THE FORCE:

Referring to **THE SEATTLE TIMES** dated 9th December 2019, the US military trainers described Afghan security forces as **incompetent, unmotivated and rife with deserters.**

> **Marine Gen Jim Mattis** had once briefed the Congress in 2010 that: *'We're on the right track now.'*

> **Marine Gen John Allen** told Congress in 2012 that: '*....the Afghan forces are better than we thought they were.'*

> **Army Lt Gen Joseph Anderson** told reporters in 2014 that: *'The Afghan national security forces are winning'.*

> **Thomas Johnson,** a Navy officer and an Adviser in *Kandahar* said: *'Afghans viewed the police as predatory bandits, calling them **the most hated institution** in Afghanistan'.*

The estimates told that more than 60,000 members of Afghan security forces were killed in this 20-year war about 17 times the number of US and NATO troops who have lost their lives. The Afghan security forces comprised of troops from regular army and about half of that number from police [*Afghan police is more of a paramilitary force than a crime-fighting agency*].

However, in secret '**The Afghanistan Papers**' - *a secret history of America's longest war* - all the above statements were proved lies; the Afghan proxy force was a long-running calamity. With most speaking on the assumption that their remarks would remain private, they told about the **Afghan security forces as incompetent, unmotivated, poorly trained, corrupt and riddled with deserters, secret agents & infiltrators.**

On another count, in one interview, **Ryan Crocker,** a former US ambassador to Kabul, told government interviewers that:

> *"....the Afghan police were ineffective not because they're outgunned or outmanned. It's because they are useless as a security force and they're useless as a security force because they are corrupt down to the patrol level."*

**Victor Glaviano,** who worked with the Afghan army as a US combat adviser in 2007-08, complained to government interviewers [2016]:

> *"Afghan troops had beautiful rifles, but didn't know how to use them, and were undisciplined fighters, wasting ammunition because they wanted to fire constantly. ......the soldiers [are] stealing fools who habitually looted equipment supplied by the Pentagon."*

By the end of year 2016, instead of ending the war as Obama had promised, there were 8,400 US troops left in Afghanistan. Less than a year later, his successor in the White House Mr Trump decided that was not enough and sent back several thousand more American troops to help the Afghans; making it nearly 13,000. The fairy progress reports, as usual before, continued to be delivered to the public, mostly based on illusion - only 2 in 10 Afghan recruits could read or write. SIGAR report interestingly noted that:

> *"Questionable motivations and loyalties snaked through the ranks of the army and police. Ethnic and tribal tensions posed a perpetual problem, with the **corps dominated by warlords** who doled out promotions based on patronage, according to the interviews."*

It took nearly a decade to get the Afghan Air Force off the ground, because the pilots were not qualified; when some became available they were not able to read operational manuals. Most motor mechanics claimed themselves as pilots *'but having no flight experience'*. The air bases were plagued by *'mischief'* as many Afghans used to steal jet fuel when they left each day - they used to sell it in small containers to the needy. Such petty corruptions were uncontrolled and widespread.

Afghan police recruits, usually on absconding, used to get their uniforms, then go back to home and sell them around; many re-enlisted them in other centres and did the same time and again. The US trainers constantly tried to plug holes in the system to prevent looting and stealing but their Afghan officers often protected them. More they miss-behaved, the more money was showered by the US on them – really awful situations.

**Michael Callen,** an economist specialized in the Afghan public sector, recalled [2015] that once he was working with a newly arrived military officer. They wanted to set up a secure system of paying salaries into bank accounts direct or through phone apps. They had to abandon the idea when after long briefing, the concerned Interior Ministry official didn't even hear our briefing – '....*he enjoyed his sleep during our stay there and finally said that Sure, if you want to go do it, go do it in places where there aren't mobile money agents. . . . Go do it in places where cell phones don't work.'*

One could understand that Afghan official's interests and motive.

> This 'all inclusive' corruption ultimately brought most disgusted Afghan security officials to question openly: '....*who represented the bigger evil – the Taliban or the Afghan government.'*

In real terms, if the US & NATO were not able to reform those Afghan lots in 2015 – they should have quit Afghanistan then – what fun in staying there for six / seven years more.

In 2017; **Shah Mahmood Miakhel,** a former Adviser to the Afghan Interior Ministry and later the Governor of *Nangahar* province, was asked:

> "....*that why is it possible that a large number of 500 security forces cannot defeat about 20 or 30 Taliban.*"

**Miakhel,** while passing on a discussion amongst village elders, replied:

> "*The security people are not there to defend the people and fight Taliban, they are there to make money by selling their uniforms, weapons or fuel.*
>
> *To a further question that OK the government is not protecting you, but you are about 30,000 people in the district. If you don't like Taliban then you must fight against them* – the response came; *that we don't want this [Ghani's] corrupt government to come and we don't want Taliban either, so we are waiting to see who is going to win.*"

The American commanders stacked their disrespect and contempt on units known as the Afghan Local Police [ALP] - about 30,000 militias organized at the village level. The US had raised them in 2010 – and trained them exclusively – but they quickly generated a reputation for brutality and drew enormous complaints. In 2016, about one third of the local police *'seemed to be drug addicts or Taliban'* - their main concern was getting fuel from their American units.

However, **Gen John Allen,** commander of all US and NATO forces during 2011-13, had described the ALP as a major success. The General held that:

> *'....the ALP stood their ground 80% of the time they were attacked. Indeed, the Taliban were more concerned about ALP than almost any other single measure taken to protect the Afghan people.'*

No one else corroborated Gen John's assessment, however.

> **Robert Perito,** a former analyst at the US Institute of Peace, also called the local police *'dysfunctional and a corrupt force, run by warlords.'*

> **Lt Col Scott Mann,** told government interviewers that: *'...the local police training expanded too rapidly between 2011 and 2013, causing the program to deteriorate.'*

However, the US and NATO deserved a large share of the blame; the training programs for the Afghan security forces – not just the police – were *ill-designed, poorly coordinated and thinly staffed.* The programs were plagued by inconsistency and constrained by the fact that US and NATO trainers served for only 6-12 months at a time. For years, the both could not find enough certified law enforcement professionals to train the Afghan police. To fill the gap, the Pentagon assigned regular troops to the job - but of no avail.

**Victor Glaviano,** (cited earlier), told interviewers [in 2016] that:

> *"....it made no sense for US infantry troops to train the police. Thinking we could build the [security forces] that fast and that well was insane. We can't even stand up a sustainable local police unit in the US in 18 months. How could we expect to set up hundreds of them across Afghanistan in that time frame?"*

See the war's ending moments now.

Quoting **Susannah George** for her analysis titled as 'How Afghan security forces lost the war' appeared in the **WASHINGTON POST** dated 25th September 2021:

> *"Building Afghanistan's national security forces were one of the most ambitious and expensive aspects of two decades of US-led war - it resulted in failure.*
>
> *The US spent billions of dollars [$88b - detailed in a separate chapter]; training and equipping police, soldiers and Special Forces. Despite years of warnings from US and Afghan officials, successive US administrations pledged that the Afghan military was capable of defending the country. President Biden said the Afghan military was 'as well-equipped as any army in the world' just a month before its collapse."*

## THE WORST STYLE OF SURRENDER:

During the taking over of various Afghan cities including Kabul in or before August 2021, not a single unit of Afghan security forces remained intact.

A sophisticated Taliban campaign aimed at securing surrender deals was laid at the heart of the Afghan military's collapse, **but layers of corruption, waste and logistical failures left the country's security forces** so under-equipped, coward and with such battered morale that it enabled the Taliban's success ultimately.

Interviews with more than a dozen members of the Afghan Special Forces, army and police in three [sample] provinces illustrated that the collapse of security forces was not abrupt. Instead, it was a slow, painful breakdown that had taken start months before the fall of Kabul. BUT where was the CIA's network through those months.

It remained a fact that the US withdrawal gained momentum and the Taliban enhanced their relentless sweep through rural Afghanistan; casualties among Afghan govt fighters also surged. In Kandahar province, as the war intensified, many of Afghanistan's police on the front line were **entering their sixth month without pay**, a widespread problem that took a toll on government forces' morale and made them vulnerable to Taliban's cash offers and safety for their own lives.

The forces were in so miserable situation that when Eid holidays were approaching, even if they were granted leave, they were NOT in a position to go home. They would have been felt too ashamed to look at their children with empty hands. When they joined Afghan-police force, all they were given was a gun — **no training or documentation or duty roasters or pay & allowances.**

[As they were not paid so next month they just sold their rifles and offered loyalties to the Taliban; then the **Taliban were paying around $2,000** for Afghan govt weapons, a price much higher than the market rate. It was **the worst style of surrender;** the historians would re-write facts about the fall of *Kandahar*.]

Afghanistan's most highly trained fighters were assigned to defensive operations as the Taliban pushed closer to provincial capitals and as the US air support had disappeared. Elite fighters were tasked with running dangerous supply missions that made them more vulnerable. Special Forces elite teams were tasked with defensive operations that put them at heightened risk of the Taliban ambush – it was not what they were trained to do. Those commandos were given this task because they were one of the few units with heavy armoured vehicles.

In the last month of surrender, the Taliban snipers had started killing the city police-men on patrol or on supply of bread & milk to the other fellow units. The Taliban came open to target the police and other security units in busy bazaars after recognizing them as Afghan govt employees.

In *Kunduz* province, the Afghan government had lost control of most village posts which were largely relying on elite units — the best trained, equipped and generally most motivated — to lead the fight. But without US supervision, the troops were being mismanaged and overworked. The elite units knew how to defeat the Taliban, but the leadership at the top was not interested to listen their *jawaans* [troops].

Special Forces fighters in Kunduz kept their equipment ready so they could jump into action at short notice. But as the US withdrew its forces, Afghan special operators were largely moved under the command of the Defence Ministry; they were no more independent then. The Defence officials set their deals with the Taliban and somewhere had sold the Units' weapons, too. The empty handed troops were sent to conduct clearing operations. How could they win the war.

In Kunduz [July 2021], an incident of friendly fire jeopardized a critical clearance operation. The captain admitted that the men in his unit were struggling to operate without US coordination and air support whereas the units never moved without American backing. The men suddenly found themselves without tools they had relied on for years. As one unit prepared to go on leave, its commander confided that he feared they would not return to the unit any more. In fact most of them had managed to fly to America with corruption-tainted arrangements with the Defence Ministry at Kabul – actually they had fled Afghanistan.

Soon after, members of the KKA fighters had to arrange a helicopter to flee from Kunduz because most territory surrounding the city was occupied by the Taliban; *airlifting troops was the only way to evacuate them.*

By late July [2021], the Taliban were closing in on nearly all the country's provincial capitals. Afghan security forces, that hadn't been killed by the Taliban till then had deserted or fled, steadily retreating from remote outposts into city centres. Those who remained on the country's front lines were some of the least capable. A wounded policeman told the **Washington Post**'s reporter that:

> *"The Taliban are everywhere now, even inside the city. He was driving an un-armoured police truck through eastern Kandahar to re-supply a checkpoint when he was caught by a Taliban ambush.*
>
> *It's because of our leadership that we are in this position; the government had suffered a great loss in a matter of weeks. **Our leaders sell our checkpoints. They've already sold our blood.**"*

One police commander said the only men from his unit willing to hold positions against the Taliban were drug addicts; it keeps them awake. *'The addicts are the only men who can stand being on the front line,'* Commander Wali said. *'If they weren't using drugs, they would go crazy';* **WP** dated 25th September 2021 is referred again.

Afghan army collapse '**took us all by surprise**' - in *Reuters' analysis* published on world media pages dated 28th September 2021.

**On 28th September 2021; US Defence Secretary Lloyd Austin told Congress that the Afghan army's sudden collapse caught the Pentagon off-guard** as he acknowledged miscalculations in America's longest war including corruption and damaged morale in Afghan ranks. While speaking before the Senate Armed Services Committee, the Secretary told that:

> *"The fact that the Afghan army simply melted away in many cases without firing a shot took us all by surprise. It would be dishonest to claim otherwise."*

The Senate and House committees overseeing the US military were holding hearings; questioning was there that saw the US Secretary of State Antony Blinken staunchly defending the administration, even as he faced calls for his resignation. **Senator James Inhofe** squarely blamed the Biden admin for a shameful end to a 20-year endeavour; further that:

> *"Biden ignored the recommendations of his military leaders and left many Americans behind after the US withdrawal. We all witnessed the horror of the president's own making."*

Many of the hardest questions were raised against the two senior US military commanders testifying: **Army Gen Mark Milley**, Chairman of the Joint Chiefs of Staff, and **Marine Gen Frank McKenzie**, Head of US Central Command.

# Scenario 238

## THE LARGEST AIR-LIFT IN HISTORY

It happened in August 2021 at the KABUL AIRPORT when America faced a humiliating defeat in the longest war of its history. Referring to Reuters in **daily DAWN** dated 2<sup>nd</sup> September 2021:

> *"Soon after taking over Kabul by the Taliban, the US military was forced to take drastic steps for evacuation including sudden stop for all flights from Kabul's International Airport for seven hours because there was nowhere for the evacuees to go. For months, the US military officials had urged the Pentagon and the White House to convince other countries to take Afghans at risk from Taliban retaliation.*
>
> *They had largely failed to secure agreements with other countries, prompting officials across the US government to rush to try to find space for the evacuees."*

President Biden administration's scramble was emblematic of failures over those few months, which culminated with a hastily organised airlift that left thousands of US-allied Afghans behind and was punctuated by a suicide **bombing outside Kabul's airport** that killed 13 US troops and scores of Afghans.

The chaotic end to America's longest war had sparked the biggest crisis of President Biden's seven months in the White House, finger-pointing within the administration and questions about whom, if anyone would be held responsible. Despite the missteps, the administration carried out one of the largest airlifts in history, *evacuating more than 120,000* Americans, Afghans and people of other nationalities amid the threat of attacks by the militant Islamic State group [ISIS]. The last US troops left the Afghan soils on Monday, the 30<sup>th</sup> August 2021.

Current and former officials & lawmakers held there was little appetite for Mr Biden to fire or demote top advisers over the handling of the US withdrawal. The Democratic president, meanwhile, strongly defended his administration's actions. Frustrated and angry officials at the

Pentagon privately blamed the lack of urgency leading up to the airlift on the State and Homeland Security departments, who in turn blamed the White House for slow decision-making.

However, a failure like this was collective. Everybody played his role to make the ship sink and then watching it from harbour smilingly.

## BIDEN DEFENDED HIS EXIT SCHEDULE:

**On 31st August 2021;** while addressing his nation, President defended his decisions over **PULL-OUT** schedule. The President made clear that:

'*I was not going to extend a forever exit,*' Biden said while defending his decision to withdraw US troops from Afghanistan - a move which led to the Taliban returning to power. *Staying longer was not an option;* it was said in an address to the nation, a day after the end of a 20-year US presence in Afghanistan.

Mr Biden praised troops for organising an airlift of more than 120,000 people wishing to flee the Taliban regime. He was widely criticised - at home and by his allies - over the abrupt manner of the US withdrawal, which led to the unexpected collapse of the Afghan security forces US troops had trained and funded for years.

The Taliban were able to reclaim control of the whole country within 11 days - finally entering the capital, Kabul, on 15th August 2021. Biden had deployed nearly 6,000 troops to seize control of the airport to co-ordinate the evacuation of US and allied foreign nationals and local Afghans who had been working for them. Thousands of people converged on Kabul Airport in the hope of being able to board one of the evacuation flights.

Taliban supporters, including those in Kandahar, were celebrating on the streets but Biden was praising his troops for the mass evacuation and promised to continue efforts to bring out those Americans who were still in Afghanistan and wanted to return - about 200 Americans altogether. Biden added in his speech:

"*A lot of our veterans and their families have gone through hell. Deployment after deployment. Months and years away from their families, loss of limbs, traumatic brain injury, post-traumatic stress.*

*I was not going to extend this forever war, and I was not extending a forever exit. The war in Afghanistan is now over.*"

*In a tweet he said the US did not need troops on the ground to defend it. His decision was 'not just about Afghanistan. It's about ending an era of major military operations to remake other countries.'*

Joe Biden tried to *'turn the page'* from a month of chaos and deaths in Afghanistan and, more broadly, from 20 years of ultimately futile US attempts at occupation and nation-building. At times he seemed defensive, noting that **Americans were warned 19 times to exit Afghanistan before** the 30th August US military withdrawal. He accused Afghan leaders, allies on whom the US had depended, of *'corruption and malfeasance'*. And he blamed Trump for negotiating what he characterised as an inadequate withdrawal agreement with the Taliban.

President Biden said the US had no vital interest in Afghanistan, and tried to reframe US foreign policy as depending less on military deployments and more on diplomacy and international cooperation *to face adversaries like China and Russia [?]*.

Public opinion polls showed Americans supported the US withdrawal from Afghanistan, only few were unhappy with how Biden oversaw the exit. White House held that the nation would be grateful for what Mr Biden accomplished and would soon forget the details of how the war ended.

On the same last day of 31st August 2021, the White House spokeswoman Jen Psaki said: *'Now, it's a 20-year war, so there's obviously a lot to dig into'*. Democrats wanted to pursue Biden's domestic agenda — expanding social programs, funding infrastructure and protecting voting rights. On the national security front, they wanted to highlight their investigation of the 6th attack on the US Capitol Hill by Trump's supporters on 6th January 2021.

How Congress would eventually proceed will depend on the level of interest from voters. Less than 40% of Americans approve of Biden's handling of the military withdrawal from Afghanistan, according to **Reuters' poll** released just after the exit-day.

National Security Adviser Jake Sullivan said a month earlier that the Biden administration would conduct a *'hot-wash'* — an after-action review — to discover what went wrong in Afghanistan and that he expected results of that review to be made public. It would simply sort out - **Who to blame?**; naturally some poor nation like Pakistan would be named to slaughter – because in America all Generals and civil officials are sacred cows whether they belong to Democrats or Republicans.

The last month in Afghanistan was a series of US failures, from the intelligence and military to diplomatic and immigration fronts, with one *core error was the failure to anticipate the speed of the Taliban's advance and collapse of the Afghan military.*

*'In some way, everyone is to be blamed in America,'* some Republicans pointed fingers at Sullivan and Secretary of State Antony Blinken as the two most responsible for setting the conditions for a chaotic evacuation and have demanded their departure.

Republicans also called for Biden to fire the US special envoy for Afghanistan, *Zalmay Khalilzad*, who negotiated the Trump administration's 2020 deal with the Taliban that set the stage for the withdrawal. However, no one gave ears to this baseless demand because the then President Trump was happy with his proceedings and it was the necessity of that time.

But when House Minority Leader **Kevin McCarthy** was asked whether he thought Biden or Blinken should be impeached, the California Republican did not answer, saying instead his focus was on getting the Americans out of Afghanistan. Defence officials told Reuters the State Department appeared out of touch with the reality on the ground in Afghanistan and had too much confidence in Afghan army, police and the Ghani government.

During a congressional hearing in June 2021, Blinken was asked if the administration was considering getting at-risk Afghans out of the country while their cases were being reviewed. His reply was:

> *"If there is a significant deterioration in security that could well happen, we discussed this before; I don't think it's going to be something that happens from a Friday to Monday."*

The Taliban seized two of Afghanistan's largest cities — *Kandahar* and *Herat* — on 13th August 2021 and took Kabul two days later.

### FOR AFGHANs ARRIVING the US:

Now see inside America....**FOR AFGHANs ARRIVING** there: During the last two weeks of August 2021, the US continued to run emergency flights from Kabul airport using mostly the military air-carriers picking up as many 'Afghani friends' as they could. Media still keeps hundreds of images and videos showing thousands of people gathered at the airport, many of them were simply hanging with the air-crafts in despair; some died by falling from when the air-crafts caught speed on ground or in air; some died in stampede; about 100 killed in IS's ambush on 27th August 2021 etc etc.

The aspired Afghans were holding and waving documents in their hands – as a proof of their associations with the US forces as contractors, suppliers, paid or voluntary intelligence workers or former recruits. No one yet has details of those Afghanis who, by share luck, succeeded in catching their flights and landed somewhere in the US territory.

The US policy was clear that evacuees who were ordered deported or who withdrew their applications to enter the US would not be returned to Taliban-controlled Afghanistan; the plans were to remove those individuals to a third country. However, the people who once landed in the US were probably not leaving even if they failed the vetting process.

The US Department of Homeland Security [DHS] flagged 44 Afghan evacuees as potential national security risks who were facilitated by the US during the two weeks after Taliban's take over of Afghanistan.

Within three weeks after take-over by Taliban, about 60,000 evacuees who have arrived on US soil, 13 Afghans remained in US Customs and Border Protection custody awaiting additional screening and review, including interviews with FBI and counter-terrorism teams.

Another 15 evacuees were considered security concerns; they were given back to US Immigration and Customs Enforcement [ICE]; some were sent back to transit sites in Europe or the Middle East. Another batch of 16 Afghans were not cleared to travel in the US and thus kept at US transit camps abroad. Two Afghan nationals were previously deported but they returned as evacuees; both were deported after convictions: one for sexual assault [2010] and the other for an armed robbery [2011].

President Biden planned to resettle 95,000 Afghans in the US, asking Congress for $6.4 billion in emergency funding to support the effort. White House officials confirmed that the vetting would be rigorous; will be tightly scrutinised by military, intelligence, law enforcement, and counter-terrorism agencies before their release.

After 17th **August 2021**, within three weeks, as many as 5,000 Afghans per day arrived at Dulles, using a United Airlines hangar as an arrival hall for flagged passengers in waiting. Relief organizations provided them meals, clothing and other provisions; most of whom were temporarily housed at eight military bases around.

Till ending first week of September 2021, amongst the 65,000 evacuees who had arrived, 11% were already the US citizens and 6% were legal permanent residents; the remaining 83% were considered *'Afghans at-Risk'* who either qualified for special immigrant visas as they had worked for the US government, or were keeping provisional immigration status known as 'humanitarian parole'.

They received work authorization, and their parole status was renewed for two years, but the White House asked Congress to approve benefits for them similar to the US refugee status-holders. American authorities had planned to allow them to apply for legal permanent residency after a year.

Several Afghans were flagged for suspected associations with terrorists, or whose phones and electronic devices contained dubious information. Afghan passengers were made to land at the two designated arrival sites only; Dulles [in Virginia] and Philadelphia Airports. DHS deployed 400 officers and agents to collect evacuees' biometric and biographical information and oversee the vetting process at transit sites in Europe and the Middle East. For the main criteria the US policy was: *'If we are assured it is not in fact derogatory information that is of concern to us, we will admit the individual.'*

## NO-ONE ACCEPTED AFGHAN REFUGEES:

Look at some of the obstacles Afghan asylum seekers faced around the world.

**Pakistan and Iran:** According to the UNHCR, Pakistan and Iran in the past had hosted the largest numbers of Afghan refugees, with nearly 1.5 million and 780,000, respectively, till ending 2020 at least. However, the interior ministry of Pakistan holds the different figures. They claimed that 3 million Afghanis were welcomed through formal two border passages during 1970s and 1980s after Soviets occupation of Afghanistan. Additionally, the same numbers of Afghanis were those who had crossed the border via traditional, non-controlled mountainous passages.

Pakistan had already shut the border crossings before the Taliban took over, but later doors were partially reopened. The Taliban were letting those with legal travel documents – but the Pakistani government ministers were issuing contradictory statements. One minister said refugees could stay in isolated, in temporary camps near the border, while Pakistan's interior minister said in mid-August: *'No Afghan refugees are coming to Pakistan'*- a traditional irresponsible behavior of Pakistani ministers since long; no one is ever sure about what they should say.

Iran's border with Afghanistan extends nearly 600 miles — mostly through desert — and Afghans have been long crossing freely to work there. Up to 3 million registered and unregistered Afghans were estimated to live in Iran. Afghans seeking to head further west often cross through Iran into Turkey or Greece.

Amid expectations of a new influx, the Iranian government instructed their border guards not to admit Afghans in 2021 whatsoever. At the same time, they set up temporary camps in border provinces for those who do cross over, though the government announced that they all would be repatriated when conditions improve. Iranian Foreign Ministry spokesman Saeed Khatibzadeh said in a briefing in ending August 2021 that Iran and Pakistan were not able to handle another surge of refugees.

**Turkey and Greece:** On the subject of potential asylum seekers from Afghanistan, Turkey and Greece shared their common stance – *'keep them out'*. Turkish President Erdogan called Greek Prime Minister Kyriakos Mitsotakis after Kabul fell to the Taliban to discuss their concerns over a potential refugee wave. Turkey has been an attractive destination country for refugees — in the past it hosted nearly 4 million Syrian refugees — and a stop on the way to Europe. Erdogan told the press:

> *"Turkey has no duty, responsibility or obligation to be Europe's refugee warehouse. The European Union should assist Afghans to prevent a migration surge [through other strategies / plans]."*

Afghans who had fled to Turkey in the past traveled over the mountains from Iran. In recent months, Turkey scaled up border patrols and fortifications. Afghans seeking to cross into the country faced a recently extended 10-foot-high wall, ditches or barbed wires and other hurdles. Turkish border guards pushed back Afghans attempting to enter during weeks of American exit, leaving thousands of Afghans massed in the Iranian border region.

Greek officials didn't allow a repetition of 2015's refugee surge, when hundreds of thousands of migrants reached Greek islands by boat from Turkey. Greece then extended a wall on its border with Turkey, and the government pledged to turn Afghans back.

**European Union:** Human Rights Watch called on European countries to lead efforts to facilitate safe passage of at-risk civilians from Afghanistan. The International Rescue Committee urged the EU to resettle at least 30,000 Afghans in the next 12 months. EU member states didn't agree to a common approach amidst divisions on policy making.

EU Commission President Ursula von der Leyen called the resettlement of vulnerable Afghans *'our moral duty'* and said the commission would provide funds to EU countries that resettle refugees - but could not get consent of a single EU member country.

EU's Chief Diplomat Josep Borrell suggested applying the temporary protection directive, a never-used mechanism since 2001 that could grant immediate, temporary protection to displaced people. A group of some 80 members of the European Parliament supported using the measure; but the idea of welcoming Afghan refugees to Europe had already been met with opposition from right-wing movements that gained support on the heels of the Syrian refugee crisis. Some EU member states, such as Slovenia and Austria, *categorically rejected the idea of taking in Afghan refugees into their territories.*

Austria, contrarily suggested, setting up *'deportation centers'* in countries neighbouring Afghanistan where European countries would send Afghans having denied asylum. EU home affairs ministers held an emergency meeting on the situation in Afghanistan, and afterwards released a statement making clear that the EU's approach would revolve around helping Afghanistan's neighbours to take in refugees and keep them there – *as if the neighbouring countries were fool nations.*

The ministers emphasized that the EU would remain determined to prevent unauthorized migrants from crossing the bloc's external borders. EU Home Affairs Commissioner Ylva Johansson said after the meeting that she would convene a forum in September 2021 to discuss resettlement priorities with member states *'and provide sustainable solutions to those Afghans who are most vulnerable'* – however, that dawn never appeared.

**Germany:** After Pakistan and Iran, Germany hosted the largest number of Afghan refugees. German Chancellor Angela Merkel had opened Germany's doors in 2015 to nearly a million refugees, mainly from Syria, Iraq and Afghanistan. That move drew immense criticism from nationalist groups and ire from the right, in Germany and across Europe. Merkel, who was set to leave office soon after, said in July [2021]: *'We cannot solve all of these problems by taking everyone in - there should be NO REPEAT of 2015'.*

The far-right Alternative for Germany [AFD] party rallied against the prospect of a 'new refugee wave.' Germany was among six EU nations that wrote to the European Commission in Brussels on 5th August 2021, calling on it to urge Afghanistan to cooperate on returns of Afghan migrants. Germany showed greater humanitarian inclinations than Austria and other such like signatories from EU.

**France:** French President Macron proposed creating a UN-led safe zone in Kabul to facilitate the departure of Afghans attempting to leave. He said several thousand remain on France's list of people in need of protection, including judges and female leaders, and pledged to try to work with partners and the Taliban to secure their departures. He also said that:

> *"We will help them as it is the honour of France to be side by side with those who share our values as much as we can - efforts would be on to evacuate Afghan human rights defenders, artists, journalists and activists.*

> *But Europe cannot alone assume the consequences of Afghanistan's fall to the Taliban."*

Dozens of French mayors offered to welcome more refugees while others spoke with a more hostile tone. Christian Estrosi, the mayor of Nice, told radio RTL: *'I am not ready to receive refugees here; that's clear.'*

## THE AGONY OF THE LEFT OVERS:

The US policy was clear that evacuees who were ordered deported or who withdrew their applications to enter the US would not be returned to Taliban-controlled Afghanistan; the plans were to remove those individuals to a third country. However, the people who once landed in the US were probably not leaving even if they failed the vetting process.

The day Afghanistan's capital fell, a contractor who had worked at the US Embassy for six years was dismissed from work early. Embassy staff had collected his family's information weeks before in preparation for a possible evacuation. But after he was told on 15$^{th}$ August to leave the embassy's grounds – *'nobody called, nobody emailed'* – perhaps the insiders knew the whole game. The contractor, who used to run a shop at the embassy, said:

> *"Everyone knows where I worked, that I worked with the Americans; I gave my mother my embassy badges and told her to put them in a box and bury it in the garden."*

The contractor eventually fled to the home of a relative in a neighbouring province. Roughly 2,500 US Embassy employees were among the 120,000 people the US evacuated by air from Afghanistan, according to President Biden. But the operation left many of America's longtime partners behind. One person familiar with the matter told they included about 2,000 US Embassy contractors and immediate family members, some of whom who had worked at the embassy for more than a decade.

**On 1$^{st}$ September 2021;** Under-Secretary of State Victoria Nuland said at a news conference that:

> *"For those who were not evacuated, we're looking at all possible options, but we're also conveying to them that their safety and security is of paramount concern to us."*

Most people kept the view that it was all an eye-wash. Biden described the operation as an *'extraordinary success,'* but thousands of Afghans considered vulnerable and eligible for evacuation fell through the cracks. They included students of American University of Afghanistan and graduates, applicants for special immigrant visas and members of Afghanistan's Special Forces who had fought on behalf of the US and luckily survived – c60,000 of their companions died in operations and ambushes.

The weapons the Taliban captured from the US camps might not be an international threat, but they gave the group more ways to control their Afghan population in its own way. With the departure of US forces from Afghanistan, many Afghans who felt threatened by the Taliban take-over were correct saying that they were in greater danger. Among the tens of thousands who managed to reach the airport and got on planes were 5,500 Americans, thousands of citizens and diplomats of US allies, thousands of Afghans who worked for the US as interpreters, translators etc.

Planning for the evacuation had begun weeks before Kabul fell to the Taliban in mid-August, but the effort began to stumble almost as soon as it started. The US officials did not expect Afghan President Ashraf Ghani to flee the country so cowardly & quickly; leaving Kabul's Security Forces to collapse; leaving the civilian side of the airport unguarded.

Stooge President Ghani's departure as the Taliban entered Kabul on 15th August 2021 was really disappointing for all policy makers in the White House and Pentagon. The Americans made every effort to know who they were dealing with and what the numbers were, making sure they had proper resources on the ground to assist them. But the whole situation had spiraled into uncertainty, frustration and ambiguity.

When the airlift was complete, the US Secretary of State Antony Blinken assured that other evacuation efforts were ongoing. It was a white lie for the whole civilized world. Many were still there; the Pentagon knew it. It was a shallow assurance that the US would keep working to help them; in fact the US commitment to them had no deadline. When the last American evacuation plane left Afghanistan, one of the embassy employee said: '.....*she became a prisoner in her own home.*'

The 23-year-old lady had recently graduated from American University of Afghanistan in Kabul with distinction - she feared for being on Taliban's 'KILL LIST' – she was too afraid even walking down her street. Referring to **the Washington Post** dated 30th August 2021:

> "*For the second time in four days Sunday, a major media outlet reported that the Taliban had been provided with a list of names of those seeking to evacuate Afghanistan. This has led critics to accuse the Biden administration of endangering those people.*"

American University, funded largely with American finances, attempted to evacuate thousands of students, faculty members and graduates but was mostly unsuccessful. Afghans associated with the school were considered at risk and were eligible for US evacuation flights. A deadly 2016 Taliban attack on this institution had killed 15 at least and left dozens wounded. But those connected to the university were not prioritized; meaning it was up to the school to navigate Taliban checkpoints without US or NATO help and make it into the military side of the airport.

**Ian Bickford,** president of American University of Afghanistan, once told that efforts to relocate students, graduates and faculty members were continuing but all they were in the process for the long haul - And they continued to appeal for the US support. However, the State Department spokesman though couldn't speak about specific cases but had affirmed the US evacuation was aimed at addressing the needs of those most at risk, including women and girls, journalists, members of religious and ethnic minorities, and such like others.

[On 15ᵗʰ August 2021; *the day Kabul fell to the Taliban, an engineer who worked for the US Army was scheduled to have his final interview at the US Embassy for an expedited visa. The interview was set for 10:45 am, but the embassy had started dismissing its staff an hour before, as news broke that the militants had reached the city's gates.*]

The engineer, in the final stages of processing for a special immigrant visa, should have been eligible for an evacuation flight. His family camped outside the airport for three nights, sleeping in an open park littered with garbage. He managed to reach the airport gates twice but was turned away both times. Taliban leaders had barred Afghans who didn't hold foreign passports or green cards from leaving Afghanistan.

[Neighbours had warned him that local Taliban fighters were asking questions about whom he worked for. The inquiries were enough to scare him off the streets. But unable to leave his home, his family was running dangerously low on food - for days, all they had was bread, tea and sugar. But the evacuation process prioritized the US citizens, legal permanent residents, special immigrant visa applicants and other Afghans at risk – not him.]

Another Afghan Special Forces officer was on the list of people to evacuate but wasn't able to get inside the military side of the airport. US forces tried to extract him and a few hundred other Afghan commandos, but the logistics repeatedly fell apart. The officer held:

*"The Americans call us and tell us to gather here. And then they say, 'No, that is the wrong place. Go to another location.' And then they say, 'Come back tomorrow'.*

4559

*Of course I'm angry. We were on the front line for the United States in this war. They told us you will be the best of the best in the Afghan army, and now look.*

*When Kabul fell, I didn't want to flee. I called my [foreign] sources and told them, if you support us, we can fight against the Taliban in Kabul. We have the training, we have the ability, and we can be the resistance."*

But there was no response to his offers. As the Taliban tightened its grip on his neighbourhood, he fled to a friend's house and then, a few days later, to another home. The night the last US evacuation plane took off, he and a friend went to watch the Taliban gunfire from the roof – '*Every hope is finished now; he can't imagine trusting the US enough to partner with its military again;*' the officer desperately cried.

Another US Embassy employee said:

*".... the silence from his longtime employer is unnerving. We are still waiting to see what they will do for us, we don't know, exactly."*

Ultimately, there was a sun-set of <u>31st August 2021</u>, hopeless for many.

# Scenario 239

## CULTURAL VALUES RE-DEFINED IN KABUL

On 17th **August 2021;** two days after the taking over, the Taliban declared an *'amnesty'* across Afghanistan and urged women to join their government, trying to calm nerves across the tense capital city of Kabul that only the day before saw chaos at its airport as people were seen mad to flee the Taliban rule.

The comments by *Enamullah Samangani*, a member of the Taliban's Cultural Commission, were the first comments on governance from a federal level across the country after their blitz across the country. While there were no major reports of abuses or fighting in Kabul, many residents stayed home but remained fearful after the insurgents' takeover saw prisons emptied and armouries vacated. Older generations remember the Taliban's ultra-conservative views during their earlier rule [1996-2001].

Back then, women were barred from attending schools or working places outside their homes. They had to wear the all-encompassing *burqa* and be accompanied by a male nearest available relative [called *mehram*] whenever they went outside. The Taliban banned music, cut off the hands of thieves and stoned adulterers. Mr *Samangani* said:

> *"The Islamic Emirate doesn't want women to be victims. They should be in government structure according to Shariah law. The structure of government is not fully clear, but based on experience, there should be a fully Islamic leadership and all sides should join. Our people are Muslims and we are not here to force them to adopt our religion Islam."*

The Taliban had sought to project greater moderation in recent years, but many Afghans remained sceptical. The world followed events in Afghanistan with a heavy heart and deep disquiet about what was ahead; UN Secretary-General Antonio Guterres was seen more worried. A resolute US President Joe Biden stood squarely behind his decision to withdraw American forces and acknowledged the *'gut-wrenching'* images unfolding in Kabul. Biden said that:

*".....he faced a choice between honouring a previously negotiated withdrawal agreement or sending thousands more troops back to begin a third decade of war. After 20 years, I've learned the hard way that there was never a good time to withdraw US forces."*

**Biden's televised address** from the White House on 17ᵗʰ August 2021 is referred.

However, despite the Taliban's statement in earlier paragraphs, there was a disturbing column in the **Washington Post** of 1ˢᵗ October 2021 telling:

- An Afghan artist in Kabul buried 15 paintings — all works of modern art depicting women — in his compound three days after the Taliban entered the capital.

- A well-known film-maker carried the same fear. Before she fled the country, she tucked away a large hard drive with more than 20 films in a secret location.

- And an aging bookseller in his tiny sidewalk shop concealed every book the militants consider damning; including two Bibles, translated into Dari and Pashto.

The main fear remained that *'if the Taliban fighters found this, they would punish me'*. And so went the cultural unravelling of Afghanistan's capital six weeks into the Taliban's resurgence. The Taliban's return to power — and its history of destroying precious art and relics it considered blasphemous —reopened the psychic wounds of the past, at once triggering anxiety and efforts by individual Afghans to protect their masterpieces. It was a different interpretation of *Afghan Culture* near most Taliban members – quite opposite to the *Islamic Culture*.

## THREATS TO ART & CULTURE:

The past 20 years of Western presence ushered in developing of arts, film, music and books, helping to transform Kabul into a cosmopolitan metropolis. A new generation of artists was influenced as much by Afghan traditions and history as by modern themes such as the war, Western music and women's rights. The Taliban rulers didn't decree what shape and form art and culture would be permitted to take shape in the new Afghanistan.

Many artists feared they would soon be governed by a hard-line vision of Islamic righteousness that could reverse the gains they enjoyed in freedoms of expression, speech and ideas over the past two decades. Sahra Karimi, a filmmaker in Kabul expressed:

*"The kind of art that we believe has a value means artists should be free to express their own thoughts, not under dictatorship or censorship. Those artists will not easily be able to work as freely as they used to do. And they were so free.*

*Even as some artists take great risks to protect their creations, many have fled the country, while others are self-censoring to avoid the wrath of the Taliban."*

Some artists had already destroyed their paintings or sculptures; stores selling musical instruments have shuttered, as had many art galleries. Wedding bands and singers stopped working as many wedding halls cancelled live music to not anger the Taliban. Afghan filmmaking went totally dead. Safiullah Habibi, the Director of Kabul's Fine Arts Institute [a government facility] told that:

*"The Taliban have not issued any statement or directions regarding the arts. But artists themselves are limiting themselves. They think the Taliban will repeat what happened in the 1990s. At that time, the arts had no place in their rule;"* **Sudarsan Raghavan's** report in **WP** of 1ˢᵗ October 2021 is referred.

**Rules 'framework' underway:** The classrooms of a few art schools in Kabul had gone empty just after Taliban's take-over. Bilal Karimi, the Taliban deputy spokesman, said the interim government was new and still *'making a framework'* for all issues concerning arts & culture; adding that:

*"Whether a form of art would be permissible or prohibited would be governed by Islamic law and* **Shariah.** *The knowledgeable people will formulate the rules, keeping in view the religious, national and historical traditions for art and cultural heritage - and whether these issues are in line with the Islamic laws or against them."*

Few Afghans expected the Taliban to fully return to its own cultural values of the mid-1990s, when it first came to power. Then the group had prohibited television, radio, movies and other forms of entertainment, declaring them immoral and socially corruptive. Their religious morality wing of police had confiscated or smashed television sets, videocassette recorders, cameras, videos and satellite dishes. Violators were given public beatings. In 2001, in the months before the Taliban was toppled following the 9/11 attacks, the Taliban had banned the Internet, too.

In 2021, the Taliban deployed sophisticated social media campaigns on *Twitter* and other Internet platforms. Taliban officials gave interviews on television and radio, and answered questions on *WhatsApp*. Their fighters in Kabul were spotted with smart-phones, taking selfies and videos. To be sure, the Taliban's lack of clarity on their cultural vision created a landscape of contradictions in Kabul.

In few neighbourhoods, art galleries remained open, though few customers come because of fear and collapsing economy situations around. On Fridays at the city's only five-star hotel, paintings of women and animals were seen on display for sale, as visiting Taliban officials walked past. Music could also be heard floating softly out of some cars – speaking of tolerant attitudes of the Ruling Taliban. And no one opted to ransack the famous *National Museum of Afghanistan*, filled with thousands of ancient cultural artefacts, as they did during their previous rule.

Kabul's established artists noted that the new rulers were seeking to improve their image to get diplomatic recognition, unfreeze billions of funds and receive international aid to bolster their tanking economy and address a spreading humanitarian crisis.

In August 2021, Taliban fighters shot dead Afghan folk singer *Fawad Andarabi* in his mountain village north of Kabul, prompting Karima Bennoune, the senior-most UN official for cultural rights, to urge governments *to demand the Taliban respect the human rights of artists.* In Bamian province, Taliban fighters destroyed two statues of leaders revered by the ethnic Shiite Hazara minority. Amongst artists and painters, most people were hiding themselves, no doubt.

In an art school in Kabul, some of the teachers still come to work even though the students were avoiding the schools. At the Fine Arts Institute, what was forbidden during the Taliban's previous rule still hangs on the walls. In one picture, one of players mounted on horses engaged in *buzkashi*, a traditional sport. The Taliban used to consider portraits of living beings blasphemous – but this time they were behaving differently.

*'Artists are a big part of our society,'* said Habibi, seated in his office with a portrait of an eagle on the wall – but it was there by all means. He sought a meeting with a senior Taliban official in the Cultural

Ministry but couldn't get appointment. Habibi hoped to convince him that art was not against Islamic law and that the institute was preserving Afghan culture. It also helps strengthen the economy by training its 700 students — 90 percent of them female — to find jobs, he had plans to argue on.

During the last week of September 2021, a Taliban group visited the institute, saying they were from the Movement's Security Services. On the ground inside, they spotted a yellow sculpture, a reproduction of one of the famed giant **Buddhas of Bamian**. The original two 6th-century statues were carved into the side of a rock face in central Afghanistan. In March 2001, the Taliban had blown them up with explosives. Here in 2021, the Taliban agents were not pleased to see the reproduction either – saying it *'haram'* because it was of a human being. Mr Habibi, the Museum's Director told them that it was our cultural heritage.

**Danger of books:** Some volumes and books that could be considered problematic for the Taliban can still be found in the city's book market, including those on religion or politics. During the Taliban's previous era, they viewed any effort to convert Muslims to Christianity a crime worthy of death. So the Bibles are still tucked behind a bookshelf. Some Afghans, he said, buy them for research purposes.

The Taliban, this time, didn't publicly weigh in on which books they would consider socially acceptable. So, many of the booksellers removed books they believed the Taliban would not condone – being against *Shariah* laws, ones with racy titles or images of women on the covers. Some Afghans also removed sensitive books from their personal libraries, in the event Taliban fighters could raid their houses while others destroyed certain books on democracy, human rights and Western literature.

## 'THEY WILL DESTROY THE ....'

Many artists in Kabul had kept their art works hidden in their homes since the Taliban took the capital. Before the Taliban seized control in August 2021, the staff of **Afghan Films - the state-run film company**, had more than 20 films in different stages of productions, including feature-length films, shorts and documentaries; said *Sahra Karimi*, the former head of Afghan Films. The second national film festival was ahead and the production was going on full bloom then - but had to discontinue due to Taliban's expected new policy and more because the government had no money in their kitty.

The staff members continued coming to work only to show their faces. Director *Karimi* had fears for the films in progress. The footage for two films left with editors who fled the country, but the rest were on the hard drive, which also contained photos, projects and other activities of the past two years. Director Karimi had to move to Slovakia after the change of government in August 2021.

In mid-1990s, the Taliban had banned moving images and destroyed reels of many films. However, *Sahra Karimi* confirmed later that:

> *".... They are now no longer as much against film, viewing television, videos and social media but they do care about the content which should be devoutly Islamic. Independent filmmakers are not going to compromise......'"*

Also of concern were decades of film archives — thousands of hours of film — that were being digitized. The archives were located inside the presidential palace, which was later occupied by the Taliban. Of course; the archives were in big danger – but not known what policy was coming up.

One artist could no longer visit the compound **where he buried his 15 paintings.** It was inside a government complex, and Taliban fighters now guard it in routine. Since August [2021], he changed home because his neighbours knew he was an artist – and finally moved in the basement of a relative's house — along with 42 of his *other* paintings. Three days before the Taliban entered Kabul, he took them out of their frames, wrapped them up in a blanket and spirited them out of a gallery.

A singer got hidden his *dambura,* a traditional lute, along with his paintings, which mostly depict humans or animals. The 38-year-old artist told the WP's representative reporter that:

> *"When we paint a human being or an animal, the Taliban says we give life and spirit to a piece of paper. Saving my own art is like saving my own life. More than a dozen of his artist friends are also in hiding."*

See a report dated <u>11<sup>th</sup> October 2021</u> published in Western media papers under the caption *'After the Taliban seized their school, Afghanistan's all-female orchestra tried to flee. Only some escaped'*:

One *Shogofa Safi*, 17, a conductor and part of the **Zohra Orchestra** at the Afghanistan National Institute of Music, left the country around

<u>25<sup>th</sup> September 2021</u>. Her other fellow girls came from homes broken by war and poverty to chase an unimaginable future as musicians. And with grit and determination they succeeded: Some played at Carnegie Hall; others at the Kennedy Centre. Many travelled the world as members of *Afghanistan's only all-female orchestra.* On <u>14<sup>th</sup> August 2021</u>, the girls were rehearsing for an upcoming concert in Colombia: next day, the Taliban seized Kabul and the girls' hopes evaporated. **Sudarsan Raghavan** wrote:

> *"This happened to Afghanistan's first and the only music school and its renowned **Zohra Orchestra** after the Taliban's return to power. It was a traumatic experience that for many of the girls and teens are still ongoing, and whose conclusion remains far from certain.*
>
> *Today, their school — the **Afghanistan National Institute of Music** — is a military base of the Haqqani network…….An evacuation operation launched in the last days of the war failed to get the girls and scores of other students and faculty out of the country before the US withdrawal was complete."*

The Taliban armed fighters often walked through the halls of the said Institute in Kabul. Once some student girls tried to escape out of the country but the Taliban stopped the girls' buses 55 yards from a US military-controlled gate into Kabul's international airport, they were sent back. A second attempt on <u>3<sup>rd</sup> October 2021</u> succeeded in taking out roughly a third of the music school with the help of famed cellist Yo-Yo Ma and others. Those who escaped included two Zohra musicians interviewed by **The Washington Post** later. But the rest didn't have valid passports and remained trapped in the capital. An 18-year-old orchestra member, who was left behind, told:

> *"I haven't practiced my violin since the day the Taliban came. The only life I want is one where I can freely play my violin. The travel documents have not been issued to me yet"*

The violinist was among the tens of thousands of Afghans left to fend for themselves under the Taliban, despite President Biden's description of the US evacuation of nearly 124,000 people as *'an extraordinary success.'*

Those who were left behind included female judges, women's rights activists, and former US military translators, artists, musicians and countless others who worked with the US or NATO forces during their stay in Afghanistan - many in hiding.

One *Wajiha Kabuli* joined [in 2015] the co-educational music school from an orphanage that funnelled in talented girls. A year earlier, the Taliban had killed her father, and her mother was ill and too poor to support her. Music was the only way to reach her goals, either financially or spiritually; now 17, a percussionist. Wajiha was in the Zohra Orchestra, which performed both traditional Afghan songs and classical music. As they toured the world, the 30-member ensemble became an emblem of Afghanistan's growing freedoms and opportunities for girls and women.

In <u>December 2014</u>, a suicide bomber targeted Kabul's **French Cultural Centre**, where the school's students were performing at a musical play. The attack killed a German national and injured 15 others. The music school's director, Ahmad Naser Sarmast, was nearly killed but survived. The Taliban claimed responsibility describing the music as an insult to Islam. Mr Sarmast said.

> *"My school was promoting gender equality, musical education, musical diversity, women's rights, girl's rights etc etc. Everything that our school was doing was against the Taliban's vision, perception and ideology."*

On the Taliban's taking over day, Shogofa Safi, 17, was playing the marimba in an orchestra rehearsal when two teachers entered. The Taliban were on the way. '*We fled the school,*' recalled Safi, who was also the orchestra's conductor.

That was the last time she and the other girls had seen their instruments.

## EVACUATION OF ART LOVERS:

Students at the music school were forced to leave their instruments behind after the Taliban took over. Within days, the school's supporters scrambled to get roughly 280 students and faculty out of the country. Portugal's government agreed to take in the musicians, and the group's backers made arrangements for them to be evacuated on a British military flight. On 27th August 2021, Kabuli, Safi and the 18-year-old violinist had received messages to pack their bags.

The next afternoon, seven buses carrying around 280 students and faculty from the school arrived at the airport gate. They were marked with an 'X' mark and Christmas signs to be identifiable by US soldiers, but between the American troops and the buses stood a Taliban checkpoint. Thousands of Afghans and foreigners, including US citizens were also trying to flee the country. They were in a bus full of girls, and the Taliban were outside and they refused buses' entry inside.

Away from Afghanistan, several groups of the school's backers were following the drama through Zoom and WhatsApp, connected with bus drivers, faculty and US troops on the ground. After waiting for several hours at one gate, the convoy drove to another gate, where Taliban fighters again blocked their entry.

Some stalwart Americans and the Congress itself sought the help of Gen Milley, the Chairman of the Joint Chiefs of Staff, to help the convoy get inside the airport, he did the best but there was no approval from the Taliban. The US soldiers were dealing with dozens of similar clusters seeking to enter the airport. The buses returned to the first gate, where the girls remained overnight. In the early morning of 29th August, the buses were half a football field away from the gate where US soldiers were positioned.

Around the capital, Taliban fighters entered wedding halls, demanding live music be halted. They confiscated or damaged the instruments, declaring them *'haraam'* or forbidden by Islamic law. Remarked one Taliban Commander that:

> *"Music is not in our religion. Since the Islamic Emirate has taken over here, music has no longer a place here."*

Against this backdrop and after their ordeal at the airport, members of the **Zohra Orchestra** confined themselves in their homes. They worried neighbours would alert the Taliban or they would be recognized if they stepped outside. To keep her skills fresh, *Shagofa Safi* was taking an online class with a teacher based in England. She played an imaginary marimba by tapping her fingers on a table to music played on her tablet. She told that: *'When the Taliban sent the bus back, I lost my dreams. My body is alive but my soul is dead.'*

Her orchestra friends felt the same way. All three girls shared the same dream: to one day attend the Juilliard School, the performing arts conservatory in New York.

On **2nd October 2021;** Safi and Kabuli received word of a second opportunity to leave Afghanistan. They were informed by their teachers to pack small bags and be ready. Their families had decided that their futures were worth the sacrifice of separation. Kabuli's mother said later that: *'I am happy my daughter is out of the country and out of danger.'*

[**This time some American senators had requested Qatar authorities to help girls' exit from Kabul.**]

After tearful goodbyes, the girls travelled next day to the airport in buses with 91 other students and faculty, including roughly half of the *Zohra Orchestra*. This time, officials from the Qatari embassy were in the vehicles, and there were no chaotic scenes at the airport. At one point, the Taliban officers questioned the validity of some of the girls' travel documents. But the Qataris convinced them to let the group leave.

Also aboard the Qatar Airways plane were graduates of the school who had played at the Carnegie Hall and Kennedy Centre in the past and master musicians with deep knowledge of traditional Afghan music. Their teacher Sarmast said:

"We should rescue this knowledge for the future which is significantly important for the preservation of the musical heritage of Afghanistan and passing it to the new generations."

Named **ZOHRA** *after the Persian goddess of music*, the orchestra was mainly made up of girls and women from a Kabul orphanage aged between 13 and 20. [Reuters]

Then in Doha, the group got prepared to leave for Portugal, which had granted visas and facilities to restart their musical studies and lives. About 180 of the school's students, faculty, staff and family members remained in Kabul, including the rest of the orchestra. Some of the student girls were not opting to go back to their village as their neighbours were the Taliban. Everyone there knew them as musicians.

In later days, the Taliban officials announced they would issue 25,000 passports, but with hundreds of thousands of Afghans seeking to leave, Sarmast had little hope his remaining students would receive theirs quickly. Shogofa told in a tele-interview from Doha that:

"I feel good, but I also feel sad. It's tragic to leave our own country. Now we can chase and continue our dreams. But we think constantly of those left behind. We hope they will soon join us. **Wherever we are, we will be ZOHRA**, and we will again stand as one community."

# Scenario 240

## HUMAN CRISIS IN NEW AFGHANISTAN

**On 15<sup>th</sup> August 2021:** The Taliban took over the reins of Afghanistan again after 20 years. They brought back their state-name as *Islamic Emirates of AFGHANISTAN*; later announced their interim cabinet but the turmoil was not over. The real-time test for the Taliban group started because, as happens in every new set-up, the group faced a massive and immediate trial in a desperately poor and diplomatically isolated country where deep-seated political and social problems had been compounded by more than four decades of war; on both counts – internally; the civil war – and externally; from Soviet and American occupations.

### HOW RICH THE TALIBAN WERE?

Referring to BBC's article at world-46554097 **[BBC Reality Check]** dated 28<sup>th</sup> August 2021:

> *"Despite the 20-year conflict during 2001-21 with deaths of tens of thousands of Taliban fighters, the group's territorial control and military strength had been increased. By mid-2021 they had estimated 70,000-100,000 fighters, up from around 30,000 in 2011.*
>
> *The group's annual income from 2011 onwards **has now been estimated at around $400m (£290m)** by the United Nations (UN). But by the end of 2018 this may have increased significantly, to as much as $1.5bn a year, according to BBC investigations."*

The Taliban got developed a number of income sources; for instance:

**Foreign Donations:** The US officials remained angry with certain countries - including Pakistan, Iran and Russia - for giving financial aid to the Taliban but the said countries always denied. However, private citizens from Pakistan and several Gulf countries including Saudi Arabia, the United Arab Emirates [UAE] and Qatar were considered to be the largest individual contributors - according to experts it could be as $500m a year. A classified US intelligence report estimated that in 2008 the Taliban received $106m from foreign sources, in particular from the Gulf States.

**Drug Trade:** The US and the West unnecessarily blame that the Taliban were involved in the illegal drug trade. It's not true as far as the organisational character is concerned; the Taliban never argued such remarks.

*Rather the Taliban take pride in having banned opium poppy cultivation for the period they remained in power during 1996-2001.* Afghanistan has been the world's largest producer of opium – and thus its derivative named heroin – but the Afghan people hold that during the foreign occupation the opium & drug trade was secretly done by some of the US and NATO security contractors and their sponsored warlords. With an estimated annual export value of $1.5-$3bn; opium has been a big business for contractors. Opium harvesting provided almost 120,000 jobs in Afghanistan in 2019, according to the UN data. A 10% cultivation tax was being collected from opium farmers – but that was done by regular Afghan government officials – not the Taliban.

A point to ponder is that during past 20 years the Taliban were hiding themselves in hilly terrains of Afghanistan with their guns and arsenal; always thinking about saving their lives OR planning to launch an ambush over the foreign forces – then *how could they involve in opium cultivation* and what area was with them for cultivation or how could they collect taxes; all seems to be a joke.

Taxes were collected from the laboratories converting opium into heroin, as well as the traders who used to smuggle the illicit drugs – but the collectors were Hamid Karzai and then Ashraf Ghani – NOT the Taliban. US Commander **Gen John Nicholson**'s conclusion in 2018's **SIGAR Report** was false and fabricated – trying to cover his colleagues and soldiers.

However, it can be understood that the Taliban might have asked the general Afghan traders to pay taxes on various goods like fuel and construction material - when travelling through areas they controlled. That's a normal routine even in settled countries. The Taliban might also have taxed supply-trucks, transport, development and infrastructure projects - including roads, schools, and clinics – which were mostly funded by the West but that, could happen in any part of the world as per routine local tax laws.

**Mines & Minerals:** Afghanistan is rich in minerals and precious stones, much of it under-exploited as a result of the years of conflict. The mining industry in Afghanistan is worth an estimated $1bn annually; most of the extraction is small scale and much of it is done illegally. The Taliban could have taken control of mining sites for their income because their operations were, of course, launched from hills and mountains.

In its 2014's Annual Report, the *UN Analytical Support and Sanctions Monitoring Team* said the Taliban received about $10m a year from 25 to 30 illegal mining operations in southern *Helmand* province – which has been the Taliban base since its first day in being – 1994-95.

The Taliban gained control of Kabul on 15<sup>th</sup> August 2021 and NEXT DAY [16<sup>th</sup> August 2021], the Biden administration froze Afghan government reserves held in US bank accounts, blocking the Taliban from accessing billions of dollars held in American banks and financial establishments. Referring to news by *Jeff Stein* on media dated 17<sup>th</sup> August 2021:

> *"The decision was made by Treasury Secretary Janet Yellen and Office of Foreign Assets Control. The State Department was also involved in discussions over the weekend, with officials in the White House monitoring the developments; they made out a statement: <u>Any Central Bank assets the Afghan government have in the United States will not be made available to the Taliban.</u>"*

This government policy was not made public then. Afghanistan was already one of the poorest countries in the world and was highly dependent on American aid that was pushed into danger zone. The Biden administration was facing hard choices over how to manage existing sanctions on the Taliban, which made it difficult to deliver international humanitarian assistance to a population facing ruin and devastation.

The Taliban was last in power from 1996 to 2001 and had returned to office after twenty years. With the group taking over again, situation could be termed as *'humanitarian crisis in the making.'* President Biden in his speech, on 16<sup>th</sup> August 2021, appeared to commit to continuing to give aid to Afghanistan, saying: *'We will continue to support the Afghan people. We will lead with our diplomacy, our international influence and our humanitarian aid.'*

However, nothing was seen on ground action till ending 2021 at least.

The IMF told that Afghanistan Central Bank held $9.4 billion in reserve assets as of April 2021 which comes up roughly as one-third of the country's annual economic output; but majority of those reserves was not held in Afghanistan. Among those, billions of dollars were kept in the US. No one in White House and Treasury was clear about the future policy for the US economic assistance to Afghanistan.

The US did not need any new authority to freeze the said reserves, because the Taliban was already facing sanctions under an executive order approved after the 9/11 [2001] attacks. Beyond the reserves, the US used to send roughly $3 billion per year in support for the Afghan military. The funding could only be spent *if the Secretary of Defence certifies to Congress that the Afghan forces are controlled by a civilian representative government that is committed to protecting human rights and women's rights.*

About 80% of Afghanistan's budget was funded by the US and other international donors. However, the fiscal gurus in Washington held that blocking the funds meant for the poor Afghan people would be dangerous. There should be no restrictions on the Afghan economy. The Chief of Eurasia Group held that: *'You'll see a lot more refugees on the back of this, a lot more radicalism on the back of this.'*

**Mark Weisbrot,** co-director of the Centre for Economic and Policy Research, a Washington think tank, said:

> *"For the US government to seize Afghanistan's central bank reserves would be a big mistake. It would be telling the Taliban that the US government wants to destroy them and their country's economy – (as a revenge of shameful defeat).*
>
> *This is far from the first time the US had cut off foreign governments from its assets, approving **similar moves against Venezuela and Libya** after leaders hostile to Washington had gained power in those countries as well."*

**Smith,** the former Obama administration official, said this important decision probably should come when Washington would decide how to handle sanctions against the Taliban. Maintaining those sanctions might chill international efforts to help Afghanistan, but it could prove politically impossible for the Biden administration to moderate — let alone lift — sanctions on the Taliban in power.

International aid flows represented roughly 43% of Afghanistan's economy in 2020, according to the World Bank.

*"It could be cataclysmic for Afghanistan if the administration does not handle the sanctions issue deftly - pointing to a similar situation in the waning days of the Trump presidency that threatened to deprive Yemenis living under the sanctioned* **Houthi government** *from aid. In that case, Biden officials removed the* Houthis *from the terrorism sanctions list — an option that could be unavailable in this (Taliban's) case."*

However, in Afghanistan, it's potentially a serious humanitarian issue that the Biden government would be thinking hard about. The US and the UN both hold the statistics that half of Afghanistan's population required humanitarian assistance in 2021, a six-fold increase from four years ago.

NATO Secretary General *Jens Stoltenberg* said at a news conference on 17th August 2021 that NATO got suspended aid to the Afghan government as well. They suspended all financial and other kinds of support to the Afghan government, because NATO would not support the Taliban regime. *"No money is transferred; no support is provided,"* held the Secretary General NATO.

Suggestion were made immediately after the Taliban's take-over by Britain's foreign minister that *'international powers may also entertain new sanctions against Afghanistan'*. Daniel Glaser, former Assistant Secretary for terrorist financing, said that cutting Afghanistan off from the reserve funds would be the obvious first move. It's the least they could do; the Taliban would not be the responsible custodians of Afghanistan's reserves.

## CHALLENGES AHEAD FOR THE TALIBAN:

Referring to an analysis available on most media pages like **daily DAWN** of 31st October 2021: There were numerous challenges facing the Afghan Taliban namely -

**Lack of trust:** Once there was widespread suspicion about the Taliban among Afghans about their thinking about concept of Islamic government. The poles apart Islamic groups had their own different reasons – but mostly subsided later. Last time when the Taliban were in power from 1996 to 2001, they imposed a harsh interpretation of Islamic law. Members of the ruling group walking past a beauty salon with images of women used to deface the images using spray paint. In their last stint, they banned women from education and public spaces, brutally executed political opponents and massacred religious and ethnic minorities such as the *Hazaras*.

However, this time, the Taliban promised a softer system around, including rights for women. The Taliban also thought about an inclusive government, holding talks with a variety of movers and shakers in Afghan politics — but excluding former US-backed President Hamid Karzai and his cabinet members. They sent representatives to the *Shia Hazara* minority, which had suffered brutal violence at the hands of the Taliban in the 1990s.

There was a relief in many parts of rural Afghanistan where people wanted an end to the violence; many Afghans said they were happy with such initial actions by the Taliban but still to see continuity in policy. Women, particularly in cities, remained fearful of stepping outside.

There was one pocket of armed resistance in the *Panjshir valley*, a traditional anti-Taliban stronghold fortress of late Ahmed Shah Masoud's group – but soon it subsided due to effective negotiations between new leadership of Taliban and the Northern Alliance. First time, the Taliban were seen NOT using war-path to show their might.

**Economic, humanitarian catastrophe:** Afghanistan was, and has been one of the poorest nations in the world. After the Taliban were toppled in 2001, huge amounts of foreign aid flowed into the country. International assistance was more than 40% of Afghan GDP in 2020; most of it stood suspended in 2021, with no guarantees about the rest.

This crunch immediately started spelling disaster, as the Taliban needed to figure out how to pay government employees and keep running critical infrastructures such as water, power and communications. The Taliban's requests to the US to release their own funds in American banks were repeatedly turned down. The UN also warned of a humanitarian catastrophe, with food stocks running low because of disruptions caused by conflict as well as a severe drought.

Western media alleged that *'insurgents (the Taliban) had large revenues — hundreds of millions of dollars'* but it was all fake estimations; it could be a tiny amount compared with Afghanistan's national requirements. The Taliban started tapping state sources of income after taking over Afghanistan afresh in August 2021, such as customs revenue from border crossings, but that too was a fraction of national needs. No Income Tax was possible as there was no business in Afghanistan;

most shops in rural districts were drone attacked by the US-Army at various times.

**HEALTH CARE CRISIS:** When the Taliban re-occupied the throne in Kabul [2021], the health care system in Afghanistan was on the brink of collapse, international aid groups had warned about threats of deepening the country's humanitarian crisis with the start of winter. Thousands of health care facilities had run out of essential medicines. Afghan doctors were not paid since months, with no pay-cheques in sight. During ending the US exit plan, there was a surge of cases of measles and diarrhoea, according to the World Health Organization [WHO].

Since two decades, aid from the World Bank and other international donors handled the country's health care system, but after the Taliban seized power, they froze $600 million in health care aid. Within the first month of the Taliban rule, the toll was becoming clear. *Jim Huylebroek and Christina* published their article on media of 12ᵗʰ October 2021:

> *"We are deeply concerned that Afghanistan faces imminent collapse of health services and worsening hunger if aid and money do not flow into the country within weeks. Afghanistan's looming harsh winter threatens greater misery and hardships."*

The unfolding health care crisis needed aid for the country – for the people – for the human being – no wonder it's under Taliban rule. Foreign aid once made up nearly 75% of the country's public expenditures, according to the World Bank, but after the Taliban seized control on 15ᵗʰ August, the US had frozen over $9 billion in the Afghan Central Bank's American accounts, and major international funders like the World Bank and International Monetary Fund [IMF] paused disbursements.

They feared that the Taliban would re-impose the brutal repression of their first reign [1996 to 2001]; Aid groups and foreign governments talked of finding a way to funnel money and supplies into Afghanistan without placing them in Taliban hands, but until then, ordinary Afghans would be constantly paying a heavy price. The consensus remained that:

> *"There needs to be some solution to the financial aid flows into Afghanistan to ensure that at least salaries can be paid, and that essential supplies — power and water being two of them — can be procured."*

However, no funds were allocated by any country or donor agency. During first week of October 2021, the US cleared the way for some aid to flow to Afghanistan, issuing two general licenses to allow Washington and certain international organizations like the UN to engage with the Taliban to provide humanitarian assistance – but red tapism was there to put hurdles as per routine. Immediate need was to ease the flow of agricultural goods, medicines and other critical resources. **Andrea Gacki**, Director of the US Treasury's Office of Foreign Assets Control, said in a statement:

> *"Treasury is committed to facilitating the flow of humanitarian assistance to the people of Afghanistan and other activities that support their basic human needs."*

Over the past 20 years, significant health gains were made in Afghanistan in reducing maternal and child mortality, to end polio and more. Those gains became at severe risk; the WHO was worried more. The International Federation of Red Cross and Red Crescent Society was looking for $38 million to fund health care and other emergency services on immediate basis across Afghanistan - but that appeal could raise only 22% funds. The international community remained deeply divided over the issue of providing aid to the Taliban-run government.

Some countries and aid organizations demanded that the new government should meet certain conditions — *like guaranteeing women's rights* — in return for aid. Others warned that making aid conditional risks plunging the country into a humanitarian disaster.

More than half a million Afghans were driven from their homes during the Taliban's four-month military campaign in summer 2021, and many of them were seen living in make-shift camps. A drought enveloped much of the country which caused a dire food shortage. Around 18 million Afghans, almost half of the Afghanistan's population, were in urgent need of food and humanitarian assistance.

In October 2021; the World Health Organization [WHO] warned that two-thirds of the roughly 2,300 health care facilities it supported had run out of essential medicines. Only about 400 were functioning then. Those facilities, the backbone of the country's health care system, were part of a $600 million project administered by the World Bank and funded by the US.

Over 2,500 health facilities installed elsewhere were no longer working, too. More than 20,000 health workers were out of work, either because the facilities were closed or their salaries were frozen. That stoked fears about a surge in deaths from basic medical ailments, and of a crippling brain drain as doctors look for work elsewhere or leave the country. One Dr Farid Rasouli, working in the anaesthesia ward at Aliabad Hospital in Kabul, said:

> *"Our doctors have not received their salaries for three months now. The hospital's medical staffs have been reporting to work each day but if we don't receive our salaries, there is a possibility we will leave our duties."*

Afghans across the country were feeling the pressure. Hundreds of people moved to the refugee settlement from the South since months before, when fighting between the Taliban and the previous government's forces intensified across southern Afghanistan. For weeks, Helmand's capital Lashkar Gah, was pummelled by air-strikes from the US and Ghani regim's forces and running battles between Taliban fighters and Afghan troops.

Hundreds of houses were destroyed and the Taliban instructed residents to leave the city. Many others in the resettlement camps couldn't find work, and they were struggling to buy basic goods as prices surged. People all over Afghanistan were facing famine, especially the refugees that were living in the camps. People there didn't have the money even to buy bread.

**Brain drain:** Beyond the cash crunch, the Taliban faced another critical shortage - skilled Afghans. As US-led forces gradually withdrew and the previous two national governments purposefully lost control; thus most Afghans with skills, experience and resources headed for exits from the country. They included bureaucrats, bankers, doctors, engineers, professors and university graduates thinking that they would face problems in the new government of the Taliban due to rising financial crunch.

The Taliban appeared aware of the impact such a brain drain could have on the Afghan economy. Their spokesman urged skilled Afghans not to leave, saying the country needed experts especially the doctors and engineers.

**Diplomatic isolation:** The Taliban's first regime was largely *'an outsider – a new class of revolutionaries'* on the global stage. This time, they were seen keen on wide international recognition, even as most nations had suspended or closed their diplomatic missions in Kabul. The group contacted regional powers such as Pakistan, Iran, Russia and China, as well as Qatar — which had previously hosted the Taliban's political activity for years - but none recognised the new regime till ending 2021 at least.

However, Moscow and Beijing did not use their veto option in the UN after language related to the Taliban was softened.

**IS Terror threat:** The Taliban took control of Afghanistan but the threat of terror attacks in the country still prevailed; their rival, the militant Islamic State group [IS], carried out a deadly suicide attack in Kabul, killing more than 100 people on 27th August 2021 at the airport during the evacuation operation. The Taliban and IS were considered both hard-line extremists before the American exit, but the latter has an even harsher and brutal interpretation of Islamic law. IS said it would continue to fight in Afghanistan, and its statements described the Taliban as *apostates*.

## SUMMITS AT ROME & THE UN:

This time the Taliban exhibited a *sharp role reversal:* They defended the Afghan people from the attacks from their own fighters as well as the foreign forces – but they were paralysed by starvation, hunger and famine at large scale. Referring to the daily '**NATION**' dated 27th September 2021:

> *"There were encouraging discussions in media as Afghanistan had a lot to offer under heads of the connectivity framework for the region – especially if seen in the back-drop of the China-Pakistan Economic Corridor [CPEC] infrastructure. However, this was a long-term endeavour requiring a lot of planning.*
>
> *The more pressing concern was the **humanitarian crisis** and **economic collapse** that could become a very real possibility given the ongoing situation in Afghanistan."*

While the US Treasury Department issued licenses to facilitate humanitarian aid and financial assistance to Afghanistan, a lot more needed to be done considering how the country's assets and reserves could remain frozen.

Another prerequisite to be achieved before grand visions of connectivity was the realisation of security and stability. Given the presence of militant groups like the TTP and ISIS on Afghan soil, it was imperative that safe havens for such outfits be eliminated at the earliest as they would continue to imperil the stability of Afghanistan, Pakistan and other neighbouring countries. Restoring stability in Afghanistan could bring far reaching positive implications for the region and its connectivity infrastructure. There were several stalled projects like the CASA-1000 power project and TAPI pipeline that could be resumed once the security situation improved.

*Chico Harlan*'s essay of 12ᵗʰ October 2021 in **the Washington Post** told the world that:

> *"With Afghanistan cut off from most of its foreign support and plunging into an **economic and humanitarian crisis**, the European Union pledged a major $1.15 billion aid package during a virtual Group of 20 summit, calling it a step to avoid catastrophe."*

But for all of Europe's urgency — part of it was driven by anxiety about **spill-over migration** — other nations, representing the largest economies, did not step forward with comparable measures.

The summit — in which President Biden participated, but Chinese President Xi Jinping and Russian President Vladimir Putin did not — ended with a general agreement about the importance of providing a lifeline to Afghanistan's people as conditions were worsening day by day. European Commission President of the EU Ursula von der Leyen said in a statement:

> *"We must do all we can to avert a major humanitarian and socio-economic collapse in Afghanistan."*

The European pledge was significant; the sum was well beyond what countries had been offering annually in humanitarian support even before the Taliban takeover. Since 2002, the US had given Afghanistan a total of only $3.9 billion in humanitarian assistance, according to USAID. But the current money was nowhere near enough to offset the distress.

Until the Taliban takeover in August [2021], Afghanistan had survived on international aid. That inflow was halted as nations cut diplomatic ties. At a UN donor conference a month before, the US had offered a relatively small funding $64 million in aid; while Italian Prime Minister Mario Draghi seemed to suggest a new US commitment of $300 million. The US was committed to work closely with the international community and using diplomatic, humanitarian, and economic means to address the situation in Afghanistan and support the Afghan people.

According to the White House summary, the leaders discussed the *'critical need to maintain a laser-focus on enduring counter-terrorism efforts'* as well as ensuring safe passage for those seeking to leave the country. Across Kabul, evidence of Afghanistan's fast-unravelling economy under the Taliban was felt everywhere. The participants also reaffirmed their commitment to provide humanitarian assistance straight to the Afghan people through international organizations rather than via the new government - the White House affirmed.

Countries in the G-20 were fairly aligned in how they would handle the new Taliban leaders: So far, none had officially recognized their government. But they could diverge on some of the more pinching issues, including what preconditions to set for diplomatic recognition and when to resume developmental aid that would be given directly to the Taliban to help the country beyond the immediate crisis. Putting simply, the West was going to put more preconditions in place for recognition including progress in women's rights issues.

A summary of the meeting released in Italy, mentioned the importance of preserving access to ***education for Afghan children*** — girls and boys — and said the rights of women and minorities must be respected. The Taliban were to be judged on their deeds. While the acting foreign minister for the Taliban, Amir Khan Muttaqi, insisted during a conference in Doha during the same days that:

> *"The international community needs to start cooperating with us, so that insecurity in the country could be addressed."*

Mr Muttaqi, however, didn't commit to restart secondary education for girls, which had been halted in August by the Taliban – an alarming issue for the whole world, not only the EU and donor agencies. Italy's Draghi had expressed disappointment while adding that:

> *"Right now there isn't any progress that we can see. It was said that the government would be inclusive; it is not inclusive. It was said the government would be representing various ethnic minorities, and gender-wise. It does not.*
>
> *The European Union still needed the Taliban to meet certain benchmarks before overall development aid — rather than this*

*one-time sum — would be unfrozen. But the Afghan people should not pay the price of the Taliban's actions thus the aid is essential to avoid humanitarian disaster and prevent 'uncontrolled migrant flows from Afghanistan' to regional countries and beyond."*

The EU aid package, some $350 million of which had already been earmarked, included funding that would be directed to Afghanistan's neighbours to *'enhance security'*. Aiding groups were warned of a pending humanitarian crisis that was grave even by the standards of a 20-year war. The economy was stalled; banks closed; the primary health-care system was on the brink of collapse. The World Food Program said a week earlier that just **5% of households were consuming enough food.** More than a million children could face acute malnutrition.

UN Secretary General António Guterres took it as a *'make-or-break moment'* in the country and warned of a heavy price if other nations didn't help Afghanistan. Draghi — famous for his role as a central banker in preserving the euro — said that:

> *"It is crucial to ensure that the banking system in Afghanistan doesn't collapse. If the banks collapse entirely, it would be very difficult to continue providing humanitarian assistance. It is very hard to see how you can help people in Afghanistan without involving the Taliban ... but that does not mean recognizing them."*

A senior Biden admin official said in that meeting at Rome that:

> *"....while not officially recognizing the government there, the United States has an interest in counterterrorism, in ensuring a safe exit for Americans and others who want to leave and in providing humanitarian aid. We are going to have to engage with the Taliban."*

Looming economic crisis overshadowed Afghan-talks at the UN, too. Afghans bury paintings and hide books out of fear of Taliban crackdown on arts and culture. As evacuation airlifts ended, the whole West got worried about those left behind in Afghanistan to face dire humanitarian crises along with Afghans.

## UN URGED THE EU & THE US FOR HELP:

**On 17th November 2021;** Afghanistan's Taliban rulers sent an open letter to the US Congress, urging American lawmakers to help unfreeze their country's assets seized after their August takeover of Kabul. In the letter,

Taliban Foreign Minister Amir Khan Muttaqi warned of a mass refugee exodus from Afghanistan unless the US unblocks the frozen assets and ends other financial sanctions against the country. Mr Muttaqi wrote that the Taliban were making this request to ensure that:

*"..... the doors for future relations are opened, assets of Afghanistan's Central Bank are unfrozen and sanctions on our banks are lifted."*

{BACKGROUND NOTE: The Biden administration had frozen $9 plus billion of assets belonging to the Afghan Central Bank soon after the Taliban captured Kabul on 15ᵗʰ August 2021 and imposed other economic sanctions on the new regime as well. America's Western allies also imposed similar sanctions.

The World Bank [WB] and International Monetary Fund [IMF] also had suspended about $1.2 billion in aid that they were supposed to release for Afghanistan in 2021. The sanctions were part of a US-led effort to persuade the militants to include non-Taliban elements in the government and protect the achievements of the last twenty years, including education for women and religious freedom for minorities.}

Washington didn't recognize the Taliban as a legitimate government in Afghanistan and a week earlier the White House had announced that Qatar would serve as its diplomatic representative in the country. Deputy Treasury Secretary Wally Adeyemo told a US Senate committee:

*"...Apparently there is no situation where Washington would allow the Taliban to access the Afghan Central Bank reserves. It's essential that we maintain our sanctions against the Taliban but at the same time find ways for legitimate humanitarian assistance to get to the Afghan people;"* daily **DAWN** dated 18ᵗʰ November 2021 is referred.

The Taliban's letter, however, reminded the US lawmakers that financial insecurity was the biggest challenge Afghanistan was facing and *'the roots of this concern lead back to the freezing of assets of our people by the American government'*.

Afghan Foreign Minister wrote that the sanctions had not only played havoc with trade and business but also with humanitarian aid to millions of desperate Afghans; adding that:

*"We are concerned that if the current situation prevails, the Afghan government and people will face problems and will become a cause for mass migration in the region and the world.*

*We hope that the members of the American Congress will think thoroughly in this regard and the American officials will view from [the] prism of justice the problems of our people arising from sanctions and unjust partisan treatment. The lawmakers are also advised not to approach this humanitarian issue in a superficial way."*

During early November 2021, the UN World Food Program had warned that years of conflict, and a prolonged drought were threatening more than half of the country's estimated 38 million people with starvation in coming winter. *The letter also assured the US Congress that Kabul's Taliban rulers intend to do things differently this time.* Practical steps were being taken towards good governance, security and transparency; Mr Muttaqi assured:

*"No threat is posed to the region or the world from Afghanistan and a pathway has been paved for positive cooperation. Afghans now understand the concerns of the international community but that it was necessary for all sides to take positive steps to build trust. Not lifting the sanctions would further damage the US reputation in Afghanistan and this will serve as the worst memory ingrained in Afghans at the hands of America."*

The UN's special representative for the country warned on the same day that *'Afghanistan is on the brink of a humanitarian catastrophe and its collapsing economy is heightening the risk of extremism.'*

Hunger forced Afghans to sell their young daughters into marriage because of that humanitarian catastrophe. It was preventable; the main cause was financial sanctions on the Taliban. Sanctions paralysed the banking system, affecting every aspect of the economy. Afghanistan was also slated to access about $450m on 23rd August 2021 from the IMF on the pre-text of *'lack of clarity about a new government'*.

The UN spokesperson [Lyons] said the paralysis of the banking sector would push the financial system into unaccountable and unregulated informal money exchanges. That, she said, *'can only help facilitate terrorism, trafficking and further drug smuggling'* that would first affect Afghanistan and then infect the whole region. A major negative development was the Taliban's inability to stem the expansion of the militant Islamic State [IS] group, which had expanded itself in nearly all provinces and was increasingly active. The number of attacks attributed to IS had increased significantly from 60 in 2020 to 334 this year of 2021 till then.

UN's Lyons had further urged the international community:

> "......to find ways to provide financial support to the Afghan people, who were 'abandoned, forgotten and indeed punished by circumstances that were not their fault. We must focus for the next three or four months on helping the most vulnerable Afghans during the coming winter [of 2021].
>
> The international community needs urgently to find a way to provide financial support to health care workers in state hospitals, staff in food security programmes, and, yes, eventually to teachers provided that girls right to education is emphatically met."

On behalf of the UN, Lyons assured council members that the UN would make every effort to ensure that funds would not be diverted to the Taliban — or by the Taliban. China and Russia also urged the unfreezing of Afghanistan's reserves but the US deputy ambassador Jeffrey made no mention of any solution except the lip service that the Afghan people should not have to pay twice for the Taliban decision.

The Taliban government was not being recognised by any country or the United Nations. Afghanistan's UN seat was still held by the representative of the previous government, Ambassador Ghulam Isaczai. Isaczai also told the council that:

> "Afghanistan is facing 'a crisis of historic proportions'. The life and dignity of millions of Afghans are threatened by a failing economy, severe food shortage and absence of security, basic rights and freedom. If the current trends continued, Afghanistan will experience near-universal poverty."

Now see an article appeared in the **AP News** dated <u>16<sup>th</sup> December 2021</u> which painted a very pathetic picture of the country after America's exit:

> "Afghanistan's health care system is on the brink of collapse and to function only with a lifeline from aid organisations. The diesel fuel needed to produce oxygen for corona-virus patients has run out. So have supplies of dozens of essential drugs. The staff, unpaid for months, still shows up for work, but they are struggling to make ends meet at home - this is the plight at the **Afghan-Japan Hospital** for communicable diseases, the only COVID-19 facility for the more than 4 million people who live in the capital of Kabul - a symptom of an extreme crisis ahead."

Dr Ahmad Fatah of one hospital said that the doctors and nurses were facing many problems here referring to three months of unpaid salaries, shortages of equipment and drugs, and lack of food...... Some of the staffs were seen in such financial difficulties that they opted to sell their household furniture to make ends meet.

Oxygen remained a big issue for them because they were unable to run the generators - the hospital's production plant was silent since months because the admin couldn't afford the diesel. And doctors were bracing for more infections in coming days of Omicron variant. Dr Shereen Agha, the 38-year-old head of the hospital's Intensive Care Unit told:

> *"Without outside help, we are not ready for omicron. A disaster will be here. The hospital is short even of basic supplies like examination gloves, and its two ambulances sit idle for lack of fuel."*

The previous government had contracted with a Netherlands-based aid group, **HealthNet TPO**, to run the hospital. But the contract expired in November [2021] and was financed under a fund managed by the World Bank, which like most of the international community had frozen their payments to the new Taliban government. The Dutch firm's Program Manager **Willem Reussing** said:

> *"The organization is in negotiations to secure funding but the donor community is very reluctant to continue support and has strict conditions. The WHO and UNICEF are only managing to maintain minimal services and do not cover the corona-virus response. The health care system ... is really on the brink of collapsing; the Afghan-Japan Hospital is a dire example - begging everyone to step in and save lives."*

When the Taliban took control of Afghanistan in August amid a chaotic US and NATO troops withdrawal, the international community pulled all funding. For a country heavily dependent on foreign aid, the consequences were devastating. The economy was deeply troubled under the previous government, with state employees often going unpaid. Last year, almost half the population was living below the poverty line, with the situation made worse by the pandemic and a drought that affected the basic price structures even.

The Taliban government wanted the international community, especially the US and the European Forums to ease sanctions and release Afghanistan's assets abroad so it could pay civil servants, including doctors and teachers. *The United Nations also sounded the alarm over a hunger crisis, with 22% of Afghanistan's 38 million people near famine and another 36% facing acute food insecurity.*

**Indira Gandhi Children Hospital**'s wards remained the worst example of inhuman treatment by the global organisations where anxious mothers sit by emaciated children waiting for medicines and food. The mothers were seen sleeping in the hospital for six - six nights or more. One mother wept while saying:

> *"I don't even have money to change his diapers. Her husband, a tailor, lost both legs in a roadside bomb several years ago, and has trouble sitting up. Work is hard to come by, and Parwana said her father and brothers are helping the family of three to survive."*

In the next bed, 1½-year-old Talwasa lying covered in blankets. Only her eyes moved behind half-closed eyelids. Her mother, Noor Bibi, who had six other children, said:

> *"We are in a very bad situation. Her husband can't find work; we only eat dried bread and can't find food for weeks and weeks."*

Deputy Health Minister Dr Abdul Bari Omar told in early December that Afghanistan had 3.5 million malnourished children, although he noted that the data was from the previous government. Dr Bari added that:

> *"It didn't happen in the last four months. Malnutrition was inherited from the previous system, but we are trying to find a solution for this problem. The former admin also had failed to resolve shortages of medical equipment. They had seen 3,000 malnutrition cases in the last four months. Of those, 250 were hospitalized and the rest were treated at home."*

Hospital workers also were struggling with shortages; they unanimously held that:

> *"We are loyal to our homeland and our profession. That's why we still continue our jobs and provide services to our patients. They have gone without salaries for five months. The hospital also is running low on drug supplies, including special food supplements for malnutrition, as well as antibiotics, analgesics and anaesthetics. Some supplies had come in from aid agencies, but just peanuts."*

Similar situation was prevailing in the National Hospital, where supplies were running low. As with most of the other state-run hospitals, its patients must buy their own drugs, with staff only dipping into emergency supplies for those who truly were not able to afford it. Sometimes doctors were forced to give smaller doses of drugs because they simply didn't have enough for the patients.

# Scenario 241

## TEHRIK-E-TALIBAN PAKISTAN [TTP]

On 13th December 2007; in a secret meeting of senior Taliban commanders hailing from the whole tribal region, called Federally Administered Tribal Areas [FATA], spread along the Pak-Afghan border and nearby settled districts of the Khyber PK province, a movement was launched named the **Tehrik-e-Taliban Pakistan [TTP]**; most of the Pakistani militants were grouped under this umbrella organization – daily *The News Islamabad* dated 15th December 2007 is referred.

To start with, the TTP was formed to pool the resources and manpower of Pakistan's militant individuals and groups to fight in self-defence in case the Pak-Army attacked their areas under the US command AND also to extend help to the Afghan Taliban taking part in '*jihad*', the holy war against America and International Security Assistance Force [ISAF] troops in Afghanistan. However, due to numerous military operations in their areas, the TTP was unable to send many fighters across the border for fighting.

Then the TTP was headed by Baitullah Mahsud, based in South Waziristan; he began fighting as a young man during the Afghan *jihad* against the Soviet occupation in Afghanistan and later joined the Afghan Taliban. Nearly a year after, one of his deputies, Hafiz Gul Bahadur, had signed a peace accord with Pakistan government in North Waziristan and thus refused to become involved in TTP's fighting against the Pak-Army. Hafiz Gul Bahadur was later joined by Maulvi Nazeer, the Taliban commander for Wana area in South Waziristan; Pakistani magazine *Newsline [July 2008]* is referred

Previously, in early 2004, the Pak-Army began its military operations in the Federally Administered Tribal Areas [FATA] and suffered heavy casualties in fierce clashes in *Kalosha* village near Wana at the hands of one Nek Mohammad. The Wana region is inhabited by the Ahmadzai Wazir tribe, historically rivals of the neighbouring *Mahsud* tribe to which Baitullah Mahsud belonged though both were **Pashtun** tribes, the ethnic group to which the Afghan and Pakistani Taliban belong. Baitullah Mahsud was a vague Taliban commander then.

## EARLY HISTORY OF THE TTP:

Nek Mohammad, only 27 years old commander then, had fought the Pak-Army bravely and ultimately concluded at a peace accord with Pakistan in *Shakai,* near Wana; where the Pak-Army's Corps Commander for Peshawar Lt Gen Safdar Hussain had publicly embraced and garlanded him. However, Commander Nek was killed in April 2004 in a US missile strike on his hideout near Wana; his death led to the collapse of the peace accord he had signed with Pakistan government.

Subsequently, **in February 2005**, a similar peace agreement with Baitullah Mahsud in *Sararogha* [South Waziristan] was signed under signatures of the same Pak-Army General; daily *The News International* dated 10th February 2005 is referred.

In 2007, serious differences emerged among the Pakistani Taliban in Wana over the presence of foreign militants belonging to the Islamic Movement of Uzbekistan [IMU]; Tahir Yuldashev from Shakai headed them. A majority of Taliban and Ahmadzai Wazir tribesmen decided to evict the Uzbek militants. Backed by the Pak-Army with arms and money, they fought the Uzbeks and their tribal supporters and finally succeeded in expelling them from Wana.

No doubt; Baitullah Mahsud was the most powerful and dangerous TTP commander those days. He was accused of involvement in assassination of the former PM Benazir Bhutto on **27th December 2007** through his men but he always denied his involvement. Other Taliban commanders working under him included Waliur Rahman, who could succeed him in case of his death, and Qari Hussain, known for his strong anti-Shia views and also for training suicide bombers and sending them on their fatal missions.

In North Waziristan, the most important TTP commander was Hafiz Gul Bahadur, who was opposed to Baitullah Mahsud and had been trying to build a rival alliance of pro-government Pakistani Taliban without any appreciable success. Two clerics who wielded considerable influence on the Taliban in North Waziristan were Maulana Sadiq Noor and Maulana Abdul Khaliq – then considered affiliated to *Jamiat Ulema-i-Islam* [JUI-F].

The impulse to extremists and fundamentalists in Pakistan would put pressure on conventional governance to follow suit and bring in an Islamic system of Government here as well. That was not a product of an Afghan Civil War but Pakistan's own ambiguous state of dealing softly with such elements. Mullah Aziz on the loose in Islamabad, killer of Governor Taseer, Mumtaz Qadri becoming a hero, succumbing to TLP etc. etc. were not Afghan Civil War issues but a consequence of tentative and weak law and order enforcement by Pakistani governments.

For Pakistan to weather the storm till Afghanistan stabilizes or settles down to reasonable levels depends on the measures and steps taken which would basically be Pakistan's own internal actions. These include *Madrassa* **Reforms,** sanitizing Islamabad of dubious elements, border management and enforcing the law.

Referring to an essay of **Pamela Constable** in ***Washington Post's Foreign Service*** desk dated <u>27<sup>th</sup> April 2009</u>:

> *"....but this season, the forested ridges [of Margalla Hills overlooking capital city of Islamabad] have taken on a new, ominous significance for jittery residents. Suddenly, the hills are being depicted as the last barrier to gangs of Islamist [Taliban] insurgents sweeping south from the Afghan border and as perfect places for suicide bombers to lurk."*

A week earlier, Maulana Fazlur Rehman, a religious party leader and the then parliamentarian had warned that:

> *"If the Taliban continue to move at this pace, they will soon be knocking at the doors of Islamabad. The Margalla Hills seem to be the only hurdle in their march toward the federal capital - he was exaggerating for effect."*

Islamabad, a docile, park-filled city of 1.5 million people, was built in 1960s as a symbol of Pakistan's modern and democratic aspirations. Its boulevards are lined with grandiose federal buildings, and its shady side streets are home to an elite class of politicians and professionals. From its first day, this orderly capital seemed immune to the religious violence but since the advent of the new century it remained no more.

In those days, the people suddenly started feeling panic, shocks and jolts by frequent televised images of 'turbaned Taliban fighters' occupying town after town in the northwest districts of Swat, Shangla, Buner and surrounding hilly terrains, only 60 miles from Islamabad – for details see:

*Scenario 55* [<u>Pak-Army in Swat</u>] of the book **JUDGES & GENERALS IN PAKISTAN VOL-II** by INAM R SEHRI; [2012 Reprint 2017] pp 694-710; published - GHP Surrey UK

In military history it's called **OPERATION RAH-E-HAQ** [meaning – straight path]; though Pakistan's army suffered big losses including a General's life but the TTP was pushed back into the tribal belt back. However, a series of suicidal bombings and threats started abruptly in Islamabad and other big cities. In the capital, many foreign missions, embassies and agencies sent their families back home; the local World Bank office moved into a heavily guarded multi-storey Serena Hotel. It became almost impossible to enter the Parliament, the diplomatic enclave and courts.

'*If a mullah tells a boy of 15 to blow himself up, how do you stop him*', the people were asking each other. Just about six months earlier, a truck full of explosives rammed into the luxury Marriott Hotel which killed 52 people and left tens as wounded. It took months to re-open and the hotel occupancy had plunged to 40%.

In March 2009, a young man approached an open camp for off-duty paramilitary guards, located in a nearby small park - the man blew himself up, killing five guards and of course himself too. In <u>Pamela</u>'s words again, the fear of a shopkeeper was that:

> "*The future looks very bleak. Fear chases us everywhere, from the moment we leave home to the moment we return at night. These blasts and attacks don't hurt the ruling class, but they destroy our business. . . . The tension is everywhere.*"

Until 2007 there was no tension in Islamabad; but that summer, the calm was shattered by a violent face-off between the government and radical chief cleric of the Red Mosque, who had turned their compound in central Islamabad into an armed camp. In confrontation, security forces stormed an allied *madrassa*, killing at least 100 people, and the leaders vowed revenge. Since then, terrorist assaults, bombings and kidnappings became regular feature all over the country. The targets included former PM Benazir Bhutto, UN officials, NATO supply convoys, police checkpoints, video shops, mosques of minority sects, an Italian eatery in Islamabad and the Sri Lankan cricket team in Lahore – for details see:

> *Scenario 46* [Red-Mosque: <u>Operation Silence</u>] of the book **JUDGES & GENERALS IN PAKISTAN VOL-II** by INAM R SEHRI; [2012 Reprint 2017] pp 528-539; published - GHP Surrey UK

There was enormous growth in the number of religious *madrassas*, some of which promoted radical visions of Islam. Even the intelligence agencies and Police knew very little about these *madrassas*, and where their funding used to come from remained a mystery. Islamabad is far better known for its top-quality academic schools and colleges, including private institutions tailored for foreign students – in those days these institutions were frequently threatened. The mature female students often commented that the people of the whole world see the TV images and think about Pakistan as a rogue and barbarian society.

The alternative was to fight against the Coalition on behalf of the Taliban. The fact that the Pakistan Army was the only Army in the world, participating in this conflict, that did not have a single man under US Command and that it operated in its own area speaks volumes for the administration then. They managed to preserve Pakistan's independent stand on not venturing into Afghanistan or Iraq or functioning under US Command.

The war in FATA, which is now being criticized by so many, was an outcome of a proposal that Pakistan Government had made to all foreign fighters (residue of the Afghan-Soviet War) to disarm and register for citizenship or then be prepared to return to their own countries. They refused both the options and said they wished to exercise the right to conduct *Jihad* within the country and from Pakistan against foreign occupiers in Afghanistan. This obviously led to a conflict in which the Pakistan Government's only objective was to establish its writ.

The political rulers of Pakistan were once seen bent over backwards to give peace a chance, so much so, that they surrendered the people of Swat to the Constitution of Sufi Muhammed while the Supreme Court, always eager to take *suo-moto* action, remained criminally silent.

### TTP TERROR ATTACKS ON INCREASE:

Agreements after agreements were signed and violated from 2001 till 2008 till the Mahsuds publicly declared war on Pakistan in January 2008 – that is when the shooting war began with **Operation Zalzala**. What was done by the Pak-Army then was need of the time and it was a realistic action. The Western media had gone critical about Pak-Army's treatment but, in fact, there was so much to be done more and the real focus was the peace.

Immediately after the fall of Kabul on 15th August 2021, Pakistan's PM Imran Khan and all his political opponents, including leaders of Islamist parties, hailed the victory and congratulated the Taliban for its historic win over American occupation. A half-dozen retired Pak-Army Generals publicly celebrated the occasion; so did the extremist groups. The Taliban's dramatic victory across the border also fired up terrorist groups waging bloody rebellion inside Pakistan; and equally encouraged hard-line religious parties with fundamentalist creed; Army, however, was seen calm and cautious.

On the Taliban's return Maulana Fazlur Rehman of JUI-F supported the Taliban but renounced and rejected any chance of violent struggle inside Pakistan. Some clerics preached about the shortcomings of democracy, and agitated for a similar *'hard struggle to have a true Islamic system in Pakistan'*. The Pakistan Institute for Peace Studies in Islamabad admitted that:

> *"....the Taliban's takeover in neighbouring Afghanistan is already affecting Pakistan in far-reaching ways. With the Taliban taking over, anti-Pakistan terrorist groups will be emboldened, but it doesn't end there - there could be an emergence of new war of narratives in the country, which will transform ongoing debates about state and society and the role that religion plays."*

The day the Taliban took over Kabul on 15th August 2021, next day the Pakistani Taliban [TTP] went active, especially in Islamabad under the command of Red Mosque's Maulana Abul Aziz. There was seen a sudden sharp increase in cross border terror attacks from Afghanistan

Pakistan had to request the Afghan Taliban's high-ups immediately though the formal government was not announced in Afghanistan or any cabinet had been named or nominated. Taliban Chief Haibatullah Akhundzada immediately set up a 3-member high-powered commission to look into Islamabad's complaints.

On 20th August 2021; Pakistani MFA spokesman Zahid Hafeez Chaudhri said in his weekly news conference:

> *"We have been taking up the issue of use of Afghan soil by the TTP for terrorist activities in Pakistan with the previous Afghan government and we will continue raising the issue with the future Afghan government as well to ensure that TTP is not provided any space in Afghanistan to operate against Pakistan."*

America's *VOA News* and other media pages told on 21st August 2021. said further:

> *"TTP leaders are being warned (by the Afghan Taliban Commission) to settle their problems with Pakistan and return to the country along with their families in exchange for a possible amnesty by the Pakistani government."*

Pakistan also clarified that there was no possibility of accepting any TTP demands; also that the amnesty would be offered in line with the country's constitution and law of the land, that require the militants to surrender their firearms. The US and the UN had also listed the TTP as a global terrorist organization.

The February 2020's Doha deal reached between the Taliban and the US, which paved the way for foreign troops to leave Afghanistan, had bound the Taliban to prevent regional as well as trans-national terrorist groups from using Afghan soil to threaten global security. Afghan Taliban govt's spokesman Suhail Shaheen told the foreign media that:

> *"This concern is legitimate, and our policy is clear that we will not allow anyone to use the soil of Afghanistan against any neighbouring country, including Pakistan. So they should not have any concern. Be it TTP or any other terrorist group they will have no place in our country and that's a clear message to all."*

At that moment, the Afghan Taliban govt was in desperate need of support from regional and international countries being in control of Afghanistan to address governance as well as critical economic challenges facing the country. Pakistani media held that:

> *"If they (the Afghan Taliban) fail to deliver on their counter-terrorism commitments, not only Pakistan but China, Russia, Iran and Central Asian countries would all be upset because they also complain that fugitive militants sheltering on Afghan soil threaten their national interests.*
>
> *Can they survive if they turn their guns against us and support TTP? This is not possible. Our trade routes are a lifeline for them, for landlocked Afghanistan."*

After 2016, Pakistan started erecting a robust fence and hundreds of forts along with its historically open border with Afghanistan; 2670 km long. The massive project effectively blocked militant infiltration in either direction. TTP militants were blamed for killing c47,000 civilians and c5,000 security personnel of Pakistan since their emergence in

*2007 in retaliation for Islamabad's decision to cooperate with Washington* in the war against terrorism.

The TTP group used strongholds in Pakistan's semi-autonomous federally administered tribal areas, known as FATA, bordering Afghanistan. But sustained Pak-Army operations forced TTP members to flee into volatile Afghan border areas and traditionally lawless FATA areas were merged into mainstream Pakistan, which have significantly reduced terrorism incidents across the whole country. In the last decade, the Pakistani Taliban [TTP] had launched nearly 1,800 attacks on Pakistani state and civilian targets; [see *Washington Post* dated 5th September 2021]; thus Pak-Army and the ISI's most immediate concern was their resurgence again. Hailing Taliban's victory in Afghanistan, the TTP claimed to have sent welcome messages to them in routine.

The TTP had 6,000 trained fighters on the Afghan side of the border; a UN Security Council report in July 2021 said; also confirmed that the Afghan Taliban and TTP maintained their relationship as usual – they had released about 5,000 of prisoners; their own Afghan Taliban, militants, miscreants including TTP members, from Afghan prisons on 24th August 2021 after their take over in Kabul.

In the meanwhile, the Chairman of Pakistan's Senate Defence Committee, Mushahid Hussain Syed, said that:

> *"Pakistan had laid down red lines to the Taliban to warn it against harbouring the TTP. There is caution because of the Taliban track record and their affinity with the sworn foes of Pakistan like the TTP. There is also optimism that this time around, the Afghan Taliban are more chastened."*

Pakistan had also, as a good gesture, asked the Taliban to convey their intention to the TTP fighters that if they like to surrender their arms in exchange for amnesty. In fact the TTP leaders wanted 'peace talks' with Government of Pakistan. Lt Gen Faiz Hameed, the head of Pakistan's ISI, also visited Kabul on 4th September 2021 to discuss security and TTP issues with Afghan Taliban leadership.

## PAK-ARMY CONTROLLED TTP:

It's also on record that since years the Pak-Army had kept a heavy boot on the TTP's face and set aside them away from their activities but, under the fresh [rogue] directions from the US Command, they were made to regroup again in 2018. Noor Wali Mehsud was nominated their new leader who was directed to launch an offensive comeback over Pakistan after the Taliban's take over two weeks earlier; *Amira Jadoon's essay, from the US Military Academy at West Point is referred.*

Jadoon also said that: *'They [TTP] see the Afghan Taliban as a pathway they can adopt.'* The Taliban takeover in Afghanistan no doubt added a volatile element to the mainstream politics play in Pakistan's streets. Ayesha Siddiqa, a researcher at the *University of London's SOAS South Asia Institute,* also held that: *'The government will be under pressure to make the state more Shariah-compliant, if Taliban next door are doing that.'*

Pak-Army's Chief, Gen Bajwa, had once said in his speech [2017] that:

> *".....there are more than 2 million students in madrassas, or religious schools, and that many were not getting a worldly education. So what will they become: Will they become clerics or they will become terrorists? We need to revisit the concept of madrassas."*

The law enforcing agencies including Pak-Army were always seen reluctant to crack down on certain religious leaders or schools out of fear of being outnumbered in a violent showdown. There were *madrassas* they wouldn't go near. The rise of extremism in Pakistan that they sailed on was gradually escalated real threat to them. Gen Talat Massood, however, acknowledged anxieties that a new government in Kabul might lead to *'Talibanization of Pakistani society'.* But those fears were overblown giving one reason or the other. Nevertheless, the fact remains that it was never two-way traffic in terms of influence.

BUT the question was of how much influence the Pakistani government could retain over Afghan Taliban as rulers of their own country and the group had announced their own interim cabinet on 7th September 2021. In that cabinet there is the Haqqani network, a named militant group in American list – but no one can ask the Taliban about there legitimacy – it's the Taliban's prerogative. Pakistan always denied the charges against Haqqani group and would continue to do so unless the US brings cogent charge sheet or evidence against Haqqani people.

Pakistan insisted that the world should go realistic and engage with the new rulers, otherwise Afghanistan could face a humanitarian crisis and economic collapse that would directly spill across the border into Pakistan.

Referring to the *APP [Article no:2822]* dated <u>11<sup>th</sup> September 2021</u> on media pages:

> *"India had been using Afghan soil against Pakistan since 2001 by investing about $3 billion on infrastructure, training of Afghan forces and other projects to establish a network for its permanent foothold and to achieve its overt and covert designs - by sponsoring terrorism against Pakistan from Afghan territory."*

It was India's move to destabilize Pakistan; the Modi's government had acted as top spoiler of regional peace.

Pakistan claimed that India had supported and trained *Dai'sh & TTP* elements to use as proxy tools for its nefarious designs against Pakistan, Afghanistan and the region. **Under the garb of training, Afghan forces, around 300 *Dai'sh & TTP* members were still under training in India on the day the Kabul fell.** For this purpose, Indian consulates, 12 as per Pak-media reports, were established along the Pak-Afghan border line, controlled and used by Indian intelligence agency, RAW, as launching pads for terrorist activities inside Pakistan.

The investigations by various agencies, including the ISI and FIA of Pakistan, pointed out that from these consulates India's RAW had planned terrorist activities like **Gurdwara attacks, Lahore blast, Gwadar attack** to discredit Pakistan. The major aim was to harm Pak-China relations – especially the CPEC cause; some media-men held that the US was happy over such activities from the said consulates in the backdrop of US-China tense / cold relations – but still wanted **DO MORE** from Pakistan.

During last week of August 2021, Pakistan handed over to the new Afghan Taliban leadership, a list of **'most wanted terrorists'** affiliated with the banned *Tehreek-e-Taliban Pakistan* [TTP] operating from the war-torn Afghanistan. Afghan Taliban Chief Haibatullah Akhundzada was moved to show his strength as per their consents given in Doha Accord; the Voice of America [VOA] also mentioned it openly.

The necessity arose suddenly; the TTP was driven out of the erstwhile tribal areas by Pakistan when it launched a full scale military offensive in 2014. Most of them found refuge across the border as Pakistan accused Indian spy agency RAW and Afghanistan's National Directorate of Security [NDS] of funding and backing that terrorist outfit.

When the Afghan Taliban swept Kabul on 15<sup>th</sup> August 2021, the TTP chief issued a statement congratulating the Afghan Taliban victory and renewed allegiance to its chief Akhundzada. As mentioned earlier, the Afghan Taliban released many TTP terrorists from jail including its former deputy chief Maulvi Faqir Muhammad a week after taking over.

Foreign Minister Shah Mahmood Qureshi, after conclusion of his four-nation tour to Tajikistan, Uzbekistan, Turkmenistan, and Iran during the last quarter of 2021, had reiterated India's spoiler role in Afghanistan.

On 14<sup>th</sup> September 2021; during an international donor conference America's Antony Blinken urged Pakistan to **get in line** with the rest of the world - but Pakistani Pakistan's PM, just in next day's interview, declined their sermon straightaway. Khan repeated his appeal at a meeting in Tajikistan with regional leaders, saying *"Afghans should not be left alone."*

The critical issue was ensuring that an immediate crisis should not occur. To withhold aid while testing the regime's behaviour could lead to economic collapse and a dangerous security vacuum. Pakistan's one Advisor, Moeed Yusuf, held that:

> *"We're putting Pakistan's dilemma more bluntly. It's like we're damned if we do and damned if we don't. India is repressing Muslims in the contested border region of Kashmir and using Afghan territory to potentially infiltrate Pakistan."*

Another worry remained about home-grown Islamist rebels; mostly the TTP. Taliban had promised to thwart such terrorist attempts but were not able to deliver. A suicide bombing in Balochistan province on 5<sup>th</sup> September 2021 was claimed by the rebel group. A security expert opined that:

> *"Pakistan would be ill-advised to stick its neck out for the Taliban. We need a coherent strategy for dealing with terrorism on both sides of the border."*

It remains a fact that in 2011, Adm. Mike Mullen, the then head of the Joint Chiefs of Staff, told a congressional hearing that *the Haqqani network was 'a veritable extension' of the ISI.* New cabinet was a tricky situation for Pakistan because the new Afghan cabinet was comprised of *both pro-Pakistan and anti-Pakistan elements.* The relationship could endure, but this time the Taliban were likely to hold the strings. Western powers had felt that by placing the *Haqqanis* in key positions, the Taliban in fact signalled about their chosen path of isolation instead of integrating into the modern international system. America threatened that *'this choice may lead to violent instability at a terrible human cost.'*

*Pamela Constable*'s article on media pages of 18<u>th</u> September 2021 described her recent interview with one Prof Shakoor Khan of a university in Mardan city of Pakistan, where a liberal student named Mashal Khan was brutally killed by conservative religious classmates in 2017; she said:

> *".....the Taliban's return to power next door is already having a deep impact. Our clerics and students are behaving as if they won a battle against mighty powers. Friday sermons are all about Taliban success stories. This can change people's minds, especially the youth – (a dangerous phenomenon in fact)."*

One should remember that there were already such pro-Taliban feelings in Pakistani society, and then the next door country became their exclusive domain in August 2021. Most Pakistanis were found afraid - the hard-liners would only become stronger with the passage of time; if suited to them.

## RED MOSQUE ALIVE AGAIN:

As discussed in above lines, the Pakistani Taliban [TTP] went alive again immediately after Afghan Taliban's take over in Afghanistan. In the capital Islamabad, the volcano of Islamist movement also erupted once more after 14 years deep slumber, snooze and sleep since 2007. For years, the Red Mosque stood as a fortress of religious rebelliousness, a nerve centre of radical Islamist preaching that attracted thousands of worshipers to hear extremely hard sermons by its long-time two pro-Taliban brothers, Maulana Abdul Aziz and [late] Ghazi Abdul Rashid.

In 2007, the mosque, also known as the *Lal Masjid,* and its next-door Islamic *madrassa* for girls [*Jamia Hafsa*] were the site of a bloody siege by Pakistani security forces after a week-long standoff with armed militants inside the compound, which left at least 100 dead. Since then, Aziz has faced numerous criminal charges but never got convicted – for details see the above referred **Scenario 46** of the book **JUDGES & GENERALS IN PAKISTAN VOL-II.**

Then, with the sudden takeover of Afghanistan by Taliban in August 2021, Maulana Aziz started telling his followers that his voice raised in

2007 was justified; it's their time again and that *The coming of the Taliban was an act of God.'* He no longer preaches at the mosque, under an agreement he made in 2020 with the government of Pakistan. Maulana further said that:

> *"The whole world has seen that they defeated America and its arrogant power. It will definitely have a positive effect on our struggle to establish Islamic rule in Pakistan, but our success is in the hands of God."*

It was the same sloganeered mission which the TTP had been using as its motto since their first day of raising guns. *Madrassas* in Pakistan have long played a major role in fostering militant Islamic groups, mostly funded by the foreign countries aimed to propagate their specific [opposing] sects of Islam. The Afghan Taliban movement was originated and nurtured in radical *madrassas* of Akora Khatak and Quetta; while *Lashkar-e-Taiba* [LeT], a violent part-group of the Taliban, was incubated in Punjab.

Amongst those home-grown groups, there was TTP which waged war against the Pakistani government for years and remained active from Afghanistan. Pakistan government rightly apprehended that the TTP could embolden its extremists to launch a new holy war in Pakistan again.

Since the first day of Afghan Taliban on victory stand, Maulana Aziz and his followers started periodically raising white Taliban flags on Jamia Hafsa's roof, defying government orders. The third time, **on 18th September** [2021], police cordoned off the area while veiled girls [students] stood on the roof, shouting taunts and vowing for Islamic Rule. Maulana Aziz threatened the police while waiving his gun. He was initially charged with rioting, sedition and other crimes under federal anti-terrorism laws, but the charges were dropped the next day – *and that is the legal practice in Pakistan; same laws are implemented differently on different people.* The Interior Minister Sheikh Rashid told the media that:

> *".....of the more than 500 madrassas and 1,000 mosques in Islamabad, we have issues with only one. Maulana comes up with an issue every day, and every day we try to resolve it."*

The fact remains that controversy over the 2007 Red Mosque siege had ignited a national outcry in Pakistan and had sparked a wave of suicide bombings and attacks by the Pakistani Taliban militants that took years to quash. Maulana Aziz was sent to prison but was ultimately *acquitted by the Supreme Court on charges of murder and other violent crimes, citing a lack of evidence and failure of witnesses to testify.* Over the years, he faced 27 legal proceedings and spent several stints in prison, but the charges were never considered substantial – mainly due to cowardice role of the pleaders and judges.

*Pamela Constable*'s report dated 25th September 2021 is available on media pages – describing that:

> "…..the government rebuilt the badly damaged mosque, an imposing redbrick compound located near government ministries, embassies and the headquarters of the national intelligence agency. It has remained a hotbed of extremist fervour, with a new library named after Osama bin Laden [OBL], but it has never again violently challenged the government's writ. In return, Pakistani authorities have tolerated its activities, up to a point, in a tacit and strategic peace agreement.

> The Red Mosque operation was and still is a sensitive issue. In recent years, Pakistan has been relatively free of terrorist attacks, and the government wants to keep it that way. Whenever a problem arises now, the authorities try to settle it peacefully."

After Taliban's victory in Afghanistan, Maulana Aziz re-affirmed that they would continue their struggle to establish Islamic rule in Pakistan. In the past, he had openly called for an *Islamic revolution* against the state but this time his strategy might invite some bargaining chips from the government. He praised the new leadership in Kabul but said they should strive to live *'even more simply'* in power - they should not meet people in offices and not to live in palaces, rather should operate from mosques. However, Maulana's rival Islamist factions held that *'….Aziz is exploiting the moment as well as his location in the capital.'* Maulana's daughter *Tayyiba Ghazi*, the vice principal at *Jamia Hafsa*, proudly described her female students as religious warriors for Islamist values.

*Jamia Hafsa* normally keeps more than 1,500 girl-students, generally between ages 5-20; these students hail from the same ethnic *Pashtun* origin as the Afghan Taliban, and usually come from the bordering area near Afghanistan. No male students are taught at this campus. *Tayyiba Ghazi* held that: *'the staffs teach our girls to be brave, and they are not scared of anyone, not the police or other forces.'*

## AFGHAN TALIBAN AND TTP ARE THE SAME [?]

The TTP, an umbrella group of armed groups originally from across Pakistan's north-western border districts, was formed in 2007, and waged a war against the Pakistani state for years before the 2014's Operation pushed most of its leadership and fighters into neighbouring Afghanistan.

Referring to the **AFP** [French News Agency] report of 15<sup>th</sup> November 2021:

> *"Since the Taliban's takeover of Afghanistan, Pakistan's offshoot of the hardline Islamist group has ramped up attacks on its side of the border, leaving Islamabad scrambling to reach a peace deal.*
>
> *Active in the remote tribal areas of Pakistan, experts say the militant group Tehreek-e-Taliban Pakistan [TTP] -- a separate movement which shares a common history with the Afghan Taliban -- plunged the country into a period of horrific violence after forming in 2007. Also made up mostly of ethnic Pashtuns, it carried out hundreds of suicide bomb attacks and kidnappings across the country, seizing control of border regions and imposing a radical version of Islamic law in territory where it held sway.*
>
> *It was a TTP gunman who opened fire on schoolgirl Malala Yousafzai in her native Swat Valley, before she won the Nobel Peace Prize.*
>
> *The group was also linked to the assassination of former Prime Minister Benazir Bhutto."*

But it wasn't until a massacre of nearly 150 children at a Peshawar Army School in 2014 that the military finally crushed the movement and forced its fighters to retreat into Afghanistan. With the Afghan Taliban back in control in Kabul, Pakistan was trying to control a TTP comeback. One TTP fighter confided that:

> *"The [TTP] fighters feel more comfortable after the fall of Kabul to the Taliban, they can now move freely in Afghanistan. They have no fear of US drone strikes. And they can meet and communicate easily."*

The group has been responsible for some of the deadliest bombings targeting civilians and security forces on Pakistani soil, including a 2014 attack on a Peshawar school in which they brutally slaughtered the women staff and 143 school-children.

In all, at least 25,622 Pakistanis were killed in attacks by the TTP and its allies since 2007, according to SATP data, with civilians accounting for 73 percent of all casualties.

The 2014 operation saw violence drop sharply, with the Pakistani military citing a 75 percent drop in the number of attacks since 2015, with 398 major and 830 minor operations conducted against the TTP and its allies.

Referring to *Asad Hashim*'s analysis Published in **AL-JAZEERA** dated 8th December 2021:

> *"With Afghan Taliban now controlling neighbouring Afghanistan, Waziristan residents fear a return to life under the TTP. The people are spending sleepless nights because of local thieves or criminals or the TTP members. Both the 'good' and 'bad' Taliban are extorting Waziristan residents for money and carrying out targeted killings."*

The situation was complex and involved a resurgence of the TTP and its allied local militias, as well as Pakistani government-backed *'surrendered Taliban'* fighters, all engaged in targeted killings of civilians, extortion, tribal councils and attacks against security forces.

During January – November 2021, at least 69 people were killed in 37 attacks across South and North Waziristan districts, according to data from the South Asia Terrorism Portal [SATP]. The attacks included targeted killings of anti-Taliban civilians, extortion-related killings, check-post raids and numerous improvised explosive device [IED] attacks targeting security forces. Media gurus attributed the rise in violence to the evolving situation in Afghanistan.

Pak-Army, however, held that *'this scenario was short-lived as Pakistan's security forces remain ready to deal with any internal [or] external threats.'* In the Waziristan districts, talk between the TTP and Pakistan government were being met with both scepticism and fear.

In North Waziristan, the birth place of the TTP, the security situation was even worse. Since Jan-Nov 2021, about 45 people were killed in 25 attacks in the district, according to SATP data, with a mix of armed actors active in the area, including the TTP and local militias led by commanders Hafiz Gul Bahadur, Sadiq Noor, Aleem Khan and others.

**Mohsin Dawar,** North Waziristan's sole member of Pakistan's Parliament told that:

> *"After the collapse of Kabul, they have gotten internal strength and confidence, and they have come onto the front foot. They had quite a*

*large presence before as well, and they were moving around as well, but it was done in a certain [hidden] way. Now they have become very visible again.*

*Everything they do; there is extortion, taking money from contractors or anyone who has any business there. There are abductions as well [and] there are killings also.*

*In one case in early November, local tribal elder Malik Laik, from the Hamzoni area of North Waziristan, was dragged out of his home and beheaded by a local Taliban-allied militia.*

*They kill brutally in order to spread fear."*

That incident, like many others in the Waziristan districts, was never reported in Pakistan's mainstream press. Statistically, it remains difficult to gauge what is or has been happening there, because the people have only one official source of information - this is ISPR [*the military's press wing*]. The fact remains that many attacks are not reported to the authorities *'out of fear'* for reprisals. The TTP's fighters had returned to the district in large numbers.

Pakistan's PM Khan announced on <u>2<sup>nd</sup> October 2021</u> that the government was in talks with the TTP for the first time since 2014, facilitated by Afghanistan's new leadership. Both sides announced a truce until at least <u>9<sup>th</sup> December 2021</u>, while they hammered out an agreement also.

The Pakistan govt's hand out said: *'Those people who want to come back and respect our law and constitution, we would like to give them amenesty.'* BUT neither side openly divulged details about the negotiating points. However, the sources told that the release of about 100 TTP fighters was a key demand from the TTP.

The fighters were also appealing to allow come out of hiding and return to the tribal areas but without the support of elders -- hundreds of whom have been killed over the years. Made up of multiple factions, some of which also swore allegiance to Al-Qaeda, the TTP had gone more dangerous. It had some 4,000 to 6,000 fighters, down from 20,000 at its peak in 2009-10.

TTP's top leadership was wiped out by military operations backed by US drone strikes after 2014 – thus the TTP in 2021 *'was not the same group as it was eight years ago'*. The October negotiations were taking place with young fighters and **TTP's third tier leaders.**

*[The said peace talks between the two sides had angered most Pakistanis, who remembered the brutal attacks on schools, hotels, churches and markets which had killed around 70,000 people.]*

The TTP vs Pakistan govt ceasefire did took place but only for a month or so. The militant TTP resumed terrorist attacks after declaring an end to a month long cease-fire on 9ᵗʰ December 2021, accusing the Pak-govt of not fulfilling its promises, including the release of key TTP leaders from jail. The agreement - brokered by the Taliban - had given Islamabad a respite for a month from attacks waged by the TTP.

Analysts monitoring insurgency in the region believe the Taliban's triumph and the US withdrawal of forces from Afghanistan definitely emboldened the TTP and boosted its morale.

Pakistani officials also approached the Afghan Taliban to ensure Afghan soil is not used by armed groups targeting Pakistan, but it was unlikely the Afghan Taliban would act in any concrete way against the TTP, whose fighters fought alongside Afghan Taliban troops against US-led NATO forces for years.

Furthermore, the Taliban care greatly about maintaining unity in their ranks – action against the TTP would undermine that and threaten to send defectors over to Islamic State-Khorasan (IS-K), something the Taliban really would never want. *The past history tells that whenever the TTP was given space and whenever they 'surrendered' they exploited it and used it to expand their influence in these areas.*

TTP Chief Noor Wali in his latest audio message of 10ᵗʰ December 2021 announced that *'the pact doesn't stand any more'*. Since then, the TTP accepted responsibility for at least 10 attacks, killing and wounding law enforcement personnel in various parts of the country. This also included an attack on 14ᵗʰ Dec instant on a police team in Rawalpindi where Pak-army's GHQ is based; and the killing of an intelligence official in *Lakki Marwat* District in KPK Province on 16ᵗʰ Dec 2021.

An Islamabad-based security official, also privy to the negotiations, told:

*"Islamabad is not in a position to fulfil most of the TTP's demands. The TTP demands to release hard-core militant leaders, such as*

*Muslim Khan and Latif Mehsud, hand them over a bordering territory and conduct talks in a third country, such as Qatar. **The TTP wants to compare itself with the Afghan Taliban which cannot be treated as such.***"

In December 2016, a Pakistani military court sentenced Muslim Khan, a top TTP leader from the Swat region in the north, to death for his involvement in killing dozens of people in terrorist attacks and kidnapping two Chinese for ransom. The TTP commander Mehsud, was brought to Islamabad in December 2014 after arresting him in Afghanistan during a raid. Pakistan govt was thus ready to fight the TTP again as per provisions of the constitution and law.

In the past, Islamabad signed several peace deals with the TTP and other Pakistani Taliban groups, but none lasted beyond a few months. Similar to the past agreements, the TTP availed mileage and legitimacy from the cease-fire and portrayed itself as a stakeholder in Pakistan's political system.

The TTP always tried to introduce, implement and enforce their own brand of Shariah [Islamic law] in the tribal [areas]; if the State will resist, it would trigger another wave of terrorism - the worst-case and more likely scenario. For residents of Waziristan, the omens were not good; they were caught in a conflict between the TTP and raids by the Pakistani security forces at times. For normal people, their lives were completely at a standstill; they were distressed, scared and afraid.

## TPP'S ATTACKS ON INCREASE:

See another analysis by ***Dr Asfandyar Mir*** appeared on media pages including **www.usip.org** on 19th January 2022:

*"In 2021, the Tehreek-e-Taliban Pakistan [TTP] insurgency escalated its challenge against Pakistan. Operating from bases in Afghanistan, and with a growing presence inside Pakistan, the group mounted an increasing number of attacks against Pakistani security forces — as well as against some critical Chinese interests in Pakistan. The insurgency also showed renewed political strength by bringing in splintered factions and improving internal cohesion.*

*With a burgeoning alliance between the Afghan Taliban and the TTP, Pakistan faces a major insurgency challenge in 2022."*

On **18th January 2022**; after an attack by the TTP on the police in Pakistan's capital city of Islamabad, the government expected more attacks by the group – because the TTP had got a new agenda from its sponsors to disrupt the CPEC program to block Chinese expansion in the region – an American cold-war plan in fact in the back-drop of the US-China economic warfare.

Year 2021's most significant development in this region was the TTP's apparent alliance with the Afghan Taliban BUT in fact was largely a by-product of the US strategy since a decade back. Based in Afghanistan, the TTP was raised and nurtured by the former Afghan government in cahoots with India; the US funding was the main source of their strength. Therefore, Pakistan often implied, the US exit from Afghanistan and the return of the Taliban would limit the TTP's threat against Pakistan.

However, the time started blowing in reverse directions for Pakistan. The TTP, on one side got energized with the Taliban's takeover and became stronger than before with the American secret funding. After the Taliban's re-taken over, almost immediately, Taliban leadership released senior TTP leaders and a large number of fighters imprisoned by the President Ghani's government. The Taliban regime also, most probably, provided the TTP's leadership with de-facto political asylum and freedom of movement within Afghanistan — from which the group was directing its campaign of violence in Pakistan.

After the Taliban's takeover in Afghanistan, the TTP Chief Noor Wali Mehsud had publicly reiterated his pledge of allegiance to Afghan Taliban leadership and claimed the TTP to be a branch of it in Pakistan. For their part, the Taliban went evasive on the future of the TTP in Afghanistan and remained non-committal on a crackdown despite the group's rising violence against Pakistan.

The Pakistani government sought the intervention of Siraj Haqqani, a top Taliban leader, for talks with the TTP — especially as the TTP's violence mounted after the Taliban took power. Pakistan's Prime Minister Imran Khan publicly took the position that a political settlement was the only way to end Pakistan's war with the TTP; **NY Times** dated 2nd October 2021 is referred.

Initial negotiations between the TTP and Pakistan, which took place in Afghanistan, made some headway. A short cease-fire was announced in early November, with reports that Pakistan had committed to the release of over 100 TTP prisoners, including some high-profile leaders, which were in detention in Pakistan. But that cease-fire was suspended by the TTP in early December, as they alleged the Pakistani government didn't keep its commitments. The Pakistani government offered amnesty for the TTP if it laid down arms and agreed to adhere to Pakistan's constitution; the cease-fire was agreed on at the request of the Afghan Taliban government.

The TTP went vague on the cease-fire; perhaps the group was using this tool to gain release of the imprisoned senior leaders and improve its battlefield position. Additionally, the TTP was asking the Afghan Taliban leadership to help it consolidate power in Afghanistan. There were indications also that some TTP leaders were unhappy with the cease-fire; however, Siraj Haqqani was pressuring the TTP on Pakistan's behest to behave well. There was deep support within the Afghan Taliban for the TTP and its 'jihad' against Pakistan.

Thereafter, on 27th January 2022; Pakistan's Security Advisor Moeed Yousaf told the nation in a telecast that Pakistan would think about revisiting its support for the Taliban government due to the safe haven the Afghan Taliban was providing to the TTP. It was unlikely because the renewed threat of the TTP was secondary in the hierarchy of Pakistan's security priorities due to its strong-hold Pak-Army – known for its vigilance.

Pakistan's preferred destination was a 'pro-Pakistan' regime in Afghanistan. In the aftermath, Pakistan also feared total state collapse in Afghanistan due to the humanitarian disaster unfolding there [details already given in a previous chapter], as well as the intriguing spill-over into Pakistan. There was another growing friction in the Pak-Taliban relationship over the border fence issue on Durand Line. With the TTP's violence continued to grow in Pakistani cities, Pak-military and intelligence faced mounting domestic political pressure. And if the Afghan Taliban stepped up their opposition to Pakistan's fencing of the border, Pak-Taliban relations could deteriorate.

While attacking mainly the security forces, the TTP claimed 32 attacks in August, 37 in September and 24 in October [2021] -- the highest monthly totals for at least five years, according to their own published data.

Across all of 2020, when the US first pledged to start withdrawing its troops from Afghanistan, it claimed 149 assaults -- three times more than in 2019.

The renewed confidence became apparent in October when the group's leader **Noor Wali Mehsud** came out of hiding and was photographed shaking hands with residents and speaking in public -- something unimaginable just a few months ago. More than a dozen Islamist factions have since July 2020 rallied under his leadership.

[*In an attempt to improve the TTP's image and distinguish them from the Islamic State's extremism, Mehsud has largely taken the group in a new direction -- sparing civilians and ordering attacks only on security and law enforcement officials.*]

**On 14th July 2021;** the TTP carried out a suicide attack in which at least 13 people, including **nine Chinese nationals,** were killed in an explosion in a bus; the people were working at a hydroelectric project in Pakistan's Kohistan District. The TTP had also carried out 95 attacks in 2020, and 44 attacks in the first six months of 2021, according to statistics compiled by the Pak Institute for Peace Studies.

The above attack on Chinese engineers clearly demonstrate that on whose agenda the TTP was / is working to sabotage the CPEC programs in Pakistan – India and the US both. The intelligentsia had held that in such situations Pakistan should not have offered or brokered peace talks or deals with the TTP – they should have launched proper planned operations against them like in Swat (2009) and in Waziristan (2014-15).

Though the TTP is fed and financed by the US through Indian hidden links in Iran and Afghanistan but the growing threat of the TTP would have implications for the US counter-terrorism priorities, too because in April 2021, al-Qaeda had publicly reposed confidence in the TTP; **CNN** dated 30th April 2021 is referred. This could be a serious threat nexus — in the past, even short-term deals had backfired by strengthening both the TTP and al-Qaeda.

Books on **THE CONTEMPORARY HISTORY OF PAKISTAN;**
4614 pages including this volume in hand.

Judges & Generals in Pakistan VOL-I
ISBN: 978-1-90859-662-8 [2012] GHP

Judges & Generals in Pakistan VOL-II
ISBN: 978-1-78148-740-0 [2012] GHP

Judges & Generals in Pakistan VOL-III
ISBN: 978-1-78148-204-9 [2013] GHP

Judges & Generals in Pakistan VOL-IV
ISBN: 978-1-78148-673-3 [2013] GHP

The Living History of Pakistan Vol-I
ISBN: 978-1-78623-705-7 [2015] GHP

The Living History of Pakistan Vol-II
ISBN: 978-1-78148-955-0 [2016] GHP

The Living History of Pakistan Vol-III
ISBN: 978-1-78623-825-2 [2017] GHP

The Living History of Pakistan Vol-IV
ISBN: 978-1-78623-827-6 [2017] GHP

The Living History of Pakistan Vol-V
ISBN: 978-1-78623-937-2 [2017] GHP

The Living History of Pakistan Vol-VI
ISBN: 978-1-78623- 130 -7 [2018] GHP

The Living History of Pakistan Vol-VII
ISBN: 978-1-78623- 141 -3 [2016-17] GHP

# About the Author

**INAM R SEHRI**
MSc (PUNJAB), MA (EXETER UK), LLB.
BORN LYALLPUR (PAKISTAN) 1948
MIGRATED (PER-FORCE) TO THE UK.
SERVED IN POLICE & FIA (1975-98)
PROFESSION: READING & WRITING
(20TH BOOK IS IN YOUR HAND)

Lightning Source UK Ltd.
Milton Keynes UK
UKHW042059300522
403760UK00003B/20